DOLLAR
OVERVALUATION
AND THE WORLD
ECONOMY

DOLLAR OVERVALUATION AND THE WORLD ECONOMY

Edited by
C. Fred Bergsten and
John Williamson

Institute for International Economics
Washington, DC
February 2003

C. **Fred Bergsten** has been director of the Institute for International Economics since its creation in 1981. He was also chairman of the Competitiveness Policy Council, which was created by Congress, throughout its existence from 1991 to 1995 and chairman of the APEC Eminent Persons Group throughout its existence from 1993 to 1995. He was assistant secretary for international affairs of the US Treasury (1977-81), assistant for international economic affairs to the National Security Council (1969-71), and a senior fellow at the Brookings Institution (1972-76), the Carnegie Endowment for International Peace (1981), and the Council on Foreign Relations (1967-68). He is the author, coauthor, or editor of numerous books on a wide range of international economic issues, including *No More Bashing: Building a New Japan-United States Economic Relationship* (2001), *Whither APEC? The Progress to Date and Agenda for the Future* (1997), *Global Economic Leadership and the Group of Seven* (1996), *The Dilemmas of the Dollar* (second edition, 1996), *Reconcilable Differences? United States-Japan Economic Conflict* (1993), and *Pacific Dynamism and the International Economic System* (1993).

John Williamson, senior fellow at the Institute for International Economics since 1981, was project director for the UN High-Level Panel on Financing for Development (the Zedillo Report) in 2001; on leave as chief economist for South Asia at the World Bank during 1996-99; economics professor at Pontificia Universidade Católica do Rio de Janeiro (1978-81), University of Warwick (1970-77), Massachusetts Institute of Technology (1967, 1980), University of York (1963-68), and Princeton University (1962-63); adviser to the International Monetary Fund (1972-74); and economic consultant to the UK Treasury (1968-70). He is author, coauthor, or editor of numerous studies on international monetary and developing world debt issues, including *Delivering on Debt Relief: From IMF Gold to a New Aid Architecture* (2002), *Exchange Rate Regimes for Emerging Markets: Reviving the Intermediate Option* (2000), *The Crawling Band as an Exchange Rate Regime* (1996), *What Role for Currency Boards?* (1995), *Estimating Equilibrium Exchange Rates* (1994), and *The Political Economy of Policy Reform* (1993).

INSTITUTE FOR INTERNATIONAL ECONOMICS
1750 Massachusetts Avenue, NW
Washington, DC 20036-1903
(202) 328-9000 FAX: (202) 659-3225
http://www.iie.com

C. Fred Bergsten, *Director*
Valerie Norville, *Director of Publications and Web Development*
Brett Kitchen, *Director of Marketing and Foreign Rights*

Typesetting and printing by Automated Graphic Systems, Inc.

Printed in the United States of America
05 04 03   5 4 3 2 1

Library of Congress Cataloging-in-Publication Data

Dollar overvaluation in the world economy / coedited by C. Fred Bergsten and John Williamson.
    p. cm.
Includes bibliographical references and index.
ISBN 0-88132-351-9
1. Dollar, American. 2. Foreign exchange. 3. United States—Foreign economic relations.
I. Bergsten, C. Fred, 1941- II. Williamson, John, 1937- III. Institute for International Economics (U.S.)

HG540.O94 2003
332.4'56'0973—dc21   2002191274

The views expressed in this publication are those of the authors. This publication is part of the overall program of the Institute, as endorsed by its Board of Directors, but does not necessarily reflect the views of individual members of the Board or the Advisory Committee.

Rudiger Dornbusch
1942-2002

This volume is dedicated to the memory of Rudiger Dornbusch, a member of the Advisory Committee of the Institute for International Economics from its founding in 1981 and a frequent participant in the Institute's conferences. Rudi was best known for his work on exchange rate theory and was also one of the most trenchant critics of the proposals for target zones for exchange rates that emerged from the Institute during the 1980s, proposals that reflected similar concerns to those that motivated the conference reported in this volume. Rudi would probably not have sympathized with many of the ideas that are presented here any more than he did with our target zone proposal—but he always delighted in taking an audience by surprise so we hope that he would have appreciated our decision to dedicate the volume to him as much as we appreciated the opportunity to benefit from his counsel.

Contents

Preface

Exchange rates of the major industrialized countries have been one of the focal points of research at the Institute throughout its history. In 1983, John Williamson invented the concept of "fundamental equilibrium exchange rates" (FEERs), which has provided the conceptual foundation for much of our work on the topic. The idea was elaborated in Williamson's edited volume *Estimating Equilibrium Exchange Rates* in 1994 and applied to all major currencies in *Real Exchange Rates for the Year 2000* by Simon Wren-Lewis and Rebecca Driver in 1998.

Exchange rate analysis has been included in numerous other Institute studies as well. William Cline and I addressed the yen-dollar relationship in *The US-Japan Economic Problem* (1985, 2d ed. 1987) and Marcus Noland and I did so in *Reconcilable Differences? United States-Japan Economic Conflict* (1993). Cline assessed the entire array of G-7 currency ratios in *American Trade Adjustment: The Global Impact* and *United States External Adjustment and the World Economy* (both 1989). Paul Krugman analyzed the impact of the currency changes of the 1980s in *Has the Adjustment Process Worked?* (1991), which was included in a broader volume that I edited on *International Adjustment and Financing: The Lessons of 1989-1991* (1992). I drew heavily on the work of my colleagues on exchange rates in writing *America in the World Economy: A Strategy for the 1990s* (1988) and *Global Economic Leadership and the Group of Seven* (with C. Randall Henning, 1996).

As described in the overview chapter, this new volume—and the conference of September 2002 on which it is based—was motivated by concerns about both the real economic impact of the strong dollar of the second half of the 1990s and the risks for the stability of the currency (and perhaps other financial) markets posed by the dollar's recent levels. The Institute sought to convene experts from a wide variety of countries and viewpoints on the topic to discuss the appropriate rate for the dollar over the medium run, the implications for other major currencies, and the policy measures that might be available to do something about it. The overview chapter summarizes the main conclusions and proposals that emerged from the conference, and the individual chapters present a range of analyses of the impact of a depreciation of the dollar on both the economies of the key countries and on the financial markets.

The Institute for International Economics is a private nonprofit institution for the study and discussion of international economic policy. Its purpose is to analyze important issues in that area and to develop and communicate practical new approaches for dealing with them. The Institute is completely nonpartisan.

The Institute is funded largely by philanthropic foundations. Major institutional grants are now being received from the William M. Keck, Jr. Foundation and the Starr Foundation. A number of other foundations and private corporations contribute to the highly diversified financial resources of the Institute. About 31 percent of the Institute's resources in our latest fiscal year were provided by contributors outside the United States, including about 18 percent from Japan. This volume and the conference on which it is based were made possible by generous financial support from Jaqui Safra, Automotive Trade Policy Council, American Forest & Paper Association, Business Roundtable, National Association of Manufacturers, American Textile Manufacturers Institute, Motor & Equipment Manufacturers Association, and National Association of Wheat Growers.

The Board of Directors bears overall responsibility for the Institute and gives general guidance and approval to its research program, including the identification of topics that are likely to become important over the medium run (one to three years), and which should be addressed by the Institute. The Director, working closely with the staff and outside Advisory Committee, is responsible for the development of particular projects and makes the final decision to publish an individual study.

The Institute hopes that its studies and other activities will contribute to building a stronger foundation for international economic policy around the world. We invite readers of these publications to let us know how they think we can best accomplish this objective.

C. FRED BERGSTEN
Director
January 2003

Overview

C. FRED BERGSTEN AND JOHN WILLIAMSON

The Institute's conference on the dollar, held in Washington on September 24, 2002, was motivated by concerns of two types. One is the array of implications the strong dollar and the very large US current account deficit and external debt have for the US and world economies. The second is the sustainability of the exchange rate of the dollar in the financial markets, especially in light of the other bubbles that have recently burst.

Facts

The value of the dollar soared from 1995, when it hit its all-time lows, until the beginning of 2002. Depending on which index one uses, the trade-weighted average foreign exchange value of the dollar rose by 30 to 50 percent over that period—not quite as large as the increase in the 1980s, but getting into the same order of magnitude. When Larry Summers was at the Treasury Department, he often said that "the charts of exchange rate movements over the last twenty years revealed the 1980s as the Himalayas and the 1990s as the foothills." In the past few years, the 1990s have become at least the Alps and maybe the Andes, if not quite the Himalayas of the 1980s.

C. Fred Bergsten has been director of the Institute for International Economics since its creation in 1981. He was also chairman of the Competitiveness Policy Council, which was created by Congress, throughout its existence from 1991 to 1995 and chairman of the APEC Eminent Persons Group throughout its existence from 1993 to 1995. John Williamson, senior fellow at the Institute for International Economics since 1981, was project director for the UN High-Level Panel on Financing for Development (the Zedillo Report) in 2001 and on leave as chief economist for South Asia at the World Bank during 1996-99.

And if one compares the current account deficits that have materialized in the two periods, then it is the recent period that deserves to be labeled the Himalayas. The adverse impact on manufacturing, as measured by the size of the manufacturing trade deficit (shown in figure 5.1 in Martin Baily's paper in chapter 5 of this volume), has been substantially larger than in the 1980s. Moreover, appreciation continued for almost two years after the US economy turned downward, including when it was in recession in 2001, an anomaly in terms of its past performance and a significant factor in intensifying the problems of the manufacturing sector.

The rising dollar, and the large and increasing current account deficits that resulted, facilitated the US economic boom of the second half of the 1990s by keeping downward pressure on prices and interest rates and by supplying large amounts of capital to fuel the investment-led economic expansion that the United States experienced during that period. One might in those particular circumstances rationalize the strong-dollar rhetoric of the Clinton administration—which actually started in 1994, when the dollar was weak and still weakening—as having been consistent with the rather satisfactory behavior of the US economy during that period. (There was never any strong-dollar *policy*. Indeed, the administration's only direct dollar operations since 1995 were to sell dollars for yen in 1998 and for euros in 2000. However, there was certainly strong-dollar *rhetoric*.)

The bad news was that the external deficit reached record levels. The current account deficit in the second quarter of 2002, the latest numbers we have,[1] came in at an annual rate in excess of $500 billion, or more than 5 percent of GDP. In her paper for the conference (chapter 3), Catherine Mann suggests that the current account deficit is on a trajectory headed toward somewhat less than 7 percent of GDP by 2005. The further increase in the external deficit in the second quarter cut US economic growth in half in that quarter, although this may have been exaggerated by the anticipation of a dock strike leading to a greater acceleration of imports than exports.

In short, the current account deficit has become very large by any standard, and is still getting larger. Moreover, this is occurring with the US net international investment position already at a negative $1.9 trillion at the end of 2001, having risen by $600 billion in 2001 alone. That net international investment position of the United States is a major consideration in the paper by Jim O'Neill (chapter 1), in which he discusses the magnitude of the correction that may be needed. The alternative view of Mann focuses instead on the share of non-US investors' portfolio wealth that needs to be invested in US assets to finance the current account deficit; she concludes that this portfolio approach suggests that it is more likely that the dollar will appreciate than depreciate in 2003.

---

1. No attempt has been made here or elsewhere to update figures beyond those available on or, where noted, shortly after the conference (September 24, 2002).

A modest correction occurred in the exchange value of the dollar during the first half of 2002. The dollar began to decline in February, after almost two years of continuing to rise despite the sluggish and even recessionary US economy, and then dropped over the subsequent six months by a trade-weighted average of 5 to 10 percent (again depending on what index is used). It dropped by more than that bilaterally against both the euro and the yen, but the average declines retraced less than 20 percent of the dollar appreciation of the previous six and a half years (see table 0.1).

However, the dollar correction of the first half of 2002 now appears to have stalled out. Since about the middle of July, the dollar has stopped depreciating and has in fact bounced back quite a bit, both on an effective trade-weighted basis and, to a lesser extent, against the yen and the euro. This poses more acutely the question of whether more correction is needed and, if so, how to get it. It is also true that demand in the United States is increasing faster than in the rest of the world, which makes it quite likely that the US current account deficit will increase further.

One of the purposes of the conference was to renew discussion of the sustainable exchange rate of the dollar and of other major currencies. The paper by O'Neill suggests that the dollar needs to correct by another 15 percent, on a trade-weighted basis, to restore a sustainable equilibrium. Baily estimates that a larger decline, of 20 to 25 percent, would be needed to cut the US current account deficit to 2.5 percent of GDP. Those estimates would suggest that the decline of the dollar that occurred during the first six months of 2002 achieved less than 40 percent of the correction that would be needed to restore a sustainable US position—and a significant part of that correction has subsequently been lost by the dollar's rebound. On the other hand, Michael Rosenberg indicates that a smaller correction is needed (chapter 2).

The dollar decline in the first half of 2002 was gradual, orderly, and virtually devoid of negative effects on financial or other markets, at least in the United States. There was no discernible effect on US inflation or US interest rates, nor any other negative impact on the US economy. Indeed, one could suggest that, with the United States still in the early stages of a recovery with substantial unemployment and underutilization of capacity, this is the optimal time to experience a currency depreciation that one may believe to be inevitable. One possible implication of this view is that (from a national US standpoint) it would be desirable to complete the correction, or at least to push it further, sooner rather than later.

Of course a dollar decline means an appreciation of other major currencies like the euro, the yen, the Canadian dollar, the Chinese renminbi, and the pound sterling. The counterpart countries have not all been as content with the adjustment as the United States has, even with the modest correction that has already occurred. Japan in particular has reacted strongly

Table 0.1 Movements in the dollar exchange rate, 1995-2002

	Fed broad (nominal)	Fed broad[a] (real)	IMF[a] index	Deutsche mark or euro	Yen
Low (1995)	88.91 May 8	84.23 July	95.85 April	1.36 April 19	80.69 April 19
High (2002)	130.61 February 27	113.09 February	130.61 February	2.28 February 1	134.81 January 25
Low (2002)	122.81 July 19	108.37 July	122.32 July	1.93 July 21	115.85 July 22
Current value	127.74 October 4	111.27 October	123.85 August	1.98 October 10	123.28 October 10
Appreciation (1995-2002, percent)	46.9	34.3	36.3	67.6	66.8
Depreciation (2002 high to low, percent)	6.0	2.7	6.3	15.4	13.9
Appreciation (2002 low to current, percent)	4.0	2.7	1.3	2.6	6.4

a. Data available on monthly basis only.

Sources: IMF, *International Financial Statistics*; Federal Reserve Bank; and Oanda.com.

against the counterpart appreciation of the yen, by attempting to jawbone the yen down on repeated occasions and intervening heavily at times to keep the yen from appreciating, or even trying to push it down. In fact this occurred again the week before the conference, when Vice Minister of Finance for International Affairs Haruhiko Kuroda again began loudly to try and jawbone the yen down. It did indeed move down after that, which is part of the counterpart to the renewed recent dollar appreciation.

Four Issues

1. Does the Dollar Need to Depreciate?

There was very general agreement at the conference that it would be better, from the standpoint of the US and world economies, if the dollar's exchange value were lower. The main qualification to this view was voiced by Baily, who presented results from standard macro models that demonstrated that under full employment conditions this would involve the United States dampening its economic growth, because releasing resources for the external sector would need higher interest rates to restrain consumption and investment. Since at present the economy is not at full employment, this would not preclude an immediate start to adjustment, but one would have to expect it to kick in before the current account deficit had been cut by 2.5 percent of GDP.

There were many different reasons for the view that the dollar needs to decline. Some worry about adverse effects on the US economy in the short run: for example, Tom Palley (chapter 7) is concerned about a "double-dip" recession (a second recession following a brief recovery) and argues that dollar depreciation could provide a needed stimulus to demand, especially in manufacturing. Some worry about a negative structural impact over the longer term: Baily notes that US manufacturing had suffered a "triple whammy" during the last two years (weak domestic demand, weak growth in overseas markets, and continued dollar strength). Some fear an eventual dollar crash and a hard landing for the US and world economies if dollar overvaluation is permitted to continue— and especially if it were to rise further. Some want to avoid further increases in the negative net international investment position of the United States. Some fear that US trade protectionism will be promoted; Mac Destler (chapter 4) notes that import volume in fact grew as rapidly from 1995 to 2000 as it did from 1982 to 1986, the period when the United States adopted its most extensive set of protectionist measures in the postwar era.

A less familiar reason is advanced by Stephen Roach (chapter 8), who seeks an inflationary impulse to counter the looming deflation that he views as the major economic problem facing the United States and the world. It is true that dollar depreciation would in itself promote deflation in the counterpart countries, but he argues that this is exactly the sort of shock they need to induce them to embark on the expansionary policies that they have been so reluctant to undertake. O'Neill argues that the euro appreciation that would accompany dollar depreciation would generate desirable, and perhaps essential, pressure on Europe to undertake both structural policy reforms and a more stimulative macro policy. (But others at the conference were doubtful that Europe was ready to respond positively.)

2. The Desirable Magnitude of Dollar Depreciation

There were much greater differences among the conference participants on how much lower it would be desirable for the dollar to move. One view, which forms the basis for O'Neill's paper, is that it is important to limit any further increase in the US negative net international investment position relative to GDP. This implies that the current account deficit should be cut by about half, which would require the dollar to depreciate by something like 20 percent from its peak. But several others who also think that the dollar should come down argue for a smaller correction on both desirability and feasibility grounds. Mann notes the very low debt service costs being incurred by the United States to date, and she and others think the United States could continue to finance larger deficits, implying that it need not adjust as much, or at all. Baily's analysis suggests that one might wish to stop depreciation when the economy hits full employment.

The main variable underlying differing views about the needed extent of the correction is differential productivity growth. US productivity growth has accelerated in recent years, whereas Japanese productivity growth fell precipitously about a decade ago, and now Daniel Gros (chapter 10) and O'Neill both suggest that something similar may recently have happened in Europe. Everyone agrees that faster relative productivity growth justifies real appreciation, but there was vigorous and unresolved debate about why this is so, and hence what it implies quantitatively.

The traditional analysis dates back to Balassa (1964) and Samuelson (1964). They reasoned that productivity growth tends to be fastest in the tradable goods industries, so a country with higher productivity growth, similar inflation, and a constant exchange rate will become more competitive than its peers over time. To offset the impact of this effect on the current account requires real appreciation (at least as measured by a broad price index that covers the prices of both tradables and nontradables[2]). But this theory suggests that the extent of the needed real appreciation

2. Though not according to a very narrow price index restricted to tradable commodities.

is some fraction of the increase in the productivity differential, which Bill Cline (chapter 9) puts at 1 percent per annum or less. Thus this might rationalize a dollar appreciation of 7 percent at most (over the seven years since 1995), a fairly small part of the actual appreciation of over 30 percent. It is this theory that is incorporated in the Goldman Sachs dynamic equilibrium real exchange rates (GSDEER) estimates that O'Neill presented to the conference.

However, most of those who argue the importance of the productivity factor are not invoking this traditional theory, which argues that real appreciation is necessary to keep the current account *constant*. Instead, they argue that faster productivity growth will pull in more capital and thus finance a *larger* current account deficit. The most conservative proponent of this view is Cline, who does not assume that the current account must be unchanged but does argue that in the longer term the ratio of net international investment position (NIIP) to GDP must be constant. Faster productivity growth in one country accelerates its growth rate, which means that its current account deficit can increase—but only as much as is consistent with maintaining NIIP/GDP constant. This turns out to allow a rather small increase (under Cline's stylized parameters, about 0.25 percent of GDP, which does not go far toward explaining the actual increase of the US current account deficit of 3 to 4 percent of GDP since the mid-1990s).

Another alternative is propounded by Baily, Rosenberg, and Mann: faster productivity growth raises the rate of return on capital, which makes a larger capital inflow profitable, which finances a larger current account deficit. If the government succeeded in thwarting that outcome by some action that depreciated the currency, inflationary pressures would develop if the economy was at full employment. To offset these pressures, the government would have to resort to restrictive fiscal and monetary policies, which would curtail growth. Far better, they argue, to let the capital flow in and finance an investment boom, even if the price is a larger current account deficit for a while and therefore higher debt. Presumably this may not be possible indefinitely, because of the rising NIIP/GDP, and eventually the Cline analysis will become relevant, but this may not be for years. Rosenberg suggests that the United States may now be able to afford a current account deficit of 3 or 4 percent of GDP, rather than the 2.5 percent that he formerly hypothesized.

Given these differing views about the importance of the recent relative increase in productivity growth in the United States, conference participants offered a fairly wide range of conclusions about the size of the adjustment needed to achieve a sustainable position. While traditional analysis suggests that the measured current account deficit needs to be reduced to something like 2 to 3 percent of GDP, some thought that the productivity miracle will enable the United States to sustain external deficits at 3 to 4 percent of GDP. The result was a large range for the preferred dollar decline, from around 25 percent to less than half that.

3. The Counterpart to the Dollar Depreciation

The mathematical counterpart to a depreciation of the dollar is appreciation of other currencies. The third big issue discussed at the conference is which currencies should be on the other side of the US adjustment. The appreciation need not necessarily be the same for all other currencies, since the impact of a uniform change would vary widely among countries. It would have a much greater impact on Canada and Mexico, for example, which trade primarily with the United States, than on the European countries, which trade primarily with each other. Moreover, some countries are likely to be in a much better position to contribute to adjustment than others.

One of the most interesting conclusions of the day was that it is no longer appropriate, or even possible, to look to Europe and Japan as the dominant or even major counterparts in the adjustment process. O'Neill points out that today these two economies account for only 30 percent of US trade. Canada, China, and other East Asian countries that have been running current account surpluses will certainly need to participate in any future adjustment operation that seeks to spread the counterpart fairly. Some considered that Mexico might also be expected to play a role, although its lack of an overall current account (or basic balance) surplus might suggest that it should instead be among the countries that could be expected to keep their effective exchange rates unchanged, which would imply a more modest appreciation vis-à-vis the dollar.

There was substantial disagreement about the appropriateness of looking to Japan to play a major role in the adjustment process, given Japan's domestic problems and its apparent inability to use fiscal or monetary policy to stimulate domestic demand. Various economists have suggested in recent years that Japan should engineer a big depreciation of the yen in order to generate some export-led growth. This proposal was endorsed in our conference by Rosenberg, who argues that Japan will have to tighten fiscal policy, because its debt is veering out of control, and will therefore need an offsetting expansionary impulse from the external sector. It also found an echo in the analysis of O'Neill, who concludes that the current yen-dollar rate is about right; in his view the yen is currently overvalued on an effective basis, but he would look to the revaluation of the euro, the renminbi, and other East Asian currencies to correct that.

In contrast, Cline's paper assumes that Japan should reduce its surplus by 15 percent of the desired reduction in the US deficit. (He argues that "Japan's share" of the US adjustment is between 10 and 25 percent, depending on whether this share is calibrated on current account surpluses, trade shares, or bilateral trade, and then selects the intermediate figure of 15 percent as the basis for his quantitative estimates.) With acceleration in Japanese growth to 2.5 to 3 percent (which many would consider optimistic), this would require an effective appreciation of 12 percent and hence an appreciation against the dollar of 21 percent, which would take the exchange rate to ¥101 to the dollar.[3] (He notes that an extrapolation of the trend appreciation exhibited by the yen—at least up to about a decade ago—would now imply an exchange rate of about ¥103 to the dollar after correcting for relative inflation rates.) He argues that it would be wrong to permanently exempt a country from international adjustment obligations and permit it to export its unemployment because of weak demand, and suggests as a compromise allowing for Japan's current difficulties by temporarily acquiescing in a yen depreciated, say, 15 percent below its long-run equilibrium (a formula suggested by the target zone literature, e.g., Williamson 1985).

Other participants, notably Mustafa Mohatarem (chapter 6) and Ernest Preeg (chapter 13), waxed indignant at the fact that Japan has often intervened to buy dollars, which in their view implies that the dollar has been artificially held up and Japan has been exporting its problems to other countries, including the United States. The shock of a yen appreciation as part of the counterpart to a dollar depreciation might in their view provide the shock needed to induce Japan to take measures that would finally get growth going again from serious bank reform and a domestic stimulus. Thus there was not even agreement on the sign of the Japanese shift—positive, negative, or zero.

A similar question concerns the proper extent of realignment of the euro. Gros addresses that issue in chapter 10. In doing so, he makes the very useful point that the Europeans should not be focusing on the dollar/euro exchange rate but rather on the real effective exchange rate for the euro, its trade-weighted average. If a number of currencies appreciate against the dollar simultaneously, then each of their trade-weighted appreciations is much less than their change against the dollar because there is no change against each other; this is particularly important in areas that trade a lot within their region, as does Europe. There was a certain amount of skepticism as to whether the Europeans are likely to take decisive actions that would contribute positively to adjustment, but that is because the European Central Bank (ECB) is still fixated on controlling inflation, not because—as in Japan—there is doubt as to whether it could do more if it chose to. The argument that a euro appreciation might be just what is needed to shock the Europeans into action is more convincing than the equivalent argument in Japan, partly because the appropriate action is much easier to diagnose, and partly because the

---

3. If one takes the more pessimistic view that Japan is unlikely to grow, the yen would need to appreciate against the dollar by 33 percent, to a level of ¥92 to the dollar.

appreciation would directly reduce the inflation that provides the motivation for the ECB's reluctance to act, but there nonetheless remained much skepticism as to whether a shock appreciation of the euro would have the desired effect.

4. Policy Instruments

No one at the conference advocated slowing US growth in order to promote adjustment, a proposal attacked by Richard Clarida in an article published after the conference ("America's Deficit, the World's Problem," *Financial Times*, October 22, 2002). On the contrary, some of the participants looked to dollar depreciation as a needed support to US growth. Suppose that policymakers indeed took that view and had agreed-on answers to the questions discussed above, involving where they would like to see the exchange rates of the dollar and of other major currencies in order to promote adjustment to a set of sustainable current account positions. Would it do any good, given that exchange rates are determined by markets and not by governments?

Most economists agree that it is possible for governments to manage exchange rates if they devote monetary policy to that end. But most also believe that monetary policy is too important to be used mainly to manage the exchange rate; it is needed to steer the domestic economy. The fourth and final issue discussed at the conference is whether other policy instruments exist that might be used to manage the exchange rate. The classic candidate is sterilized intervention, and the final session of the conference was devoted to three papers that discuss whether it can and should be used to try to manage exchange rates.

Kathryn Dominguez (chapter 11), who has worked on the subject before, argues in her paper that the new evidence from the 1990s confirms that one can get some traction through sterilized intervention, provided a series of exacting conditions are satisfied: that the intervention reinforces the fundamentals, that it catches the markets by surprise, that it is announced so as to make clear the authorities' intent, and that it is conducted among at least the two authorities directly involved.

Ted Truman (chapter 12) takes a decidedly more skeptical view of the potency of intervention. This is not so much because he denies that it can ever work, but because it may cause various types of collateral damage: it may distract the authorities from addressing more fundamental problems, it may send false signals, and it may exacerbate domestic economic problems. Truman also performs the useful task of examining whether, as is sometimes claimed, a decision to use monetary policy to manage the exchange rate would usually tend to result in monetary policies that would be stabilizing to the domestic economy, and he concludes that it would be stabilizing only about half the time. To use intervention counter to the sense of monetary policy would be to risk sending a false signal about monetary policy.

Ernest Preeg (chapter 13) argues that the massive intervention by Japan and China has led to severe undervaluation of their currencies and should therefore be condemned under the International Monetary Fund's (IMF) proscription of "currency manipulation." Preeg and Mohatarem argue that this intervention is the equivalent of an export subsidy that should also be countervailable under the international trade rules.

Preeg's view can be contested on several grounds: a Trumanesque belief that currency intervention is largely ineffective because assets are close to perfect substitutes; a recognition that at least in the case of China the intervention is undertaken in furtherance of a policy of pegging the exchange rate, which is an option explicitly allowed by the IMF Articles; a view that what is needed is not a general prohibition of significant intervention, but some international discipline to ensure that large-scale intervention is undertaken only to push exchange rates toward a level that the international community agrees is desirable; and a belief that Japanese intervention is undertaken so that the Japanese government can claim to be doing something, not because it expects it to have much effect. But even those at the conference who subscribed to one or more of these reasons for questioning the damage done by "currency manipulation" seemed to agree that the IMF, the G-7, and the US government have done little to prevent such large-scale intervention from proceeding unquestioned. Most thought that Japan (at least) should desist. And even if the implicit interpretation of the undefined word "manipulation" still follows the pre-1977 Articles that prohibited competitive devaluation but not the maintenance of an exchange rate that happened to have become undervalued through time, it would make sense to adopt an explicit interpretation that follows common sense in defining manipulation to include large sustained interventions such as those in China.

In this context, several participants in the conference leveled strong criticisms at the US Treasury for its failure to address this question despite its having a statutory responsibility to do so. Under the provisions of the Omnibus Trade Act of 1988, the Treasury is required to submit semiannual reports to the Congress on developments in the exchange markets and how they affect the trade position of the United States. In particular, the Treasury is mandated to be alert to "currency manipulation" through which other countries take actions in the exchange markets that deliberately work to the disadvantage of US trade.

In its most recent reports, in early and late 2002, the Treasury has accurately reported the active intervention of Japan but indicated no intention of doing anything about it, even criticizing it. Such inertia is seemingly inconsistent with both the letter and spirit of the law, which is clearly intended to deter competitive depreciations by other countries.

Are there any new policy initiatives vis-à-vis the dollar that should be adopted by the United States, the G-7, or anybody else? The administration, including the Treasury, has not used the term "strong dollar" for over a year. Nevertheless, they have said that there is no change in that past policy and, when asked about the Japanese intervention utterances a few weeks before the conference, former Treasury Secretary Paul H. O'Neill said that "the dollar is trading in a reasonable range," implying that he was not unhappy with where things were. Is this appropriate, or are any changes in policy needed?

One option, which is suggested in some of the papers in this volume, is that at a minimum the United States should oppose actions by other countries that would promote renewed dollar appreciation or limit dollar depreciation, notably intervention by Japan, China, and other countries to buy dollars and thus keep the dollar from declining even when market forces are pushing it in that direction.

One could of course go further, with US or G-7 statements that they do not want to see any renewed dollar appreciation. The market might then perceive itself as faced with something of a one-way option, which would encourage the dollar to resume its depreciation.

An even more ambitious agenda would include giving some guidance to the markets as to where the authorities would like to see exchange rates settle down. Palley suggests a new Plaza Accord.

Concluding Remarks

The conference thus addressed the range of issues raised by the strong exchange rate of the dollar, the large and growing US external deficit, and the counterpart surpluses elsewhere around the world. It reached a fairly strong consensus on the need for an eventual correction of the dollar overvaluation, but less agreement on the timing of that correction, the amount of adjustment needed (10 to 25 percent), and the distribution of that adjustment among other countries via counterpart movements in their currencies (some for Japan and Europe, though less than in previous "coordination" exercises, with significant contributions from Canada, China, and other East Asian countries). There was little agreement, however, on either the desirability of official action to promote the needed correction or how such action could be conducted, though most were critical of Japanese intervention to weaken the yen.

Three key questions for further research became evident. One concerns the correct analysis of the implications of changes in the rates of productivity growth on current account positions and nominal exchange rates. Three alternative theories presented by different authors were listed above, but no attempt was made to adjudicate between them. The second topic involves developing models that can illuminate alternative geographic distributions of adjustment responsibilities in a world where China and other countries in East Asia, as well as Canada, are running large current account and/or basic balance surpluses. The third concerns how the IMF (and conceivably the World Trade Organization) could play a more active and effective role in monitoring and disciplining intervention in the currency markets so as to reduce the risk that intervention will impede adjustment or increase the instability of the international monetary system. One possibility would be to agree on a set of "reference rates" (Williamson 2000), which impose only one obligation: to ensure that any intervention pushes market exchange rates toward, rather than away from, those rates. This would be a way of securing the desired discipline over Japanese and Chinese intervention policy, without forgoing any benefits that might come from using sterilized intervention to push the dollar down. It might also achieve any advantages that intervention may bring through what Truman calls the "coordination channel," while reducing or eliminating the need for actual intervention.

References

Balassa, Bela. 1964. The Purchasing-Power Parity Doctrine: A Reappraisal. *Journal of Political Economy* 72 (December): 584-96.
Samuelson, Paul A. 1964. Theoretical Notes on Trade Problems. *Review of Economics and Statistics* 46 (March): 145-54.
Williamson, John. 1985. *The Exchange Rate System.* Washington: Institute for International Economics.
Williamson, John. 2000. *Exchange Rate Regimes for Emerging Markets: Reviving the Intermediate Option.* Washington: Institute for International Economics.

1

Features of a Dollar Decline

JIM O'NEILL

Any future decline in the value of the dollar—either designed by policy-makers to help reduce the US current account deficit or reflecting a loss of confidence in the US economy that undermined the ability to attract sufficient foreign capital to cover the current account deficit—would need to involve a wide range of currencies. Unless a well-organized policy to weaken the dollar against a broad basket of currencies that reflected the modern trade patterns of the US were orchestrated, the dollar might eventually fall more against currencies that are less important for the current account and those of countries that are less well positioned to cope.

Earlier this year, we at Goldman Sachs updated some research that we conducted in 1999 arguing that the US balance of payments was unsustainable (O'Neill and Hatzius 2002). This research tried to determine what would be necessary to stabilize the net foreign liability position of the United States. Specifically, we showed that to prevent net foreign liabilities from going above 40 percent of GDP by 2007, the United States would have to see a permanent improvement in the current account balance by around $200 billion, some 2 percent of GDP. We went on to show that if this were to be solely the result of a decline in the dollar, a decline of as much as 43 percent on a trade-weighted basis could be necessary. In reality, of course, other countervailing influences would be likely to play a role, and a significant increase in foreign domestic demand relative to the United States would be likely to vastly diminish the need for such a large move in the dollar.

It does seem as though something must be done in the coming years to stabilize the US net foreign liability position even if, as it appears, this

---

Jim O'Neill is head of global economic research at Goldman Sachs International.

Table 1.1 Weights of seven currencies as computed in the Fed's broad trade-weighted dollar index (1985 and 2002, in percent)

Currency	1985	2002
Japanese yen	20.6	13.3
Canadian dollar	19.7	17.0
Euro	18.8	16.3
Pound sterling	4.9	4.3
Mexican peso	4.5	10.4
Korean won	3.6	4.3
Chinese yuan	1.8	8.0

Source: Federal Reserve.

is not currently obvious to the markets. And if the necessary shifts in relative domestic demand do not occur, then ultimately the dollar might decline as precipitously as predicted in our model to achieve a better balance. Stronger domestic demand seems particularly important given the current fragile state of demand outside the United States, particularly in the euro zone and even more in Japan.

Our own estimates for currency equilibrium, further discussed below, suggest that the fair value for the dollar appears to have risen in recent years, reflecting the stronger productivity performance of the US economy relative to others. This approach does not suggest that a large dollar decline against all the major currencies would currently be appropriate.

Three different alternatives for the future would be consistent with a recent appreciation in the equilibrium value of the dollar. The first is that the future US current account deficit may turn out to be lower than current trends suggest as a result of improved efficiencies associated with the productivity improvements, generating increased exports and/or reduced imports. Of course, there are no imminent signs of this. Second, it is possible that the United States can sustain a higher current account deficit than before. Perhaps FEER[1]-like models should consider that possibility, as better-quality capital flows can be sustained as a result of the healthier economic conditions. Third, of course, relative productivity trends may change again, and if Japan and the euro zone economies improve their productivity growth in the future, then this would imply a renewed decline in the equilibrium exchange rate of the dollar, more compatible with the current message from FEER-like models.

Whichever is the correct explanation, it would be unwise to force an adjustment on economies that might find it difficult to cope with an immediate loss of export opportunities. It is argued below that this is particularly important with respect to Japan. In relation to this point, it is also important to be aware of the very large shift in US foreign trade relationships since the 1980s. Table 1.1 compares the current and earlier

---

1. Fundamental equilibrium exchange rate.

weights for several countries as computed in the broad trade-weighted dollar index formulated by the Federal Reserve Board (Leahy 1998). The Fed's index is based on three separate indices for imports, exports, and third-party competition. As the table shows, today China carries a weight of 8.0 percent, more than that of Germany (about 5.4 percent). The weight for Mexico has also risen sharply, and China and Mexico together have a greater weight than either the euro zone or Japan. In fact, the euro zone and Japan have a combined weight of only around 30 percent, less than the combined weights of Canada, China, and Mexico.

It would be inappropriate to look to currencies that make up just 30 percent of the trade-weighted exchange rate of the dollar to provide the counterpart appreciation needed to improve the US current account. Movement of the dollar against a broader group—certainly one that involved the currencies of Canada, China, Korea, and possibly Mexico in addition to those of the euro zone (and only modestly Japan)—might seem more viable.

The Extent of Dollar Overvaluation

We estimate equilibria for currency rates according to our Goldman Sachs dynamic equilibrium real exchange rates (GSDEER) model. In addition to accepting the Williamson rationale (Wren-Lewis and Driver 1998) that real exchange rates are not stable and need to reflect equilibria for both internal and external balance, the GSDEER model argues that the Balassa-Samuelson model (Balassa 1964 and Samuelson 1964) holds for the major currencies also. The GSDEER model estimates the real exchange rate as a function of relative productivity in the different economies. We use data from the Organization for Economic Cooperation and Development (OECD) on labor productivity and estimate nominal exchange rates deflated by either producer prices or GDP deflators. (The 1996, 2001, and 2002 editions of our annual *Foreign Exchange Market* give a more detailed explanation and some econometric estimates.)

The GSDEER method suggests that the dollar is currently overvalued by around 15 percent on an effective trade-weighted basis, with the equilibrium having risen somewhat in recent years, reflective of the relative improvements in US productivity.

Against a narrower basket of major currencies (the Fed's major trade-weighted index), we estimate that the dollar is now overvalued by a smaller degree, just under 10 percent. This reflects the dollar decline against these currencies earlier this year as well as some rise in the equilibrium associated with the rise in US productivity.

Some evidence to support the modest increase in the equilibrium value of the dollar can be seen in the overall performance of the US balance of payments in recent years. Although the current account balance has

Figure 1.1 United States: BBoP vs. current account

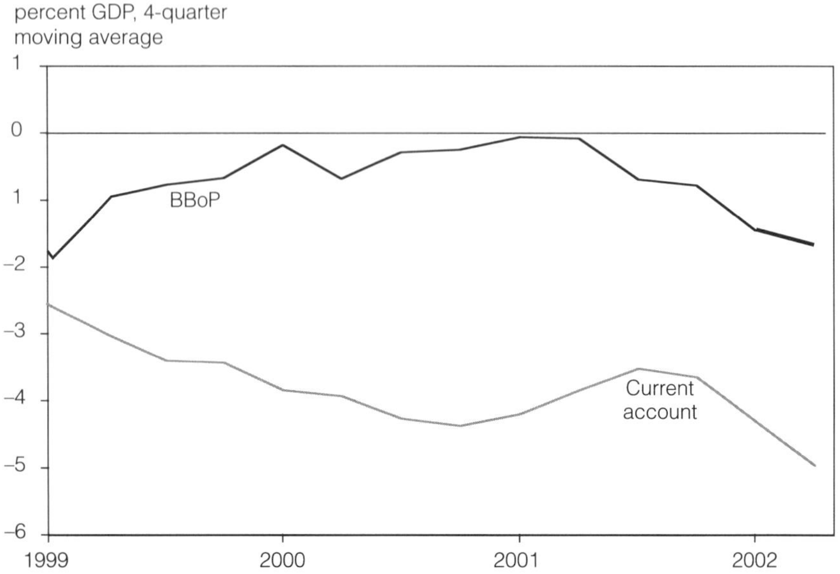

percent GDP, 4-quarter
moving average

BBoP = broad basic balance of payments

Source: US Department of Commerce and Goldman Sachs calculations.

deteriorated despite the weakness of the overall economy since late 2000, substantial net inflows of capital have persisted. It was only in the past few months that net inflows of foreign direct investment, bonds, and equities were unable to offset the deteriorating current account deficit.

The combined balance of the current account, net direct investment, and portfolio flows can be described as a broad basic balance of payments, and as can be seen in figure 1.1, this aggregate has stayed close to balance as a percentage of GDP until the past few months. Now the broad balance has moved into deficit, and the overall balance is starting to depend on more short-term inflows.

The degree of positive capital flows may have partially reflected the belief that rising relative US productivity might offer better returns on investments than elsewhere or a view that the current account balance might be lowered in the future, as discussed earlier.

The underlying current account deficit will presumably become more of a problem for the dollar if quality capital flows slow more quickly, resulting in increasing dependence on short-term flows. This would then increase the risk of a forced abrupt improvement in the current account deficit, raising the risk of a sharp decline in US domestic demand and a sharp decline in the dollar.

The likely alternatives for the dollar in the coming years can perhaps be bounded by the following cases. A decline of 15 percent would result in a return to fair value reflecting relative productivity levels and would

Figure 1.2a   US dollar/Japanese yen: GSDEER, 1974-2002

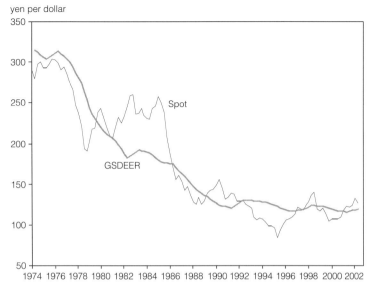

yen per dollar

GSDEER = Goldman Sachs dynamic equilibrium real exchange rates
Source: Goldman Sachs.

allow for a more equitable balance of world capital flows and an improved US current account. At the other extreme, a decline by close to 40 percent could result if markets are forced to adjust the US current account abruptly and significantly. To reduce the risk of an abrupt adjustment, policymakers may need to work toward adjusting the global pattern of demand to secure a better balance.

The Yen and the Japanese Economy

According to our basic research on currency equilibria, the yen is actually close to equilibrium against the dollar, with our latest specific point estimate suggesting a fair value currently around 119 yen to the dollar. In fact, our simple models of productivity-adjusted exchange equilibria actually show that the yen is overvalued on a trade-weighted basis. In this regard, it is difficult to believe that the yen should play a lead role in any policy-induced dollar decline to improve the US current account balance. It should play a role, but probably not a lead role.

Historically, our estimates have been reasonably similar to those of FEER-type models. In recent years, however, our estimates show that the equilibrium of the yen has declined. Against the yen, as can be seen in figure 1.2, the fair value of the dollar has improved, reflecting the improvements in US productivity relative to Japan, and this has more than compensated for Japan's negative inflation.

Figure 1.2b Japanese yen trade-weighted index, 1984-2002

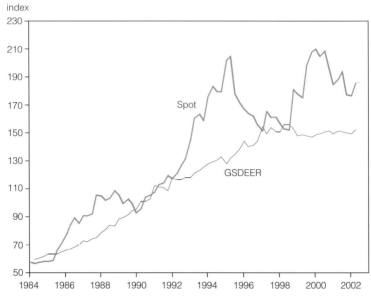

index

Spot

GSDEER

Source: Goldman Sachs.

Figure 1.2c Productivity in the United States and Japan, 1990-2002

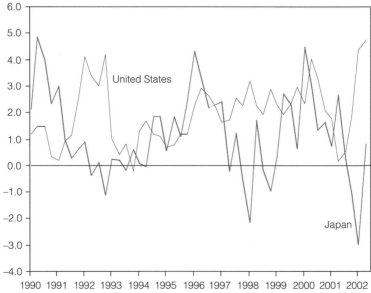

year-over-year change, percent

United States

Japan

Source: Japanese Cabinet Office; Japanese Ministry of Public Management, Home Affairs, Posts and Telecommunications; US Department of Labor; and Goldman Sachs calculations.

Table 1.2 Components of the Japanese yen in the Goldman Sachs trade-weighted index

Country or region	Weight
United States	25.43
Euroland	24.84
Korea	6.21
Taiwan	5.30
United Kingdom	5.29
Canada	4.91
China	3.56
Hong Kong	3.22
Singapore	2.82
Australia	2.12
Switzerland	2.05
Thailand	1.93
Malaysia	1.47
Sweden	1.44
Mexico	1.31
Indonesia	1.19
India	0.92
The Philippines	0.65
New Zealand	0.41

Source: Goldman Sachs.

We also find that the yen appears to be overvalued on a trade-weighted basis, which is not surprising considering that the other Asian economies have a considerable weight in Japan's trade (table 1.2). Each of the Chinese yuan, the Hong Kong dollar, the Korean won, and the Taiwan dollar seems cheap relative to the yen. In addition, the euro is an important part of the trade-weighted yen exchange rate, and according to our estimates, the euro remains undervalued relative to the yen.

Analysis of the breakdown of world export performance supports our valuation. The latest OECD estimates of relative export share of world exports show that Japan's share is still declining despite the level of the yen (figure 1.3). Much of the loss appears to have coincided with gains by China rather than by the other G-7 nations, although some Euroland economies have gained modestly.

This analysis may surprise those who simply observe Japan's persistent current account surplus and accumulation of foreign exchange reserves, both of which would rather bluntly suggest that the yen is in fact undervalued. Our research implies that the ongoing trade surpluses are more a reflection of weak imports and perhaps the depressed level of Japanese domestic demand rather than of high exports. As with other major economies, imports in Japan are greatly determined by the level of demand rather than the exchange rate; if Japanese demand had been significantly stronger over the past decade or so, Japan's trade surpluses might not have been as high as they are.

Figure 1.3 Share of world exports, 1989-2001

percent

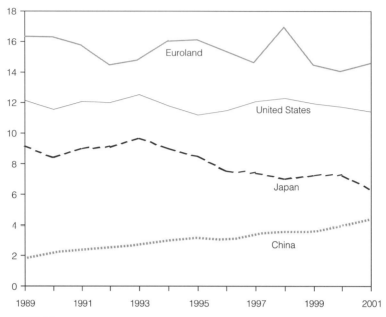

Source: IMF, Eurostat.

In this context, it is especially difficult to argue that the yen should play a lead role in any policy-induced decline in the dollar. In addition to our evidence of fair value for the yen, the current weak state of the Japanese economy must be taken into account. As figure 1.4 shows, Japanese GDP growth has strongly underperformed the United States since 1991, and in fact we now believe that Japan's long-term growth potential is just about 0.9 percent, while that of the United States is just under 3.0 percent. This is a far cry from the 1970s and 1980s, when Japan also ran large current account surpluses but had stronger trend growth.

Japan needs to undertake significant economic reform in order to strengthen its economic performance and to raise its long-term growth trend in view of its demographic and financial challenges. It would be difficult for Japan to absorb a trade-weighted yen appreciation on top of these severe challenges in the coming years.

This suggests that other currencies important to Japan, such as the Chinese yuan, the Korean won, and the euro, would need to strengthen more than the yen in any decline of the dollar for the trade-weighted yen to weaken.

The Broad Balance of Payments

Back in 1999, we started to give more attention in our analyses to the basic balance of payments rather than the current account balance as a

Figure 1.4   Real GDP comparisons: United States vs. Japan, 1991-2002

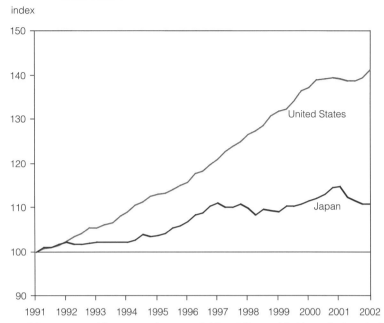

index

Source: US Department of Commerce, Japanese Cabinet Office, and Goldman Sachs calculations.

key driver of currencies. We did this primarily in order to understand the euro better in its infancy, but the approach is also applicable to the yen.

We define the broad basic balance of payments (BBoP) as the combination of the current account, net foreign direct investment flows, and portfolio flows of both bonds and equities. If all three are analyzed together, there appears to be a good correlation between the BBoP as a percentage of GDP and the trade-weighted exchange rate. The BBoP can be regarded as perhaps the best guide to commercial supply and demand for a currency and the remaining parts of the balance of payments are effectively hot money or short-term money flows (except for reserve changes).

The current account usually dominates the Japanese BBoP, but as can be seen in figure 1.5, this is not always the case. For example, in 1996-97, when the yen declined sharply, the BBoP was actually in modest deficit despite the current account surplus, reflecting large Japanese portfolio outflows. Again in the last year or so, Japan's BBoP has declined despite an upward turn in the current account surplus.

In 1998 the yen continued to weaken despite a significant improvement in Japan's current account and BBoP. The decline of the yen was being sustained by large speculation, particularly in the hedge fund community. Not surprisingly, when US and Japanese authorities joined in intervening to buy yen, the underlying BBoP allowed the yen to recover rapidly.

Figure 1.5 Japan: BBoP vs. current account, 1990-2002

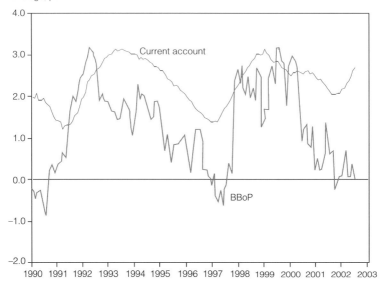

GDP, 12-month moving average, percent

BBoP = broad basic balance of payments

Source: Bank of Japan and Goldman Sachs calculations.

A Note on Foreign Exchange Intervention by Japanese Authorities

A considerable amount of attention is devoted to Japan's large-scale accumulation of foreign exchange reserves and the effectiveness of this intervention, and indeed, other papers in this conference focus on the topic. Two points on the subject deserve mention here. First, it is not always the case that the Japanese authorities intervene to sell yen. As noted above, in 1998, they were joined by the US Treasury in intervening to buy yen. Second, because of the weakness of the Japanese financial system, private-sector risk taking has been so limited in recent years that at times the intervention in the yen by the Ministry of Finance may be designed to close the balance of payments identity and to halt a large, destabilizing rise in the yen, as opposed to being based on the belief that the intervention will be successful in depreciating the yen. Indeed, in view of the chronic weakness of the Japanese economy, it could be argued that both the current and the capital accounts of the balance of payments have been artificially distorted.

The Euro and the Euroland Economy

The Euroland economy is also fragile, and so any policy-induced decline in the dollar to improve the US current account could also cause problems

Figure 1.6   Euro/US dollar: GSDEER, 1978-2002

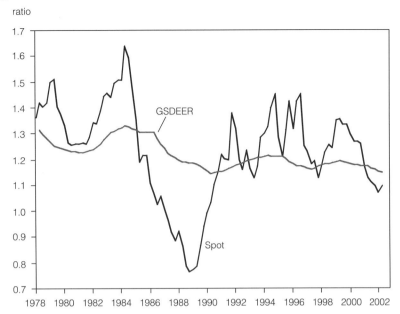

GSDEER = Goldman Sachs dynamic equilibrium real exchange rates

Source: Goldman Sachs.

for the euro zone. However, our GSDEER models suggest that the euro is significantly undervalued; with a stronger exchange rate, a better balance of monetary, financial, and economic conditions might help both the Euroland and the world economies. In this light, a policy-induced decline in the dollar that involved a major role for the euro might appear to have more benefits and would, together with a dollar decline against other currencies, make more sense than one greatly focused against the yen.

As mentioned earlier, China carries a greater weight than Germany in the trade-weighted exchange rate of the United States, and as we will see below, the euro zone does not have a large current account surplus. Nonetheless, the case for a policy-induced rise in the euro is reasonable. Figure 1.6 shows our GSDEER estimate for the exchange rate between the euro and the dollar. As can be seen, the euro appears to be significantly undervalued. Indeed, our point estimate is currently 1.19,[2] implying that the euro is still undervalued by around 20 percent. We also find that the euro is even more undervalued on a trade-weighted basis—some 24 percent—primarily because of undervaluation against the pound sterling and the Swiss franc as well as the yen.

---

2. Our latest estimate of dollar/euro equilibrium is 1.15, updated since the conference in September 2002.

Figure 1.7 Productivity: United States vs. Euroland, 1975-2002

year-over-year change, percent

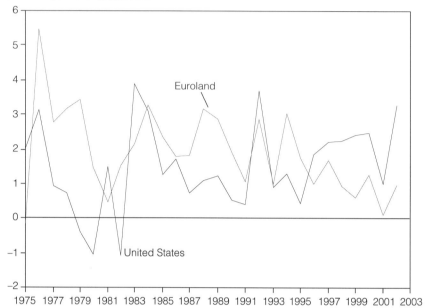

Source: Organization for Economic Cooperation and Development.

Two further points are worth making. First, as can be seen in the figure, the equilibrium for the dollar has also improved against the euro, once again because of relative US productivity improvements. A few years ago, the implied GSDEER estimate of the dollar-euro rate was in the mid 1.20s. Second, there is only modest evidence that Euroland is benefiting from the low valuation of the euro. As shown earlier in figure 1.3, the euro zone had some gains recently in its share of world exports, but the gains are modest. This latter fact serves to remind us that any estimate of equilibrium for the euro may be more open to doubt than estimates for most currencies because of the euro's infancy. It is worth noting that anecdotal evidence from many industries around Europe suggests that the euro is relatively cheap, especially in Switzerland and the United Kingdom.

Figure 1.7, which charts the rates of productivity change of Euroland and the United States since the 1970s, shows that the United States has performed better since the mid-1990s. This is a result of both improved productivity growth in the United States and slower productivity growth in Euroland. The latter reflects poorer economic performance in many of the larger economies.

We believe that the trend GDP growth potential of the euro zone has probably weakened to somewhere between 2.0 and 2.25 percent, after being around 2.5 percent when the European Monetary Union (EMU)

Figure 1.8 Real GDP comparisons: Euroland vs. United States, 1991-2002

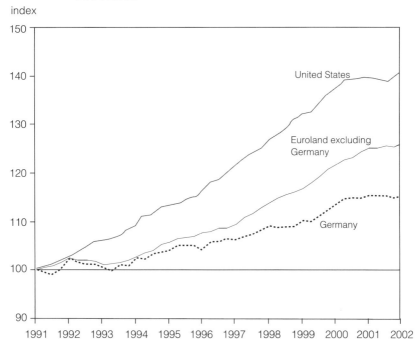

index

Source: US Department of Commerce; Eurostat; Goldman Sachs calculations.

was launched in 1999. Of course the theory of EMU suggested that the process should help boost the trend growth rate, not weaken it.

Within the euro zone, a number of countries have seen their productivity performance deteriorate, but none more so than Germany, and it may well be that the trend growth performance of Germany is now somewhere around 1.75 percent, instead of the 2.5 percent it appeared to be historically. As figure 1.8 shows, Germany has lagged badly behind the rest of the euro zone's economic growth since the early 1990s.

Rebalancing Economic Conditions

Euroland needs a stronger trend growth rate, and economic reforms are necessary to achieve them. It is also possible, however, for the euro zone to have a different, more beneficial balance of financial conditions. Table 1.3 shows the impact a broad decline in the dollar would have on a number of different regions and what the consequences for GDP growth

Table 1.3 Impact of US dollar depreciation

	Depreciation of US dollar of:		
	10 percent	20 percent	30 percent
Impact on Goldman Sachs trade-weighted index (percent)			
United States	−10	−20	−30
Euroland	3	5	8
Japan	3	7	10
United Kingdom	2	3	5
Impact on MCI/FCI (basis points)[a]			
United States	−50	−100	−150
Euroland	26	52	77
Japan	27	54	81
United Kingdom	56	111	167
Impact on real GDP growth (policy unchanged)			
United States	+0.50	+1.00	+1.50
Euroland	−0.26	−0.52	−0.77
Japan	−0.27	−0.54	−0.81
United Kingdom	−0.37	−0.74	−1.11
Advanced economies	−0.01	−0.03	−0.04
Rate reduction needed to offset depreciation[b]			
Euroland	29	57	86
Japan	n.p.	n.p.	n.p.
United Kingdom	57	114	171
Impact on real GDP growth (full policy offset)			
United States	+0.50	+1.00	+1.50
Euroland	0.0	0.0	0.0
Japan	−0.27	−0.54	−0.81
United Kingdom	0.0	0.0	0.0
Advanced economies	+0.16	+0.32	+0.48

MCI = Monetary Conditions Index; FCI = Financial Conditions Index; n.p. = not possible

a. The MCIs consist of weighted averages of short-term long-term interest rates and trade-weighted exchange rates, and FCIs add the impact of changes in equity markets.

b. The yield curve is assumed to remain constant.

Source: Goldman Sachs.

would be, both with and without economic policy change. The first section of the table shows the impact on the trade-weighted exchange rate. For example, a generalized 10 percent decline in the dollar would have a 10 percent effect on the trade-weighted index for the dollar, all else remaining equal. It would strengthen the trade-weighted euro and yen by about 3 percent and the trade-weighted pound sterling by about 2 percent. A 30 percent decline in the dollar would strengthen the trade-weighted euro by about 8 percent. The second section shows the impact on local financial conditions. The dollar has a weight of 5 percent in our US financial conditions index, and the exchange rate has a weight of about 10 percent for the euro zone and Japan. As the UK economy is the most open, the weight is even higher. The third section shows what the impact of the dollar decline would be via the resulting change in financial conditions on real GDP. We would estimate that US GDP growth would be boosted after a year by about 0.5 percent from a loosening of 50 basis points in financial conditions and 1.5 percent from a loosening of 150 basis points.

The euro zone and Japan would be negatively affected by similar magnitudes. Of course, Japan could not react to soften financial conditions easily, as interest rates are already zero. In addition to the yen valuation issue we mentioned earlier, this again serves to remind us that a weaker dollar might be bad news for Japan. However, there would be scope for the euro zone and the United Kingdom to respond, and the fourth section of the table shows the change in interest rates that would be needed in order to keep financial conditions unchanged.

The final section shows what the net consequences would be for each country or region as well as the total GDP consequences for the advanced economies. This shows that a trade-weighted dollar decline can help boost world GDP growth, but that a Euroland policy response would be needed.

The Euroland BBoP

As far as the determinants of the euro exchange rate are concerned, the BBoP seems to be important. Figure 1.9 shows that the euro's movements have coincided rather closely with the path of the BBoP. Initially the euro fell as the BBoP moved into significant deficit, and more recently it has recovered as the BBoP has moved back into surplus.

Unlike Japan's BBoP, the balance for the euro zone is not dominated by the current account but by portfolio and foreign direct investment (FDI) flows. Indeed, as figure 1.10 shows, the euro zone has run a current account balance close to zero for much of its life so far. It has moved recently into a small surplus, perhaps some further indication of the undervaluation of the euro. The BBoP has improved even more sharply than the current account in the last year as both net FDI and net portfolio flows have shifted dramatically. This has happened despite the fact that the United States has continued to outperform the euro zone in terms of economic growth and productivity. This suggests that the euro can continue to appreciate even if Euroland's growth rate is below that of the United States. We would argue that the growth differential compared with expectations about that growth differential are more important than the growth differential alone.

If the United States continues to grow more slowly than expected, the euro might strengthen further despite the weak growth rate of the euro zone. Of course it would be better for the Euroland economy if the euro strengthened more as a result of Euroland's growth exceeding expecta-

Figure 1.9 Euroland: BBoP vs. TWI, 1998-2002

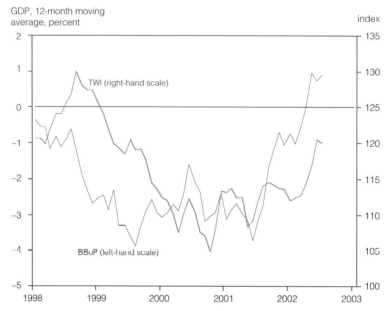

BBoP = broad basic balance of payments; TWI = Trade-weighted index
Source: European Central Bank; Goldman Sachs data and calculations.

Figure 1.10 Euroland: BBoP vs. current account, 1998-2002

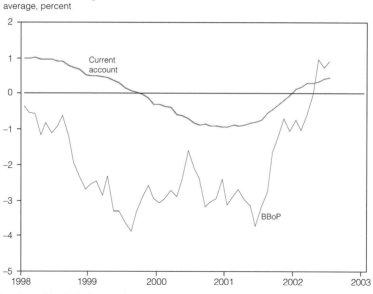

BBoP = broad basic balance of payments.
Sources: European Central Bank and Goldman Sachs calculations.

tions; and if policy could be changed to help bring about both, that would be good for both the euro zone and the rest of the world.

Figure 1.11 illustrates the dramatic shift in FDI-related flows in the past year. The graph shows our estimate, based on announced deals that are yet to be completed, of the pending "pipeline" of cash mergers and acquisitions (M&A) flows between the euro zone and the rest of the world. After showing significant outflows for much of the euro's life, the current pipeline shows a small pending inflow. This reflects the end of the technology, media, and telecommunications boom as many leading Euroland companies can no longer afford to make overseas acquisitions; indeed, many have to sell them. The US M&A pipeline with the rest of the world is shown for comparison. As can be seen, the opposite trend is evident, with the United States now experiencing net outflows. It is quite likely that if policy could improve the outlook for the Euroland economies, pending inflows might improve even more. While structural reforms and a more welcoming stance on corporate ownership might have a big impact, a significant decline in interest rates might help also.

As for net portfolio flows (figure 1.12), there have been some notable fluctuations in both net bond flows and net equity flows. In recent months net equity flows have been shifting back to the United States.[3] Net bond flows have shifted from a large net inflow to the United States in the past few months, and net equity flows have slowed, in contrast with the picture of large net outflows for much of 2000 and early 2001. The recent shift of flows back to the United States after a brief period of net inflows to the euro zone primarily reflects foreign selling of Euroland stocks as US-based investors have been disappointed by the lack of Euroland growth and the absence of policies to stimulate better opportunities.

It seems likely that if growth performance could be improved, these flows would be helped. A significant easing of monetary policy could help to achieve these changes, as could any changes in the implementation of Euroland's Stability and Growth Pact. It may well be that a policy-induced decline in the dollar could help to achieve them, adding to the momentum of the euro, aiding a move closer to equilibrium, and achieving more domestic-led economic growth.

---

3. The charts are based on the cross-border net flows that Goldman Sachs sees between the United States and the euro zone (the y-axis labels have been removed to preserve client confidentiality).

Figure 1.11a   Net Euroland cash mergers and acquisitions pipeline* with the rest of the world

billions of US dollars

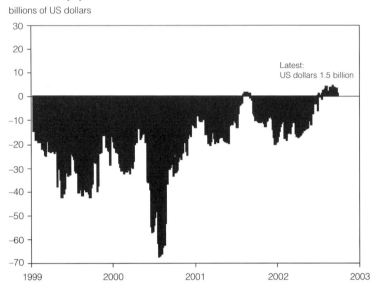

Latest:
US dollars 1.5 billion

* = Euroland mergers and acquisitions abroad.
Source: Thomson Financial SDC and Goldman Sachs calculations.

Figure 1.11b   Net US cash mergers and acquisitions pipeline* with the rest of the world

billions of US dollars

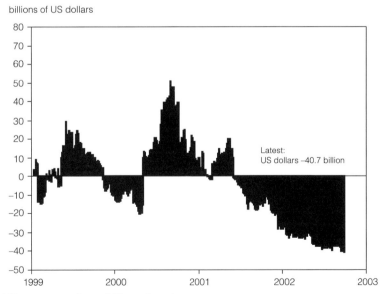

Latest:
US dollars –40.7 billion

* = US mergers and acquisitions abroad.
Source: Thomson Financial SDC and Goldman Sachs calculations.

Figure 1.12a   Net Goldman Sachs bond flows from Euroland to the United States, 2000-02

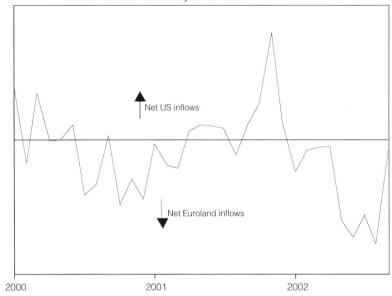

Net US inflows

Net Euroland inflows

2000   2001   2002

Source: Goldman Sachs.

Figure 1.12b   Net Goldman Sachs equity flows from Euroland to the United States, 2000-02

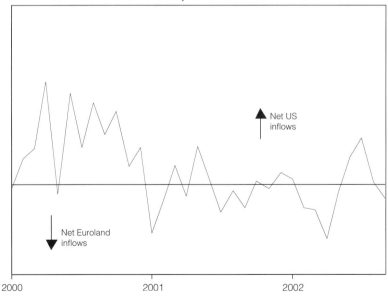

Net US
inflows

Net Euroland
inflows

2000   2001   2002

Note: See footnote 3.

Source: Goldman Sachs.

Conclusion

This analysis has shown that a policy-induced decline in the dollar would need to take into account the changes in rates of productivity growth in recent years as well as the remarkably different patterns of trade that the United States has today compared with in the late 1980s. In addition to arguing that the yen should not play a lead role in any policy-induced decline in the dollar, the analysis argues that the dollar would need to decline against a broader basket of currencies, including those of Canada, China, Korea, and possibly even Mexico. We have shown that the yen is close to equilibrium against the dollar and overvalued on a trade-weighted basis and that given Japan's weak economic health, a yen-led strengthening of a dollar decline would not be helpful.

We have also shown that although the euro zone has a small current account surplus, our models suggest that the euro remains significantly undervalued. In addition, unlike Japan, the euro zone has scope to expand financial conditions in response to a decline of the dollar, which would help to achieve a better balance of domestic-led and world growth.

References

Balassa, Bela. 1964. The Purchasing-Power Parity Doctrine: A Reappraisal. *Journal of Political Economy* 72 (December): 584-96.

Leahy, Michael P. 1998. New Summary Measures of the Foreign Exchange Value of the Dollar. New York: Federal Reserve Bulletin, October.

O'Neill, Jim, and Jan Hatzius. 2002. *US Balance of Payments: Still Unsustainable*. Goldman Sachs Global Economics Paper No. 70. London, March.

Samuelson, Paul A. 1964. Theoretical Notes on Trade Problems. *Review of Economics and Statistics* 46 (March): 145-54.

Wren-Lewis, Simon, and Rebecca L. Driver. 1998. *Real Exchange Rates for the Year 2000*. POLICY ANALYSES IN INTERNATIONAL ECONOMICS 54. Washington: Institute for International Economics.

2

The Dollar's Equilibrium Exchange Rate: A Market View

MICHAEL R. ROSENBERG

In theory, a currency's value should gravitate over time toward its real long-run equilibrium value. If we were able to estimate this value, investors would be able to identify the likely path that an exchange rate will take on a long-term basis and position their portfolios accordingly. Unfortunately, there is no uniform agreement among economists either on what exchange rate level represents a currency's true long-run equilibrium value or on the method that should be used to estimate its value. For instance, the method with the widest following among economists and strategists—the purchasing power parity (PPP) approach, which equates a currency's fair value with the trend in relative price levels—is also widely recognized to have serious limitations because other fundamental forces have often played an important role in driving the long-term path of exchange rates.

The purpose of this paper is to describe how equilibrium exchange rate modeling can be useful for foreign exchange market participants. One of my principal goals is to demonstrate that equilibrium exchange rate modeling is not purely an arcane academic exercise. I begin by discussing the fundamental equilibrium exchange rate framework pioneered by John Williamson. I then survey several modeling attempts that use the FEER framework as well as others undertaken in recent years to estimate where the dollar's equilibrium value versus the euro lies.

Michael R. Rosenberg is managing director and head of global foreign exchange research at Deutsche Bank. Prior to joining Deutsche Bank in May 1999, he was managing director and head of international fixed income research at Merrill Lynch for 15 years.

Most model-based estimates suggest that the dollar is significantly over-valued versus the euro. I suggest that those estimates might be understating the dollar's true equilibrium value. Specifically, I raise the following questions: Is it possible that "new economy" forces raised the dollar's equilibrium value beginning in the second half of the 1990s? If so, what level of the dollar is now consistent with long-run equilibrium? I then consider whether a portion of the dollar's rise in the second half of the 1990s might have been a disequilibrium phenomenon. One could argue that overoptimistic assessments of "new economy" forces might have caused the dollar to overshoot its fair value. In addition, the excessively wide US current account deficit that has arisen in recent years, and which the United States might soon find problematic to finance, also suggests a possible dollar overshoot.

Assuming it is agreed that the dollar is now overvalued, although not by how much, I consider what kind of adjustment in the dollar's value one should expect to help bring the dollar back into line with fair value. If "new economy" forces have indeed raised the dollar's equilibrium value, it might not have to fall by much from its present level to bring it into line with fair value. History suggests, nonetheless, that investors should be braced for the possibility that the dollar might overshoot its equilibrium level—whatever that level is—to the downside, as it has in previous cycles.

Finally, I address the question of the Japanese yen. Although some would argue that favorable external balance considerations in Japan should lift the yen's equilibrium value over time, I suggest that unfavorable internal balance considerations in Japan—specifically, its persistent economic slump and financial-sector problems—are likely to drive the yen's equilibrium value lower over time.

Market Participants and Equilibrium Exchange Rate Estimates

In practice, estimates of long-run equilibrium often vary considerably, depending on which model is used. The problem for foreign exchange market participants is to determine which of these models will yield the most reliable estimate of the dollar's equilibrium value. Consider the dilemma posed by a recent European Central Bank (ECB) working paper (Detken et al. 2002) that examined four models of the euro's equilibrium value. The study found that all four models agreed that the euro was undervalued, but the estimated magnitude of its undervaluation varied widely from model to model—from 5 percent to 27 percent. From an investor's perspective, the failure of these models to agree on what level of the euro represents long-run equilibrium could have a major bearing on how much foreign exchange risk one would be willing to undertake.

Investors who believe that the euro is only moderately undervalued might prefer to maintain a portfolio posture that is close to neutrally weighted toward the euro. Those who believe that the euro is significantly undervalued and thus has considerable upside potential might prefer to aggressively overweight the euro in their portfolios.

Because different models often yield different estimates of a currency's long-run equilibrium value, market participants are often unwilling to risk significant amounts of capital on the basis of such estimates. This is especially true for fund managers whose performances are evaluated over relatively short time spans. It is no wonder, then, that many fund managers today concentrate less of their energies on long-term equilibrium exchange rate models and more on shorter-run forecasting tools such as momentum-based trading rules and order flow, sentiment, and positioning indicators.

If equilibrium exchange rates are so difficult to estimate and very few investors are willing to commit capital on the basis of such estimates, one might ask why foreign exchange market participants would have any interest in such models. The answer might be that, although it is probably impossible to pinpoint where true long-run equilibrium lies, an equilibrium exchange rate modeling framework might nevertheless help investors better understand the forces that give rise to long-term cycles in exchange rates.

The dollar has exhibited a tendency both to rise and to fall over long-term cycles, and the lion's share of those cycles have been driven by upward and downward revisions in the market's assessment of the dollar's real long-run equilibrium value. Not only are exchange rate cycles long—often lasting five years or longer—but also the magnitude of the dollar's movements in each cycle has tended to be quite large. Indeed, at the end of each long exchange rate cycle, there has been a tendency for the dollar to overshoot its equilibrium value by a wide margin. Knowing that the dollar rises and falls over long-term cycles and that sustained shifts in equilibrium exchange rates are largely responsible for those long cycles, investors might profitably concentrate more of their attention on the forces that determine equilibrium exchange rates, whether their investment time horizons are short or long.

Equilibrium Exchange Rate Assessment: The FEER/IMF Approach

The failure of the PPP approach to hold over medium-term and, in some cases, long-term horizons has led economists to consider alternative approaches to assessing long-term value in the foreign exchange markets. For instance, the International Monetary Fund (IMF) (Isard et al. 2001) favors the macroeconomic balance approach to long-term exchange rate determination. In this approach, the long-run equilibrium exchange rate

Figure 2.1 The IMF's macroeconomic-balance approach to long-run exchange rate determination

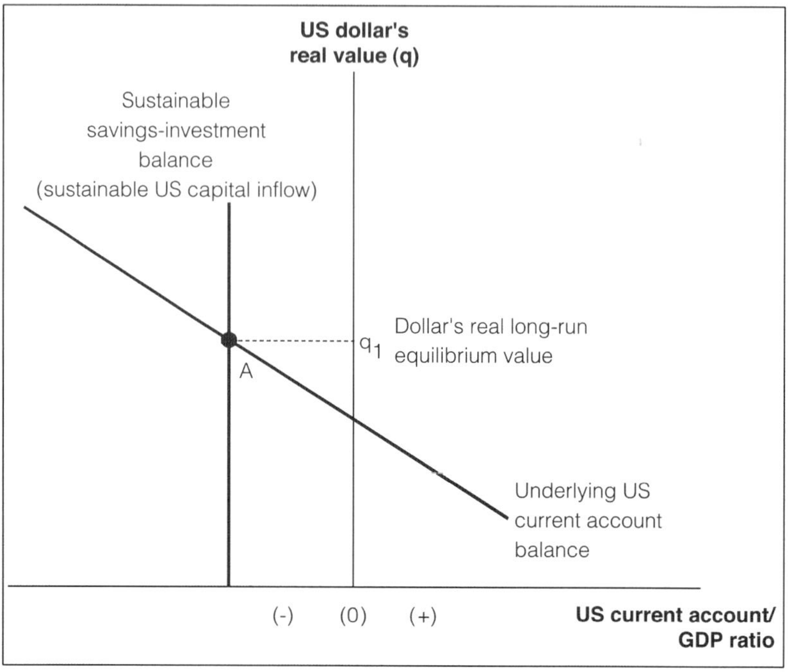

Source: Adapted from Isard et al. (2001, 8).

is defined as the rate that would equalize a country's sustainable savings-investment balance with its underlying current account balance. If there is a sustained shift in a country's national savings, investment, or underlying current account, then in this model the real long-run equilibrium exchange rate should adjust accordingly. This method is quite similar to the fundamental equilibrium exchange rate (FEER) approach pioneered by John Williamson (1994), which serves as the foundation for most equilibrium exchange rate modeling efforts. In recent years, a variety of other approaches have been undertaken, such as the NATREX model and behavioral/dynamic equilibrium exchange rate models, with each offering certain advantages over the others.

Figure 2.1 illustrates how the dollar's equilibrium value is determined using the IMF's three-step exchange rate assessment approach. In step 1, a US trade equation is estimated to calculate how the US underlying current account position would typically behave in response to changes in the dollar's real value. As illustrated in the figure, the US underlying current account position (the US external payments position that would prevail if all countries operated at full employment) is shown to vary inversely with changes in the dollar's real value, q. In step 2, the US normal or sustainable domestic savings-investment imbalance is estimated. In a global context, where capital is permitted to flow freely, domestic investment need not equal domestic savings. If domestic investment exceeds domestic savings, the imbalance can be financed by attracting capital from overseas. The critical issue is to determine how much foreign capital a country can attract on a sustained basis to finance an excess of investment over domestic savings. If it is estimated that the United States cannot attract, on a sustained basis, capital inflows that exceed, say, 2.5 percent of US GDP, then the gap between US domestic investment and domestic savings could not exceed 2.5 percent of GDP on a sustained basis. Since the gap between US domestic investment and domestic savings equals the US current account deficit, this would imply that the US current account deficit could not exceed 2.5 percent of GDP on a sustained basis as well.

Step 3 in the IMF's approach combines steps 1 and 2 to arrive at an equilibrium estimate of the dollar's value. In figure 2.1, the dollar's equilibrium value is determined at the point where the US underlying current account schedule intersects the US sustainable savings-investment gap schedule at point A. This is shown as q_1 in figure 2.1. In the IMF's framework, it is possible for the US savings-investment gap (and therefore the current account imbalance) to exceed its long-run "sustainable" level on a short-term basis or possibly even a medium-term basis as long as foreign capital can be attracted to finance the gap. Nonetheless, in the long run the savings-investment imbalance could not exceed its sustainable level, since it is presumed that there is an upper limit on a country's ability to attract foreign capital on a sustained basis. That upper limit determines where the vertical savings-investment gap schedule is positioned, where the savings-investment gap schedule and the underlying current account balance schedule will intersect, and thus what exchange rate level will represent the dollar's real long-run equilibrium level.

Using this FEER framework, a number of economists have attempted to model the dollar's equilibrium value in recent years. A recent OECD study (Koen et al. 2001) surveyed these modeling attempts, with specific emphasis on the equilibrium level of the US dollar/euro exchange rate (table 2.1). Although equilibrium estimates vary widely, with dollar/euro ratios ranging from 0.87 to 1.45, the median estimate of long-run fair value for the dollar appears to fall into the range of 1.10 to 1.20, which is broadly in line with our purchasing power parity estimates.

If these equilibrium exchange rate estimates were perceived by the investment community to be on the mark, and with the dollar hovering well below these levels, we would expect that a large number of fundamental-based investors would currently be holding significantly long-euro/short-dollar positions, since this would put them in position to profit from an expected drop in the dollar's value toward its long-run equilibrium level. But this is not what we in fact find. Rather, according to recent investor positioning surveys, most fundamental-based managers appear to be holding neutral positions in both the euro and the dollar.

Table 2.1 Selected estimates of the US dollar's medium/long-run "equilibrium" value versus the euro

Study	Key explanatory variables/model	Equilibrium exchange rate estimate (dollar/euro)
Wren-Lewis and Driver (1998)	FEER model	1.19-1.45
Borowski and Couharde (2000)	FEER model	1.23-1.31
Alberola et al. (1999)	Ratio of nontraded/traded goods prices, net foreign assets	1.26
Chinn and Alquist (2000)	M1, GDP, short-term interest rates, CPI, ratio of nontraded/traded goods prices	1.19-1.28
Lorenzen and Thygessen (2000)	Net foreign assets, R&D spending, demographics, ratio of nontraded/traded goods prices	1.17-1.24
Duval (2001)	Consumption, multifactor productivity, real long-term yield spread, ratio of nontraded/traded goods prices	1.15
Clostermann and Schnatz (2000)	Real long-term yield spread, oil price, government spending, ratio of nontraded/traded goods prices	1.13
Teïletche (2000)	Productivity, government spending, real long-term yield spread, M1, industrial production	1.09
OECD PPP estimates	GDP PPP	1.09
Gern et al. (2001)	Short-term real interest rate differential	1.03
Schulmeister (2000)	PPP for tradables	0.87
Deutsche Bank (2002)	PPP (long-run average)	1.20

M1 = the most liquid measure of money supply; CPI = Consumer Price Index; FEER = fundamental equilibrium exchange rate; PPP = purchasing power parity

Source: OECD Working Paper Number 298, June 2001 (except Deutsche Bank).

Have global fund managers become overly conservative in their investor positioning, or is it possible that market practitioners might have a less pessimistic view of the dollar's equilibrium value than the one implied by the model-based equilibrium exchange rate estimates reported in table 2.1?

"New Economy" Forces and the Dollar's Equilibrium Value

Why might market practitioners have a less pessimistic view of the dollar's equilibrium value than the one implied by most model-based estimates?

**Figure 2.2   The dollar's 7-year rise vs. the deutsche mark
(1995-2002)**

deutsche mark/US dollars

Source: Datastream.

I believe a strong case could be made that the market's assessment of the dollar's real long-run equilibrium value might have been pushed significantly higher beginning in 1999 as the marketplace embraced the notion that "new economy" forces would not only raise the speed limit at which the US economy could safely grow without igniting inflation, but might also have raised the sustainable current account deficit that the US could safely run without triggering a major downward adjustment in the dollar's value.

To fully appreciate the role that "new economy" forces might have played in influencing the market's assessment of the dollar's equilibrium value in the late 1990s, it is instructive to break down the dollar's rise over the 1995-2000 period into two phases. (Note that the euro was introduced in January of 1999, and that I use the trend in the deutsche mark/dollar exchange rate to illustrate my point.) As shown in figure 2.2, the dollar rose by 50 pfennigs in the three and a half years between the spring of 1995 and the fall of 1998, and then rose another 50 pfennigs between the fall of 1999 and the fall of 2000. (Over the intervening period between the fall of 1998 and the fall of 1999, the deutsche mark was unchanged from point to point.)

The first phase of dollar strength versus the deutsche mark, between 1995 and 1998, can be explained largely by the widening in US/German real long-term interest rate differentials that took place over that period

Figure 2.3 Deutsche mark/dollar exchange rate and US/German real interest rate differential (10-year bond yield less increase in CPI, 1993-2002)

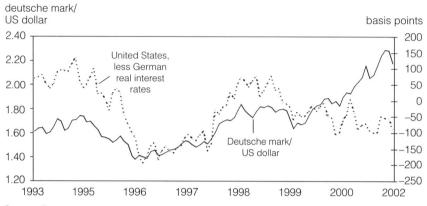

Source: Datastream.

(figure 2.3). The second phase of dollar strength began in the fall of 1999. Note, however, that the trend in real yield spreads over the 1999-2000 period argued for a weaker, not a stronger dollar. Yet the dollar soared a full 50 pfennigs in just 12 months between the fall of 1999 and the fall of 2000. What could have caused the dollar to rise so sharply in so short a time?

In my view, the dollar was propelled higher by an upward revision in the market's assessment of its real long-run equilibrium value during that period. This reassessment was sudden and dramatic, following closely on the heels of a sudden and dramatic upward revision in market expectations about the US economy's long-run growth prospects.

Consider the annual survey of professional forecasters conducted by the Federal Reserve Bank of Philadelphia. The survey asks professional forecasters each February: What annual rate of growth do you expect US real GDP and productivity to average over the next 10 years? The survey results are reported in figures 2.4 and 2.5. As shown, the projected average long-term US real GDP and productivity growth rates barely changed from one year to the next in the 1990s. Each year, polled economists projected that long-term US real GDP growth would average around 2.5 percent per annum, a fairly modest pace, while long-term productivity growth would average a mere 1.5 percent per annum.

Then something happened between the 1999 and 2000 surveys. Suddenly, economists raised their estimates of long-term US real GDP growth from 2.5 percent per annum to over 3 percent, and at the same time raised their estimates of long-term US productivity growth from a bland 1.5 percent per annum to a brisk 2.5 percent. Normally, one would have expected any changes in the US long-term growth outlook to have taken place gradually over a number of years, not suddenly. But in 1999-2000,

Figure 2.4   Long-term expectation of US real GDP growth

expected 10-year growth rate (percent)

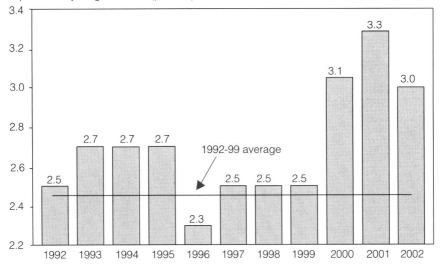

Source: Federal Reserve Bank of Philadelphia, Business Outlook Survey, February 2002.

Figure 2.5   Long-term expectation of US productivity

expected 10-year
growth rate (percent)

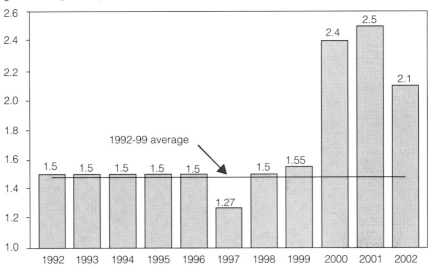

Source: Federal Reserve Bank of Philadelphia, Business Outlook Survey, February 2002.

Figure 2.6 "New economy" forces and the rise in the US sustainable current account deficit

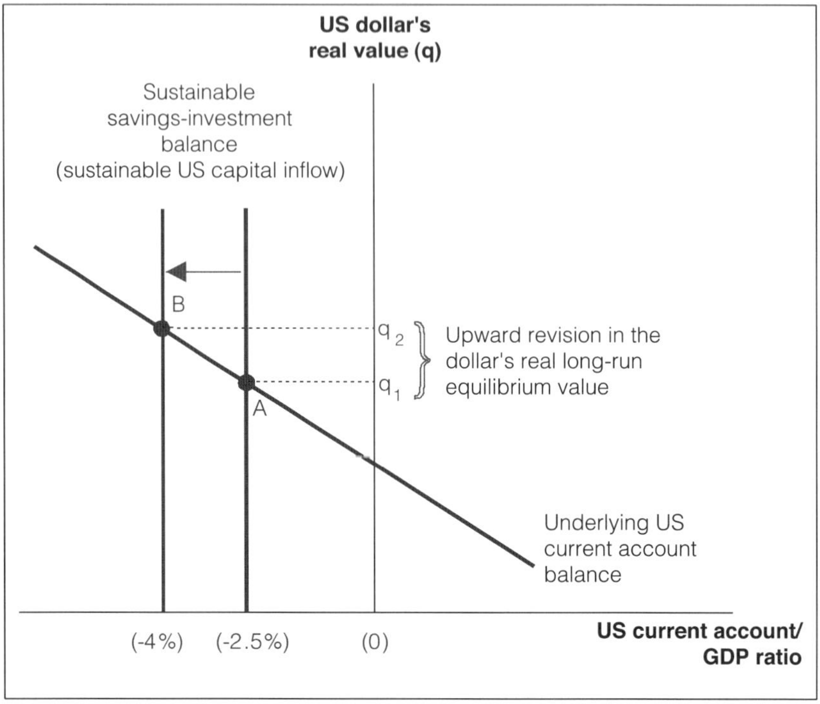

Source: Adapted from Isard et al. (2001).

it appears that expectations about long-term growth prospects in the US not only soared, but that the change occurred virtually overnight.

The US economy had been growing faster than the Euroland and Japanese economies over much of the 1990s. According to the Philadelphia Fed survey results, though, it was not until very late in the decade that economists and market participants began to take notice of something special occurring in the US that might distance the American economy from the rest of the world on a sustained basis. The US economy was undergoing a major investment boom in both absolute terms and relative to the rest of the world in the 1990s, with most of the investment boom concentrated in the information technology (IT) arena, where US industry held a dominant global position. The IT-led investment boom, in turn, contributed to the surge in US productivity growth that began in the second half of the 1990s. Based on the Philadelphia Fed's survey results, the initial gains in US productivity growth were probably viewed as transitory, but by the end of the decade, they were expected to be permanent.

In my view, the upward-adjusted long-term growth and investment outlook compelled the market to revise sharply upward its estimate of the dollar's real long-run equilibrium level in 1999-2000. Figure 2.6 illustrates how the IT-led investment boom might have raised the dollar's real long-run equilibrium value. The figure is similar to figure 2.1 but assumes that the late 1990s surge in US investment spending led market participants to expect a permanently wider gap—say 4 percent of GDP—between US investment and US savings than the 2.5 percent gap that might have previously been the case. A permanently wider gap between US investment and savings would give rise to a leftward shift in the US savings-investment balance schedule, which would then intersect the underlying US current account balance schedule at point B in figure 2.6, resulting in an upward revision in the dollar's equilibrium value from q_1 to q_2.

A permanently wider gap between US investment and savings would be possible only if the US were able to attract additional capital from abroad on a sustained basis. A sustained increase in capital inflows would be possible only if the rate of return on US assets were sufficiently attractive to induce foreign savings to move offshore and into the United States on a permanent or semipermanent basis. If the United States could suddenly attract greater capital inflows on a sustained basis, it could then more easily finance a larger current account deficit on a sustained basis.

How large the sustainable current account deficit might now be is anyone's guess, but if the long-term trend in US productivity growth has risen from 1.5 percent per annum to roughly 2.5 percent, then perhaps the sustainable current account deficit that the United States could now safely run might have risen from 2.5 percent of GDP to 3.5 to 4 percent of GDP. This possibility is illustrated in figure 2.6, where the boom in US investment spending is shown to have contributed not only to a rise in the dollar's equilibrium value, but also to a rise in the sustainable current account deficit that the United States could now safely run.

Was the Dollar's Rise in 1999-2000 Entirely an Equilibrium Phenomenon?

The dollar was not the only financial asset that soared in value over the 1999-2000 period. The marketplace's embrace of "new economy" notions also helped propel US equity values to unprecedented heights. Indeed, the NASDAQ index tripled in value between the fourth quarter of 1998 and the first quarter of 2000. With the benefit of hindsight, it is clear that a large part of the surge in the NASDAQ index was a bubble phenomenon that has subsequently reversed. However, much of the dollar's gain over that same period remains essentially intact. Does this imply that the dollar's rise was largely an equilibrium phenomenon? From my perspective, although a significant portion of the rise probably was, a certain portion of it was also probably a disequilibrium phenomenon that will eventually need to be reversed. Several factors lead me to this conclusion.

First, although a large part of the rise in US investment spending in the second half of the 1990s was productive, there was probably also a considerable amount that should be deemed excessive, particularly during the height of the IT bubble period. Anecdotal evidence suggests that investment spending was especially excessive in the Internet and telecom sectors. This might have contributed to an unsustainable leftward shift of the US savings-investment balance schedule beyond the leftwardly shifted savings-investment balance schedule depicted in figure 2.6. US investment has indeed turned down sharply since its peak pace in 2000, so a decline in the dollar's equilibrium value should be expected, assuming the decline in investment is sustained. In figure 2.6, the savings-investment balance schedule should shift back to the right, with a concurrent downward move in the dollar's value toward its upwardly revised real long-run equilibrium level, q_2.

Second, even if one were to embrace the idea that the recent gains in US productivity will prove sustainable, a case could still be made that a portion of the dollar's rising trend was not an equilibrium phenomenon. The reason is that the US productivity gains registered during the second half of the 1990s were not evenly distributed across all sectors of the economy. A recent McKinsey & Company study (2001) found that only six of the leading 59 sectors of the US economy, representing 28 percent of US real GDP, contributed to the 1995-2000 productivity gains. These sectors were heavy users of new technologies. The other 53 sectors, representing 72 percent of US real GDP, contributed virtually nothing to the productivity gains of that period.

It appears that the gains in productivity registered by the 28 percent that invested heavily in new technologies were so great that they were able to boost the aggregate productivity performance of the entire US economy in 1995-2000. That, in turn, helped drive the dollar higher over that period. For the 28 percent of the US economy that enjoyed strong productivity gains, the dollar's rise has not seriously dented their overall competitiveness, since the positive effect of strong productivity gains has helped offset the negative effect of a rising dollar. However, the other 72 percent of the US economy must now struggle to compete in world markets with an overvalued exchange rate and without an offsetting gain in productivity. That would explain why a large number of US firms are now loudly complaining that the dollar's strength is undermining their long-run competitiveness. If a small but dynamic sector of the US economy is largely responsible for the dollar's gains, then a case could be made that the dollar's value is currently too high for a large segment of the economy and that a weaker dollar might therefore be warranted.

Third, although one could argue that "new economy" forces might have raised the size of the sustainable US current account deficit, that does not mean that the United States can now run any size deficit that it wishes. If, for example, the sustainable US current account deficit limit has risen from, say, 2.5 percent of GDP to 3.5 to 4.0 percent of GDP, then a deficit that exceeded this revised limit would have to be eliminated. Data for the second quarter of 2002 indicate that the US current account deficit as a percentage of GDP widened to a new record of 5 percent, and it is highly unlikely that a deficit of this magnitude will prove sustainable. According to studies by Catherine Mann (1999) and Caroline Freund (2000), current account deficits that have reached a threshold of over 4 percent of GDP have tended to set corrective forces in motion—including corrective currency adjustments. With the US now having passed this threshold, the dollar would thus appear to be in a vulnerable position.

The major problem facing the US at the present time is that in order to finance its record shortfall in the last year, the US has had to absorb 70 percent of world net foreign savings, according to the IMF's September 2002 Global Financial Stability Report. It is unlikely, however, that the United States will be able to have free access to such a large share of world net savings indefinitely. If growth prospects elsewhere in the world pick up, the United States will likely have to make do with a smaller share.

At present, the United States is actually in a rather weak position to attract the needed capital inflows to finance its current account deficit. Normally, when a country runs a larger current account deficit, it often must push interest rates higher to attract the necessary capital from abroad to finance its current account imbalance. One would therefore expect a country's current account shortfall to move roughly in line with domestic-foreign yield spreads, with larger deficits associated with wider domestic-foreign yield spreads and vice versa.

Indeed, that has been the case for the United States over much of the past 15 to 20 years (figure 2.7). But in the past three years or so, something has gone awry with this relationship. At the same time that the US current account deficit widened to record levels in the 1999-2002 period, US-foreign yield spreads have actually narrowed, and quite appreciably so. What this indicates is that the United States did not have to go out of its way to attract the necessary capital to finance the record surge in its current account deficit. Instead, it was able to finance its record shortfall with huge net inflows into the US equity market (figure 2.8), surging net foreign direct investment inflows (figure 2.9), and capital flight from emerging markets (figure 2.10). As figures 2.8 to 2.10 indicate, however, these sources of capital now appear to be drying up. With the current account deficit still widening, the dollar's vulnerability clearly has risen, especially given the fact that the trend in US-foreign yield spreads is moving in a direction that will discourage capital flows into the United States.

Fourth and finally, although it is true that professional forecasters did revise significantly upward their long-term projections of US GDP and

Figure 2.7   US current account deficit and the US/German short-term interest rate spread

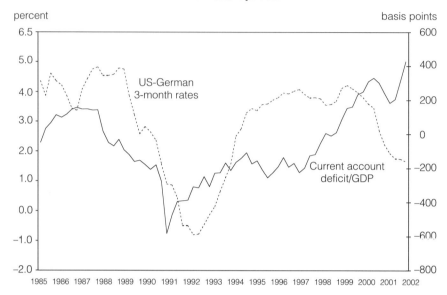

Source: Datastream.

Figure 2.8   Net foreign purchases of US equities

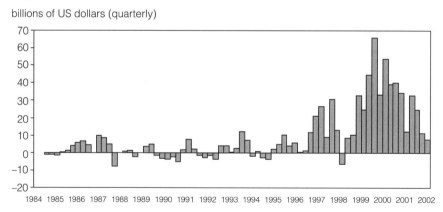

Source: Datastream.

Figure 2.9 Net foreign direct investment in the United States

billions of US dollars

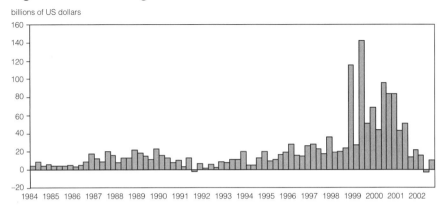

Source: Datastream.

Figure 2.10 Capital flows into emerging markets (net private capital flows)

billions of US dollars

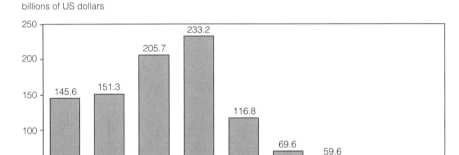

Source: IMF *World Economic Outlook* December 2001.

productivity growth, which was deemed to be positive for the dollar on a longer-term basis, a careful reading of figures 2.4 and 2.5 above indicates that professional forecasters did scale back their long-term projections for both US GDP growth and productivity in the most recent (2002) survey. To the extent that the dollar's equilibrium value was pushed higher by upbeat estimates of long-term US economic growth prospects, one would expect that a less upbeat projection of long-run US growth prospects should be accompanied by a downward revision in the dollar's equilibrium value. If long-run US growth prospects are scaled back further in the 2003 survey, which seems likely, then a further downward adjustment of the dollar would be called for.

How Far Can the Dollar Actually Fall?

Summing up my thoughts so far, it appears to me that a sizable portion of the dollar's rise was an equilibrium phenomenon brought about by "new economy" forces but that an equally sizable portion might have been a disequilibrium phenomenon caused by an excessive increase in US investment spending that is now being reversed. In addition, the outsized US current account shortfall might not be easily financed in the future, particularly with US-foreign yield spreads moving in a direction that will discourage capital inflows. Furthermore, the sharp rise in the dollar's value might have made a large segment of the US economy less competitive. Finally, overly optimistic long-term forecasts of US GDP and productivity growth now appear to be in the process of being scaled back.

This then raises the question of just how far the dollar will need to fall from present levels to bring it back into line with its long-run fair value. The answer largely depends on what one assumes the long-run sustainable US current account deficit to be. If the ratio of the sustainable US current account deficit to GDP is 2.5 percent and the US current account shortfall is 5 percent of GDP, then a sizable decline in the dollar's value from present levels will be required to bring the actual deficit in line with its long-run sustainable level. If the sustainable current account shortfall were closer to the range of 3.5 to 4 percent of GDP, then only a modest decline in the dollar would be required.

According to the Federal Reserve Board's econometric model, a sustained 10 percent drop in the dollar's trade-weighted value over the next two years should boost US exports by roughly 9 percent and cut imports by roughly 6.5 percent to 7 percent. That should be enough to reduce the US current account deficit by roughly 1 percent of GDP, which would then bring it in line with a target range of 3.5 to 4 percent of GDP. However, the trade-weighted dollar would need to fall by about 25 percent from present levels to satisfy a 2.5 percent of GDP target.

Assuming agreement that the dollar must fall in the future, how certain are we that the decline will stop once the dollar hits its estimated long-run equilibrium level? History would suggest that once the dollar begins to decline in earnest, there is a very good chance that it will overshoot its fair value (whatever that level is) to the downside.

Historically, the dollar has exhibited a tendency to rise and fall over long-term cycles, with each cycle lasting for five years or longer. Dollar cycles often begin from a point of significant overvaluation or undervaluation on a PPP basis. From those maximum over- or undervalued levels, the dollar typically enters a first phase of adjustment by falling or rising

Figure 2.11   US dollar purchasing power parity (Deutsche Bank
PPP estimates based on 1982-2000 averages)

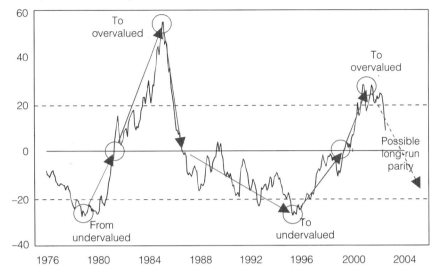

percent over/under PPP
level (vs. deutsche mark)

Note: The zero line represents the long-run equilibrium level of PPP.

Source: Datastream, Deutsche Bank estimates.

to correct the initial misalignment. But market forces seldom stop driving
the dollar lower or higher once PPP has been restored. Rather, the dollar
often enters a second phase in which the marketplace drives the dollar well
beyond its estimated PPP value, and in the process creates a new and
rather large PPP misalignment with the opposite sign of the dollar's initial
misalignment. This process then repeats itself over succeeding cycles.

Figure 2.11 illustrates the dollar's pattern of long cycles followed by
PPP misalignment over the past 25 years. As shown, the dollar became
highly undervalued (by more than −20 percent versus the deutsche mark)
in the late 1970s, and then rose dramatically in the first half of the 1980s
until it became grossly overvalued in 1984-85. The dollar then fell steadily
between 1985 and 1995, at which point it became highly undervalued
again. The dollar then rose sharply between 1995 and 2000, until it once
again became significantly overvalued.

From this perspective, the dollar appears to have entered a new down
cycle in the past two years that—if the five-year-plus pattern of cycles
continues—will carry forward to at least 2005. A fall in the dollar to its
estimated PPP value would take it to a dollar/euro range of 1.15 to 1.20.
The dollar's true long-run equilibrium level might be higher or lower
than this, depending on whether one assumes the long-run sustainable
current account deficit is closer to 2.5 percent or 3.5 to 4 percent of GDP.

The risk suggested by figure 2.11 is that the dollar could easily overshoot to the downside in the next few years to levels well beyond our PPP estimates, if the dollar's tendency to move in long-term cycles and overshoot its fair value at turning points persists.

Whither the Yen?

While I am comfortable with the idea that the dollar should weaken on a trend basis versus the euro, I believe the dollar will take an entirely different path versus the yen. The yen can be a frustrating exchange rate to forecast even during the best of times. But it is likely to prove particularly frustrating in the coming years, because the underlying trends on the internal and external balance fronts in the United States and Japan have diverged so greatly.

Exchange rates are normally determined by the joint interaction of internal and external balance forces, but determining where equilibrium lies can be a problem if one country is suffering a serious deterioration on its external balance front while the other country is suffering a serious deterioration on its internal balance front. The key question for forecasters is how to weigh such conflicting trends to come up with an estimate of a currency's equilibrium value.

This is clearly the dilemma faced by investors today when analyzing the fundamental forces driving the yen versus the dollar. For example, Japan's economy has been suffering from a serious internal balance problem for over a decade. Moreover, there are significant risks that this problem could become even more serious if global economic activity slows significantly and world equity markets continue to slide. A slowdown in global growth could undermine Japan's export-led recovery, while weaker equity prices could lead to a further deterioration in Japanese banks' balance sheets. If that happens, bank lending would be constrained further and a financial bailout of the Japanese banking system might need to be considered. Under such a scenario, the Bank of Japan would come under greater pressure to step up its quantitative easing of monetary policy, which would in all likelihood contribute to a significant weakening of the yen.

From a longer-run perspective, Japan faces a number of serious internal balance problems. These include the following:

1. Japan has been in a decade-long slump that is displaying no sign of reversing.

2. Japan's standing in global competitiveness surveys has been slipping steadily in recent years.

3. S&P, Moody's, and Fitch have issued a series of ratings downgrades on Japanese government debt.

4. Capital spending has been persistently weak, which has led to a sustained decline in Japanese productivity growth.

5. Bankruptcies are running at record levels.

6. Bank lending has contracted in each of the past four years.

7. Banks' nonperforming and problem loans have grown steadily in recent years and are now estimated to be around ¥150 trillion, roughly 30 percent of GDP.

8. The financial health of the Japanese government's Fiscal Investment and Loan Program (FILP) has been called into question (a recent NBER study [Doi and Hoshi 2002] suggests that "as much as 75 percent of the FILP loans are bad" and estimates that losses could amount to roughly ¥80 trillion, or 16 percent of GDP).

9. Japan's huge budget deficit and gross government debt as a percentage of GDP will place limits on the ability of policymakers to stimulate growth in the future through fiscal channels.

In addition, with deflationary expectations so deep-seated, the IMF indicated in its latest annual assessment of Japan that the Bank of Japan needs to do more on the quantitative easing front. According to the IMF's monetary model of the Japanese economy, a 25 percent increase in Japan's monetary base should boost consumer prices by 1.0 percent. Although Japan's monetary base is currently rising at a 25 percent year-over-year pace, that may not be sufficient if underlying deflationary forces are pushing Japan's consumer price index down by more than 1 percent per annum. The IMF noted that, on the basis of lessons learned from past deflationary episodes in other industrialized countries, Japanese monetary base growth might need to rise far more rapidly to push the rate of change in Japan's consumer price index into positive territory on a sustained basis. If the Bank of Japan does indeed move in this direction, one should expect that a policy shift of this magnitude would exert considerable downward pressure on the yen's value (figure 2.12), as has been the case in all other countries where monetary easing has been undertaken in earnest.

With Japan's government debt dynamics on an unsustainable path, it is highly likely that Japan will need to engineer a long-run fiscal consolidation effort to bring its deficits under control. Using the FEER framework depicted in figure 2.1, Japan's savings-investment balance schedule appears

Figure 2.12 The yen and Japanese/US monetary policies
(using BoJ notes in circulation series)

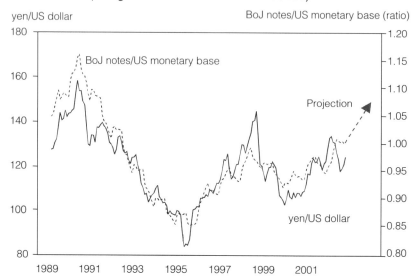

Note: 6-month moving averages of year 2000 adjusted monetary-base series.
Source: Datastream.

destined to shift sharply to the right for a long time to come, which will be yen negative. Combining this with the monetary policy path that the Bank of Japan looks set to pursue, the long-term policy mix in Japan is likely to be one of significant fiscal restraint coupled with monetary ease. The Mundell-Fleming model would argue that such a policy mix is a recipe for a long-term decline in a currency's value (figure 2.13).

In fact, the yen has been underperforming the dollar for the past seven and a half years. As shown in figure 2.14, long-dollar positions have significantly outperformed long-yen positions since the spring of 1995. The cumulative excess return (currency returns plus positive carry) from being long-dollar/short-yen between April 1995 and October 2002 is a fairly hefty 85 percent. There were a number of instances when holding on to a long-dollar/short-yen position proved costly—such as the fall of 1998, the summer of 1999, and the spring and summer of 2002—but from a longer-run standpoint, one would have earned far more by being long the dollar than long the yen over the past seven and a half years.

Looking ahead, I am optimistic that the long-run trend of dollar outperformance versus the yen will remain intact. Japan's internal balance problems are unlikely to improve for a long time to come and may indeed worsen. I believe that Japan's deep-seated internal balance problems will more than offset any positives that might emerge on Japan's external balance front.

Figure 2.13 The monetary/fiscal policy mix and the determination of exchange rates

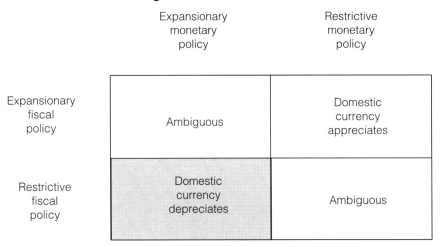

	Expansionary monetary policy	Restrictive monetary policy
Expansionary fiscal policy	Ambiguous	Domestic currency appreciates
Restrictive fiscal policy	Domestic currency depreciates	Ambiguous

Figure 2.14 Excess return on long-dollar/short-yen positions (since April 1995)

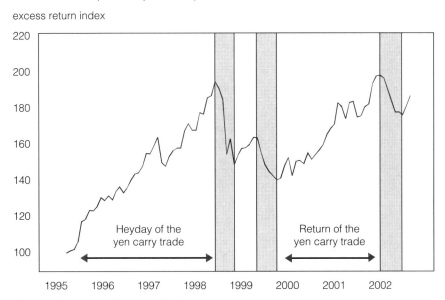

excess return index

Heyday of the yen carry trade

Return of the yen carry trade

Source: Datastream, Deutsche Bank estimates.

References

Alberola, E., S. Cervero, H. Lopez, and A. Ubide. 1999. Global Equilibrium Exchange Rates: Euro, Dollar, 'Ins,' 'Outs,' and Other Major Currencies in a Panel Cointegration Framework. IMF Working Paper 99/175. Washington: IMF.

Borowski, D. and C. Couharde. 2000. Euro, dollar, yen: Pour une approche multilatérale des taux de change d'équilibre. *Revue Économique* 51, no. 3.

Chinn, M. and R. Alquist. 2000. Tracking the Euro's Progress. *International Finance* 3, no. 3: 357-73.

Clostermann, J. and B. Schnatz. 2000. The Determinants of the Euro-Dollar Exchange Rate: Synthetic Fundamentals and a Non-Existing Currency. Deutsche Bundesbank Discussion Paper no. 2/00.

Detken, C., A. Dieppe, J. Henry, C. Marin, and F. Smets. 2002. Model Uncertainty and the Equilibrium Value of the Real Effective Euro Exchange Rate. ECB Working Paper No. 160. Frankfurt: European Central Bank.

Doi, Takero, and Takeo Hoshi. 2002. FILP: How Much Has Been Lost? How Much Will Be Lost? In *Structural Impediments to Growth in Japan.* NBER Conference Proceeding. Cambridge, MA: National Bureau of Economic Research, March.

Duval, R. 2001. Estimation du taux de change réel d'équilibre de long terme euro/dollar par une approche dynamique synthétique. Photocopy.

Freund, Caroline L. 2000. Current Account Adjustment in Industrial Countries. Federal Reserve Board of Governors International Finance Discussion Paper No. 692. Washington: Federal Reserve Board of Governors.

Isard, Peter, Hamid Faruqee, G. Russell Kincaid, and Martin Fetherston. 2001. Methodology for Current Account and Exchange Rate Assessments. IMF Occasional Paper No. 209. Washington: International Monetary Fund.

Koen, Vincent, Laurence Boone, Alain de Serres, and Nicola Fuchs. 2001. Tracking the Euro. OECD Economic Department Working Paper No. 298. Paris: Organization for Economic Cooperation and Development.

Lorenzen, H. and N. Thygessen. 2000. The Relation between the Euro and the Dollar. Paper presented at the EPRU Conference on Perspectives on Danish and European Economic Policy, Copenhagen, November 9-10.

Mann, Catherine L. 1999. *Is the US Trade Deficit Sustainable?* Washington: Institute for International Economics.

McKinsey Global Institute. 2001. *US Productivity Growth, 1995-2000.* Washington: McKinsey and Company.

Schulmeister, S. 2000. *Die Kaufkraft des Euro innerbalb und außerhalb der Währungsunton.* WIFO-Studie.

Teïletche, J. 2000. La parité euro/dollar durant les décennies 80 et 90: Peut-on trouver une spécification raisonable et à quel horizon? Photocopy (December).

Williamson, John, ed. 1994. *Estimating Equilibrium Exchange Rates.* Washington: Institute for International Economics.

Wren-Lewis, S. and R. Driver. 1998. *Real Exchange Rates for the Year 2000.* POLICY ANALYSES IN INTERNATIONAL ECONOMICS 54. Washington: Institute for International Economics.

3

How Long the Strong Dollar?

CATHERINE L. MANN

When the dollar started to depreciate at the beginning of 2002, many pundits nodded: This was expected. After all, the US current account deficit in 2000 and 2001 hovered around 4 percent of GDP, and, based on second-quarter data, the figure for 2002 was headed for around 5 percent. For industrialized countries the rule of thumb is that a current account deficit of 4 to 4.5 percent of GDP is a "danger point" for the home currency. On this basis, my 1999 book *Is the US Trade Deficit Sustainable?* suggested that the current account deficit could widen for another two to three years. So, the dollar was depreciating right on schedule! But was I right in my prediction for the right reasons? Is sustainability analysis based on the current account deficit the best framework for explaining the depreciation of the dollar so far this year? Or is there another perspective on the current account deficit that has more salience in explaining the dollar's behavior in 2002 and for considering its likely direction for 2003?

In this essay I outline two views of external sustainability and the dollar and conclude that the current account deficit-to-GDP analysis, although valuable for tying down long-term trends for a currency, is not the more important framework for understanding the behavior of the dollar in 2002 or 2003. Rather, an analysis framed around the global investor—rather

Catherine L. Mann, senior fellow at the Institute for International Economics since 1997, previously served in policymaking institutions in Washington, including the Federal Reserve Board of Governors, President's Council of Economic Advisers at the White House, and the World Bank. Outstanding assistance from Jacob Funk Kirkegaard is thankfully acknowledged. This paper draws on some of the author's previous work (Mann 1999, 2002).

than focused on the US economy—yields insights that better aid our understanding of the recent and near-term behavior of the dollar. This alternative perspective on sustainability is based on portfolio allocation theory and takes into account the size of net foreign purchases of US assets, the increase in global financial wealth, and investors' portfolio preferences for risk, return, and diversification.

Considered in this light, depreciation pressures are created by the high share of US assets in the portfolio of the global investor (the consequence of decades of large US external deficits). Particularly in early 2002, the significant flow of US assets into the global marketplace at a time when global financial wealth had not been expanding very much and when the relative returns to US assets seemed to have narrowed put depreciation pressure on the dollar. But possibilities for additional appreciation, particularly in 2003, derive from the likely return to relatively more attractive (or less unattractive) investment possibilities within the United States. The global investor, and therefore the dollar, is caught between a desire for diversification and an appetite for return.

Dollar Depreciation in 2002: Much Ado About Nothing?

Many analysts discussing dollar depreciation in 2002 focus on the euro and the yen and start the clock at the beginning of the year (figure 3.1, top graph). Indeed, from February to mid-July the dollar depreciated some 12 percent against the euro and the yen—a rapid enough change to worry German exporters and precipitate Japanese intervention. But that's not the only way to look at the dollar. Considering a longer perspective, say, from 1995, and looking at the dollar in real terms and against a broad currency basket, there is not much action to report—only about 5 percent depreciation (figure 3.1, bottom graph)—about half of which reversed since mid-July. Are the different time periods and measures of the dollar relevant for perspectives on sustainability of the current account deficit?

The exchange value of the dollar can be viewed as a summary statistic incorporating numerous forces and factors: monetary policy stance, domestic savings relative to investment, long-term potential GDP growth, relative productivity of the United States vis-à-vis other major countries, depth of financial markets, and sentiment barometer. That is why it is so difficult to forecast exchange rates.

In this paper I present two views of what drives the dollar, each a collage of the factors listed above. View 1 is the traditional "current account view" on sustainability. In this view, the focus is on the US real economy. Are the current account deficit and negative net international investment position "large" with respect to the US economy? This view focuses on

Figure 3.1 Views on dollar depreciation

US dollar exchange rate index, January 2 - December 1 2002

Source: Pacific Exchange Rate Service.

FRB monthly broad dollar indices, January 1995 - November 2002

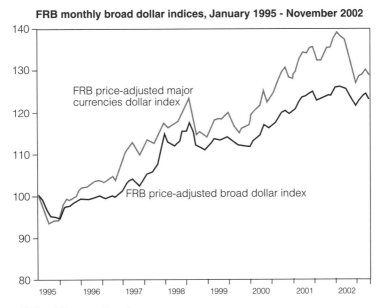

Source: Federal Reserve Board.

US economic conditions and on what the magnitude of the stock and flow of external obligations imply for US spending and economic growth.

View 2 is the "global wealth portfolio view" on sustainability. Are the flow of US financial assets into the global marketplace and the current stock of US assets in the global wealth portfolio "large" with respect to global investor wealth? This view focuses on conditions in both the United States and other global economies when considering what the stock and flow of US assets imply for allocation of global financial wealth.

Concepts of Sustainability and Benchmarks

Sustainability has two sides, which mirror these two views of what drives the dollar. From the standpoint of the US economy, sustainability has to do with how much the US economy can afford to borrow from the rest of the world by running a current account deficit and building up a negative net international investment position on which it must ultimately make good. Sustainability from the standpoint of the rest of the world has to do with the extent to which investors in other countries are willing to buy and hold US assets in their portfolios of wealth given other investment choices with other risk-return profiles as well as their diversification preferences for the allocation of exposures in their portfolio.

In either concept, a sustainable situation is one in which the stock or flow imbalance generates no economic force of its own to change the trajectory of the imbalance. For example, a sustainable current account trajectory is one where the feedback effects from the current account deficit or negative net international investment position through net investment service payments to consumption or business investment spending, are relatively weak in comparison to other macroeconomic forces that affect these spending categories. A sustainable net capital inflow is one where the feedback effect from global wealth allocation to the dollar is relatively weak in comparison to other macroeconomic forces that affect asset prices and portfolio choices. From an econometric standpoint, the question is whether or not the external imbalance would be a significant variable in a regression for US spending (in the US economy view) or foreign portfolio allocation (in the global portfolio view), and in either case, in a model of the exchange value of the dollar.

Sustainability Benchmark for the Current Account Deficit

A large and persistent current account deficit portends a negative net international investment position that grows ever larger. Eventually the financial payments (such as interest and dividends) arising from this negative net international investment position (NIIP) will become large enough to cut into current consumption and business investment. At that time, the current account deficit itself (and its accumulation in the NIIP) changes domestic absorption (the sum of consumption, investment, and government spending), reducing import growth, and changing the trajectory of the current account toward a sustainable path.[1]

At some point, an economy running a current account deficit today has to stem the widening of that deficit and the accumulating negative NIIP so that they grow less rapidly than the capacity of the economy to service the debt—that is, the NIIP-to-GDP ratio (and, by arithmetic, the current account deficit-to-GDP ratio) need to stop becoming ever more negative. The US current account deficit seems very big, but is it big relative to the US economy in this "sustainability" sense?

In a world of certainty everyone can "do the math," but only empirical analysis can help determine a sustainability benchmark for the real world. For industrialized countries, a current account deficit-to-GDP ratio of somewhere between 4 and 5 percent appears to be associated with the onset of economic forces (including a monetary policy response, a reduction in income, and, in some cases, a real depreciation of the currency) that reduce consumption and (particularly) business investment, thus changing the trajectory of the current account and returning it to sustainable territory (Chinn and Prasad 2000, Freund 2000, Mann 1999). Similarly, econometric analysis finds, for a group of industrialized countries, that a large negative net international investment position is associated with a depreciation of the relevant exchange rate, although the magnitude of net international investment that is associated with the exchange rate change is less clear (Gagnon 1996). The US current account deficit-to-GDP ratio was in the "danger zone" for two years before the dollar started depreciating in early 2002. Is the average experience of industrialized countries less pertinent to the sustainability of the US current account deficit? If so, why might this be?

Sustainability Benchmark for the Global Wealth Portfolio

If significant net capital inflows are to be sustained, global investors must be willing to purchase US assets at current prices and prospects, including the going rate of return and exchange rate. If the global demand for US assets at current prices is lower than what the US economy is offering in the global marketplace by running a current account deficit, then foreign investors may demand a higher return, or they may sell (or not purchase) US investments, putting depreciation pressure on the dollar.

---

1. The literature on balance of payments crises has a somewhat different trigger. There, foreign currency interest service exceeds the level of foreign exchange reserves, precipitating the change in imports, current account trajectory, and exchange rate.

At that point, the "needed" net capital inflow into the United States is unsustainable.

How much the global investor is willing to invest in the US economy is a function of several factors, including the risk-return profile of US assets relative to financial assets of other countries, the growth of the investor's portfolio of wealth, transaction costs, information asymmetries, and regulation (Branson and Henderson 1985, Frenkel and Mussa 1985, Levich 1998). The US offering of financial assets in the international marketplace is very big, but is it big relative to global wealth in this "sustainability" sense?

Estimating a sustainability benchmark based on the global investor's portfolio is difficult because the empirical record is thin and international financial markets are quite innovative, tending to quickly make a benchmark obsolete (Isard and Steckler 1985, Meade and Thomas 1993, Ventura 2001). One approach is to consider US net capital inflows relative to global savings. By this measure, the US current account deficit absorbs about 6 percent of world savings (Cooper 2001). But even if home bias[2] is gradually attenuating with financial innovation and deregulation, clearly not all of global savings is available to be invested in international, much less US, assets (Lewis 1999). Suppose a global investor allocated his or her portfolio on the basis of relative real GDP shares; about 30 percent of the portfolio would be US assets. But portfolio weights based on GDP do not reflect the importance of return differentials for investment decisions, nor regulatory constraints on where investors can put their wealth. A third possible benchmark comes from relative stock market capitalization, which embodies both longer-term wealth creation and shorter-term valuation effects. If the global investor chose a portfolio to mirror the relative size of equity markets around the world, the share of US assets would be about 55 percent (based on Morgan Stanley Capital International [MSCI] data).

What evidence can we bring to bear on the sustainability question from the point of view of the global investor that will help us explain the behavior of the dollar in early 2002 and help inform us about the future direction of the dollar?

The US Current Account Deficit, Foreign Purchases of US Assets, and the Dollar

Considering 2002 and looking forward into 2003, which concept of sustainability matters more for the behavior of the dollar? Has and will the dollar react to the current account deficit-to-GDP ratio (or its close cousin the

---

2. Home bias is the term used to acknowledge that investors tend to hold a higher share of domestic assets in their portfolio of wealth than is to be expected based on risk, return, and diversification preferences alone.

Table 3.1 Assumptions for scenarios for current account balance and global financial wealth

	2002	2003	2004, 2005
US real GDP[1,2] (percent)	2.3	2.5	3.7, 3.5
World real GDP[3] (percent)	2.0	3.0	3.5

1. Macroeconomic Advisers, November 11, 2002: 2002, 2003.

2. *Economic Report of the President* 2002: 2004-05.

3. Macroeconomic Advisers, November 11, 2002: 2005 assumed equal to 2004.

NIIP-to-GDP ratio), which measures the domestic economy's exposure to the external imbalances? Or has/will the global investor's wealth exposure to US assets been/be the relatively more important factor affecting the dollar?

Simple scenarios for the current account and global financial wealth are based on public forecasts for US and global growth (table 3.1). As detailed below, these scenarios suggest that the concept of sustainability based on the current account deficit-to-GDP ratio is not the key concept for explaining the dollar's behavior in 2002 nor for considering sustainability in 2003. Rather, the concept based on global portfolio allocation suggests that the supply of US assets offered to the global marketplace has been large compared to the increase in global wealth. This relatively heavy demand that the global investor buy US assets, at a time when US relative returns appear less generous than in the late 1990s and when the global portfolio is flush with US assets, is the key reason for the dollar depreciation of the first half of 2002, and will be an important consideration in 2003.

The Dollar and the Current Account Deficit

Consider first the concept of sustainability based on the current account deficit. Reasonable assumptions for US and global growth in 2002, 2003, and through the medium term yield a current account deficit-to-GDP ratio of 4.5 percent in 2002, rising to 4.9 percent in 2003, and to 6.1 percent in 2005 (figure 3.2, top graph). In 2002 and 2003, as well as for the past two years, the ratios exceed the benchmark value determined from the current account experience of other industrialized countries.

For the United States, however, the external imbalances have not yet translated into large financial costs. Although the net international investment position turned from positive to increasingly negative in the 1990s, the United States still enjoyed net service receipts of $15 billion (0.15 percent of GDP) in 2001 (figure 3.2, bottom graph). By way of comparison, inventory changes of $30 billion or more (seasonally adjusted annual rates) frequently occur from quarter to quarter in the US economy, and

Figure 3.2 Current account and sustainability: Base case, no dollar change

US current account as a share of GDP

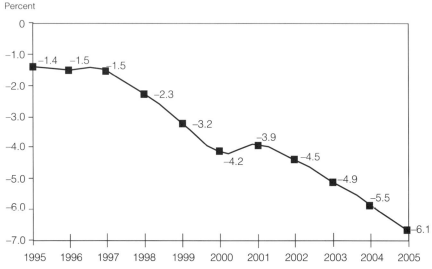

Source: Department of Commerce, and author's calculations.

Net investment income and NIIP as share of GDP

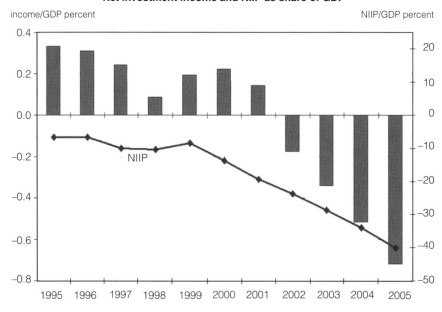

Note: Bars represent net investment income.

Source: Department of Commerce, and author's calculations.

consumption alone is more than $7 trillion. Therefore, as large as these current account deficits appear to be in 2002 and even 2003, they are not yet large enough to engender financial costs that force an adjustment in domestic spending. Moreover, even as the negative NIIP increases to 24 and 29 percent in 2002 and 2003, respectively, what little empirical evidence there is for industrialized countries relating the NIIP-to-GDP ratio to the exchange rate suggests that the "trigger" benchmark is much larger. For many member countries of the Organization of Economic Cooperation and Development the NIIP-to-GDP ratio is stable at 40 to 50 percent.

According to the theory that underpins the current account view of sustainability, a high-productivity country that issues assets mostly in its own currency at a low interest rate (such as US government obligations) and with a high share of marketable assets (such as equity and corporate bonds) can continue along a trajectory of increasing the current account deficit for a longer period than can a country that borrows in currencies other than its own, at high interest rates, and using fixed-maturity, fixed-payment bank debt. This constellation of domestic real economy and external financing closely matches the characteristics of the US economy and net financing (figure 3.3). This mix of financing is part of the reason for the surprisingly positive net service obligations noted above. Finally, figure 3.3 also shows that net foreign purchases of US assets have exceeded $400 billion every year since 1995, topping $1 trillion in 2000. The United States attracts far more capital inflow than needed to finance the current account deficit.

Even considering arguments of forward-looking expectations, all told, the current account view on sustainability is not a plausible story for why the exchange value of the dollar started to depreciate at the start of 2002.

The Dollar and the Global Portfolio

Consider now the concept of sustainability based on global financial markets. The data for the first quarter of 2002 (annualized rate) (figure 3.3) show a dramatic slowing of net foreign purchases of US assets, which is consistent with the depreciation of the dollar in the first half of 2002.[3] The second-quarter rebound in net financing to annualized rates similar to the "dot-com years" and the stabilizing of the dollar in mid-2002 are also notable. Is there evidence from the standpoint of the global investor's portfolio that would help explain what we observe in terms of net financial flows? We need to consider both the marginal investment choice, since

---

3. Recent empirical work (Tille, Stoffels, and Gorbachev 2001; Alquist and Chinn 2002; and Brooks, Edison, Kumar, and Sløk 2001) finds statistically significant relationships between the dollar/euro exchange rate and transatlantic capital flows.

Figure 3.3 Net foreign purchases of US assets by asset type

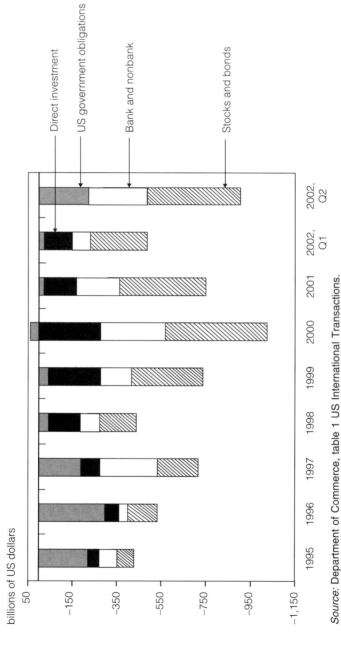

billions of US dollars

Source: Department of Commerce, table 1 US International Transactions.

this determines whether net capital inflows into the United States will be sustained at the going exchange rate, but also the average exposure of the global investor's portfolio of wealth to US assets—that is, portfolio diversification—since diversification affects allocation.

Our knowledge of the portfolio of the global investor is limited. The *Economist* surveys a set of global portfolio managers quarterly about their portfolios (figure 3.4, top graph). Based on these surveys, the share of US equity assets in the equity portion of the overall portfolio stood at around 30 percent in 1993 to 1995, rose dramatically between 1995 and 1997 to about 50 percent, stabilized again through 2000, and then rose a bit more to about 55 percent through the third quarter of 2002.[4]

Increased average holdings of US assets comes from a higher marginal investment in US assets as the global portfolio grows. Although we cannot observe this directly with available data, the bottom graph of figure 3.4 shows a calculation of this marginal investment allocation. In simple terms, this calculation is the ratio of the net flow of US assets into the global financial markets (this flow is proxied by the current account) to the increase in non-US global net financial wealth (calculated from a base of non-US G-7 net financial wealth). (See the appendix for more details.) Based on these calculations the modest marginal allocation of US assets in the global portfolio of the early 1990s doubled in the mid-1990s and became dramatically large from 1998 to 2001. The pattern of marginal allocations is consistent with the changes in average holdings from the *Economist* survey, is consistent with the relative performance of the US economy in the later 1990s and early 2000s, and matches the dramatic net foreign purchases of US assets (figure 3.3), particularly during the bubble period in the US stock market.

How can these measures of the average and marginal investment allocations help us understand the behavior of the dollar in 2002? By the end of 2001, the global investor's portfolio had become less diversified.[5] At the same time, the calculations suggest that the net offering of US assets in the global financial marketplace in 2002 has been large, even in historical experience, in comparison with the projected increase in global financial wealth. This is partly because of continued large US current account deficits (the numerator) but, more importantly, because of slug-

---

4. Also shown is the so-called MSCI-neutral portfolio, which is what portfolio allocation "should" be if the investor merely holds a portfolio to mirror global market capitalization. Clearly the *Economist* investors follow the MSCI but they do not hold a completely neutral portfolio. For more discussion see Mann and Meade (2002).

5. We do not have a complete picture of the geographic allocation strategy in the portfolio of the global investor, including in bonds, cash, and other assets. In the example that follows, the equity portion of the portfolio is taken as a proxy for the overall portfolio. Of course even if the equity component of the portfolio is becoming less diversified, the overall portfolio could still be sufficiently geographically diversified.

Figure 3.4 Global financial wealth and sustainability: Base case, no dollar change

US share of equity assets in the global portfolio

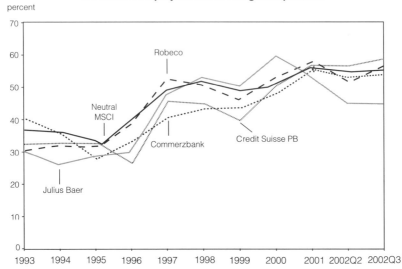

MSCI = Morgan Stanley Capital International index
Source: Data from *The Economist,* calculations by author.

US share of change in (non-US) global wealth
(70 percent home bias of global investor)

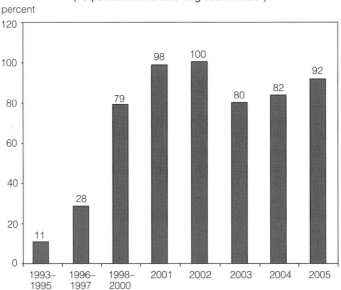

Note: Bars represent 50 percent G-7, 25 percent non-G-7 advanced economies, 25 percent developing Asian countries.
Source: Author's calculations.

Figure 3.5 Stock market differential and the dollar/euro exchange rate (Xetra Dax-S&P500 indices spread and dollar/euro exchange rate, October 1, 2001 [= 100] to November 27, 2002)

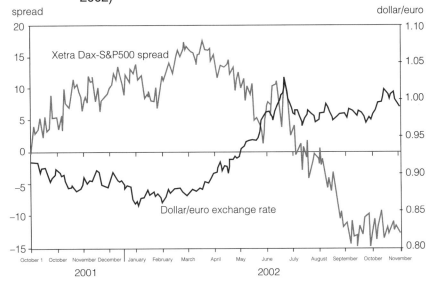

Sources: Yahoo Finance; Federal Reserve.

gish global growth and thus smaller increases in global wealth (the denominator). Finally, at least in the early months of 2002, differentials between major stock market indices in Europe and the United States widened (figure 3.5) as the relative rate of return on US assets seemed to be less attractive, and revelations of mismanagement by Enron, Tyco, WorldCom, and other major companies increased the risk premium on US assets.

All told, lack of diversification, slow growth in global wealth, a too-generous offering of US assets in the marketplace, narrowed US relative returns, and a higher perceived accounting risk on US investments help to explain the dollar depreciation in the first half of 2002.

Whither the Dollar in 2003?

Given the assumptions for US and global growth (summarized earlier in table 3.1) that underpin both the current account view of sustainability and the global portfolio view of sustainability, what are prospects for the dollar in 2003? Several scenarios frame possible sources of pressure on the dollar that differ considering the two views of sustainability.

In the simplest scenario, suppose there is no change in the value of the dollar in 2003. How the current account deficit and global investor allocation evolve relative to their respective sustainability benchmarks helps determine the plausibility of this scenario. Returning to figure 3.2 (the current account view of sustainability), for 2003 the current account deficit-to-GDP ratio is well into the danger zone based on the industrialized-country benchmark. But the NIIP-to-GDP ratio (and its medium-term trajectory) remain small compared to other OECD country experiences, and although the net service payments might rise to 0.3 percent of GDP, they remain small as well. Therefore, despite a large current account deficit per se, it leads to few forces that would herald a change in consumption habits, a change in the trajectory of the current account, and a depreciation of the dollar in 2003.

In the global portfolio view, on the other hand, this unchanged-dollar scenario implies that the global investor must allocate about 80 percent of the increase in wealth to US assets, much as they did in the 1998 to 2001 period (see figure 3.4 bottom graph). But this would happen at a time when the US share in the portfolio has risen sharply and seems historically high. Is this investor choice realistic? If it is, then there will be little pressure on the dollar in 2003 coming from either the current account view or the global investor view of sustainability. If not, the global portfolio view might portend another round of dollar depreciation from the period of pause in the second half of 2002.

What factors might affect the portfolio allocation decision and therefore affect prospects for the dollar? The global investor could simply continue to increase the share of US assets in his portfolio, moving further away from a diversified allocation, and the dollar would stay about stable. Regulatory and institutional changes in foreign markets, particularly the European financial markets (or China's capital account liberalization), could make those markets relatively more attractive destinations for financial investment, causing the investor to move assets into those markets and allocate less to US investments so the dollar would depreciate.[6] But these structural changes could also increase financial leverage and reduce "home bias," both of which would grow the financial portfolio and increase the share of wealth that can be invested in international assets, including US assets. A "wealth stock" effect vs. "relative return" effect would determine whether more or less investment in US assets resulted and what direction the dollar might take. A full analysis of all these factors is beyond the scope of this paper.

Instead, consider much simpler dollar stories based on alternative scenarios for the allocation of global net financial wealth (figure 3.6 and table 3.2). In the first scenario (global GDP share), the marginal allocation of global financial wealth in US assets returns to the mid-1990s average of

---

6. Mann and Meade (2002) discuss the implications for portfolio allocations and the dollar/euro exchange rate of a change in the institutional structure of European financial markets.

Figure 3.6 Global financial wealth: US share of change in (non-US) global financial wealth

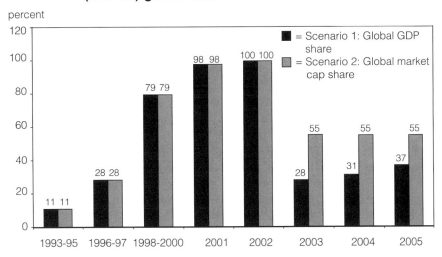

Source: Author's calculations.

Table 3.2 US current account/GDP and dollar depreciation (percent) scenarios targeting US share of the global equity portfolio

	2002	2003	2004	2005
Scenario 1 target: Equity share drops to global GDP share (33 percent)	−4.5	−1.7	−2.1	−2.4
Scenario 2 target: Equity share stays at MSCI share in global financial wealth (55 percent)	−4.5	−3.3	−3.7	−3.6

MSCI = Morgan Stanley Capital International index

about 30 percent, which is also the US share in global GDP (one of the possible global portfolio benchmarks noted earlier). In order for this marginal allocation to be achieved in 2003, the dollar would have to depreciate by nearly 50 percent from current levels![7]

The significant change in the value of the dollar under this first scenario has predictable effects on the path of the current account deficit, but also yields some financial results that are not realistic (table 3.2). In the current

---

7. As with any partial equilibrium scenario, the change in the dollar is taken to affect the current account deficit and the marginal allocation of global financial wealth, but not US GDP growth or the growth of global wealth.

account view, the dramatic crash of the dollar needed to bring the US portfolio share back to the US share in global GDP pushes the current account deficit-to-GDP ratio well into the territory of long-term sustainability, as judged by Williamson and others.[8] (Although ultimately the dynamics of trade flows take over and the deficit widens again.) But, beyond what happens in the US marketplace, what might happen in other countries? The dollar crash implies a radical shift in the investment strategy of the global investor toward other financial markets amounting to about $350 billion in investor capital in 2003. Investors could buy domestic assets, but suppose this shift is into other international assets. Based on the MSCI neutral portfolio weights, the reallocated portfolio implies capital flows of about $220 billion into assets of Europe and the United Kingdom, about $81 billion into assets in Japan, and about $60 billion into assets in other regions. These are huge net capital flows that would be associated with very large movements in their current accounts, thus underlining the implausibility of the scenario.[9]

In the second scenario (global market cap share), the marginal allocation of global financial wealth in US assets returns to the 2001-2002 average share of equities in the global portfolio of wealth (55 percent), which approximates the global weight based on stock-market capitalization. In order for this to be the marginal allocation throughout the projection, the dollar would have to depreciate about 20 percent from late November 2002 levels in 2003, and then depreciate a bit further in 2004 and 2005.[10]

The results from this second scenario are more reasonable and rather intriguing. The immediate effect of the 24 percent depreciation narrows the current account deficit to 3.3 percent of GDP; the further small dollar depreciations (which keep the marginal allocation at 55 percent) stabilize the current account deficit at 3.7 percent of GDP, which is well within the industrialized-country benchmark. Thus, there is a symmetry between the benchmarks based on global market cap and industrialized-country current account. But, the global market cap benchmark may be a tighter

---

8. John Williamson and Molly Mahar (1998) judged that the long-term US current account deficit should be 2 percent of GDP (1 percent if measured properly).

9. It is interesting to note, however, that if, following the 48 percent depreciation (which is necessary to get to the long-term average portfolio allocation of 33 percent), the dollar then depreciates about 10 percent per year in 2004 and 2005, the marginal allocation of the global investor in US assets would be stabilized at 33 percent of global financial wealth and the current account deficit would be stabilized at 2.2 percent of GDP, just about the Williamson and Mahar target.

10. The dynamics of the trade deficit and the net service payment on the NIIP cause the current account gap to widen again immediately after any one-off dollar depreciation. So a continuous dollar depreciation is necessary to keep the current account deficit from widening. For more on how the dynamics of the US current account are driven by trade elasticities and debt service, see Mann (1999, chapter 8).

benchmark. Whereas the US current account deficit-to-GDP ratio has room to rise toward the industrialized-country benchmark of 4 to 4.5 percent, this would push the average share of US assets in the global portfolio beyond the 55 percent benchmark based on global market capitalization. While the global investor certainly has allocated a higher fraction of his or her increase in wealth to US assets, this occurred when the US economy clearly was out-performing the rest of the world (late 1990s).

All these scenarios taken together, including the unchanged dollar, suggest that the offering of US assets to the global investors is "large" with respect to the growth in global wealth but that the current account deficit is not large with respect to the US economy. The view of sustainability that matters most for the dollar in the near term is the one based on the global portfolio. Does this mean that the dollar is ripe for further depreciation?

The fundamental factor underpinning the scenarios is the share of US assets in the global portfolio, either the average share of wealth or the marginal share of the increase in global wealth. In either case, it's about diversification and based on this motive alone, the dollar should experience further pressure for depreciation. However, risk and return motives are equally, if not more, important for the global investor's marginal allocation decision. Into 2003, what can we say about prospects for risk and return on US and other international assets? The long-run growth estimates of 3-3.5 percent for the United States, 2-2.5 percent for Europe and 1 percent for Japan suggest continued superior performance by the US economy and therefore, on average, higher returns to holding US assets. A restored faith in the US economy, dashed hopes for a revival of growth in Japan, and insufficient structural reforms in Europe give appreciation momentum to the dollar for 2003, even as the share of US assets rises in the portfolio of the global investor. Will return trump diversification? Answering this question determines the direction for the dollar in 2003.

Appendix 3.1
Calculating Global Non-US Investable
Net Financial Wealth

The starting point for constructing a measure of global non-US investable net financial wealth lies in the OECD Net Financial Wealth data for the G-7 nations from 1992-2000.[11] These were used to generate current dollar-denominated non-US G-7 net financial wealth by dividing the OECD net financial wealth figures (which are presented as a percentage of nominal

---

11. Available in Annex table 57, "Household Wealth and Indebtedness," OECD Economic Outlook, vol. 2001/2, no. 70, p. 261.

personal disposable income, PDY) by the national PDY-to-GDP ratio.[12] Local currency unit (LCU) wealth is then computed by multiplying the net financial wealth-to-GDP ratio by LCU GDP. Current dollar-denominated wealth is generated using annual dollar-exchange rate averages.[13]

The national G-7 current dollar-denominated net financial wealth (α) is computed as follows:

$$\alpha_i = (\beta_i / \chi_i^* \gamma_i / \lambda_i)$$

where

  β_i = national G-7 net financial wealth as a percentage of nominal PDY,
  χ_i = national G-7 PDY/nominal GDP ratio,
  γ_i = national G-7 LCU nominal GDP, and
  λ_i = national G-7 LCU/dollar annual average exchange rate.

The total non-US G-7 current dollar-denominated wealth ($\Sigma\alpha_i$) is then grossed up to non-US world levels by dividing by the non-US G-7 nominal GDP-to-non-US world nominal GDP ratio.[14] World net financial wealth (μ) is computed as follows:

$$\mu = (\theta/\rho)$$

where

  θ = non-US G-7 current dollar-denominated net financial wealth ($\Sigma\alpha_i$), and
  ρ = non-US G-7 current dollar GDP/non-US world current dollar GDP ratio.

A home bias of 70 percent is assumed when determining how much of the world's net financial wealth is available for purchases of US assets, that is, only 30 percent of the total world net financial wealth (μ) is global non-US *investable* net financial wealth (Lewis 1999).

---

12. Personal disposable incomes are available at G-7 national statistical agencies: UK, www.statistics.gov.uk/; Canada, www.statcan.ca/start.html; Germany, www.bundesbank. de/; France, www.insee.fr/fr/home/home_page.asp; Japan, www.stat.go.jp/english/data/ nenkan/1431-04.htm. No numbers could be located for Italy, which was then assumed to be equal to the average of Germany and France. As no number for Japan for 2000 could be located, PDY/GDP fraction is assumed to grow from 1999 by the 1998-99 growth rate. Furthermore, few historical data for Canada were available, and hence the Canadian fraction was frozen at 0.65, halfway between the US 2001 figure and the Continental European average of France and Germany.

13. National LCU GDP figures and average exchange rates are from the IMF *World Economic Outlook* September 2002 database at www.imf.org/external/pubs/ft/weo/2002/02/data/ index.htm.

14. World current dollar-denominated GDP data are from the World Bank, http:// devdata.worldbank.org/dataonline/.

The above figures are data to the year 2000. For the period 2001-05, the 2000 non-US global net financial wealth figure is increased annually at the Macroeconomic Advisers' November 11, 2002, real multilateral trade-weighted GDP year-over-year growth rate plus inflation. Inflation is a weighted average of the inflation rates for three groupings of the G-7 nations, the non-G-7 advanced economies,[15] and "developing Asia,"[16] with the weights at 50 percent, 25 percent, and 25 percent, respectively. All inflation rates are GDP weighted according to the 2001 current dollar-denominated GDP from the IMF *World Economic Outlook* September 2002 database. Inflation figures are annual for 2002 and 2003, with the 2003 rate assumed constant for the period 2004-05.

The calculations for 2001-05 assume the following:

- Stable consumption shares: PDY/GDP is held at the 2000 figure based on the OECD data. This is a reasonable assumption based on the examination of historical data.

- Stable financial leverage: Net financial wealth/GDP is held at the 2000 figure based on the OECD data. An examination of the historical pattern of this ratio shows that it moves around with changing economic conditions. However, there is no obvious empirical or theoretical rationale to make any specific assumption other than the one chosen.

- Stable home bias: It is assumed that home bias is unchanged at 70 percent. Home bias changes as a result of both cyclical and structural factors. However, there is no obvious empirical or theoretical rationale to make any specific assumption other than the one chosen.

References

Alquist, Ron, and Menzie D. Chinn. 2002. Productivity and the Euro-Dollar Exchange Rate Puzzle. NBER Working Paper Series 8824. Cambridge, MA: National Bureau of Economic Research.

Branson, William, and Dale W. Henderson. 1985. The Specification and Influence of Asset Markets. In *Handbook of International Economics*, vol. 2, ed. Ronald W. Jones and Peter B. Kenen. New York: Elsevier, North-Holland.

---

15. Data for the non-G-7 advanced countries are from the *World Economic Outlook* September 2002 database. This grouping consists of the following countries: Australia, Austria, Belgium, Hong Kong, Cyprus, Denmark, Finland, Greece, Iceland, Ireland, Israel, Korea, Luxembourg, Netherlands, Norway, Portugal, Singapore, Spain, Sweden, Switzerland, and Taiwan.

16. Developing Asia as taken from the *World Economic Outlook* September 2002 database consists of the following countries: Afghanistan, Bangladesh, Bhutan, Cambodia, China, Fiji, India, Indonesia, Kiribati, Laos, Malaysia, Maldives, Myanmar, Nepal, Pakistan, Papua New Guinea, the Philippines, Samoa, Solomon Islands, Sri Lanka, Thailand, Tonga, Vanuatu, and Vietnam.

Brooks, Robin, Hali Edison, Manmohan Kumar, and Torsten Sløk. 2001. Exchange Rates and Capital Flows. IMF Working Paper 01/190. Washington: International Monetary Fund.

Chinn, Menzie, and Eswar S. Prasad. 2000. Medium-Term Determinants of the Current Accounts in Industrial and Developing Countries: An Empirical Exploration. NBER Working Paper 7581. Cambridge, MA: National Bureau of Economic Research.

Cooper, Richard. 2001. Is the U.S. Current Account Deficit Sustainable? Will It Be Sustained? *Brookings Papers on Economic Activity* 1:2001: 217-26.

Frenkel, Jacob, and Michael Mussa. 1985. Exchange Rates and the Balance of Payments. In *Handbook of International Economics,* vol. 2, ed. Ronald W. Jones and Peter B. Kenen. New York: Elsevier, North-Holland.

Freund, Caroline. 2000. Current Account Adjustment in Industrial Countries. Federal Reserve Board of Governors International Finance Discussion Paper No. 692. Washington: Federal Reserve Board of Governors.

Gagnon, Joseph. 1996. Net Foreign Assets and Equilibrium Exchange Rates: Panel Evidence. Federal Reserve Board of Governors, International Finance Discussion Paper No. 574. Washington: Federal Reserve Board of Governors.

Isard, Peter, and Lois Stekler. 1985. U.S. International Capital Flows and the Dollar. *Brookings Papers on Economic Activity* 1:1985: 219-36.

Levich, Richard M. 1998. *International Financial Markets: Prices and Policies.* Boston: Irwin/McGraw-Hill.

Lewis, Karen K. 1999. Trying to Explain Home Bias in Equities and Consumption. *Journal of Economic Literature* 37, no. 2 (June): 571-608.

Mann, Catherine L. 1999. *Is the US Trade Deficit Sustainable?* Washington: Institute for International Economics.

Mann, Catherine L. 2002. Perspectives on the U.S. Current Account Deficit and Sustainability. *Journal of Economic Perspectives* 16, no. 3 (Summer).

Mann, Catherine L., and Ellen E. Meade. 2002. Home Bias, Transaction Costs, and Prospects for the Euro: A More Detailed Analysis. Institute for International Economics Working Paper No. 02-03, reprinted as Deutsche Bank Research Note, October 2002.

Meade, Ellen E., and Charles P. Thomas. 1993. Using External Sustainability to Model the Dollar. In *Evaluating Policy Regimes: New Research in Empirical Macroeconomics,* ed. Ralph C. Bryant, Peter Hooper, and Catherine L. Mann. Washington: Brookings Institution.

Tille, Cédric, Nicolas Stoffels, and Olga Gorbachev. 2001. To What Extent Does Productivity Drive the Dollar? *Current Issues in Economics and Finance,* August. New York: Federal Reserve Bank of New York.

Ventura, Jaume. 2001. A Portfolio View of the U.S. Current Account Deficit. *Brookings Papers on Economic Activity* 1:2001: 241-53.

Williamson, John, and Molly Mahar 1998. Appendix A: Current Account Targets. In *Real Exchange Rates for the Year 2000,* POLICY ANALYSES IN INTERNATIONAL ECONOMICS 54, by Simon Wren-Lewis and Rebecca L. Driver. Washington: Institute for International Economics.

Wren-Lewis, Simon, and Rebecca L. Driver. 1998. *Real Exchange Rates for the Year 2000.* POLICY ANALYSES IN INTERNATIONAL ECONOMICS 54. Washington: Institute for International Economics.

4

The Dollar and US Trade Politics

I. M. DESTLER

As a general rule, the United States is one of the least exchange-rate conscious of countries. Unlike Tokyo residents, who see flashing downtown signs displaying the latest number of yen to the dollar—akin to New York signs flashing the Dow—Americans don't tend to think of the dollar in relation to another currency. The image of a shrinking dollar evokes domestic inflation, not devaluation of the dollar in currency markets. The dollar's exchange value is therefore not central to our politics, as other currencies' values can be to theirs.

But for the growing portion of US economic actors who are engaged in international transactions or who compete with those who are, the dollar does matter. For that reason, changes in the international value of the dollar have had an important impact on US trade politics, dating from at least the Nixon administration. Overvaluation before 1971 helped fuel protectionism and the threat of statutory import quotas in 1970. Conversely, by 1973, negotiated devaluation and further downward floating of the dollar had led to visible, month-by-month improvement in the US trade balance just as executive branch trade officials were lobbying the House to pass the trade bill authorizing the Tokyo Round. They found this trend most helpful. Similarly, trade troubles early in the Carter administration were triggered in part by the mid-1970s dollar resurgence; the overwhelming final vote for the law implementing the Tokyo Round agreements in 1979 was facilitated by a dollar decline in 1977 and 1978.

I. M. Destler is a visiting fellow at the Institute for International Economics and a professor at the School of Public Affairs, University of Maryland.

The most dramatic case was in the 1980s, of course. The huge (40 percent), generally unanticipated rise in the dollar fueled an unprecedented surge in the volume of US imports while exports stagnated—their nominal level in 1986 was below that of 1980. The political impact is well remembered: the biggest upsurge in demands for trade protection since the 1930s and the demoralization of protrade internationalist business. Interestingly, the balance of trade politics began to right itself with the Plaza Accord of September 1985, and the dollar declined from that year forward. The reason lay not only in the actual improvement of the trade balance that eventually followed; the anticipated effect allowed the Reagan administration and other protrade forces to assert that the overall numbers would get better, but (given the J-curve) not right away. In fact, US exports doubled between 1986 and 1992, and a particularly sharp rise in 1988 coincided with the modification, in a congressional conference committee, of some of the rougher provisions in the omnibus trade legislation completed in August of that year.

As these examples suggest, a strong dollar inflicts a "double whammy" on expansion-minded trade policy. It stimulates imports, arousing industries that compete with these imports to enter the political arena. It dampens exports, reducing the trade policy interest of industries that typically act as a counterweight to protectionism. Thus, as a general rule, a rise in the dollar is a useful leading indicator of the rise of producer protectionism. By contrast, a weaker or declining dollar is trade policy's friend.

Other things being equal, therefore, a rise in the dollar worsens the merchandise trade balance. But the dollar figures understate the economic impact, especially on the import side, because foreign products come in cheaper than before. So the rise in import volume exceeds the rise in import value. From 1982 to 1986, for example, the value of US imports rose by 48 percent, from $248 to $368 billion. That in itself seems like a staggering increase in a period of diminishing inflation, but the quantity of imports rose even faster, by 65 percent, as measured by the Department of Commerce's quantity index.

Similar statistics give us a sense of the political burden carried by current US trade policy. Although the dollar did not rise as rapidly in the late 1990s as it did in the early 1980s, import volume (again measured by the quantity index) rose 63 percent between 1996 and 2000. Since then, US imports and exports have both fallen significantly. (In all cases the statistics refer to merchandise imports, excluding services, chosen because goods producers remain the economic actors with the greatest impact on trade politics.)

The political response at the onset of this decade has been decidedly less ferocious than that of the 1980s. One reason is that the US economy has been, until recently, in much better shape overall, with higher growth and lower unemployment. Another is that US producers have had an additional decade and a half to internationalize. Still, the strong dollar has contributed notably to the problems of steel and agriculture, the two issues that sullied President Bush's free trade reputation last spring. And it meant that this administration, unlike its Nixon and Reagan predecessors, had to sail into a strong exchange rate wind to win Trade Promotion Authority (aka fast track).

As this and previously cited examples suggest, the main political reaction to high dollar valuation has been to attack not the exchange rate itself but its effects, particularly on the import side. But there have been a variety of other responses. One, seen mainly during the Reagan administration but of equal economic relevance today, is to call for changes in fiscal policy as a means of reducing the overall US savings deficit. A related reaction, more relevant in the 1980s than today, is to call for easing of US monetary policy. Another political response, visible now as well as then, is to charge other nations with currency manipulation and promote US pressure on them to desist. A fourth is to call for changes in policy toward exchange rates themselves—seeking to change what the treasury secretary either says or, together with the Federal Reserve Board, does in foreign exchange markets.

A conference like this one is testimony to the fact that the dollar has become an issue in and of itself. Whether this will lead to compensating political action is uncertain at best. Fortunately for US trade policy, it is likely that the dollar will fall significantly from present levels before there is another trade vote in Congress as important as those of 2001 and 2002.

5

Persistent Dollar Swings and the US Economy

MARTIN NEIL BAILY

The dollar has experienced two large sustained upward movements in the past 30 years, and both of these episodes were associated with large trade and current account deficits. Large swings in the dollar cause shifts of resources back and forth between the tradable and nontradable sectors, and these adjustments may be costly. A great deal of concern has been expressed about the impact of dollar variations on the manufacturing sector. Organizations representing both labor and management have complained that the strong dollar is hurting their constituencies and have suggested policies ranging from a new rhetoric from government officials[1] to exchange rate intervention and even capital controls.[2] In this paper I

Martin Neil Baily, senior fellow at the Institute for International Economics, was chairman of the Council of Economic Advisers of President Clinton from 1999 to 2001 and a member of President Clinton's cabinet. The author would like to thank his colleagues at the Institute for International Economics for many helpful comments, especially C. Fred Bergsten, Robert Lawrence, Catherine Mann, Mike Mussa, Ted Truman, and John Williamson. Karen Johnson and David Wilcox of the Federal Reserve and their staffs, Joel Prakken of Macroeconomic Advisers, and David Heuther of the National Association of Manufacturers gave substantial assistance or advice; and Pavel Trcala provided excellent research assistance.

1. See Jasinowski (2002).

2. See Palley (2002), a study for the AFL-CIO. C. Fred Bergsten of the Institute for International Economics does not represent either of these constituencies but has argued for a change in rhetoric and possibly for exchange rate intervention on the grounds that a disequilibrium exchange rate imposes costs on the economy. Bergsten and John Williamson, also of the Institute, favor the establishment of target zones for the dollar and the euro. See Bergsten (2002).

examine how the manufacturing sector has actually been affected by swings in the dollar and by other economic forces.

In addition, I look at macroeconomic effects of dollar changes. How did the macroeconomy accommodate to the dollar adjustments of the 1980s and 1990s? And what would be the macro effects for the US economy in the future if the dollar were to fall enough to reduce the current account deficit from the level of 4.2 percent of GDP reached in 2000 to about 2.5 percent?

I am not attempting to predict where the dollar will move in future years. It has fallen somewhat since its peak in the spring of 2002, but it still remains high relative to its recent historical average, and the US current account and trade deficits are very large. A substantial decline in the dollar is possible, and even likely, over the next few years. So it is worthwhile exploring the macro consequences of such a dollar decline. This would involve a readjustment of the savings-investment balance, requiring a reduction in the growth of consumption and investment, as well as an inflationary impact.

Examining the potential impact of a decline in the dollar can raise a hornet's nest of objections from economists. The dollar is not exogenous but a market-determined price, so instead of asking what would be the consequences of a lower dollar, it is more appropriate to ask what the consequences would be of some shock to the world economy that would also result in a decline in the real value of the dollar. Another area of concern for economists is that the value of any dollar index depends on a large vector of bilateral exchange rates, and the outcome of changes in the relative prices of the dollar can depend on exactly which countries adjust more and less.

Ideally one would explore exchange rate adjustments within a meaning-ful multicountry general equilibrium framework that allowed examina-tion of a variety of possible shocks to the system.[3] However, there is an advantage in focusing on a US-based model to explore the consequences for the US economy. I will be using the Macroeconomic Advisers model, which has a clear track record in following the historical movements of the US economy and has shown the ability to make useful predictions of the future. Multicountry models introduce the danger that specification errors in the model of some other country will throw off the results for the United States.

In terms of the shock that causes a dollar decline, there is a case for adjusting the model equation that determines the exchange rate. This is the preferred approach of Macroeconomic Advisers and also used by the international staff at the Federal Reserve Board. The idea is to capture either shifts in expectations (the exchange rate risk premium), or the

---

3. See, for example, Bryant, Hooper, and Mann (1993).

impact of portfolio effects that cannot be modeled well in the econometric exchange rate equation. I discuss this point further below.

To anticipate the main findings: First, for the manufacturing sector as a whole it is hard to find signs that swings in the dollar over the period 1973-2000 have had a large negative impact. This is also true when three specific industries are considered, autos, steel, and high tech (computers and semiconductors). US manufacturing has done relatively well in the period of floating exchange rates (although the unionized part of manufacturing has done less well). Second, the past two years have been unusually difficult ones for manufacturing. The sector has been hit very hard in this recession by three blows at once. There has been a sharp fall in the domestic demand for manufactured goods; the dollar has remained strong during this downturn—actually rising throughout 2001; and there has been economic weakness in the other major world economies. Third, because of continuing capital inflows and because of the growth of services trade, the value of the dollar is likely to remain indefinitely above the level that would result in balanced trade in manufactured goods. A manufacturing trade deficit will likely be a persistent feature of the US economy. Fourth, looking forward, the US current account deficit could be reduced to around 2.5 percent of GDP by a devaluation of 20 to 25 percent. Fifth, such an adjustment, should it take place, would benefit the goods-producing and service-producing sectors of the US economy and would slow sharply the growth of net foreign indebtedness. It would, according to the simulation model, come at a rather high price in terms of much higher interest rates, a slower GDP growth, and a substantial sacrifice of consumption and investment. Sixth, the exchange rate adjustment can be made gradually or more sharply. The benefits come more quickly and the costs are higher in the latter case, and there is some overshooting of the exchange rate on the downside.

US Manufacturing During the Period of the Floating Dollar, 1973-Present

The theory of comparative advantage provides the rationale behind the drive for worldwide trade expansion. The analysis of the gains from trade is generally developed under the assumption of balanced trade, but with open capital markets and flexible exchange rates, there can be and have been very large trade deficits and surpluses for different countries. The adjustment costs imposed on the tradable goods sector of the economy by fluctuating exchange rates are not ignored in the literature, but they are not given great prominence.[4] For the United States, dollar swings,

4. The ability of the US economy to adjust to trade was explored in Lawrence (1984). The Globalization Balance Sheet project at the Institute for International Economics, led by J. David Richardson, has explored the costs of adjustment. In a paper written contemporaneously

generally seen as driven by capital flows, impose an adjustment cost on all tradable goods and services, and notably on manufacturing.

For a company exporting a commodity product (one that has very close substitutes) with a price set in terms of local currency in the export market, a rise of 30 or 40 percent in the exchange rate is large enough to eliminate all of the profit margin in many cases. Exporting can become unprofitable in the face of an elevated dollar. In the first instance, this can create large instability in profits for companies involved in exporting and a loss of foreign market share.

Companies in import-competing industries face a similar problem. A company that had thought its competitive position was very strong could find itself losing contracts to foreign producers because it cannot match the prices available in world markets.

As witness to the importance of these issues in practice, the National Association of Manufacturers collected comment letters from a variety of small manufacturers throughout the United States and sent them to Treasury Secretary Paul H. O'Neill.[5] For example, an Ohio machine tool maker wrote about the "devastating impact" of the undervalued euro on his company and his industry. "Between 1990 and 1998 our exports represented an average of 25 percent of our business. In 1999 exports represented only 7 percent of our bookings and there have been NO export orders in 2000. Our employment is down 33 percent." An Indiana maker of veneer machinery reports, "Foreign companies tell us they wish to buy our machinery but cannot afford it with the difference in currency value. Our foreign sales have dropped over 90 percent in the last four years." And there are many, many more such stories.

The pressure of the high dollar has been linked to a weakness in business profitability in recent years. Corporate profits before tax of nonfinancial corporations nearly doubled between 1992 and 1997 (current dollars) and then were fairly flat until 2000, even though the output of this sector continued to grow strongly. In 2001, profits fell 31 percent (profits as measured in the national income and product accounts).

When exporting or import-competing companies experience a drop in orders or a sharp downward price movement, they often respond by reducing employment. US labor unions see the rise in the dollar after 1995 as a central reason for the weakness in manufacturing employment over the past few years. Thomas Palley (2002), in a report for the AFL-

---

with this one, Robert Blecker (2002) argues that the "overvaluation of the dollar has caused massive damage to the US manufacturing sector as a whole, and was an important contributing factor in the surge of imports that caused a crisis for the US steel industry in the late 1990s and early 2000s."

5. Available from the National Association of Manufacturers in Washington. Excerpts presented at the hearings by the House Committee on Small Business, June 12, 2002, testimony by Tony Raimondo, Behlen Manufacturing Company.

CIO, finds that the manufacturing trade deficit in 2000 had reached over 20 percent of manufacturing value added, having grown dramatically since 1991. Figure 5.1 shows this measure of trade impact. The United States has run persistent trade deficits in manufactured goods since 1983, and those deficits have widened dramatically since 1998. Palley notes that manufacturing employment fell nearly 2 million from 1998 to March of 2002.

In this section, I examine the performance of US manufacturing during the period of the floating dollar after 1973, and especially in the past ten years. In the next section I look in more detail at three industries that have figured large in the discussion of the trade effects of the dollar: steel, autos, and high tech.

Manufacturing Employment, 1973-2000: The US and Other Advanced Economies

Changes in the level of employment in a given sector in a given country depend on its productivity growth and the increase or decrease in the demand for its products. Total demand for a product is the sum of domestic demand and net foreign demand. Domestic demand, typically by far the largest component, follows secular trends and is subject to short-term movements, notably cyclical changes.

Looking at the trends, an industry that experiences rapid productivity growth will generally reduce its prices over time, relative to other goods and services, and this will help bolster demand. For example, the volume of semiconductors produced in the United States has increased sharply over time as the quality-adjusted prices have fallen dramatically. Demand for an industry's products may also increase over time if people buy more of them as their income increases. And there may be factors external to an industry at work, such as the price and availability of substitute products.

For many mature or traditional manufacturing industries the secular trends are working against employment. Productivity continues to rise over time, but the combination of falling prices and rising incomes does not provide enough impetus to demand to increase employment. The classic example of this phenomenon is outside of manufacturing, namely in agriculture, where both income and price elasticities are low; here, a strong productivity performance over at least a century has reduced employment to very low levels. The service sector provides many examples of the opposite case, where low productivity growth is combined with rising employment—legal and business services, for example.

The manufacturing sector as a whole seems to be more like agriculture than services on a secular basis. Output has grown over time, but not fast enough to keep employment up, given strong productivity growth. The key reason for believing there is a secular trend weakness in manufac-

Figure 5.1 Manufacturing trade balance as a share of manufacturing value added, 1975-2000

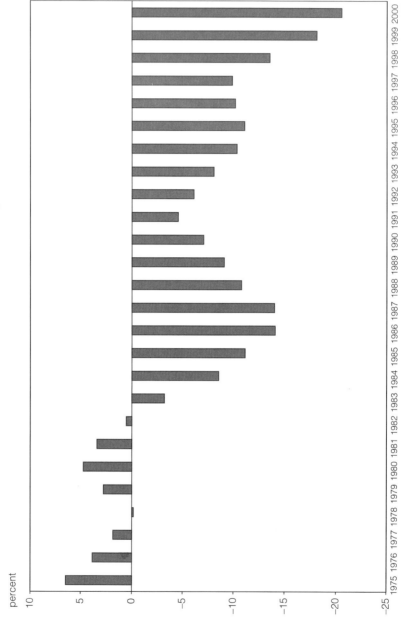

percent

Sources: Bureau of Economic Analysis, International Trade Administration, and author's calculations.

turing employment is that this pattern is typical of advanced economies. Figure 5.2 shows how the level of total hours worked (employment times average annual hours per employee) has changed over the period 1973-2000 for the large industrial economies. The pattern of declining employment is very marked. In fact, Canada is the only one of the large economies that has experienced employment growth since 1973. Germany and Japan are both manufacturing powerhouses in international markets and have run consistent manufacturing trade surpluses over this period. Yet both countries have experienced much sharper declines in employment than did the United States. Viewed against the example of its developed-country competitors, the US manufacturing sector performed well in terms of maintaining employment over the 27-year period after the start of floating exchange rates. There are two reasons for this. First, the level of productivity in US manufacturing was (and is) very high, so there was less restructuring to be done in the United States. Second, the United States has been successful in developing new industries where demand growth has been very rapid—instruments, computers, and semiconductors, for example.

Canadian manufacturing since 1973 has actually had slower output growth than that in the US, but also far slower productivity growth, in part because of a much smaller high-tech sector. In the 1990s, Canadian manufacturing employment benefited from the weak Canadian dollar, proximity to the United States, and the robust growth of the US GDP. The North American Free Trade Agreement (NAFTA) also encouraged the expansion of trade between the two countries.

Countries that are still in the process of industrializing can be expected to show increases in manufacturing employment, just as the United States did in the first half of the 20th century. But the tendency for manufacturing employment to decline shows up rather early in the industrialization process nowadays, as technology transfer and a more favorable regulatory environment allow developing countries to move toward developed-country productivity levels in manufacturing more quickly than in service industries. Total hours worked in manufacturing have shown a declining trend in Korea since 1988 and in Taiwan since 1987.

As well as being driven by trends, the movements of employment in manufacturing in the short run are highly cyclical. Fluctuations in GDP during the business cycle are disproportionately concentrated in manufacturing, especially durable goods manufacturing. The impact of the episodes of cyclical downturn in 1974-75, 1980-82, and 1990-92 are strongly evident in the time-series pattern of employment shown in figure 5.2.

There have been two periods with a strong dollar since 1973, and there is no question that these periods put temporary downward pressure on US manufacturing employment. The high dollar during the periods 1984-86 and 1997-2000 clearly had an impact on employment, and it is evident

Figure 5.2 Total hours worked in manufacturing by country, 1973-2000

index 1973 = 100

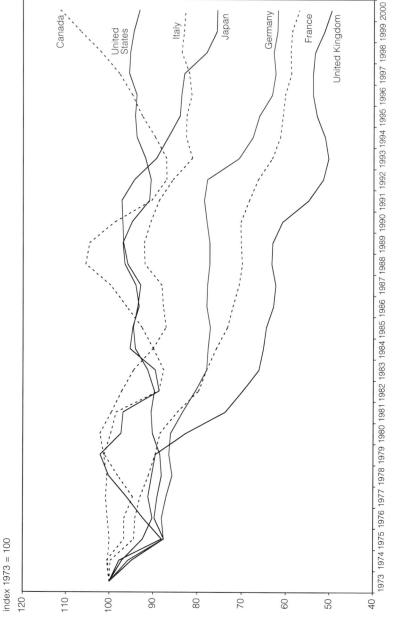

Note: Total hours is employment times hours worked per employee.

Source: Bureau of Labor Statistics.

Figure 5.3 US manufacturing employment in the past decade

thousands of workers

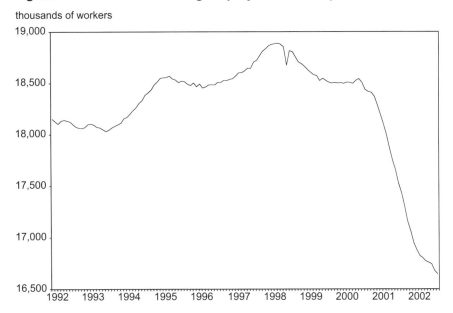

Source: Bureau of Labor Statistics.

in figure 5.2, especially allowing for some lag between dollar movements and trade movements. It is striking, and it is not a coincidence, that during both of these strong-dollar periods, through mid-2000, the cyclical factors were working to sustain employment, and so the overall impact on employment was rather modest.

The two large upward movements of the dollar were driven by the ability of the US economy to attract large capital inflows. Relative to the rest of the world, when the US economy is growing strongly, the return on capital rises; in addition, interest rates rose with the large budget deficits of the 1980s, attracting capital from around the world. In practice, therefore, the two strong-dollar episodes since 1973 have coincided with times of strong cyclical growth in US demand, thereby minimizing the extent of adjustment or resource reallocation that has been required.

As noted above, the offsetting effect of dollar movements and cyclical movements applies only through mid-2000. I turn now to the 1990s expansion and the subsequent downturn.

Manufacturing Employment and Productivity, 1992-2002

Figure 5.3 shows seasonally adjusted monthly employment from January 1992 through September 2002, the most recently available (preliminary) datum. Because of a recession that had started in 1990, manufacturing employment remained sluggish until mid-1993 (the "jobless recovery"). Employment then grew by 860,000 from July 1993 to April 1998 before starting to decline gradually, with about 350,000 jobs lost through August 2000. At that point, the US economy tipped into a sharp growth recession followed by a mild overall recession, and an additional 1.86 million manufacturing jobs were lost through September 2002. The manufacturing job loss in this recession has been far more severe than in the recession of the early 1990s.

What are the forces at work over this 10-year period—and in the downturn in particular? First, the rate of productivity growth increased in the 1990s, especially after 1995. Manufacturing output per hour increased at 2.6 percent a year from 1979 to 1990, followed by a rate of 3.2 percent a year from 1990 to 1995 and 3.8 percent a year from 1995 to 2001. A higher rate of output growth would have been needed just to hold employment constant.

The strength of manufacturing productivity growth during the downturn and the start of the recovery is surprising. It grew by 2.6 percent a year from mid-2000 until the second quarter of 2002, despite sustained weakness in manufacturing output. After September 11, 2001, productivity was particularly striking, increasing at an annual rate of 5.9 percent over the three quarters from the fourth quarter of 2001 through the first half of 2002. Manufacturing employment continued to decline even though the sector was turning the corner in terms of output. Uncertainty about the economic outlook likely encouraged employers to make layoffs faster than in prior periods of demand weakness.

Second, during the 1990s expansion there was a shift of US investment. There was strong growth in investment in the expansion, but much of that growth was concentrated in information processing equipment and software. The information technology (IT) hardware sector has modest levels of employment, and rapid real output increases were met by extraordinary increases in productivity. The software sector is not part of manufacturing. Thus the investment boom in the 1990s, especially after 1995, was very strong in terms of increasing the real capital stock, but not in terms of the output of the traditional areas of manufactured goods. As the United States has become more of an information economy, this has changed the magnitude and mix of the demand for manufactured goods.

Third, the slowdown that started in 2000 and the recession of 2001 were concentrated in manufacturing. Even though the overall downturn (so far) has been very mild in terms of GDP, the drop in the domestic demand for goods was sharp. Figure 5.4 shows the deviation from trend of the domestic demand for goods (GDP of goods plus goods imports minus goods exports) from 1990 to the first quarter of 2002.[6] The time trend over

---

6. The data are in current dollars, although the corresponding real values move in very much the same pattern. GDP of goods includes the value added in manufacturing, but also

Figure 5.4   Domestic demand for goods: Deviation from trend, 1990-2002

percent of trend

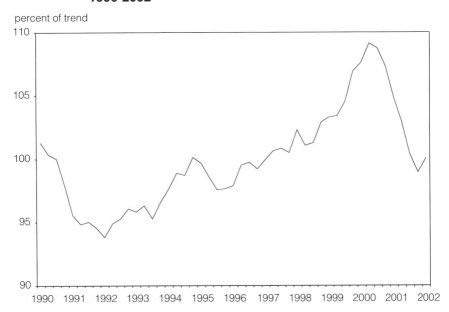

Source: Bureau of Economic Analysis, and author's calculations.

this period has been removed. The figure shows that the downturn of 2000-02 resulted in a very sharp decline in goods demand, and the employment decline was also large. Trend-adjusted domestic demand for goods fell by 9.3 percent from the second quarter of 2000 through the fourth quarter of 2001, while manufacturing employment declined by 7.2 percent over the same period.[7] The decline in US manufacturing employment occurred in parallel with a decline in the demand for manufactured goods by US consumers and businesses.

Last but not least, the pattern of the dollar as the 1990s expansion ended was very different from the movement of the dollar as the 1980s expansion ended. The dollar started to decline in 1985 and came down quickly and substantially. As the growth of domestic demand slowed in the United States, the competitive position of US manufacturers sharply improved, helping to sustain US growth. By contrast, the dollar remained very strong even after the 1990s expansion slowed and ended, and in fact it continued

---

the value added in upstream and downstream industries, notably wholesale and retail. The figure shows how much US residents were choosing to spend on goods, plus changes in inventories.

7. The employment series were not trend adjusted, but figure 5.1 showed that there was not a large trend, and certainly not a significant upward trend.

Table 5.1 The impact of trade in goods on GDP growth

Periods	Contributions to real GDP growth average of the quarterly figures (percent)		
	Goods exports	Goods imports	Net exports
1997Q1 - 2000Q2	0.54	−1.40	−0.86
2000Q3 - 2002Q2	−0.29	−0.09	−0.38
Contribution to the growth slowdown	−0.83	1.31	0.48

Source: Bureau of Economic Analysis, http://www.bea.gov, table S.2.

to rise until February 2002. Dollar movements in 2000, 2001, and early 2002 exacerbated the cyclical downturn in manufacturing.

Keep in mind, however, that even though dollar movements were hurting manufacturing, foreign trade generally acts as an automatic stabilizer for the economy, and for manufacturing specifically, and it did so in this downturn. One way to show this is to look at the contributions to real GDP growth coming from the different components of GDP, as computed by the Bureau of Economic Analysis. Table 5.1 shows how exports, imports, and net exports of goods added to or subtracted from real GDP growth over the period leading up to the growth slowdown and the period after the growth slowdown started (1997Q1 through 2000Q2 versus 2000Q3 through 2002Q2). The table shows that growth in goods exports contributed to overall GDP growth in the period before the start of the slowdown, adding 0.54 percent a year to the annual average growth rate. Goods imports, on the other hand, subtracted 1.4 percent a year from the rate during those same boom years. The net impact of goods trade was to reduce GDP growth by 0.86 percent a year—during a period when GDP growth averaged over 4 percent a year.

After the downturn started, there was a falloff in exports, and this reduced overall growth by 0.29 percent a year. The strong dollar and the weakness in the rest of the world economies adversely affected US growth. On the other hand, the turnaround in imports was even more dramatic. Imports declined, and since imports are a subtraction from GDP, this import decline reduced almost to zero the negative contribution to GDP.

The net effect of goods trade was to reduce GDP growth both before and after the middle of 2000, but the reduction in growth was far greater during the boom years (−0.86) than during the downturn (−0.38). On balance, goods trade mitigated the decline in growth by nearly half a percentage point a year (0.48). These findings reinforce the message from figure 5.4. The sharp drop in manufacturing employment that started in mid-2000 was the result of the shift in domestic demand for manufactured goods. The high dollar and the weakness of overseas economies reduced but did not entirely eliminate the role that trade in goods plays as an automatic stabilizer to the manufacturing sector and the whole US economy.

Profits in Manufacturing

Figure 5.5a shows the real profits earned by the domestic operations of all nonfinancial US corporations from 1973 through the first quarter of 2002 (adjusted by the implicit price deflator for nonfinancial corporate output). Profits are strongly cyclical, turning down in 1974-75, in the early 1980s, and in the recent downturn. The rapid rise of profits for much of the 1990s is remarkable, a runup that reached its peak in the third quarter of 1997. After that, profits weakened until mid-2000 and then fell sharply until the third quarter of 2001. They have made a modest comeback since then and remain at a substantially higher level than in the late 1980s.[8] The fall in profits with the downturn was to be expected, but the profit weakness after 1997 is more puzzling. One possibility is that companies were overreporting profits in the bubble frenzy of the 1990s, but eventually ran out of ways to use creative accounting. Another possibility is that the strong dollar was exposing domestic operations to severe competitive pressure.

The path of profits in the 1980s suggests a more limited role for the dollar, with the cycle as the primary cause of variations. The dollar reached a peak in March 1985, while profits increased strongly from 1983 to 1985, reaching a peak in the third quarter of that year. The dollar then fell sharply, but profits weakened through early 1987.

Figure 5.5b explores this idea further, dividing total profits of nonfinancial corporations into those generated by domestic manufacturing industries and nonmanufacturing industries (same deflator as above).[9] (Unfortunately, the industry profit data do not include the capital consumption adjustment (CCA). For the total nonfinancial sector this makes a big difference to profits in the second half of 2001, when economic profits (including CCA) are much stronger than reported profits because of tax law changes.)[10]

Although there is international trade in services, it is a trivial part of the total of US output of services, so figure 5.5b provides a good comparison of the tradable and nontradable sectors. In the cyclical peak 1989-90, the level of profits in manufacturing and nonmanufacturing were similar. In

---

8. In part this is because interest rates dropped in the 1990s and so the debt service burden on nonfinancial corporations declined.

9. Since many corporations have both manufacturing and nonmanufacturing operations, the breakdown reflects the best estimates of the Bureau of Economic Affairs staff and is not precise.

10. See *Survey of Current Business,* April 2002, 5-7.

Figure 5.5a Nonfinancial corporate profits, domestic US operations, 1987-2002

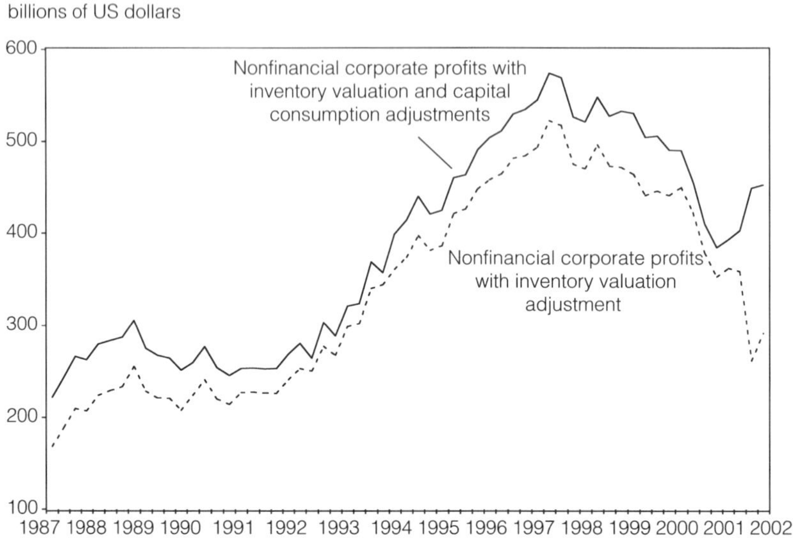

billions of US dollars

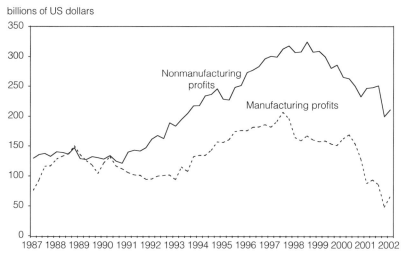

Nonfinancial corporate profits with inventory valuation and capital consumption adjustments

Nonfinancial corporate profits with inventory valuation adjustment

Figure 5.5b Nonfinancial nonmanufacturing and manufacturing corporate profits

billions of US dollars

Nonmanufacturing profits

Manufacturing profits

Note: Corporate profits with inventory valuation adjustment. Deflated with gross product price index for nonfinancial industries.

Source: Bureau of Economic Analysis, www.bea.gov, table 6.16c.

the subsequent recession, manufacturing profits fell substantially, while nonmanufacturing profits dipped only very slightly and then started to grow strongly, reaching a peak in the third quarter of 1998. Manufacturing profits never caught up. They grew strongly through the third quarter of 1997, but reached only two-thirds of the level of nonmanufacturing profits. Manufacturing profits peaked in 1997, a year earlier than for nonmanufacturing profits, and fell sharply.

In nonmanufacturing, profits fell from their peak of $324 billion (1996 dollars) in 1998 to $248 billion in the second quarter of 2001, a 27 percent decline. In manufacturing, profits fell from $206 billion in their peak of 1997 to $93 billion in mid-2001, a much larger decline of 79 percent. Manufacturing profits were hit sooner and harder than in the nonmanufacturing sector. (Reported profits fell more after mid-2001, but the absence of CCA makes the data hard to interpret).

The fact that profits turned down in the nontradables sector a year and a half before the cyclical slowdown started (over two years before the recession started) suggests that not all of the profit weakness was the result of either the recession or the dollar. Creative accounting may have been at work, in both manufacturing and nonmanufacturing sectors.

This comparison between sectors, however, reveals that profits in manufacturing were facing stronger pressures than in the rest of the economy.[11] There was an expansion of globalization in the 1990s, which increased competitive pressure most strongly in the tradable goods sector. Manufacturers in the 1990s spoke about their lack of pricing power, presumably indicating they had had more of it in previous times, when there was less competitive pressure. Unless a US manufacturing industry has some form of strong trade protection, it faces very high competitive intensity. Any company in such an industry will face profit pressures and continually be forced to cut costs or develop new products (raise productivity) in order to be profitable. This can be hard on the producers—workers and firms—but is a benefit to consumers.

Investment in Manufacturing, the Dollar, and Capital Movements

More problematic than simply an increase in competitive pressure is the possible impact on manufacturing investment of the large, sustained swings in the dollar, which depress profits when the dollar is high even for companies that are competitive internationally in the long run. Presumably a low dollar inflates US manufacturing profits. Such currency swings, up and down, increase the risk of operating in tradable goods industries and could reduce the level of investment in those activities if the capital market is risk averse.

---

11. Blecker (2002) finds that manufacturing profits were strongly affected by variations in the dollar.

How would that show up? Paradoxically, if this view is correct and dollar fluctuations had increased the variability of manufacturing profits and discouraged investment in this sector, the result would be that average returns to manufacturing companies over an extended period would be higher over the long run than in nonmanufacturing. The variability of returns would have to be compensated by higher average returns. With the possible exception of some high-tech areas in the 1990s, that does not seem to be the case.

A Persistently High Dollar?

It is possible that the variations in the dollar are taking place around a mean value that results in a deficit in manufactured goods. A currency can remain above the level implied by balance in manufactured trade over an extended period if there are other sources of dollar inflows that push the dollar exchange rate up. For example, a country that suddenly discovers oil or natural gas will find its trade position and the value of its currency fundamentally altered. Instead of paying for large energy imports, the country would reduce its import bill sharply or even start to export energy. The "Dutch disease" is the famous example of this, when Holland discovered natural gas and started selling it in large quantities. This raised the value of the Dutch currency and caused the manufacturing sector to suffer a competitive disadvantage. The discovery of oil in the North Sea had a similar effect on UK manufacturing, visible in the very sharp declines in UK manufacturing employment over the period 1973-2000.[12] Note that a country as a whole need not be harmed by the discovery of energy and can benefit from it, but there is an adjustment in manufacturing that will result in fewer manufacturing jobs as long as the energy supply holds out.

Is there a similar problem in the United States? Not from oil or gas. After being self-sufficient in energy for over 60 years of the 20th century, the United States has become a large net importer of energy. I noted earlier that the United States had fared better than other countries in manufacturing employment since 1973, and some of this is the result of the ever-increasing need to pay for oil imports by exporting manufactured goods. This depressed the dollar relative to the counterfactual of remaining energy independent. If there is a strain of the Dutch disease in the United States, it is a different variety.

Another factor affecting the competitive position of manufacturing is that the United States has a comparative advantage in agriculture and services. The trade surpluses in these sectors generate a net inflow of

---

12. UK manufacturing also had low productivity and required major restructuring, especially in formerly nationalized industries.

funds that sustains the dollar. Historically, these surpluses have made a difference, but not a big difference. Going forward, if the growth of services trade continues to be rapid and the surpluses grow, this could be an important factor keeping manufacturing trade in deficit. The simulations discussed below highlight this issue.

Perhaps the biggest factor keeping the dollar persistently high is capital flows. The US has traditionally been a low-saving economy relative to other advanced countries, such as Japan and Germany. In the 1980s, national saving was pushed down because of exploding federal budget deficits. In the 1990s national saving was kept low despite a shift from federal budget deficits to surpluses, because the already low private saving rate dropped even lower. Hence one can make the following case. The United States is chronically a low-saving economy, and this means that when the business cycle is strong and domestic investment booms, foreign capital is drawn in to finance it (directly or indirectly). This raises the dollar, gives rise to periods where the dollar is higher than its long-run trend value, and hurts manufacturing profits and employment. When the dollar falls, it may reverse the short-term problem, but it does not give rise to a period of large trade surpluses.

Another part of the same story is the willingness of foreign investors to buy US assets. The argument is sometimes made that "too much" foreign capital is flowing into the United States and distorting the dollar. To evaluate this argument, it is helpful to distinguish the types of capital inflows. An important fraction of the increased capital inflow in the 1990s was foreign direct investment (FDI).

FDI into the United States over the period 1996-2001 was $1.07 trillion, an increase of $826 billion over the period 1990-95. Both the magnitude of the FDI and its increase are important. The increase in FDI is equal to two-thirds of the increase in the current account deficit over the same period. Of course capital outflows and other inflows also increased, but FDI clearly played an important role in the increase in the net capital inflow.

An important fraction of the FDI went to US manufacturing. Figure 5.6 shows FDI into US manufacturing over the period 1990-2001. From 1996 through 2001, the period of the high or rising dollar, $356 billion of FDI went into US manufacturing. This represented one-third of all FDI into the United States. One-third is far larger than the share of manufacturing in the US economy, so foreign direct investors were favoring US manufacturing operations and supplying large amounts of capital to it. The inflow of capital did help fund investment, and hence jobs, in US manufacturing.[13]

---

13. Not all of the FDI was for new facilities. However, other types of capital inflow also helped manufacturing investment. Foreigners bought equities and bonds of US manufacturing companies, lowering their cost of capital.

Figure 5.6 Manufacturing foreign direct investment in the United States, 1990-2001

billions of US dollars

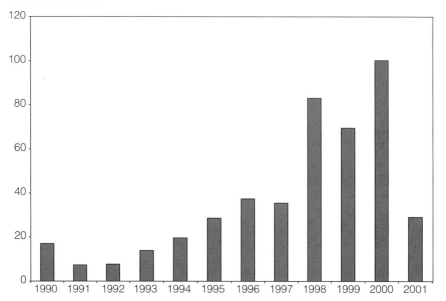

Note: Capital inflows without a current cost adjustment.

Source: Bureau of Economic Analysis (international accounts data).

The flow of foreign capital into US manufacturing is an important signal of the value given to the United States as a location for manufacturing activity. Foreign investors in the 1990s expected the US manufacturing sector to be profitable over the long run, even though the dollar was moving up so strongly.

Of course money is fungible. Not all of the FDI was for investment in new manufacturing facilities; some of the funds went to buy out the existing owners who then were free to do other things with the proceeds. However, whenever a foreigner purchases a US asset, this increases the supply of capital to the United States. It increases the availability of funds, which are then allocated by the market to different uses. The first-round effect of capital inflows to the United States is to increase the funds available to all industries, including manufacturing. The inflow of funds offsets the low US national saving rate. The macroeconomic simulations described in later sections provide more information on the impact of the capital inflows.

Aggregate manufacturing data have provided some insights into the impact of the dollar on manufacturing. To probe the issues further, however, it is worth looking in more detail at three specific industries that have faced particular pressures.

Box 5.1 Estimates of hysteresis in trade and wages

Hysteresis in Trade. One possible problem associated with swings in the value of the dollar is that when the dollar is high, this could cause a permanent loss of trade competitiveness for the United States. Reasons for this are that, first, US companies in export or import-competing industries may go out of business or cut back on their investments or R&D or export promotion. When the dollar comes down again, they may be unable to compete as effectively. Second, and parallel, foreign companies may use a period when the dollar is strong to expand their market shares or dealer networks in the United States. When the dollar goes down again they will use the enlarged base to continue to export strongly. These effects could create hysteresis such that net exports to the United States are larger after a period of dollar strength even if the dollar has gone back down to the level at which it started. Although this view has some surface plausibility, it is not clear a priori why ups and downs of the dollar should work asymmetrically. What does the evidence show?

Paul Krugman (1989) found empirical evidence to support the idea of trade hysteresis, but subsequent research has not generally supported this view. In particular, Robert Lawrence (1990) examined the episode of the high dollar in the 1980s and found no support for the hysteresis hypothesis. The trade equations he estimated for the period up to 1980, which did not assume the existence of any hysteresis, tracked actual trade over the 1980s very well, including the period after the dollar came back down.

The analysis is complicated because of the Houthakker-McGee effects in estimated trade equations. The pattern of US trade over time strongly suggests that if the United States grows at the same rate as the rest of the world and the dollar remains constant, then the US trade deficit will worsen. Or, alternatively, the dollar must fall over time if there is to be a constant deficit or surplus in US trade in goods and services (constant share of the economy). The causes of this remain cloudy. One reasonable possibility is that the expansion of production capacity and the spread of technology worldwide are gradually changing the terms of trade of the United States. But it has proven hard to model convincingly the forces driving this trend. The most important point is that the trend shift in the US trading position that the effect implies does not seem to be driven by swings in the dollar; indeed, the pattern predates the era of floating exchange rates. The existence of the trend means that when Lawrence rejects the hypothesis of hysteresis, this does not imply that the same value of the dollar would induce the same US trade balance in 1990 as it did in 1980 (adjusting for any GDP growth differentials over the period). It does say that the period of the strong dollar in the 1980s did not leave a permanent legacy of US trade weakness.

Hysteresis in Wages. There is a broad literature suggesting that globalization may have contributed to the widening of the wage distribution in the United States over the past 20 years.[1] There is economic theory and common sense behind the idea that as the United States increases its trade with countries with a large supply of low-skill workers, this will lower the relative wages of low-skill workers in the United States. The difficult issue is in determining how important the trade effects are. The main arguments suggesting that the effects are small are that the United States does most of its trade with Canada, Europe, and Japan, where wage levels are similar to US levels, and that the tradable goods sector in the United States is small relative to the total US labor market; to what extent can a fairly small tail

(box continues next page)

Box 5.1 *(continued)*

wag a very large dog? An alternative explanation of wage trends is that there have been shifts in the relative domestic demand for labor of different types, perhaps tied to shifts in technology. One recent study has traced a direct link not just from general trade expansion to the US wage distribution, but from dollar swings to the wage distribution. Linda Goldberg and Joseph Tracy (2002) have analyzed Current Population Survey data and concluded that when the dollar rises, this increases the gap between low-skill and high-skill workers. But when the dollar falls, the gap does not return to its former level. There is a kind of relative wage hysteresis suggested by their results.

This study is carefully done and interesting, but also puzzling to the point that the overall results are hard to accept. The impact of an increase in the dollar, in their analysis, produces a substantial increase in the wages of highly educated workers and a decline in the wages of workers with low educational levels. And this effect is true across all industries. It is not concentrated only in tradable goods industries, nor does it start in tradable goods industries and spread to the whole economy. A decrease in the dollar does not reverse these effects. I find it hard to understand a sustainable labor market equilibrium in which dollar swings over time would drive the variance of wages higher and higher. I note also that low-skill workers started to improve their wage position in the United States during the period 1995-2000, even though the dollar rose strongly.[2]

1. See, for example, Borjas, Freeman, and Katz (1997).

2. See *Council of Economic Advisers* (2001) and Juhn, Murphy, and Topel (2002).

Case Studies of Specific Manufacturing Industries

Steel

There are two very different perspectives on the US steel industry.[14] One view is that it is a viable productive industry in the process of structural change, where the main competitive threat to high-cost domestic companies does not come from abroad but from more cost-efficient producers in the United States. The second view is that the US industry faces a dire threat from unfair competition overseas. Steel plants operate with high fixed costs and low marginal costs. Foreign governments have subsidized the construction of steel capacity, resulting in global overcapacity. Foreign companies thus have an economic incentive to dump steel on the US market at prices below the unsubsidized full average cost of production. The US industry is therefore in dire need of either a lower dollar or trade protection, or both. Understanding these alternatives is essential to understanding how the dollar has affected this industry.

14. See, for example, Crandall (2001) and Economic Strategy Institute (2001).

The US steel industry emerged from World War II as the dominant industry in the world, with massive scale and productivity advantages over competitors elsewhere. Over time, the steel industries in such countries as Germany, Japan, and Korea were built or rebuilt as these economies invested heavily in developing their own steel capacity. The dominant technology for many years was the large integrated steel mill, which starts with iron ore, carries out the whole steel manufacturing process, and produces a large range of products. In the postwar period there have been technological advances in integrated steel mills, based on scale, design, and layout. The result is that newer integrated mills built around the world are more productive and have lower marginal costs than the older integrated mills in the United States. For example, the steel facilities of POSCO (Pohang Steel Company), the government-owned Korean integrated producer, are among the most productive in the world (Baily and Zitzewitz 1998). Korea imported its steel technology from best-practice equipment suppliers worldwide. Unlike industries such as autos or machine tools, basic steel technology is not very hard to transfer from developed to developing countries, since much of it is embodied in the capital goods.[15]

As economies develop economically and industrialize, the domestic demand for steel grows rapidly, which stimulates the growth of steel capacity. As economies mature, however, demand growth slows or even stops with the shift to services and to lighter products and newer materials. This pattern was intensified in Japan, which experienced strong growth in the demand for steel during its boom years in the 1980s and faced labor shortages. The industry overinvested in capacity and in automation and then found itself with severe overcapacity and an uneconomic level of capital intensity in the 1990s. Europe and other regions have also had problems with overcapacity, and the former Soviet Bloc countries had dramatic overcapacity once they transformed into market economies and cut back their defense industries.

The integrated steel producers in the United States, which had been very profitable in the 1950s, have gradually found their competitive position eroding. Their high operating costs were increased further by rapid wage increases in the 1970s (Lawrence and Lawrence 1985) and increases in the costs of retirement pension and health care costs.

An important innovation in the steel industry was developed in the United States. Minimills start with steel scrap instead of iron ore and use an electric arc furnace to melt the scrap for reuse in new steel products. They have much lower capital costs per ton of steel produced. In addition, the minimills, which started small and remained lean, have avoided the excessive bureaucracy and overstaffing that plagued the integrated pro-

---

15. Certain specialty steels require more sophisticated technology and high labor skills.

ducers. Nucor and other minimills have adopted practices such as cross-training workers to handle multiple tasks, limiting the number of products produced in a given mill, and using continuous improvement programs to increase productivity. In 2000, minimills were estimated to have had a 21.8 percent cost advantage over integrated mills for sheet steel products. This understates the advantage of the minimills, because integrated mills have abandoned other products where their cost disadvantage is even greater. At $376 per ton, minimill costs per ton in 2000 were close to those in Korea ($378) and Brazil ($389), despite the strong dollar of that year (World Steel Dynamics 2000).

Another sign of their strong cost position is that the minimills have expanded their capacity. An additional 9 million tons of flat-rolled mini-mill capacity came on-line in 1997-98, whereas no new integrated raw-steel capacity has been built in the United States since the 1970s. In 2001, mini-mills had 50 million tons of steel capacity in the United States, out of a total capacity of 120 million tons (Crandall 2001). Minimill production is larger than the volume of imports, which have averaged just under 30 million tons between 1994 and 2001.

Figure 5.7a illustrates the situation of the US steel industry, showing output, hours, and productivity for blast furnaces and basic steel products (SIC 331). It shows that US output has remained fairly flat over the period 1973-2000, with evidence of some cyclical losses in recessions. Productivity over the period has soared. This has been the result of increases in market share by the minimills, the closing of the least efficient integrated mills, and a push to reduce costs within both integrated and minimills as a result of the high competitive intensity in the industry. New technologies, such as computerized control of the manufacturing process, have also improved productivity. As a result employment has been weak over the whole period. Based on this figure, there is no evidence that employment in the industry was greatly affected in the mid-1980s or the late 1990s, when the dollar was strong. Hours declined slowly when the dollar was weak (1990-95) and when the dollar strengthened (1995-2000). Figure 5.7b shows employment in a broader definition of the steel industry that includes iron and steel foundries (SIC 332) and shows employment through early 2002 (the figure also shows auto employment, which I will discuss shortly). With this broader definition of the steel industry, one could argue that the dollar had some impact on employment, although it was small.

Based on import levels, it looks as if trade was actually cushioning the impact of the downturn, not worsening it. According to US Geological Survey data (iron and steel statistics, Mineral Commodity Summaries), consumption of steel in the United States was flat between 1997 and 2001. Imports fell by 36 percent over this period, including a 27 percent reduction between 2000 and 2001, when consumption fell by less than 1 percent.

Figure 5.7a   Steel industry employment, output, hours, and productivity (SIC 331), 1973-99

index 1973 = 100

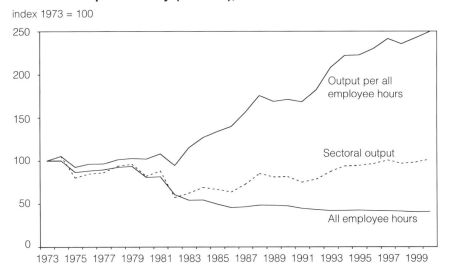

Figure 5.7b   US auto and steel industry employment, 1987-2002

thousands of workers

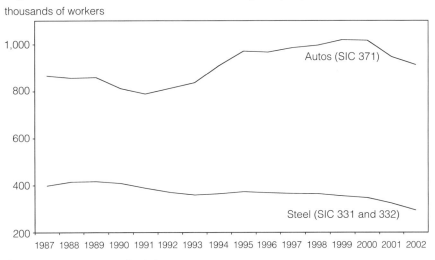

Source: Bureau of Labor Statistics.

In summary, there is some degree of truth to both of the perspectives of the steel industry that were presented above. Capacity decisions around the world have often not been made on the basis of rational discounted cash-flow analysis. And industries where fixed costs are high typically find it difficult to maintain a stable equilibrium in the absence of a tacit or explicit cartel (even then, it can be difficult). Aluminum, petrochemicals, oil, and airlines come to mind. The US steel industry is vulnerable to imports of steel from countries that have overinvested and have excess capacity. It is also vulnerable to imports from countries that have very low cost structures—low wages in Russia or cheap, high-quality iron ore in Brazil, for example. At the same time, the plight of the unionized integrated steel producers does not seem to depend primarily on either imports or the strong dollar. A fall in the dollar would certainly help, but this segment of the industry is at a fundamental comparative disadvantage relative to the domestic minimills, and a reduction in the dollar will not fundamentally change that relationship. Moreover, during the recent downturn, the fall in imports has been greater than the fall in domestic production.

Autos

There are some broad similarities between the steel and auto industries in the United States. The US auto industry was also the world's best-practice industry in the 1950s and 1960s and was dominated by a few large companies. A significant innovation occurred in the production process that disrupted the domestic equilibrium, although in the auto case it originated in the Japanese industry—the Toyota production system, which emphasized incremental improvement, lean production, and new approaches to product design.

The advantages that US companies had in design and production in the 1950s led them to invest overseas. US-built automobiles were not suitable for conditions outside the United States, but US nameplates developed a strong position in overseas markets. Japanese companies had developed alliances with the Big Three automakers before World War II, but these were broken in the 1930s with friction between the two countries. After the war the Japanese companies, with some industrial policy intervention, developed their own auto industry, and by the late 1960s Japanese companies were exporting to the United States. They used the advantage of low labor costs and rapidly rising productivity, fueled by the Toyota production system. Early imports to the United States were low-quality vehicles that were much smaller than the typical US car, so the Japanese market share was small. But when oil prices rose rapidly in the 1970s and when emissions restrictions were introduced, smaller, lighter cars became much more desirable and imports surged. Chrysler moved close to bankruptcy.

Trade restrictions were imposed on Japanese companies in the form of "voluntary" quotas, but this simply accelerated a trend toward direct investment in the United States and Canada. A key feature of the Toyota production system is "design for manufacturing," in which parts are simplified and made easier to assemble. Productivity both in auto plants in Japan and in Japanese nameplate plants in the United States moved well above the level of the Big Three average. Also, a bonus of this effort to raise productivity was that the simpler designs were more reliable, so a quality differential opened up between the Japanese and US nameplates.

Under increasing pressure from Japanese companies as well as rising imports of luxury autos from Germany, the Big Three have moved aggressively to raise their own productivity and quality and to cut costs. Modified versions of the Toyota production system were introduced into US plants, notably with the Ford Taurus in the 1980s. Improvements in productivity within existing plants were limited because of resistance from both plant managers and production workers, so an additional two-pronged strategy has been followed. First, a number of older, less efficient plants have been closed completely. And second, the US producers have been able to move consumers into SUVs, pickups, and minivans, where profits and value added per worker are higher and the competition from the Japanese and German companies has been less strong. Although the Big Three continue to lose market share in cars and reportedly make little or no profit from their production, the market share of light trucks and minivans is now over 50 percent.

Figure 5.7b shows the overall employment picture in this industry (SIC 371), showing continued employment growth through the 1990s despite the rise of the dollar after 1995. Figure 5.8 summarizes the movements of output, hours, and productivity over the longer period since 1973. The figures include US employment and production of both Big Three and foreign nameplates as well as parts suppliers. Although clearly sensitive to the business cycle, US auto industry output rose strongly in the 1980s and 1990s, roughly doubling from 1983 to 1999. Employment over the longer period did not do so well. It increased in the 1990s, but by 2000 was only just back to its 1973 level, and it has fallen since 2000. Productivity increases were strong and accelerated after 1995. They have had the effect of cutting employment for a given level of output, although of course they have also kept prices down and increased the industry's international competitiveness, both of which have encouraged output growth.

The high value of the dollar in the 1990s did not create the long-term dynamics that have driven this industry, but it did exacerbate the pressures on the domestic industry. Specifically, net imports of motor vehicles and parts into the United States rose from $56.9 billion in 1995 to $110.6 billion in 2000. Most of those net imports came from Canada, Japan, Mexico, Germany, and Korea, whose currencies were weak against the dollar after 1995.

The situation of the Big Three unionized auto producers is better than that of the integrated steel producers. They are more profitable, they have substantially improved their performance, and they retain considerable

Figure 5.8   Motor vehicle industry employment, hours, output, and productivity (SIC 371), 1973-2000

index 1973 = 100

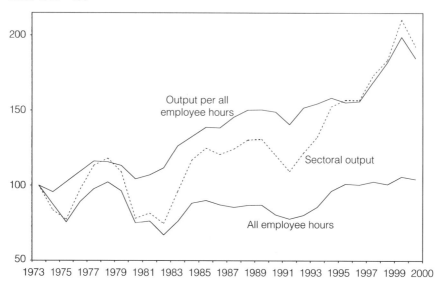

Source: Bureau of Labor Statistics.

assets, such as customer brand loyalty and skills in financing. But the challenges facing these companies are substantial. According to Harbour and Associates (2002), in 2001 Toyota, Honda, and Nissan earned an average $1,377 in profit per vehicle. In contrast, Chrysler lost $1,679 per vehicle, Ford lost $1,913, and GM made a profit of only $337.[16] In such a highly competitive market, the pressure on the Big Three to raise productivity further will remain very intense, and the potential for large output increases is limited. It will be hard to avoid further declines in employment for this segment.

Decisions on where to locate new plants by the foreign nameplates are based on political as well as economic factors. But at current exchange rates, production is cheaper in Canada and Mexico than in the United States. Unless there is some exchange rate adjustment, net US imports of autos and parts from within the NAFTA region will keep rising.

Profitability and Legacy Labor Costs in the Steel and Auto Industries

Figure 5.9 shows real profits in three domestic industries, motor vehicles and parts, primary metals, and electronics and electrical equipment. The

---

16. As reported by Jeremy Grant, "Detroit Fights Back," *Financial Times,* August 6, 2002. Data are from *The Harbour Report 2002.*

Figure 5.9   Corporate profits in selected manufacturing industries, 1987-2001

billions of US dollars

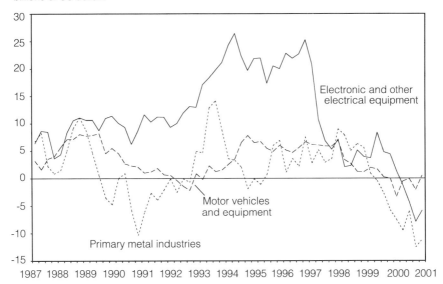

Note: Corporate profits with inventory valuation adjustment. Deflated with gross product price index for nonfinancial industries.

Source: Bureau of Economic Analysis.

last of these I will discuss shortly. The primary metals sector includes nonferrous metals, but it gives a sense of how the steel industry has fared in profits.

Neither the auto industry nor the primary metals industry has been a huge moneymaker over the period 1987-2001 (the same problems in the profits data described above affect the profits for 2001). Profitability has been cyclical and was hit hard by the combination of a weak economy and a strong dollar, with the weakness showing up before 2000.

The integrated steel mills and the Big Three automakers face a similar problem that is adversely affecting their profits. They reached agreements with their workers many years ago to provide retirement benefits into the future that they thought would be manageable but that have turned out to be extremely costly as the industries have faced full global competition. As the base of employed unionized workers has fallen, the cost of servicing the retired workforce has risen as a proportion of total labor costs. The proportion of the auto industry that is unionized (motor vehicles and motor vehicle equipment) has fallen from 59 percent in 1983 to 48 percent in 1990 and 37 percent in 2001. For the steel industry (blast furnaces, steelworks, rolling and finishing mills, and iron and steel foundries) the percentages are 60 percent in 1983, 49 percent in 1990, and 40 percent in 2001.[17] The high legacy labor costs are a major problem for these industries.

The Information Technology Sector

US-based companies largely developed the information technology sector and make up most of the leading companies in the industry today. This industry is still in a phase of rapid innovation, and the structure of the US market system has proven to be a major advantage in this phase— through the venture capital industry, mobile workers, the educational institutions, and the culture of Silicon Valley. In addition, first-mover advantages have proven decisive in some sectors of the industry and, to an extent, in the success of Silicon Valley itself, which has attracted people and ideas from all over the world. Historically, the Department of Defense provided financial support for R&D and purchase the resulting products, which helped some of the first movers get started.

The success of US companies in this sector has not meant, however, that the production of IT hardware, and its associated employment, has been concentrated in the United States. The industry has become global, with components manufactured around the world where costs are lowest. Much of the production is carried out in Asia, for two reasons. First, the labor-intensive parts of the value chain have located in low-wage countries. Second, industrial policy in several countries favored the development of a high-tech sector so that loans were provided to build semiconductor fabrication plants and other capital-intensive facilities. In the 1980s, there was substantial concern in the United States that industrial policy in Asia would damage the high-tech sector in the United States (Tyson 1992).

Industrial policies in the IT sector in Asia have a mixed record, however. Japan used market access as a lever to encourage IBM to share technology in the computer mainframe industry, and using this, it developed a strong industry of its own. However, the mainframe industry went into sharp decline, and the Japanese computer companies were left behind by the PC revolution. Korea used loans from government-owned or -influenced banks to fund the development of its semiconductor industry, and Korea remains a major producer of memory chips today. However, its industry has been slow to move up the technology ladder and has a relatively low-productivity, low-profit industry compared to the US semiconductor sector (Baily and Zitzewitz 1998). Semiconductor companies in Korea suffered financial problems in the late 1990s. Andrew Grove (1999) argues that getting out of the memory chip business was a vital step in Intel's success as it developed its microprocessors and other higher-value chips.

---

17. The data are compiled by Barry Hirsch and David Macpherson; see http://www.unionstats.com.

Figure 5.10 Semiconductors and computers output and output per hour, 1987-2000

index 1987 = 100

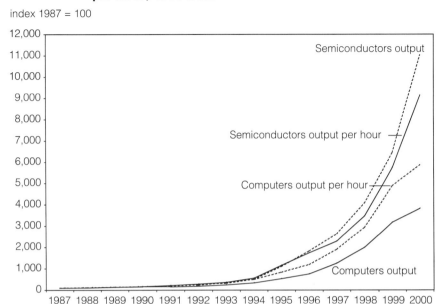

Source: Bureau of Labor Statistics.

Productivity, as measured by the Bureau of Labor Statistics, increased at phenomenal rates in both the semiconductor and computer industries in the United States—22.8 percent a year in semiconductors and 26.7 percent in computers in the 1987-2000 period (figure 5.10).[18] These rates of growth meant that employment in the computer sector fell substantially over this period and grew only modestly in semiconductors (figure 5.11). In neither industry is there any sign that the rising dollar during the 1995-2000 period was the major determinant of employment performance. The big decline in computer employment occurred before 1995 as the industry completed the transformation to PCs. Semiconductor employment rose strongly after 1993.

The profit figures shown earlier in figure 5.9 (which are profits on US-based assets), on the other hand, are consistent with a view that the industry may have been affected by the rising dollar. Profits soared with the strong economic growth and the weak dollar of the early 1990s before flattening out and then dropping sharply in the late 1990s, even as eco-

18. The computer makers did improve their manufacturing capabilities substantially, but much of the productivity growth in this industry should be attributed to the component makers. Figures on output per hour are from the Bureau of Labor Statistics Web site.

Figure 5.11 Employment in computers and semiconductors, 1987-2000

thousands of workers

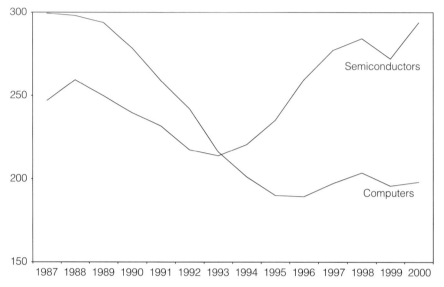

Note: Computers SIC 3571 (electronic computers). Semiconductors SIC 3674 (semiconductors and related devices).

Source: Bureau of Labor Statistics.

nomic growth continued. The bust in the tech sector then greatly exacerbated this decline.

Although the domestic profits in this industry may have been lowered by the high dollar, the industry's dynamics suggest that other factors were probably much more important. The pace of innovation, the ability of innovators to expropriate returns from their innovations, and the volatile pattern of demand for the industry's products are the factors that industry observers stress.

Lessons from the Experience of US Manufacturing

The value of the dollar certainly affects manufacturing employment, so that, other things being equal, manufacturing employment would have been higher with a lower value of the dollar. The partial effect of a lower dollar would have helped preserve employment in that sector. It is a mistake, however, to attribute cyclical effects and secular trends to the dollar. And the review of aggregate and industry data above suggests that these trends are much more important over the long run. Key conclusions are as follows:

- The past two years represent a unique period for manufacturing. Even though the recession has been relatively mild in the economy as a whole, the decline in domestic demand for manufactured goods has been severe. The dollar continued to rise until February 2002 and has fallen only modestly since then. The economies of the rest of the world remain weak. The combination of domestic weakness in goods demand, a high dollar, and foreign demand weakness have resulted in a severe manufacturing downturn.

- Between 1973 and 2000, US manufacturing employment did relatively well during the period of dollar flexibility. Employment fell only slightly, whereas almost all advanced economies have faced much greater declines. Even middle-income countries such as Korea and Taiwan have experienced falling employment in manufacturing. There appears to be a clear trend decline in manufacturing employment among all advanced countries (except Canada), because productivity growth exceeds demand and output growth in this sector. This is the case whether countries run trade surpluses or deficits.

- The 1990s expansion, despite its overall strength, was not very favorable to manufacturing employment. Productivity growth accelerated, and the investment boom was concentrated in IT, where manufacturing employment is small.

- Foreign trade generally serves as an automatic stabilizer, in the sense that imports weaken more than exports in a recession. This was true in the 2000-02 downturn also, but the persistence of the high dollar into the downturn greatly reduced this effect. In contrast, the dollar declined after 1985, well before the cyclical peak. (Note that these comments ignore the impact of the dollar on inflation.)

- Neither the case studies nor the data from aggregate manufacturing provide strong evidence that the two episodes of a very strong dollar in the mid-1980s and late 1990s have resulted in large structural adjustment costs so far. With the exception of 2000-02, the dollar has been strong when the economy has been strong, cyclically, with offsetting impacts on manufacturing employment.

- The structural adjustments taking place in the steel and auto industries are strongly associated with increased domestic competition from non-union companies. The structural changes taking place within the US industry are as important as or more important than foreign competition to the overall adjustment problems facing these industries.

- With the rise in the dollar there was a large increase in auto imports from Canada and Mexico. In the absence of any exchange rate adjustment among the NAFTA countries, the economic incentives favor increasing the share of North American production outside the United States.

- There is a tendency for the dollar to remain persistently above the level that would be consistent with balance of trade in manufactured goods. In part this is because of a US comparative advantage in agriculture and services. In addition, it is because the United States is a low-saving economy and because opportunities for investment in the rest of the world seem limited, so capital flows to the United States. There are offsetting advantages to the United States because of its access to foreign capital, but there is a case for increased national saving in the United States.

Macroeconomic Adjustment: The Experience of the 1980s and 1990s

In this section I turn to the adjustment processes at the macro level. The best place to start is with the simple identity implied by the National Income and Product Accounts (NIPA). The definition of GDP when subject to a little manipulation implies as an identity that national saving minus investment equals net exports:

Net private saving + budget balance − (gross investment − depreciation) = net exports

Net national saving is the sum of net private saving and the government budget balance (positive for a surplus or negative for a deficit). Investment includes equipment, structures, residential housing, and inventory change. The depreciation of physical capital is a large, hard-to-measure item in the United States, accounting for about 12 percent of GDP in the 1990s.

Figure 5.12 shows each of the five elements in this identity expressed as a percentage of GDP over the period 1959-2001. These are calculated from nominal dollar values, since the nominal shares reflect the choices made in each year about how to allocate total GDP produced in that year.[19]

The top line of the figure shows that investment is strongly cyclical but has no particular trend over the period. It moved to a slightly higher level after the 1960s and has fluctuated since then, mostly but not entirely with the cycle.

One important period is from 1984 to 1989. The US economy went into deep recession in 1982 and then recovered strongly. Investment grew rapidly through 1984, but then started to decline as a share of GDP.

---

19. The chain-weighted real values do not add up and are intended to assess growth rates. The real shares of different expenditure categories in real GDP become very distorted for years not close to the base year.

Figure 5.12 Elements of the national accounts identity

percent GDP (current dollars)

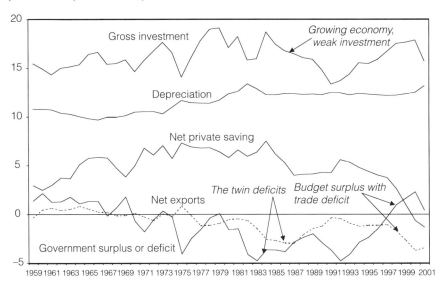

Sources: Bureau of Economic Analysis, National Income and Product Accounts Tables, and author's calculations.

Given that solid economic growth continued for several years, investment spending was surprisingly weak in the second half of the 1980s.

The investment boom of the 1990s is evident in the figure. Over this period information technology equipment became increasingly important, and this equipment has rapidly declining prices, so the rise in investment share was accompanied by an even faster rise in real investment.

Depreciation, which is hard to measure anyway, is fortunately not much of a story. It moved up after the 1960s, offsetting the upward shift in gross investment, but has been a very stable share of GDP since then. In painting the broad-brush picture, we can take depreciation as a constant.

Much of the action in figure 5.12 comes from the last three lines: net saving,[20] the budget balance, and net exports. All three series are cyclical, particularly the latter two. Unemployment was high in 1975-76, 1982-83, and 1992-93, and during these times the budget moved strongly toward

---

20. Net saving is calculated as a residual. It is GDP minus depreciation, minus consumption, minus taxes, plus transfers. This differs from reported saving numbers because of the discrepancy between the income and product sides of the NIPA. The above identity does not hold for gross domestic income. The trends of net private saving shown here are very similar to the reported saving rate, but because of the growth in the statistical discrepancy, saving in figure 5.12 falls further in the last couple of years.

Figure 5.13 Cyclically adjusted elements of the national accounts identity, 1959-2001

percent of GDP (current dollars)

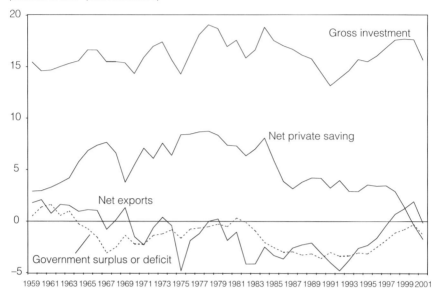

Source: Bureau of Economic Analysis, and author's calculations.

deficit and net exports moved strongly toward surplus.[21] Cyclical movements create a negative correlation between these series.

The unemployment rate was used to construct cyclically adjusted values for the shares of gross investment, net saving, the budget balance, and net exports,[22] and the adjusted values are shown in figure 5.13. In this chart, a positive association between budget and trade deficits emerges. The combined federal, state, and local budgets went into a trend of worsening deficits in the 1970s and into even larger structural deficits in the 1980s. Net exports moved into a parallel pattern of deficits over this period, which economists referred to as the "twin deficits."[23]

The argument about the twin deficits is now the stuff of textbooks, but to summarize briefly, the idea was that the rising budget deficits sharply reduced government saving (increased government dissaving). Since

---

21. The NBER-dated cycle peaks and troughs give the economy's turning points. The budget deficit and net exports respond more to the gap between actual and potential GDP, which is reflected in unemployment rates. Unemployment movements lag significantly behind peaks and troughs.

22. Current, leading, and lagged values of the unemployment rate were used.

23. See Mann (1999) for a discussion of the twin deficits of the 1980s and why they became uncoupled.

there was no offsetting rise in private saving, in fact private saving as a share of GDP started to fall after the mid-1980s; this meant that the impact of the budget deficits was largely pushed onto the trade account, resulting in a large trade deficit. In essence, an inflow of foreign capital was used, directly or indirectly, to finance the large government deficits.

The mechanism bringing about this relation was that real interest rates rose, pulled in capital, pushed up the dollar, and caused a trade deficit. The combination of a very expansionary fiscal policy and a restrained monetary policy changed the equilibrium in the capital market. The government was supplying large amounts of bonds, and to absorb these bonds, interest rates had to rise. The availability of high real interest rates in the United States attracted foreign capital, which made up the gap between domestic saving and domestic investment. But the effect of the capital inflow was a soaring dollar—it rose from an index value of 88 in June 1980 to a peak of 127 in March 1985, an increase of 37 percent.[24] The strong dollar, in turn, restrained exports and encouraged imports, and the trade deficit emerged, with net exports hitting –3 percent of GDP in 1987.

The twin deficits story was actually more complex than this. First, the rise in real interest rates also cut into investment, some parts of which are interest sensitive. As noted above, investment was fairly weak in the late 1980s, given a strongly growing economy. The deficit did crowd out domestic investment to an extent. Second, there are lags in the adjustment of trade flows to the exchange rate. The trade deficit continued to worsen until 1987, two years after the fall in the dollar started—a familiar J-curve effect that occurs because export growth is slow to increase and imports are more expensive in dollar terms as the dollar falls. This means that capital inflows were actually increasing in 1986 and 1987 with a falling dollar. The dollar had to fall enough that it was then expected to appreciate again, so foreigners were willing to buy larger and larger amounts of US assets.

Official reserve holdings of the dollar increased during that period, as foreign governments feared an even faster dollar decline than actually took place. Official foreign holdings of US assets rose by $120.8 billion in 1986-88, representing 28 percent of the US current account deficits in those years. Foreign governments were funding a significant proportion of the US current account and budget deficits.

The dollar index fell to 98.5 in March 1987, down 26 percent from its March 1985 peak. With modest ups and downs, the dollar continued to drift lower after that, into the 1990s, reaching a low of 84.2 in July 1995,

---

24. The broad price-adjusted exchange rate index from the Federal Reserve. Conventional percentage changes, based on changes in an index divided by the initial values, can be misleading. The figures used here are the change in the index divided by the average of the initial and final values. The change in the log of the exchange rate is also 37 percent.

41 percent below its 1985 peak. The yen in particular was very high, averaging 84.5 yen to the dollar in the second quarter of 1995, despite a very weak Japanese economy.

The dollar then started to rise again, reaching an index value of 113.1 in February 2002, 29 percent above its low in 1995. The upward swing in the dollar, therefore, was not as great as had occurred in the 1980s.

Simulating the Counterfactual of No Dollar Increase

What would have happened if the dollar had not gone through the down and up cycle that it experienced in the 1990s? To give an answer to that question I report the results of a macroeconometric model run in which the dollar is held constant at its 1997 level. The model used is from Macroeconomic Advisers (MA), but this run was not carried out by them.[25] This simulation, unlike those reported below, simply fixes the value of the dollar and does not specify the shocks that would have had to occur for this to take place. The results should be viewed with appropriate caution, but they provide a starting point to look at the impact of the dollar swing of the 1990s. The model run incorporates a Fed reaction function, which targets consumer price index (CPI) inflation and real GDP growth.

Table 5.2 shows a summary of the effects. The figures for real GDP growth indicate that the swing in the dollar actually had a stabilizing effect. The boom in 1998-99 would have been even stronger without the dollar's rise, and the downturn in 2000-01 would have been sharper. The rise in the dollar reduced US growth at a time when it was running much faster than potential growth. Over the six-year period as a whole, real GDP growth is actually slightly slower overall with a constant dollar. The reason for this pattern is shown in the net export figures. The rapid expansion of the trade deficit in the 1990s curtailed the boom that was overheating the economy. Consumption and gross investment would have been markedly lower with a constant dollar, as imports would have been much less and exports more. The model does not track manufacturing output, but it is clear that in this simulation, manufacturing output would have been stronger through 1999 without the dollar increase, as goods imports would have been lower and exports higher. The United States would have run up a much smaller level of net foreign indebtedness. Consumption and investment would have been lower throughout the period because of the higher cost of imported goods and services. Another

---

25. The numbers were generously provided by David Heuther of the National Association of Manufacturers. I am grateful for his assistance. The results presented here do not necessarily reflect the views of the NAM.

Table 5.2 Simulating the effect of a constant dollar in the 1990s

	1996	1997	1998	1999	2000	2001
Real GDP (percent change)						
History	4.1	4.3	4.8	4.4	2.8	0.5
Constant dollar	4.1	4.3	5.1	4.7	2.4	− 0.5
Consumption (percent change)						
History	3.1	4.1	5.0	5.2	4.2	3.1
Constant dollar	3.1	3.9	4.2	4.6	3.3	2.0
Gross investment (percent change)						
History	11.4	12.1	12.1	7.0	3.1	− 14.8
Constant dollar	11.4	12.0	11.2	5.7	1.0	− 19.2
Net exports (billions of 1996 dollars)						
History	− 89.0	− 113.3	− 221.1	− 316.9	− 399.1	− 408.7
Constant dollar	− 89.0	− 108.1	− 145.8	− 134.5	− 134.8	− 90.0
GDP price index (percent change)						
History	1.9	1.8	1.1	1.6	2.3	2.0
Constant dollar	1.9	2.0	1.8	1.8	2.7	2.5
CPI (percent change)						
History	3.2	1.9	1.5	2.6	3.4	1.9
Constant dollar	3.2	2.2	3.1	3.2	4.3	3.0

Source: See text on page 116.

substantial cost of the constant dollar is that inflation would have been higher. The rate of change of the GDP price index in the constant dollar simulation exceeds the actual historical rate of increase quite substantially. For the CPI, which includes the prices of imported goods, the impact would have been even greater—CPI inflation would have been twice as high in 1998. Of course the Federal Reserve could have acted to offset the higher inflation (more so than is built into the model's reaction function), but that would have come at the expense of employment and GDP growth. If the Fed had fully offset the higher inflation, it is not clear that manufacturing employment would have been higher in the 1990s.

On balance, therefore, the simulation results are pretty much what one would have expected. US consumers benefited over the period from the high dollar, and so did the level of investment. A large current account deficit means that we were consuming and investing more than we were producing. Given the Fed reaction function built into the model, the boom and bust cycle is greater with a constant dollar. The constant dollar would have meant less pressure on import-competing industries and a stronger export performance.

Paying for the "Excesses" of the 1980s and 1990s

With the exception of manufacturing, the constant-dollar simulation run suggests some advantages from the large current account deficits of the

Figure 5.14   Net US indebtedness and balance on income

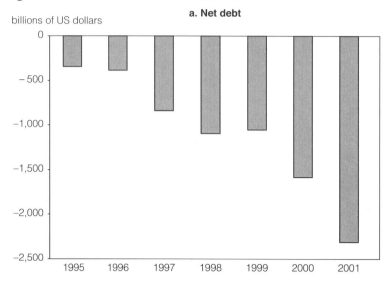

a. Net debt

billions of US dollars

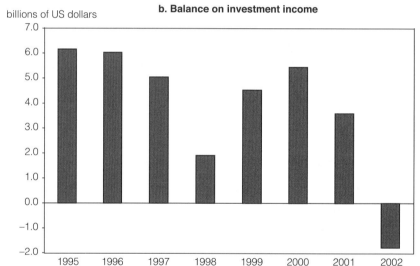

b. Balance on investment income

billions of US dollars

Source: Bureau of Economic Analysis.

1980s and 1990s. But this can give a misleading picture, because the increased debt burden that is a legacy of this period may weigh down American living standards in the future. Simulations to follow will add more to this story, but it is worth noting here that the burden so far of the debt that was accumulated in the 1990s has been surprisingly small.

Figure 5.14a shows the increase of net indebtedness over the period 1995-2001. After being a net foreign creditor until 1988, the United States has shifted to being a very large net debtor. This has changed the United States from being a net recipient of foreign income to being a net payer of income. In 1983, net foreign income payments to the United States peaked at $36.4 billion, or about 1 percent of GDP. As figure 5.14b shows, this net inflow had fallen by the mid-1990s and had turned negative by the first quarter of 2002. The most remarkable aspect of the data, however, is that the net income flow remained positive for so long. Moreover, the net outflow in 2002 so far is tiny. In 2001, for example, the United States was a net debtor of around $2.3 trillion, and yet the net income flow was positive and over $3 billion. The United States clearly earns much higher returns on its assets overseas than the returns earned by foreigners on assets held in the United States.

These data indicate that foreign borrowing has been a cost. Going from a net inflow of 1 percent of GDP to zero or a net outflow represents a burden to the United States. Clearly, however, the burden is amazingly small; the net cost of borrowing has been tiny. A recent Bureau of Economic Analysis study of FDI in the United States (*Survey of Current Business*, 2002) suggests one reason for this. The rates of return earned by foreign companies investing in the United States tend to rise over time. Much of the foreign investment in the United States has been made recently, and the owners have faced start-up costs and adjustment costs to operating in the United States. For a given size of the net indebtedness, it seems likely that the net outflow of income from the United States will rise in the years to come.

As Robert Lawrence pointed out to me, however, since much of the investment in the United States has been in acquisitions or portfolio investments, it is less clear that the rate of return will rise. It may be that the reason for the low levels of returns is that foreign investors have made bad investments, purchasing their share of overvalued companies or overvalued equities. Buying NASDAQ or S&P stocks looked like a great investment to a lot of people, but the returns for those who bought in the late 1990s have been very poor or negative. It is tempting for Americans to gloat a little over selling the Brooklyn Bridge to gullible world investors, but the level of returns that foreigners have earned in the past will affect their willingness to continue lending in the future. That influences the assumptions examined in the simulations described in the following section.

Reducing the Current Account Deficit in the Future

I turn now to the question of how the US economy would adjust to a lower current account deficit in the future. The approach once again is to use simulations from a macroeconometric model, again from MA, and this time the simulations were carried out by Joel Prakken and Macroeconomic Advisers (MA).[26] These are "authorized" runs, although none should be seen as predictions by MA—or by me for that matter; they are "what-if" simulations. The first run, or "baseline," simply lets the MA model run without any added factors or adjustments. The second run, "gradual dollar decline," adjusts the equation of the model that determines the exchange rate. That equation is based on rate-of-return differentials but includes a term allowing for the propensity of foreigners to hold US assets.[27] Since in the 1980s the dollar declined rather rapidly once it started down, the third simulation looks at a "fast dollar decline." The fourth simulation, "faster growth in the rest of the world," looks at the effect of a five-year growth spurt in the rest of the world. Growth is about 1 percent a year higher for five years—a new economy boost of the type experienced by the United States in the period 1995-2000. In all of the runs there is an assumed Fed reaction function, which targets inflation and unemployment. The unemployment rate in all of the runs remains very close to the nonaccelerating inflation rate of unemployment (NAIRU), which is just over 5 percent.

Table 5.3 presents the results of these simulations. I have given only a fraction of the full set of results, but because the table still contains a lot of numbers, I will focus on a few high points. First, in the baseline run, the dollar actually rises slightly over the next few years before declining by a modest amount. Without any constraints on US borrowing overseas, the model indicates that the US economy will keep running large current account deficits and corresponding large capital inflows. The rate of growth of real GDP is just over 3 percent a year, close to the potential growth rate in the model. Consumption growth, at below 3 percent a year, is slower than GDP in the baseline, as the private saving rate is assumed to recover. So even with continued large current account deficits, consumption in the baseline simulation grows much more slowly than the 4 percent rate achieved in the period 1995-2000. Investment grows more rapidly than GDP, although again more slowly than the real investment boom of the 1990s. The rapid rate of decline of IT capital goods prices helps sustain strong investment.

---

26. I am grateful to Joel Prakken for his assistance not only in running the model but also in helping figure out the most interesting runs, the best assumptions to make, and the inferences to be drawn from the results.

27. In econometric equations it is very hard or impossible to find statistically significant portfolio effects on the dollar. But reason suggests they are there. As foreigners build up larger and larger shares of US assets in their portfolios, they will demand higher returns in order to induce a given capital inflow to the United States. The adjustment of the exchange rate equation can be seen as a way of introducing this portfolio effect. In the Fed's macro model, the impacts of different exchange rates are examined by adjusting the assumed risk premium in the exchange rate equation. This is very similar in practice to what is done here in the MA model.

Table 5.3 The impact on the United States of a gradual dollar decline or faster growth abroad

| | Levels | | | | | Growth rates | | |
	2001	2002	2007	2012	2017	2002-07	2002-12	2002-17
FRB broad foreign exchange rate (index 2001 = 100)								
Baseline	100	100.9	102.8	100.2	96.6			
Gradual dollar decline	100	100.6	90.9	85.8	82.8			
Fast dollar decline	100	99.4	85.8	79.2	79.7			
Faster growth in rest of world	100	100.9	99.5	105.3	100.6			
Real GDP (billions of chained 1996 dollars)								
Baseline	9,215	9,424	11,094	12,978	14,906	3.32	3.25	3.10
Gradual dollar decline	9,215	9,425	11,031	12,771	14,447	3.20	3.08	2.89
Fast dollar decline	9,215	9,426	10,964	12,535	14,051	3.07	2.89	2.70
Faster growth in rest of world	9,215	9,424	11,049	12,849	14,823	3.23	3.15	3.07
Consumption (billions of 1996 dollars)								
Baseline	6,377	6,577	7,586	8,791	9,859	2.90	2.94	2.74
Gradual dollar decline	6,377	6,576	7,435	8,396	9,304	2.48	2.47	2.34
Fast dollar decline	6,377	6,576	7,185	8,144	9,049	1.79	2.16	2.15
Faster growth in rest of world	6,377	6,577	7,473	8,711	9,862	2.59	2.85	2.74
Investment (billions of 1996 dollars)								
Baseline	1,575	1,572	2,123	2,696	3,394	6.19	5.54	5.26
Gradual dollar decline	1,575	1,572	1,983	2,411	2,880	4.75	4.37	4.12
Fast dollar decline	1,575	1,573	1,885	2,196	2,564	3.68	3.40	3.31
Faster growth in rest of world	1,575	1,572	2,034	2,621	3,312	5.28	5.24	5.09

(table continues next page)

121

Table 5.3 The impact on the United States of a gradual dollar decline or faster growth abroad (*continued*)

	Levels					Growth rates		
	2001	2002	2007	2012	2017	2002-07	2002-12	2002-17
Government (billions of 1996 dollars)								
Baseline	1,640	1,710	1,862	2,013	2,152	1.71	1.65	1.54
Gradual dollar decline	1,640	1,710	1,862	2,016	2,157	1.72	1.66	1.56
Fast dollar decline	1,640	1,710	1,863	2,019	2,161	1.73	1.68	1.57
Faster growth in rest of world	1,640	1,710	1,862	2,014	2,152	1.72	1.65	1.55
Net exports (billions of 1996 dollars)								
Baseline	−416	−486	−486	−467	−290			
Gradual dollar decline	−416	−485	−245	20	282			
Fast dollar decline	−416	−483	18	199	365			
Faster growth in rest of world	−416	−486	−315	−454	−319			
Goods exports (billions of 1996 dollars)								
Baseline	785	763	1,069	1,421	1,845	6.98	6.41	6.06
Gradual dollar decline	785	764	1,096	1,452	1,829	7.50	6.64	6.00
Fast dollar decline	785	764	1,107	1,432	1,744	7.70	6.48	5.65
Faster growth in rest of world	785	763	1,105	1,428	1,858	7.67	6.46	6.11
Goods imports (billions of 1996 dollars)								
Baseline	1,271	1,320	1,722	2,178	2,621	5.46	5.14	4.68
Gradual dollar decline	1,271	1,319	1,529	1,765	2,054	2.99	2.95	2.99
Fast dollar decline	1,271	1,318	1,314	1,573	1,855	−0.06	1.78	2.31
Faster growth in rest of world	1,271	1,320	1,631	2,209	2,695	4.32	5.29	4.87
Services exports (billions of 1996 dollars)								
Baseline	292	297	421	573	762	7.23	6.79	6.47
Gradual dollar decline	292	297	423	575	752	7.33	6.83	6.38
Fast dollar decline	292	297	427	571	725	7.50	6.73	6.12
Faster growth in rest of world	292	297	457	620	815	8.97	7.62	6.95

Services imports (billions of 1996 dollars)

Baseline	222	226	261	298	310	2.88	2.80	2.12
Gradual dollar decline	222	226	239	251	265	1.13	1.05	1.07
Fast dollar decline	222	226	205	237	262	−1.95	0.47	1.00
Faster growth in rest of world	222	226	252	309	332	2.14	3.18	2.59

Current account balance (billions of US dollars)

Baseline	−393	−498	−643	−845	−935	5.27	5.43	4.29
Gradual dollar decline	−393	−498	−548	−558	−550	1.92	1.14	0.66
Fast dollar decline	−393	−501	−345	−433	−484	−7.19	−1.45	−0.23
Faster growth in rest of world	−393	−498	−522	−749	−885	0.98	4.17	3.91

Current account balance as percent of GDP

Baseline	−3.9	−4.8	−4.8	−5.0	−4.3
Gradual dollar decline	−3.9	−4.8	−4.1	−3.3	−2.5
Fast dollar decline	−3.9	−4.8	−2.6	−2.5	−2.2
Faster growth in rest of world	−3.9	−4.8	−3.9	−4.4	−4.2

US indebtedness to rest of world (billions of US dollars)

Baseline	−2,266	−2,665	−5,475	−9,210	−13,648	15.49	13.20	11.50
Gradual dollar decline	−2,266	−2,665	−5,430	−8,234	−10,997	15.30	11.94	9.91
Fast dollar decline	−2,266	−2,666	−4,813	−6,934	−9,078	12.55	10.03	8.51
Faster growth in rest of world	−2,266	−2,665	−5,238	−8,307	−12,499	14.47	12.04	10.85

US indebtedness to rest of world as percent of GDP

Baseline	−22.5	−25.6	−41.1	−54.2	−63.4
Gradual dollar decline	−22.5	−25.6	−40.6	−48.2	−50.9
Fast dollar decline	−22.5	−25.6	−35.6	−40.2	−41.9
Faster growth in rest of world	−22.5	−25.6	−39.3	−49.3	−58.7

(table continues next page)

123

Table 5.3 The impact on the United States of a gradual dollar decline or faster growth abroad (*continued*)

			Levels			Growth rates		
	2001	2002	2007	2012	2017	2002-07	2002-12	2002-17
GDP price index								
Baseline	109.4	110.6	120.2	131.1	144.4	1.68	1.71	1.79
Gradual dollar decline	109.4	110.6	121.1	133.8	149.4	1.83	1.92	2.02
Fast dollar decline	109.4	110.6	123.2	137.6	154.3	2.17	2.21	2.24
Faster growth in rest of world	109.4	110.6	120.6	131.2	143.7	1.74	1.72	1.76
Consumer price index								
Baseline	177.1	179.8	201.5	227.1	262.0	2.30	2.36	2.54
Gradual dollar decline	177.1	179.9	205.4	237.1	278.7	2.69	2.80	2.96
Fast dollar decline	177.1	180.0	212.5	248.3	293.0	3.38	3.27	3.30
Faster growth in rest of world	177.1	179.8	202.9	226.9	259.6	2.45	2.35	2.48
Foreign real GDP index								
Baseline	116.6	119.0	142.2	167.2	194.5	3.62	3.46	3.33
Gradual dollar decline	116.6	119.0	140.9	163.4	188.2	3.44	3.22	3.10
Fast dollar decline	116.6	119.0	137.8	161.1	183.6	2.97	3.08	2.93
Faster growth in rest of world	116.6	119.0	147.6	175.3	203.1	4.40	3.95	3.63

Foreign consumer price index

Baseline	202.4	206.4	234.6	263.6	302.5	2.59	2.48	2.58
Gradual dollar decline	202.4	206.4	235.7	269.4	313.8	2.69	2.70	2.83
Fast dollar decline	202.4	206.4	240.3	277.0	324.5	3.09	2.99	3.06
Faster growth in rest of world	202.4	206.4	235.2	264.3	301.2	2.65	2.50	2.55

Federal funds rate (percent)

Baseline	3.89	1.74	4.50	5.57	6.32	20.88	12.30	8.97
Gradual dollar decline	3.89	1.75	5.99	7.99	10.05	27.96	16.43	12.38
Fast dollar decline	3.89	1.77	7.34	11.21	13.14	32.97	20.31	14.32
Faster growth in rest of world	3.89	1.74	5.68	5.99	7.24	26.62	13.13	9.95

10-year Treasury note yield (percent)

Baseline	5.02	4.71	5.95	6.90	7.72	4.78	3.89	3.34
Gradual dollar decline	5.02	4.71	6.89	8.84	10.88	7.90	6.50	5.74
Fast dollar decline	5.02	4.72	8.56	11.05	13.63	12.65	8.88	7.33
Faster growth in rest of world	5.02	4.71	6.82	7.35	8.39	7.67	4.54	3.92

Foreign bond yield (percent)

Baseline	4.09	4.21	6.43	7.42	8.78	8.86	5.84	5.03
Gradual dollar decline	4.09	4.21	6.79	8.76	11.10	10.05	7.62	6.68
Fast dollar decline	4.09	4.21	8.10	10.29	13.34	14.02	9.36	8.00
Faster growth in rest of world	4.09	4.21	7.55	7.08	9.20	12.40	5.34	5.36

Source: See text on pages 119-20.

125

In the baseline run, foreign GDP is expected to grow as fast as or a little faster than US GDP, unlike in the 1990s boom. This reduction in the growth differential, together with the modest decline of the dollar in the second half of the period, allows the deficit in net exports to decline over time, absolutely and as a share of GDP. The current account deficit continues to grow in dollar terms and stays fairly flat as a share of nominal GDP. The rise in US net indebtedness increases the net outflow of factor payments and keeps the current account deficit high.

In the gradual dollar decline scenario, the dollar index is 12.3 percent below the baseline in 2007 and 15.4 percent lower in 2017. In this simulation, real net exports turn positive by 2012. The current account remains negative, however, but is reduced absolutely and as a percentage of GDP, compared to the baseline. By 2012, the current account deficit is only two-thirds of the baseline, and it is down to 59 percent by 2017. The big driver of the reduction in real net exports from the lower dollar is the reduction of real imports. By 2017, real net imports, with a lower dollar, are about $570 billion lower than in the baseline, a reduction of 24 percent.

An interesting feature of the gradual dollar decline simulation is that even though real net exports become strongly positive and goods imports are curtailed, there remains a deficit in real goods exports, equal to $225 billion or 1.6 percent of real GDP. Part of this is oil imports, but a substantial fraction would represent a continued real deficit in manufactured goods. Earlier I mentioned that the competitiveness problems faced by segments of the steel and auto industries were not just vis-à-vis the rest of the world but also in relation to other domestic segments of their own industry. Somewhat parallel at the aggregate level is the fact that US service industries have become more competitive in foreign trade than US manufacturing industries. The volume of trade in services has been increasing strongly over time, and the United States has maintained a surplus in services trade despite the strong dollar ($70 billion in 2001 in 1996 dollars). In this simulation run, a substantial surplus in services trade develops ($490 billion in 2017, equal to 3.4 percent of real GDP).[28]

There is a substantial penalty to growth, consumption, and investment from the lower dollar. Real GDP grows more slowly than in the baseline model by 0.2 percent a year over the 15 years, resulting in a level of GDP that is down by $460 billion or 3.1 percent of GDP compared to the baseline after 15 years. Since the Fed reaction function keeps unemployment close to the NAIRU in both simulations, this loss of GDP is on the supply side, with lower investment and a smaller capital stock in the dollar decline simulation. Inflation is higher also, running 0.2 percent a year higher for the GDP deflator and 0.4 percent a year for the CPI (which is affected directly by higher import prices).

---

28. Catherine Mann (2002) has stressed the importance of the growing trade in services and the potential for growth in services trade if other countries open their markets.

Consumption and investment take bigger hits than GDP, since they must adjust to the reduction of net exports. Consumption is down $555 billion or 5.8 percent after 15 years, growing more slowly by 0.4 percent a year. Investment is down 16.4 percent after 15 years, and the investment growth rate is reduced by 1.1 percent a year over the whole period. Interest rates are substantially higher with a lower dollar, 2.2 percentage points on the Federal Funds rate and 2.3 points on the 10-year Treasury. The higher interest rates offset the stimulus of lower net exports and serve to crowd out investment and durable goods consumption.

One surprising result is that foreign GDP is lower and foreign interest rates are higher with a lower dollar. If the flow of saving to the United States is being reduced, then in principle there should be more funds available overseas, creating the potential for higher growth. The reason for the effect is that the rest of the world is assumed to be unable to absorb the additional saving effectively—they have been relying on the United States as the main driver of demand growth for the whole world.

One of the main payoffs to the lower dollar simulation is that the net indebtedness of the United States is down $2.65 trillion in 2017, a 21.5 percent decrease compared to the baseline.

This simulation run tracks the impact over time of a reduction in the propensity of foreign residents to demand dollar assets. It "predicts" a gradual decline in the dollar as a result. In practice, at least based on the mid-1980s (and to a degree the early 1970s), when the dollar starts to decline, it falls rapidly. There may be a speculative component to dollar swings that is not easy to capture econometrically. When the dollar starts to fall, it could set up reinforcing movements out of dollar-denominated assets that result in a rather sharp dollar decline. The fast dollar decline simulation traces out the impact of a quicker adjustment. Since much of the impact on the economy in this fast decline occurs over the six years 2002 to 2007, table 5.4 is added to show the year-by-year effects.

In this simulation the dollar has fallen nearly 20 percent by 2004, and by 2006 total net exports in the NIPA tables has turned positive, although net exports of goods remain negative. The current account deficit remains negative also, at 2.4 percent of GDP. So if we were to see a rapid decline of the dollar by 20 percent, the model simulation predicts that this would reduce the US current account deficit below 2.5 percent of GDP by 2006.

The consequences for the rest of the economy are fairly tough. Real GDP in 2007 is down 1.2 percent compared to the baseline; real consumption is down over 5 percent; and investment is down nearly 12 percent. To induce this readjustment, interest rates are much higher, with the Federal Funds rate and the 10-year yield both exceeding 10 percent. Given the interest rate environment of recent years, a switch like that would be very disruptive. The housing market would look a lot different than it does today.

Table 5.4 The impact on the United States of a fast dollar decline

	2002	2003	2004	2005	2006	2007
FRB broad foreign exchange rate (index 2001 = 100)	99.4	88.3	79.7	76.6	82.1	85.8
Real GDP (billions of chained 1996 dollars)	9,426	9,714	10,023	10,377	10,664	10,964
Consumption (billions of 1996 dollars)	6,576	6,714	6,770	6,847	6,976	7,185
Investment (billions of 1996 dollars)	1,573	1,648	1,671	1,714	1,757	1,885
Government (billions of 1996 dollars)	1,710	1,749	1,782	1,811	1,838	1,863
Net exports (billions of 1996 dollars)	-483	-440	-231	-21	68	18
Goods exports (billions of 1996 dollars)	764	826	924	1,015	1,071	1,107
Goods imports (billions of 1996 dollars)	1,318	1,360	1,289	1,213	1,210	1,314
Services exports (billions of 1996 dollars)	297	317	343	373	400	427
Services imports (billions of 1996 dollars)	226	223	211	198	195	205
Current account balance (billions of dollars)	-501	-557	-490	-380	-307	-345
Current account balance as percent of GDP	-4.8	-5.1	-4.2	-3.1	-2.4	-2.6
US indebtedness to rest of world (billions of dollars)	-2,666	-3,170	-3,708	-4,153	-4,504	-4,813
US indebtedness to rest of world as percent of GDP	-25.6	-28.9	-32.0	-33.8	-34.9	-35.6
GDP price index	110.6	112.7	115.6	118.4	120.9	123.2
Consumer price index	180.0	186.1	194.0	201.6	207.7	212.5
Foreign real GDP index	119.0	122.9	126.4	129.7	133.2	137.8
Foreign consumer price index	206.4	212.0	218.2	225.3	232.8	240.3
Federal funds rate (percent)	1.77	3.98	6.49	8.07	7.73	7.34
10-year Treasury note yield (percent)	4.72	5.41	6.59	7.66	8.48	8.56
Foreign bond yield (percent)	4.21	4.51	5.19	5.88	6.98	8.10

Source: See text on page 127.

Financial institutions would have to make a large adjustment, and household portfolios would be greatly affected.

Inflation is higher with the fast drop in the dollar, with the rate of increase in the GDP price index being half a percentage point higher through 2012 and CPI inflation taking a big hit over the next five years, running a full percentage point higher from 2002 to 2007.

The simulation also suggests that the rest of the world would not do well with this scenario either. Foreign GDP is lower and foreign interest rates higher, and other countries fail to adapt effectively to the loss of demand generated in the United States.

The simulation of faster growth in the rest of the world shows most of its impact in the early years of the simulation—during the time the assumed "new economy" period is occurring. The net exports deficit is sharply lower in 2007, while real GDP consumption and investment are less affected than in the lower dollar case. As long as it lasts, faster growth overseas is an easier way for the United States to lower its trade deficit than a lower dollar. By the end of the simulation run, however, there is only a modest change in the US outcome relative to the baseline case. In fact, the net export deficit is little changed from the baseline, as goods imports increase strongly in the latter years of the simulation.

Lessons from the Simulation Results and Questions Raised

If the dollar does come down substantially, over a few years or over the next 15 years, the simulations reported here suggest that the results could be fairly costly for the United States. For one thing, the very favorable inflation-unemployment trade-off that the US economy enjoyed in the 1990s would change. In addition, the growth of real consumption and investment would be noticeably lower. Manufacturing is likely to do relatively well, although if the Fed were to fight inflation more aggressively than assumed here, then overall demand weakness might limit the benefits to this cyclically sensitive sector. The simulation results are sobering and reveal important implications of a potential dollar adjustment.

The simulation model uses assumptions that are entirely reasonable, but there are alternative possibilities that can be considered. The reason GDP growth is lower in the simulations is that investment is lower, and this feeds into a standard neoclassical production framework. Productivity growth is reduced. My own work on productivity makes me cautious in assessing the impact of slower or faster investment on productivity. The increase in productivity growth after 1995 may have been largely the result of an increased pace of business innovation, rather than just greater use of IT. As long as the pace of innovation continues, this can sustain strong productivity growth.

Another aspect of the simulation results that can be questioned is the extent of inflation pass-through. There is currently a view in Washington that the impact of currency depreciation on inflation is lower than it used to be. Depreciations do not trigger increases in inflation the way they used to.[29] The evidence for this comes partly from inflation equations estimated from a range of countries.

Robert Gordon (1998), on the other hand, has argued that variations in the dollar have had an important impact on recent US inflation experience. He finds that much of the favorable inflation experience of the 1990s was the result of the strong dollar. A dollar decline, should it occur, would run that process in reverse and provide a serious inflation shock. Gordon suggests that "a 10 percent decline in the nominal effective exchange rate of the dollar would imply a 6-7 percent increase in import prices and 0.6-0.7 percent extra overall inflation, spread out over more than a single year" (personal communication, August 5, 2002).

The MA model is not directly comparable to Gordon's analysis, since it takes a variety of feedback effects into account and uses a Fed reaction function, but overall it is closer to the Gordon view than the "Washington" view. The simulation results may be a bit pessimistic in terms of the adverse inflation impact of a dollar decline.

The model's findings about the relative performance of manufacturing and services in international trade are intriguing and make sense, given the strong relative productivity level of US service industries. But predicting trends in this area is tricky. Some business consulting groups predict explosive growth in offshore outsourcing of service activities from the United States to low-wage countries, notably India, where the English-speaking population is large and wages are low, and China, in which large numbers of people are learning English. Moreover, not all offshore outsourcing of services requires knowledge of English.[30] It is uncertain how US net trade in services will play out over time.

The final and most important question raised by the simulations is whether some of the very tough macroeconomic implications, such as the very high interest rates, would actually come about. In particular, are the results from the simulations consistent with actual past experience? The dollar came down rapidly and by a large amount in the 1980s, and the effects did not seem so bad. In the mid-1980s, Stephen Marris (1985) warned of a "hard landing" from a sharp decline in the dollar. He correctly predicted that the dollar would fall and fall hard. He incorrectly predicted that the consequences for the US economy would be severe.

---

29. This is based on work at the IMF and the Federal Reserve Board in Washington. See, for example, Gagnon and Ihrig (2002).

30. This is based on discussions at McKinsey & Company, although specific predictions of the growth of offshore services were made by other groups.

The first point, by way of reconciliation between the simulations and past history, is that when the dollar fell after 1985, there was still a lot of cyclical slack in the economy. The unemployment rate in 1985 was 7.2 percent, compared to 5.6 percent in September 2002. After the dollar decline in the 1980s, there was still plenty of room for growth faster than the rate of growth of potential GDP. Second, the cohesion of the Organization of Petroleum Exporting Countries collapsed and oil prices fell very sharply in January 1986. This kept inflation low for a while. Third, the adjustment to the dollar decline of the mid-1980s was actually painful. GDP growth slowed and so did productivity growth. Inflation increased in the late 1980s and the economy ended up in a recession in 1990 (which started before the rise in oil prices, according to the NBER). The consequences for the economy of the fall in the dollar in the 1980s were not nearly as bad as Marris feared, but they were negative.

Policy Implications

As a market-oriented economist, I start with the presumption that free trade and free movements of capital will improve overall world economic efficiency. Production is allocated to the lowest-cost producers and capital seeks the highest rate of return. Empirical studies have supported the connection from trade to growth.[31] The empirical case for the benefits of free capital movements is less clear, however, and observation also suggests that asset prices, including the dollar, are subject to persistent swings that are hard or impossible to relate to the underlying economic fundamentals. They seem driven in part by volatile expectations, including speculative bubbles.

Asset price fluctuations can be costly. Investors lose their pensions in a stock market collapse, homeowners find they have lost the equity in their homes, and, in the case of the exchange rate, workers and companies find themselves out of a job or out of business, not as a result of the fundamental forces of comparative advantage, but because of exchange rate swings lasting several years at a time. Ideally, it would be better if exchange rates did not overshoot their long-run trend values.

The discussion in this paper points to some of the costs of dollar swings, in terms of adjustment costs in manufacturing and also because of macroeconomic adjustment. The costs revealed in this paper do not seem high enough to justify policies that could inflict significant distortions on the economy, however. In manufacturing, some of the adjustment difficulties faced by workers and firms in the sector will not go away even with a stable dollar. And in the case of the macroeconomy, there are benefits when the dollar rises and penalties when it falls, so the net costs over

---

31. See, for example, Frankel and Romer (1999).

time may not be large. One of the biggest problems caused by exchange rate swings is not addressed here directly but is relevant to the analysis of manufacturing. Episodes of a very high dollar undermine support for globalization and open trade. This has been particularly the case in the past two years, as recession has combined with a high dollar. It is one thing to tell workers and companies that the fundamental forces of technology have left them uncompetitive. It is another to tell them that they have been caught by the excess volatility of the exchange rate.[32]

The existence of a market "failure" and the adverse consequences that follow do not mean that there is a policy that can solve the problem. At this point I leave it to others to debate the pros and cons of an active exchange rate policy. I myself come out rather skeptical that such a policy can be effective, or will be beneficial if it is effective. As Alan Greenspan has noted in the context of stock market bubbles, asset price swings are hard to identify ex ante and hard to do anything about.

Two policy measures that I believe would be helpful and would ameliorate the impact of dollar swings are as follows. First, a policy of running government budget surpluses on average over the business cycle is called for. The existence of social security, together with a lack of foresight among many families, means that there is undersaving in the United States. A policy of positive government saving would partially offset this problem and would result in a smaller capital inflow to the United States and a smaller current account deficit on average.

Second, the costs of labor market adjustment could be reduced; one way to do this is to offer wage insurance to workers who are laid off as a result of trade. This idea, which was developed in 1986 (Litan and Lawrence 1986), was revived, and some new cost estimates were prepared, in recent work by Lori Kletzer and Robert Litan (2001). The proposal is feasible and not very costly, and it has won support in Washington. Wage insurance can be enacted in a way that does not undermine work incentives—indeed, it may enhance them. Ideally, adjustment assistance should be provided more broadly than simply to those affected by trade. As Davis, Haltiwanger, and Schuh (1996) point out, job loss on a large scale is the norm in manufacturing, in good times and bad. Facilitating adjustment and relocation are potentially of broader value, but wage insurance for trade adjustment is a good place to start.

References

Baily, Martin Neil, and Eric Zitzewitz. 1998. Extending the East Asian Miracle: Microeconomic Evidence from Korea. *Brookings Papers on Economic Activity, Microeconomics*: 249-322. Washington: Brookings Institution.

32. See the discussion by I. M. Destler in this volume.

Bergsten, C. Fred. 2002. Testimony on U.S. international economic and exchange rate policy, before the Senate Committee on Banking, Housing, and Urban Affairs, May 1.

Blecker, Robert A. 2002. Let It Fall: The Effects of the Overvalued Dollar on US Manufacturing and the Steel Industry. Washington: American University. Photocopy, October.

Borjas, George J., Richard B. Freeman, and Lawrence F. Katz. 1997. How Much Do Immigration and Trade Affect Labor Market Outcomes? *Brookings Papers on Economic Activity* 1997:1-90. Washington: Brookings Institution.

Bryant, Ralph, Peter Hooper, and Catherine Mann, eds. 1993. *Evaluating Policy Regimes: New Research in Empirical Macroeconomics.* Washington: Brookings Institution.

Bureau of Economic Analysis. 2002. *Survey of Current Business.* Washington, April.

Council of Economic Advisers. 2001. *Economic Report of the President.* Washington, January.

Crandall, Robert W. 2001. *The Futility of Steel Trade Protection.* Report prepared through Criterion Economics. http://www.criterioneconomics.com.

Davis, Steven J., John C. Haltiwanger, and Scott Schuh. 1996. *Job Creation and Destruction.* Cambridge, MA: MIT Press.

Economic Strategy Institute. 2001. *Cross-Border Cartels and the Steel Industry.* Washington, May 24.

Frankel, Jeffrey, and David Romer. 1999. Does Trade Cause Growth? *American Economic Review* 89, no. 3 (June).

Gagnon, Joseph E., and Jane Ihrig. 2002. Monetary Policy and Exchange Rate Pass-Through. Washington: Federal Reserve Board. Photocopy, March.

Goldberg, Linda, and Joseph Tracy. 2002. Exchange Rates and Wages. NBER Working Paper No. 8137, revised. New York: Federal Reserve Bank of New York, June.

Gordon, Robert, J. 1998. Foundations of the Goldilocks Economy: Supply Shocks and the Time-Varying NAIRU. *Brookings Papers on Economic Activity* 1998:1 (297-346). Washington: Brookings Institution.

Grove, Andrew S. 1999. *Only the Paranoid Survive: How to Exploit the Crisis Points That Challenge Every Company.* New York: Random House.

Harbour and Associates. 2002. *The Harbour Report 2002.* Richmond, VA.

Jasinowski, Jerry. 2002. Testimony on U.S. international economic and exchange rate policy, on behalf of the National Association of Manufacturers, before the Senate Committee on Banking, Housing, and Urban Affairs, May 1.

Juhn, Chinhui, Kevin Murphy, and Robert Topel. 2002. Current Unemployment, Historically Contemplated. *Brookings Papers on Economic Activity* 2002:1 (79-136). Washington: Brookings Institution.

Kletzer, Lori, and Robert E. Litan. 2001. *A Prescription to Relieve Worker Anxiety.* International Economics Policy Briefs No. 01-2. Washington: Institute for International Economics, February.

Krugman, Paul. 1989. *Exchange Rate Instability.* Cambridge, MA: MIT Press.

Lawrence, Robert Z., and Colin Lawrence. 1985. Manufacturing Wage Dispersion: An End-Game Interpretation. *Brookings Papers on Economic Activity* 1985:1 (47-116). Washington: Brookings Institution.

Lawrence, Robert Z. 1984. *Can America Compete?* Washington: Brookings Institution.

Lawrence, Robert Z. 1990. U.S. Current Account Adjustment: An Appraisal. *Brookings Papers on Economic Activity*, 1990:2 (343-92). Washington: Brookings Institution.

Litan, Robert E., and Robert Z. Lawrence. 1986. *Saving Free Trade.* Washington: Brookings Institution.

Mann, Catherine L. 1999. *Is the US Trade Deficit Sustainable?* Washington: Institute for International Economics.

Mann, Catherine L. 2002. Perspectives on the U.S. Current Account Deficit and Sustainability. *Journal of Economic Perspectives* 16, no. 3: 131-52 (Summer).

Marris, Stephen. 1985. *Deficits and the Dollar: The World Economy at Risk.* POLICY ANALYSES IN INTERNATIONAL ECONOMICS 14. Washington: Institute for International Economics.

Palley, Thomas I. 2002. *The Over-Valued Dollar and the Danger to Economic Recovery.* Study for the American Federation of Labor and Congress of Industrial Organizations. Washington: AFL-CIO, April.

Tyson, Laura D'Andrea. 1992. *Who's Bashing Whom? Trade Conflict in High-Technology Industries.* Washington: Institute for International Economics.

World Steel Dynamics. 2000. *Steel Strategist* 26 (July). Englewood Cliffs, NJ. http://www.worldsteeldynamics.com.

6

Impact of the Strong Dollar on the US Auto Industry

G. MUSTAFA MOHATAREM

2002 is shaping up to be another banner year for auto sales in the United States. Calendar-year-to-date sales have been running at a pace slightly above 17 million units. If this pace were maintained through the remainder of the year, 2002 would go down as the fourth best sales year ever. Annual auto sales have exceeded the 17 million mark—a level that was considered unattainable as recently as the mid-1990s—for three straight years, including the recession year of 2001.

Given the strength of auto sales, one would think that US auto manufacturers, auto suppliers, and their workers would be celebrating. But we are not. Despite the strong sales, auto manufacturers and suppliers are struggling to turn a profit, and many autoworkers have been laid off or are threatened with layoffs. Credit ratings for US auto manufacturers have been downgraded, and many suppliers are faced with bankruptcy. While there are many reasons for the current challenges facing American-owned auto manufacturers, the strong dollar—and the artificially weak Japanese yen—stand out among the primary causes.

Before I address why the strong dollar is depressing profits for domestic auto manufacturers and their suppliers, let me briefly discuss the recent performance of the US auto industry.

G. Mustafa Mohatarem has been chief economist at General Motors Corporation since 1995. He was the lead contact for General Motors with the United States and other governments during the Uruguay Round of General Agreement on Tariffs and Trade (GATT) negotiations, as well as the negotiations for the Canada-US Free Trade Agreement and the North American Free Trade Agreement.

Figure 6.1   Vehicle sales around business cycle peaks (business
cycle peak = 100 percent)

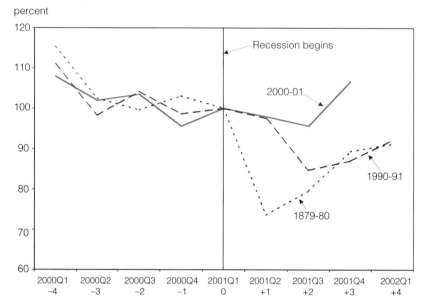

Source: General Motors.

Immediately after the terrorist attacks of September 11, 2001, consumer
confidence fell by roughly 10 points. Historically, falling consumer confidence has led to sharp reductions in vehicle sales: "When the economy
catches a cold, the auto industry catches pneumonia." It looked like it
would be no different this time. In the days immediately after September
11, vehicle sales fell by more than 35 percent. Customer traffic in our
showrooms evaporated, suggesting that sales would remain depressed.

We recognized that without some bold measures, the industry could
be headed for a deep downturn. At GM, we responded with our "Keep
America Rolling" program, which offered consumers zero-interest financing on all GM products. The response to this and similar programs by
many of our competitors exceeded all expectations. Vehicle sales surged
to a record 21.5 million annual rate in October 2001 and remained a strong
18.2 million in November. The industry ended the year having sold over
17.4 million vehicles in 2001, the third best year ever.

Figure 6.1 illustrates the impact of early incentives on vehicle sales by
contrasting auto sales in this recession and the recessions of 1990-91 and
1979-80. As the figure shows, in a typical recession, auto sales can drop
off 15 to 25 percent from their trend level. In this downturn, auto sales
maintained their very strong pace. Alan Blinder noted in an op-ed piece
(*Washington Post,* December 11, 2001) that the sales stimulus provided by
"Keep America Rolling" and similar programs drove "auto sales to record

Figure 6.2 Unit sales, vehicles (cars and light trucks), **1990-2002**

unit sales (millions)

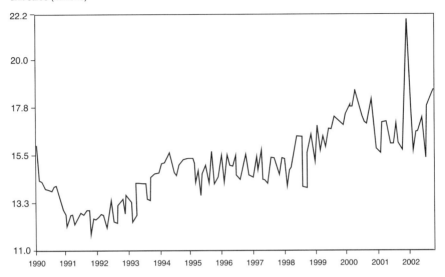

Source: Bureau of Economic Analysis.

highs while other categories of consumer spending were slumping. . . . The zero percent financing programs thus amounted to a kind of 'privatized' stimulus policy—wonderfully timed, well-targeted, and effective. Would that Congress have done so well?''

GM estimates that for the industry as a whole, the zero percent interest programs generated roughly 500,000 additional sales. This is a very conservative estimate, as it assumes that the US economy would have stabilized after the September 11 attacks even without our incentive programs. In any case, using Bureau of Labor Statistics (BLS) methods, the 500,000 additional vehicle sales—an addition of more than $10 billion to the US GDP—translate into 115,000 avoided layoffs in auto and related supplier industries during the lowest point of the recession.

Of course, the auto manufacturers can't take all the credit for the strength of vehicle sales in the period since the attacks. Aggressive easing of interest rates by the Fed certainly lowered the cost for automakers offering zero or low interest rates. In addition, the Bush tax cut added to disposable income. But as Blinder pointed out in his op-ed piece, "Waiting for Congress to pass the much-needed economic stimulus bill is beginning to look like waiting for Godot. Fortunately for the US economy, two large private industries—automobiles and homebuilding—have stepped up to provide the stimulus that the government has thus far failed to deliver."

From a slightly longer-term perspective, auto sales have been exceptionally strong since the mid-1990s (figure 6.2). The 1990s started on a sour note for the US auto industry. With the economy in a recession, auto sales fell precipitously. While sales recovered as the economy emerged from recession, the sales recovery was muted. Many analysts who follow the industry argued that auto sales would remain weak for an extended period because customers were more interested in computers, boats, and home improvements. Fortunately, the pessimists were proved wrong as industry sales improved steadily through the 1990s. Auto sales exceeded the 15 million mark—which was considered the benchmark for a strong sales year—for an unprecedented five consecutive years before jumping above 17 million for three years.

The 1990s also marked the revival of the US auto industry and American-owned auto manufacturers. In the 1980s and early 1990s, it had become conventional wisdom that American auto companies would not survive the competitive challenge from Japan. Yet by the end of the decade, it was the Japanese auto companies that were struggling.

What Happened?

The first factor was the economy. The US economy thrived in the 1990s, while Japan's economy was stagnant. The strong US economy led to strong vehicle sales—again, more than 15 million each year since 1995. In contrast vehicle sales in Japan trended down steadily and are now at levels last seen in the early 1980s. US auto companies benefited greatly from strong domestic sales. While Japanese companies also benefited from the strength of the US market, it was not sufficient to offset their weak domestic market.

The second factor was restructuring. The threat of foreign competition forced US auto companies to restructure their US operations in the 1980s and 1990s. In contrast, Japanese companies delayed restructuring in Japan in the hope that domestic recovery would make such restructuring unnecessary.

Another factor was business strategies. In the late 1980s, American auto companies chose to invest heavily in light trucks and trucklike vehicles such as sport utility vehicles and minivans. In contrast, all the major Japanese auto companies invested heavily in luxury cars. Thus, when the market for sport utility vehicles and minivans took off in the United States, American auto companies were the primary beneficiaries. In contrast, the market for luxury cars did not develop to the extent that Japanese companies had anticipated. Moreover, an effective response by German auto companies prevented the Japanese companies from gaining share at their expense.

Finally, exchange rates were a factor. Like many other US manufacturers, the domestic auto companies benefited from the dollar's substantial

Figure 6.3   Japanese yen per US dollar, 1985-2002

yen/dollar

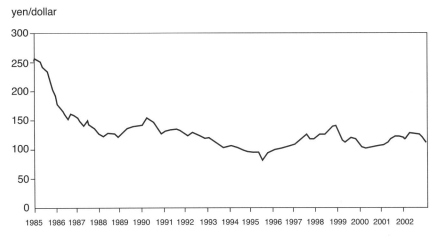

Source: Federal Reserve Board.

Figure 6.4   Japanese import car share versus the yen, 1978-2001

percent   yen/dollar

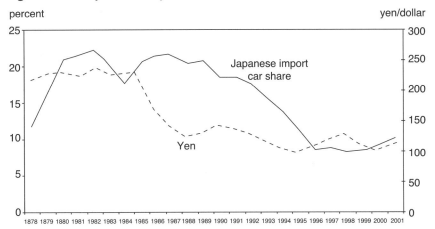

Source: Automotive Trade Policy Council.

depreciation from 1985 to 1995 (figure 6.3). The stronger yen resulted in declining imports from Japan (figure 6.4) and increased production in the United States by both domestic manufacturers and by the Japanese manufacturers in the United States (figure 6.5).

In short, as Michael Moskow, president of the Chicago Fed stated (quoted in *USA Today,* February 28, 1997), the Midwest economy in general, and the US auto industry in particular, were the surprise stories of the 1990s. Written off as part of the rust belt in the early 1980s, the auto

Figure 6.5 Index of industrial production, motor vehicles and parts (SIC 371), 1990-2002

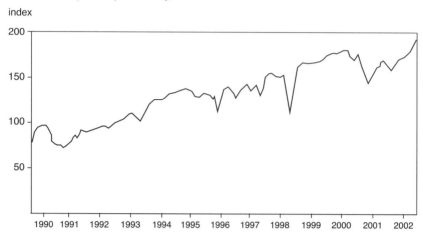

Source: Federal Reserve Board.

industry flourished in the 1990s. The combined annual profits for GM, Ford, and Chrysler averaged over $13 billion per year from 1993 to 2000.

For the Japanese companies, in contrast, failure to restructure combined with a weak domestic economy and an appreciated currency left them with excess capacity and excess borrowing. By the end of the decade, Renault had taken controlling interest in Nissan, Ford had taken management control over Mazda, and DaimlerChrysler had taken over Mitsubishi. Even healthy companies such as Suzuki and Fuji Heavy Industries sought alliances with GM. Who would have thought a decade ago that Nissan, the second largest auto company in Japan, would fall under the control of a foreign firm—Renault? Or that the GM group (GM, Isuzu, Suzuki, and Fuji Heavy Industries) would become the second largest seller of cars in Japan?

The good news for American auto companies would have continued into the new millennium were it not for the fact that the government of Japan decided to embark on an export-led growth strategy again. In particular, as the yen began to appreciate in late 1998, Japan started to intervene in the currency markets heavily in 1999. During the year, Japan bought more than $75 billion in order to weaken the yen (figure 6.6). By the start of 2000, the heavy intervention combined with frequent comments from Japanese officials threatening additional intervention succeeded in halting the yen's appreciation. However, Japan was not satisfied with simply halting the appreciation of the yen. It continued to intervene and to jawbone the currency lower. By the end of 2001, Japan had succeeded in pushing the yen down to around 134 yen to the dollar.

Many analysts continue to question the effectiveness of Japan's intervention. Indeed, there is a strong belief among economists that interven-

Figure 6.6 Japanese foreign currency exchange reserves, August 1997-August 2002

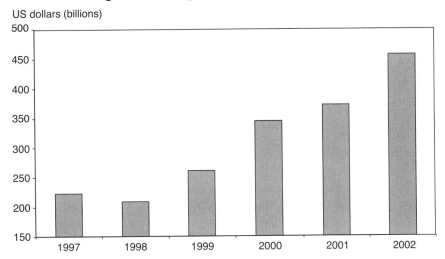

US dollars (billions)

Note: All data are for August of the year indicated.

Source: Automotive Trade Policy Council.

tion only has a short-term impact on exchange rates. Their view is based on attempts countries have made to defend their currency. Japan proves that as long as inflation is not a concern, a country can intervene to lower the value of its currency without any limits.

One measure of Japan's intervention is change in reserves. As shown in figure 6.6, Japan's reserves rose by roughly $200 billion, from around $250 billion to $450 billion, between August 1999 and August 2002. Certainly no one believes that a hard-currency country needs reserves of this magnitude. For example, US reserves are around $50 billion. In any case, Japan has made no secret of its intervention or of its desire to drive the value of the yen lower.

What difference did this make in the auto industry? The change in the value of the yen from 116 yen to the dollar in January 2001 to 126 yen to the dollar in May 2002 added about $3,000 in additional margin on a Nissan Maxima originally priced at $25,989. The margin differential is obviously much greater if one considers the differential between, say, 100 to 105 yen to the dollar—what I believe to be equilibrium exchange rate and roughly the value in January 2000—and the weakest point in the current cycle, around 135 yen to the dollar at the end of 2001.

Is it any surprise, then, that 2001 marked the turning point in the relative performance of the Japanese and US auto companies? Armed with a subsidy of $3,000 to $3,500 per unit, the Japanese companies were soon reporting improving profits and increasing share in the United States.

Honda and Toyota, the two strongest Japanese automakers, reported all-time record profits in 2001. Nissan's turnaround made Carlos Ghosn a household name in Japan. Interestingly, both Toyota and Honda attributed the entire improvement in their profits to the depreciation of the yen.

Using the change in profits reported by Honda and Toyota in 2001, it appears that Toyota's profits improve by ¥20 billion for every one-yen fall in the yen against the dollar. For Honda, which has a higher level of production relative to sales in the United States, the improvement is around ¥12 billion. Using a longer data set, Morgan Stanley estimates that Toyota's profits change by $125 per unit for each percentage point change in the value of the yen against the dollar ("Weaker Dollar May Change Strategic Outlook," *Equity Research,* May 31, 2002).

If it was only profits that were being increased, US automakers would be less concerned. But with auto sales in Japan stagnant, Japanese auto companies have taken advantage of the weak yen to increase market share in the United States. In the past two years, the share of the US auto market captured by imports from Japan has jumped by 1.2 percentage points. The Korean manufacturers, who also enjoy a weak currency, have gained another 1.2 percentage points, and the European manufacturers have gained about 0.8 percentage points. In total, the import share has gained 3.2 percentage points. Of course, the Japanese also have gained share through increasing local production, which also benefits from the weaker yen. But, contrary to public-relations statements from Japan, much of the gain has come from imports. Indeed, Morgan Stanley estimates a 0.75 percent correlation between Japanese import share and longer-term movements in the yen versus the US dollar.

It has been suggested that US manufacturers can offset the currency changes through hedging. That is not true, however. US companies can and do hedge their own currency exposure, but they can't hedge their competitive exposure. More important, they shouldn't have to. The auto industry is already intensively competitive. It should not be forced to compete against subsidized competitors.

Indeed, intervention on the scale that Japan has engaged in is no different from other forms of subsidies that governments offer. That is why the World Trade Organization has explicit provisions against currency manipulation. That is also why the International Monetary Fund proscribes manipulation of currency values. And that is why the Omnibus Trade Act of 1988 required the US Treasury Department to monitor currency manipulation by other countries and to take appropriate measures to prevent other countries from manipulating their currencies to gain a competitive advantage for their producers.

There is only one reason that Japan is intervening in currency markets today—to give its firms an unfair competitive advantage.

Of course, US automakers have to focus on things under their control—products, manufacturing efficiency, and supply chain management—and they are doing that. Productivity at GM, for example, has increased substantially, and quality has improved even more as the time required to bring new products to market has declined. However, it is difficult to overcome a currency disadvantage of 20 percent or more.

Nor is this a short-term problem. Japanese, Korean, and European auto manufacturers are plowing their profits back into products and production facilities, some of which are in the United States. In other words, not only are they getting a short-term advantage, they could well be gaining a longer-term advantage.

Conclusion

The second half of the 1990s marked a revival of fortunes for the American auto industry. The strong US economy and demand for vehicles, a competitive value of the dollar, strong products, improved quality, and restructuring of manufacturing allowed the domestic manufacturers to compete successfully with foreign-owned manufacturers. GM and Ford solidified their positions as the number one and two manufacturers in the world. And, although Chrysler merged with Daimler, the combined company—DaimlerChrysler—became the number three manufacturer. In the meantime, Japanese auto companies struggled with a weak home market and an appreciated yen.

The new millennium has started with another reversal. The American companies are struggling to earn a profit while the Japanese companies are again in ascendancy. To be sure, some of the American companies' problems and the Japanese companies' recent success can be attributed to market factors. However, an even larger contributor to the relative performance has been Japan's intervention to lower the value of the yen. The weak yen has lowered the cost of vehicles imported from Japan by roughly $3,000 on a $25,000 vehicle. It is no surprise that Japanese companies are reporting record profits and expansion around the world while American companies are announcing significant cutbacks in capacity and employment.

7

The Overvalued Dollar and the US Slump

THOMAS I. PALLEY

Dangers of the Dollar Bubble

Over the past seven years the value of the dollar has appreciated dramatically against almost all major currencies. Since bottoming out in 1995, the real value of the dollar has steadily risen against both the Federal Reserve's broad basket of currencies (which includes all major trading partners in Europe, East Asia, and Latin America) and against the Fed's basket of currencies for major industrialized counties.[1] Relative to the broad basket, the appreciation has been 32 percent as of September 2002, and relative to the major industrialized currencies basket, it has been 40 percent. This appreciation pushed the dollar to a 16-year high in early 2002, and it remains stubbornly close to this peak despite the much ballyhooed recent talk of a weakening dollar. Thus, as of September, the broad basket of currencies was just 1 percent below the February 2002 peak.

From 1996 through mid-2000 the US economy was in the grip of a powerful economic expansion that obscured the accumulating negative

Thomas I. Palley is director of the Globalization Reform Project at the Open Society Institute (OSI) in Washington, DC. Prior to joining OSI, he was assistant director of public policy at the AFL-CIO. This paper is an expanded and updated version of "The Over-valued Dollar: Policy Complacency and the Deepening of America's Slump," New Economy 8 (December 2001), 242-47. The author thanks Blackwell Publishing for permission to use this earlier material.

1. In these exchange rate indices, each country is given a weight equal to its share of trade with the United States; the exchange rate is also adjusted to take account of differences in cross-country inflation rates.

effects of this appreciation. The rising dollar did help control inflation by keeping a lid on import prices, but there was already a cost in manufacturing jobs, which began to decline in early 1998. Even if a strengthening dollar could once have been justified, that justification has long since ceased. Today the US economy is in the grip of an economic slump, and overvaluation of the dollar is obstructing recovery by undermining manufacturing. Robust consumption spending—financed by home price appreciation and mortgage refinancings—has helped mitigate the slump, but there is now an imminent danger that continued dollar overvaluation could trigger a deep double-dip recession. Unwinding the dollar's overvaluation should therefore be an urgent policy priority.

In the aftermath of the US stock market bubble, many have wondered about resemblances between the United States and Japan. There can be no doubt that the United States is different in both the scale of its bubble and its capital market arrangements. That said, however, there are also clear similarities, and one of these may be the exchange rate. Japan's asset bubble burst in 1990, yet the yen continued appreciating until 1995, thereby deepening Japan's economic difficulties. One reason for the strong dollar is continuing robust financial flows into the United States driven by investor hopes that asset markets will resume an upward course. In this, the United States may be similar to Japan. A second reason is the strength of US consumption spending, which, although unsustainable, has mitigated the recession. Given simultaneous weakness in foreign economies, this has made the United States look relatively attractive, thereby increasing capital inflows and appreciating the dollar. This shows how asset market considerations can drive the dollar without regard to the impact on economic activity and employment. It is a serious policy problem. The stock market bubble has shown the destabilizing nature of asset price inflation, and the dollar's appreciation represents another instance of asset inflation, this time located in foreign currency markets. Yet, thus far policymakers have shown little inclination to engage with the question of how to guard against asset market bubbles.

Short-Term Damage: Manufacturing and the Recession

The overvalued dollar is inflicting both short- and long-term damage on the US economy. The damage is inflicted via the impact of the overvalued dollar on exports, imports, business investment spending, and the financial position of the US economy.

The trade deficit is the major damage transmission channel, and it especially affects manufacturing, since the deficit is largely accounted for by manufactured goods trade. In 2001, nonagricultural goods exports accounted for 65 percent of all exports, and nonpetroleum goods imports accounted for 81 percent of total imports. The immediate damage comes from the draining of demand for domestically manufactured goods, thereby causing manufacturing job losses. Between April 1998 and September 2002 the United States lost 2.2 million manufacturing jobs, of which 1.9 million were lost after July 2000. These losses can be substantially attributed to the overvalued dollar, which has reduced export demand for US manufactures while simultaneously displacing domestic production through increased imports of foreign manufactures. Before 1998, manufacturing employment was growing, but since then the strong dollar has placed persistent downward pressure on manufacturing employment. Indeed, the manufacturing sector lost jobs in 1999 and 2000, when the overall economy was still booming. The United States has some of the most efficient manufacturing industry in the world, and for the past decade US manufacturing has posted rapid productivity growth that has lowered unit labor costs. However, these efficiency gains have been swamped by the dollar's appreciation, which has lowered prices of foreign competitors' products. The bottom line is that even US industry cannot compete when confronted by a 30 percent price disadvantage imposed by currency markets.

These impacts of the overvalued dollar are documented in a recent study by the National Association of Manufacturers (2002). The study reports that US exports have fallen $140 billion since August 2000, accounting for the loss of over 500,000 factory jobs. Moreover, these export-related job losses are only those of one side of the ledger. Surging imports that have grabbed market share have also caused job losses. In 2001 the deficit in goods trade was $426.7 billion, approximately 25 percent of manufacturing GDP. Reducing this deficit by $200 billion to the level that prevailed in 1997-98, before the overvalued dollar began to bite, would add 12.5 percent to manufacturing GDP. This in turn would translate into approximately 2.1 million additional jobs.[2] This calculation shows how the entire job loss in manufacturing over the past four and a half years can be attributed to the ballooning trade deficit.

Analytically, the trade deficit impact of the dollar works via the twin channels of exports and imports. This effect is clearly shown in figure 7.1. The solid line represents the Federal Reserve's broad trade-weighted real dollar index, which includes exchange rates for all major US trading partners and is adjusted for cross-country differences in inflation. The broken line represents the ratio of US goods imports to goods exports. When the dollar is strong, imports go up and exports go down, and the

---

2. Manufacturing GDP in 2000 was $1,567 billion. Reducing the goods trade deficit by $200 billion to $226 billion represents 12.8 percent of manufacturing GDP. Manufacturing employment in April 2002 was 16.8 million, and increasing this by 12.8 percent would add 2.14 million additional manufacturing jobs.

Figure 7.1 Real broad dollar index and import/export ratio, 1980-2001

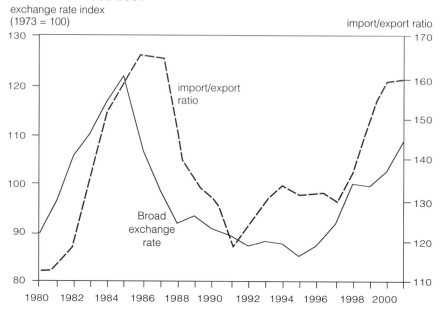

Source: *Economic Report of the President*, February 2002; and author's calculations.

ratio therefore rises. The figure shows a clear robust positive relation that is supported by the following regression:

$$D(GM/GX) = 1.91 + 1.07D(\text{broad exchange rate});$$
$$\text{adjusted } R^2 = 0.41; \text{Durbin-Watson} = 2.16$$

where $D(GM/GX)$ is the change in the ratio of goods imports to goods exports, and D(broad exchange rate) is the change in the lagged broad exchange rate. The regression indicates that a one-point increase in the broad exchange rate results in a 1.07 point increase in the import-export ratio (with a t-ratio of 3.7).

Furthermore, the impact of exchange rate movements has become larger over the past two decades because the US economy has become more engaged in trade. This is shown in figure 7.2, which shows exports and imports as a share of GDP. In 1980 exports and imports were 18.3 percent of GDP, but by 2001 they were 23.8 percent of GDP. Even more dramatic is the change in manufacturing openness, defined as manufacturing exports and imports as a share of manufacturing GDP. This is shown in figure 7.3.[3] In 1980 manufacturing exports and imports were 60 percent

---

3. Manufacturing exports are measured as goods exports minus agricultural exports. Manufacturing imports are measured as goods imports minus petroleum and petroleum-based products.

Figure 7.2 Exports plus imports as a percentage of GDP, 1980-2001

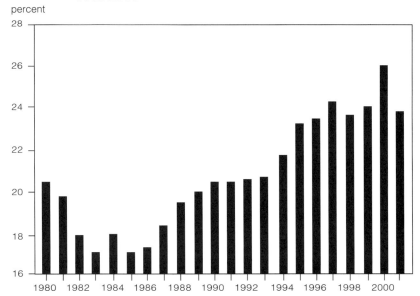

Source: Economic Report of the President, February 2002, updated by *Economic Indicators* published by the Joint Economic Committee, April 2002.

Figure 7.3 Manufacturing exports plus imports as a percentage of manufacturing GDP, 1980-2000

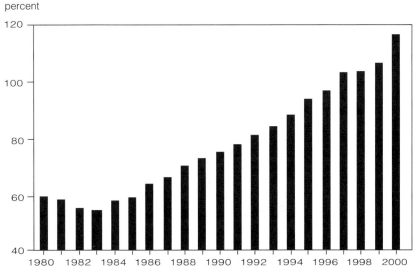

Source: Economic Report of the President, February 2002, and author's calculations as described in footnote 3.

Figure 7.4 Real broad dollar index and manufacturing profit share

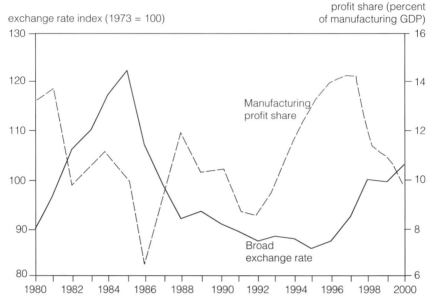

exchange rate index (1973 = 100)

profit share (percent of manufacturing GDP)

Source: Economic Report of the President, February 2002, and author's calculations.

of manufacturing GDP, but by 2000 they had risen to 116 percent of manufacturing GDP. The value of manufacturing trade (exports plus imports) now exceeds the total value of manufacturing output. Manufacturing exports are 46 percent of manufacturing output, and manufacturing imports are 70 percent of manufacturing output. Given this exposure, overvaluation of the dollar whipsaws the manufacturing sector.

A second indirect damage channel is investment spending, which is negatively affected for two reasons. First, by reducing exports and domestic sales, an overvalued dollar contributes to excess capacity, which diminishes the need to invest. Second, by making foreign goods cheaper, an overvalued dollar lowers profitability and reduces firms' ability to finance investment. In August 2002, manufacturing capacity utilization was 74.6 percent, 6.3 percentage points below the average for the period 1967-2001, and manufacturing capacity utilization in 2002 is running at its lowest level since 1983. Figure 7.4 shows the Federal Reserve's broad currency index and the manufacturing profit share, and it reveals a clear inverse correlation. These heuristic arguments can be supported by formal econometric analysis; Blecker (2002) reports that the dollar enters negatively and statistically significantly in regressions of the manufacturing profit share and the manufacturing investment rate. Indeed, a hallmark of the current recession has been the collapse in business fixed investment spending.

The policy implications are clear. The overvalued dollar has contributed significantly to the current recession, and it now risks triggering a double-dip recession. The benefits of Federal Reserve easing, mortgage refinancings, tax cuts, and increased government spending have all been diluted to the extent that spending has bled into imports. The inventory rebuilding of the first half of 2002 also had weaker employment effects to the extent that it relied on imports. A robust sustained recovery will require renewed business investment spending, but the likelihood of such spending is reduced as long as the overvalued dollar undermines domestic manufacturers' competitive position and creates incentives to shift production offshore.

Long-Term Damage: Manufacturing and Financial Stability

Not only has the overvalued dollar inflicted short-run damage on the US economy, it has also inflicted long-run damage. In September 2002 US manufacturing employment fell to 16.6 million jobs, equal to the level of January 1962. This decline threatens the long-run commercial outlook for the US economy. The threat is illustrated in the aircraft industry, where Boeing has been forced to make significantly larger cuts to production schedules than has Airbus.[4] Given that airlines order on a "fleet" principle, sales lost today mean lost future sales, as airlines tend to stick with their current supplier when placing new aircraft orders.

In the textile industry, there were on average two mill closures a week in 2001, and there were 240 mill closures between 1997 and September 2002.[5] Modern textile-making equipment from these closures is being sold overseas in secondhand markets at rock-bottom prices. In this fashion, US capacity is being permanently reduced while that of foreign competitors is built up.

Loss of manufacturing jobs carries a high cost. Manufacturing is widely recognized as a principal engine of productivity growth, and there is evidence of positive productivity spillovers from manufacturing to non-manufacturing (Palley 1999). Some of the greatest gains from "new economy" information technologies may come from application of these technologies to manufacturing. A shrinking manufacturing sector results in a smaller base for productivity growth and on which to apply the new

---

4. See "Boeing's Bleak Outlook: It's a Desert Out There," *The Economist*, January 24, 2003, and "Airbus: Battering Boeing," *The Economist*, July 18, 2002.

5. These statistics are drawn from "Crisis in US Textiles," posted on the Web site of the American Textile Manufacturers Institute, http://www.atmi.org. 1997 was a record year for US textile industry profitability, fiber consumption, shipments, and exports. According to ATMI, "Since then the dollar's relentless rise, particularly against the currencies of major Asian exporters, has shattered the competitive structure of the industry, causing a huge import surge while collapsing major export markets."

information technologies. Consequently, the United States is at risk of having slower productivity growth in the future, which will result in lower living standards.

A second cost of lost manufacturing jobs concerns wages and income distribution (Palley 1999). Historically, manufacturing jobs have been "good" jobs in the sense of paying above-average wages and health benefits. Moreover, these jobs have gone disproportionately to those with educational attainment of a high school diploma or less, a group still constituting 75 percent of the labor force. Manufacturing jobs have historically provided a ladder to the middle class for this large group, and there is solid empirical evidence that increasing the share of manufacturing jobs in total employment improves income distribution. Eliminating these jobs is therefore tantamount to kicking away the ladder, and the decline in manufacturing employment stands to entrench America's deteriorated income distribution.

A widespread misapprehension is that declining manufacturing employment is an inevitable feature of economic development, and a parallel is often drawn with the experience of US agriculture. However, this parallel is misleading. First, the decline in agricultural employment occurred as the United States became agriculturally self-sufficient and a net exporter of agricultural products, whereas the decline in manufacturing is marked by increasing import dependence. Second, while it is true that the manufacturing share of employment tends to decline owing to manufacturing's faster productivity growth, this need not mean a falling absolute level of manufacturing employment. Instead, manufacturing employment can actually grow slightly over time. This is illustrated by the Canadian experience. Figure 7.5 shows manufacturing employment in the United States and Canada for the period 1990 to March 2002. After the recession of the early 1990s, manufacturing employment in both countries bottomed out in 1993. Thereafter, in Canada it proceeded to rise steadily, from 1.8 million in 1993 to 2.3 million in 2000, making for a 28 percent gain over seven years. Moreover, manufacturing employment has held constant since then, and was 2.3 million in March 2002.

The difference in the Canadian and US experiences holds a number of important lessons. First, there is no automatic tendency for manufacturing employment to fall. Canada and the United States have similar economic endowments, measured in terms of quality of governance, capital stock, and labor force educational attainment. Yet in Canada manufacturing employment has significantly grown, whereas in the United States it has not. Moreover, during the 1990s the United States had more favorable macroeconomic conditions than Canada, since it enjoyed a stronger consumption and investment boom and had lower interest rates. The one significant difference between the two economies was the exchange rate, with the US dollar showing sustained appreciation relative to the Canadian dollar.

Figure 7.5   Manufacturing employment in the United States and Canada, 1990-March 2002

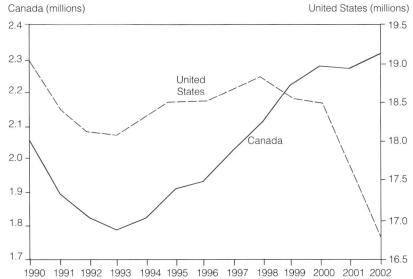

Canada (millions)   United States (millions)

Source: Economic Report of the President, February 2002, and author's calculations. Canadian data provided by the Canadian Labor Congress.

Some have claimed that the loss of US manufacturing jobs is due to the global economy's slowdown. But if this were so, there should have been a similar loss of jobs in Canadian manufacturing, which is not the case. Nor can the US recession entirely explain the loss of jobs, since Canadian manufacturing is enormously dependent on the US market, which absorbs 85 percent of Canadian exports. If the US recession were decisive, Canadian manufacturing should also have been negatively affected.

As noted earlier, the overvalued dollar and the decline of manufacturing are both intimately linked with the problem of the trade deficit. A declining manufacturing base threatens to entrench structurally the large US trade deficit, which risks creating conditions conducive to financial instability. The ability to run a trade deficit requires a willingness of foreigners to finance the deficit. If that willingness diminishes, lacking a domestic manufacturing base capable of replacing imported goods, the US economy could become constrained to grow more slowly with higher unemployment.

This danger is illustrated in figure 7.6, which shows the manufacturing trade deficit as a percentage of manufacturing output. In 1980 the United States had a small surplus on manufacturing trade equal to 2.04 percent of manufacturing GDP, but since then this surplus has turned into a widening deficit. As of 2000, the manufacturing trade deficit was 24.56

Figure 7.6 Manufacturing trade deficit as a share of manufacturing output, 1980-2000

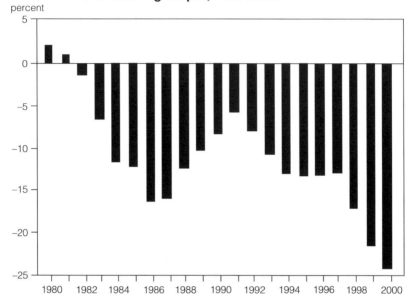

Source: Economic Report of the President, February 2002, and author's calculations as described in footnote 3.

Table 7.1 Selected US trade and international financial wealth statistics (percent)

As percent of GDP	1990	1995	2000	2002Q1
Trade balance, goods	− 1.9	− 2.4	− 4.6	− 4.1
Current account balance	− 1.4	− 1.4	− 4.2	− 4.3
Net US international financial position	− 2.8	− 4.6	− 16.0	− 22.6
Foreign financial asset holdings in United States	33.1	44.2	62.5	65.1

Source: Blecker (2002).

percent of manufacturing GDP. The size of this deficit suggests that the United States may now be critically short of manufacturing capacity, exposing it to a risk of stagflation triggered by financial instability.

The logic is as follows. For much of the past 20 years the United States has run large current account deficits that have been financed by a combination of borrowing from abroad and selling US-owned assets to foreigners. Having been the world's largest creditor in 1980, the United States has become the world's largest debtor. This change is captured in table 7.1, which shows how persistent trade deficits have contributed to a deterioration in the US net international financial position and an increase in foreign-owned US financial assets. Moreover, this changed financial

Figure 7.7 The balance on the US foreign income account, 1980-2000

billions of US dollars

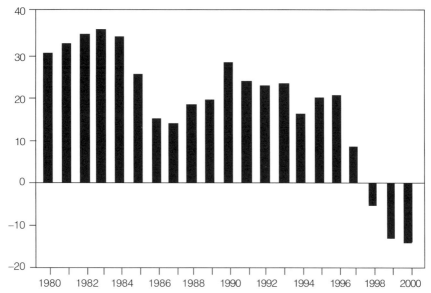

Soruce: Economic Report of the President, February 2002.

circumstance is feeding back on the current account deficit, since the United States must now pay interest and dividends to foreigners. The balance on international income turned negative in 1998 for the first time since before World War II, and in 2001 the income account was in deficit to the tune of $19.1 billion. These changes, illustrated in figure 7.7, promise to grow as a result of compounding of interest on past loans and investments.

The increased size of foreign asset holdings means that even a minor rebalancing of foreign portfolios away from the United States could have large financial market effects. In the event that foreign investors lose their appetite for US financial assets, US financial markets will stand exposed to reduced demand, which will lower asset prices and raise interest rates. The dollar also stands to weaken precipitously as asset holders exit US markets. Higher interest rates would then choke off economic activity, while a sharp decline in the dollar would make for significant imported inflation because of dependence on imported manufactured goods. Hence, stagflation.

The nexus of the trade deficit and financial instability described above can be understood through the metaphor of a bathtub. Water in the tub represents accumulated indebtedness, and water entering through the tap represents new borrowing. As long as there is room in the tub, more water—that is, new debt—can flow in. But once the tub reaches its limit, the water immediately starts to overflow. This metaphor captures the nature of financial crises. One minute everything appears sound, and the next, financial markets are in turmoil. No one knows exactly what the US financial instability threshold is, but the United States has run large trade deficits for 20 years and the current account deficit was 4 percent of GDP in 2001. Historically, deficits of this magnitude have proved harbingers of instability. Policy prudence therefore suggests a course of smooth gradual adjustment now, rather than risking larger future disruptions.

Global Economic Problems Stemming from the Overvalued Dollar

It is not only the domestic economy that is being hurt by the overvalued dollar. So too is the global economy. Although foreign economies benefit from the overvalued dollar to the extent that it lowers their export prices and increases export sales to the United States, foreign economies also bear several costs.

One cost comes from imported inflation resulting from the fact that most commodities are priced in dollars. This is illustrated by the European experience where, after the introduction of the euro in January 1999, inflation surged because of higher oil prices. The near-tripling of dollar-denominated oil prices that took place over the period 1999-2001 interacted with the 35 percent fall in the value of the euro relative to the dollar to cause higher inflation. This prompted the European Central Bank to raise interest rates, which slowed the European economy.

A second cost is related to debt service for developing countries. Most developing countries have significant dollar-denominated foreign debts. A rise in the value of the dollar makes it more difficult to service this debt, requiring countries to export more to meet their debt service obligations. By increasing the debt service strain, the overvalued dollar creates financial instability in developing countries. Moreover, this comes on top of the problem of higher dollar costs of imported oil, which also has a negative effect on developing countries.

The third and most important cost pertains to the US economy, which is the locomotive of the global economy. If the US economy is pushed back into a double-dip recession as a result of the overvalued dollar, the global economy will be profoundly and negatively affected. A double-dip recession can be expected to significantly reduce US imports, and these losses stand to far outweigh the sales gains at the margin that foreign economies gain as a result of the overvalued dollar. In effect, the negative income feedbacks resulting from a dollar-induced double-dip recession will dominate any positive relative price effects on foreign country exports.

Arguments for a "Strong" Dollar Do Not Wash

The arguments against an overvalued dollar are compelling, yet some continue to argue that a "strong" dollar is desirable. One argument is that the strong dollar helps keep down inflation by lowering import prices and keeping the lid on prices of domestic manufacturers. This argument had some support in the late 1990s when the United States was in the midst of a huge credit-driven boom, but that is no longer the case. Inflation is not an imminent economic danger, and there are reasons to believe that deflation is actually the greater danger, given the highly indebted state of the US economy. In these circumstances, slightly higher inflation could be a benefit to the extent that it reduces debt burdens.

A second argument is that a strong dollar is needed to finance the trade deficit. This argument has the reasoning backward. There is a need to finance the trade deficit because the dollar is hugely overvalued. Absent this overvaluation, exports would be higher and imports lower, which would diminish the trade deficit and the amount needed to finance it.

The above financing argument can also apply to claims that the US trade deficit is the product of inadequate domestic saving rather than the overvalued dollar. These undersaving claims misunderstand the nature of the national income identity from which they derive. The national income identity is given by

$$\text{(private saving } - \text{ private investment spending) } +$$
$$\text{(taxes } - \text{ government spending) } = \text{(exports } - \text{ imports)}$$

The logic of this identity can be understood through the logic of credit markets, which require that for every lender there be a borrower. The trade deficit represents foreign lending to the United States, and by implication there must be either a private-sector borrower (when private saving is less than private investment) and/or a public-sector borrower (when taxes are less than government spending). A higher-valued dollar drives up the trade deficit, thereby inducing additional foreign borrowing, the counterpart of which must by definition be a domestic saving shortfall.

Exchange Rate Intervention Works

Having made the case that an overvalued dollar is economically damaging, I turn now to the problem of what is to be done. Some argue that foreign exchange market flows are simply too large and that effective intervention is no longer feasible in a world of globally integrated financial markets. In making this claim, intervention opponents point to the many instances where massive intervention has failed to sustain exchange rates. Most recently, there is the case of Turkey in 2002. Other recent cases include Brazil in 1999, Russia in 1998, and the East Asian economies in 1997. A classic example concerning developed economies is the United Kingdom in 1992. In each of these instances, market forces proved too powerful, and central banks ultimately had to accept lower exchange rates.

Missing in the discussion of dollar intervention is the fact that there is a significant difference between intervention designed to lower the value of a currency and intervention designed to support a currency's value. Turkey, Brazil, Russia, East Asia, and the United Kingdom were all instances where national central banks were pitted against market participants in an attempt to defend exchange rates. The resources available to these banks were restricted to limited holdings of foreign reserves, and given the huge leverage possessed by market participants, they were inevitably defeated. However, intervention by a strong currency bank is a different matter, since it is selling its own currency, of which it has unlimited supplies.

Evidence for the success of intervention is provided by the Plaza Exchange Rate Accord of September 1985, when the G-7 finance ministers agreed to bring down the value of the dollar, and there followed a smooth depreciation that lasted 18 months. On a more systematic level, research by Dominguez and Frankel (1993) reports evidence that exchange rate intervention was successful in the 1980s. Their conclusions are reaffirmed in a recent state-of-the-art survey of the literature on exchange rate intervention by Sarno and Taylor (2001) and in a recent intervention event study by Fatum and Hutchison (2001). Ito (2002) also provides implicit support for the effectiveness of intervention by reporting how the Bank of Japan made systematic profits on its interventions during the 1990s. Currency markets appear to be significantly driven by psychology, momentum trading, and herd behavior, which explains why econometric models do so poorly in attempts to predict the exchange rate. That said, this also explains why robust coordinated central bank market interventions accompanied by coordinated central bank "open-mouth operations" can change market psychology and the direction in which the herd is moving.

If successful exchange rate intervention is feasible, that still leaves the question of when intervention is warranted. When it comes to exchange rate settings, policymakers can be guided by real exchange rate measures that track the real value of currencies and take account of differences in country inflation rates. A theoretical framework for analyzing this issue is provided by Williamson (1985) through his concept of fundamental

Table 7.2 Total reserves excluding gold (end-of-period, in billions of US dollars)

Country	1990	1995	2001
Japan	78	183	395
China	30	76	216
Hong Kong	24	55	111

Source: Blecker (2002).

equilibrium exchange rates. In arriving at decisions, the policy process should also ensure that those who are economically affected are consulted. In this connection, it is noteworthy that the National Association of Manufacturers, the AFL-CIO, and the American Farm Bureau Federation are all currently calling for a weaker dollar.

Economic policymaking involves judgments. Adjusting interest rates results in changes in asset prices. Central banks willingly engage in interest rate management because they recognize the pervasive effect of interest rates on economic activity. The same holds for the exchange rate. Just as interest rate policy is set on the basis of sensibly informed judgments about the economy, so, too, exchange rate policy should be conducted in similar fashion.

China and Japan: Two Special Policy Concerns

The value of the dollar needs to be brought down against the broad index of currencies. However, the Japanese yen and the Chinese renminbi are especially problematic. In the case of the yen, the Japanese government has repeatedly engaged in strategic interventions to gain competitive trade advantage. In the case of the renminbi, China has run persistent large trade surpluses, yet capital controls prevent the renminbi from appreciating. In both cases, these policies have resulted in large accumulations of foreign reserves that have blocked the yen and the renminbi from appreciating. The scale of accumulations is shown in table 7.2.

With regard to the yen, Japanese government policy appears driven by the hope that a weak yen will sufficiently stimulate exports to pull the economy out of recession. However, the reality is that Japan is a relatively closed economy, with exports constituting only 11 percent of GDP, while a significant portion of imports are nonsubstitutable primary products. Therefore the base on which depreciation operates is too small for yen depreciation to solve Japan's domestic economic problems. Instead, yen depreciation risks exporting Japan's problems to the United States and to other East Asian trading rivals. This risks triggering financial instability and a cycle of competitive devaluation in the East Asia region. The clear policy implication is that Japan must abandon its attempt to depreciate its way out of recession.

With regard to the renminbi, the problem is that China is using an artificially undervalued currency to spur export-led growth. According to the International Monetary Fund's *Direction of Trade Statistics Yearbook* (2000), in 1999 (the latest available data) China had a trade surplus of $68.7 billion with the United States and of $28.7 billion with the European Union. China is also a massive recipient of foreign direct investment (FDI) and the dominant destination of such investment in the developing world. In a free market, China's exchange rate should appreciate under these conditions. However, China has pursued an aggressive interventionist and mercantilist exchange rate strategy that has prevented its currency from appreciating. The result has been continuing trade surpluses that threaten global deflation. Jobs are being lost in the US manufacturing sector, and China is also effectively sucking all the demand out of the global economy, leaving nothing for other developing countries. In this fashion, the developing economies are being pushed into permanent stagnation. Once again the policy implication is clear. As a member of the international economic community, China must abandon its mercantilist exchange rate policy and allow its currency to appreciate as market forces dictate.

Policy Recommendations

The recognition that currency markets can damage economic activity points to broader issues of international economic governance. The existing international policy framework treats trade and finance as separate independent arenas, yet it is clear that trade outcomes are profoundly affected by currency markets. Milton Friedman's (1953) old defense that exchange rates are determined by market fundamentals and that market speculators will inevitably pull exchange rates back to levels warranted by these fundamentals is now discredited, as the empirical literature on purchasing power parity conclusively proves.[6] Instead, exchange rates appear to behave like asset market prices, and exchange rate bubbles driven by speculative expectations can persist for long periods. Today's dollar problem shows that exchange rate misalignment is not just a problem for developing countries.

Recommendation 1. An immediate policy recommendation is for the US Treasury to explicitly revoke its earlier "strong dollar" rhetoric. Such rhetoric has likely contributed to the dollar's appreciation by creating market expectations that the Treasury stands ready to intervene in the event of dollar weakness. When linked with the willingness of many

---

6. Obstfeld (2001) provides a survey of the empirical literature on purchasing power parity.

foreign governments to accept weaker currencies to gain international competitive advantage, the Treasury's rhetoric has likely fostered perceptions of a "one-way" bet that places persistent upward pressure on the dollar. Revoking this rhetoric will help erase such perceptions.

Recommendation 2. Japan must abandon its attempt to depreciate its way out of recession. This is a policy that will not work for Japan, yet risks exporting Japan's problems. China must abandon its mercantilist exchange rate policy and allow its currency to appreciate as market forces dictate.

Recommendation 3. The European Central Bank must be enjoined to lower interest rates and adopt a more progrowth monetary policy stance. There is clear evidence that the European economy is slowing dramatically, and this has had a dampening effect on investor demand for euro-denominated assets.[7] By increasing growth, an interest rate reduction stands to appreciate the euro by making European assets more attractive.

Recommendation 4. Leaders of the G-7 should initiate a second Plaza Accord. They should publicly acknowledge that the dollar needs to be brought down smoothly from current levels and that their central banks will act to do so through coordinated market intervention. An appropriate benchmark would be 100 to 110 yen per dollar and 1.10 to 1.20 dollars per euro.

Recommendation 5. In addition to these changes in country policies, there are deeper structural failings in foreign exchange markets that point to a need for permanent coordinated exchange rate policies. Acting together, with the onus of intervention falling predominantly on central banks of stronger currencies, the international community should establish procedures to prevent future damaging currency misalignments. American workers suffered from the dollar bubble of the mid-1980s, and they are suffering again from today's dollar bubble. Exchange rates are too important and potentially disruptive to be left to unfettered speculation, and the community of central banks should establish procedures for monitoring and correcting exchange rate excesses.

Recommendation 6. There is a need to reconsider existing arrangements of unfettered capital mobility. The goal should not be to prevent capital mobility, but rather to give central banks the ability to slow inflows when they deem necessary. One possibility is application of speed bumps in the form of temporary nonremunerated reserve requirements on capital inflows. These have been used to good effect in Chile.

Recommendation 7. The fact that exchanges rates can become significantly distorted points to the need for exchange rate considerations to be addressed in trade agreements. In serial fashion across countries, exchange

---

7. The IMF's *World Economic Outlook,* September 2002, reports of Europe that "there are signs of core inflation starting to come down, and . . . the recovery has appeared increasingly hesitant" (27).

rate depreciations have destroyed US manufacturing jobs and capital investments without regard to underlying productive efficiency. Such depreciations swamp the benefit of tariff reductions achieved through trade negotiations, and amount to an exchange rate subsidy for US competitors. Trade policy must explicitly address this problem and can no longer be pursued as if trade and exchange rates are unrelated.

In the global trade-exchange rate game, US policymakers have persistently abdicated their responsibilities, leaving US manufacturers unprotected against the exchange rate manipulations of rival governments. Some of the major manufacturing US trading partners, such as Japan and Korea, manipulate their currencies to give their exports a competitive edge. This has been documented by Calvo and Reinhart (2000), who term developing countries' practice of managing their currencies "fear of floating." Although governments nominally commit to a floating exchange rate regime, they actually engage in systematic intervention to prevent appreciations.

The old Bretton Woods system of fixed exchange rates guarded against this type of unfair practice, but that system suffered from the need for large disruptive periodic exchange rate adjustments, and it could not withstand the powers of speculation created by liberalization of capital flows. The system that has replaced Bretton Woods encourages unfair exchange rate gaming, and it also allows exchange rates to be set by capital flows irrespective of trade deficits. There is no going back to the Bretton Woods arrangements. However, placing exchange rate provisions in trade agreements, having a coordinated G-7 exchange rate policy centered on strong-currency central banks leading interventions, and making small modifications to the rules governing capital flows so as to allow central banks to slow inflows would go a long way to making the international financial system work more fairly and productively. Implementing such an agenda will require policymakers to escape the existing efficient-financial-markets ideology that has them abdicating their powers of responsible governance. In the meantime, this ideology promotes a policy of dollar complacency that is deepening America's economic slump.

References

Blecker, R. A. 2002. Exchange Rates in North America: Effects of the Over-valued Dollar on Domestic US Manufacturing and Implications for Canada and Mexico. Paper presented for the conference "Can Canada and Its NAFTA Partners Conduct Independent Macroeconomic Policies in a Globalized World?" University of Ottawa, Ottawa, Canada, September 20-21.

Calvo, G., and Reinhart, M. 2000. Fear of Floating. NBER Working Paper No. 7993. Cambridge, MA: National Bureau of Economic Research.

Dominguez, K. M., and J. A. Frankel. 1993. *Does Foreign Exchange Intervention Work?* Washington: Institute for International Economics.

Fatum, R., and M. M. Hutchison. 2001. Is Sterilized Foreign Exchange Intervention Effective After All? An Event Study Approach. UCSC Working Paper No. 02-02 (August 2001) and *Economic Journal,* forthcoming.

Friedman, M. 1953. The Case for Flexible Exchange Rates. In *Essays in Positive Economics.* Chicago: Chicago University Press.

International Monetary Fund. 2002. *World Economic Outlook, September 2002: Trade and Finance.* Washington: IMF.

Ito, T. 2002. Is Foreign Exchange Intervention Effective? The Japanese Experiences in the 1990s. NBER Working Paper No. 8914. Cambridge, MA: National Bureau of Economic Research.

National Association of Manufacturers. 2002. Overvalued Dollar Puts Hundreds of Thousands Out of Work. Washington, March. Available at http://www.nam.org.

Obstfeld, M. 2001. International Macroeconomics: Beyond the Mundell-Fleming Model. IMF Staff Papers No. 47. Washington: International Monetary Fund.

Palley, T. I. 1999. Manufacturing Matters: The Impact on Productivity Growth, Wages, and Income Distribution. AFL-CIO Public Policy Department, Economic Policy Paper No. E031. Washington: AFL-CIO.

Palley, T. I. 2001. The Over-valued Dollar: Policy Complacency and the Deepening of America's Slump. *New Economy* 8 (December): 242-47.

Sarno, L., and M. Taylor. 2001. Official Intervention in the Foreign Exchange Market: Is It Effective and, If So, How Does It Work? *Journal of Economic Literature* 39 (September): 839-68.

Williamson, J. 1985. The Exchange Rate System. POLICY ANALYSES IN INTERNATIONAL ECONOMICS 5. Washington: Institute for International Economics.

8

All Eyes on the Dollar

STEPHEN S. ROACH

On Wall Street these days there is an obvious sense of urgency to the macro conundrum. As I see it, a US-centric global economy is feeling the full force of America's postbubble shakeout. Lacking in autonomous sources of domestic demand, anemic growth in the non-US world awaits a jump-start from the once powerful American growth engine. And that just isn't happening. The impacts of America's summer flirtation with a double-dip recession have been magnified in the rest of the world. Europe is floundering, Japan is veering back toward another crisis, and an inventory-led rebound in global trade is leading to a peaking of the cyclical upturn elsewhere in Asia. All this and only a double-dip scare! Can you imagine what would have happened had there actually been a recessionary relapse in the US economy?

This is hardly idle conjecture. I would currently place a probability of greater than 50 percent on a US double-dip at some point in the next 6 to 9 months. In that context, the task ahead for global stabilization policy is hardly simple. As I see it, the authorities are confronted with a triangulation of trade-offs. First, there is the need for the United States to purge its postbubble excesses—the root cause of a Japanese-like tendency for periodic recessionary relapses over the next several years. Second, there is the imperative for the rest of the world to wean itself from excessive dependence on the US economy. And, third, there is the urgent need for global policymakers to do everything in their power to avoid deflation. Achieving any of these objectives is tough enough. Pulling it all off simultaneously is a different matter altogether.

Stephen S. Roach is managing director and chief economist at Morgan Stanley.

It's not all that difficult to come up with policy prescriptions that might resolve each of these objectives in isolation from one another. Slow growth is the antidote for the purging of America's postbubble excesses. A dip or two—however painful—would accelerate the process, presumably leading to a slowdown in domestic demand that would be required to boost saving, pay down debt, and facilitate a long overdue current account adjustment. A return to policy austerity—both fiscal and monetary—by US policymakers would be required to achieve such an outcome, in my view. As for the growth-starved rest of the world, the policy prescription is precisely the opposite—progrowth fiscal and monetary policies that would jump-start domestic demand overseas and break the unhealthy and excessive dependence of other nations on the United States. Nor is there much debate about deflationary remedies—aggressive monetary and fiscal stimulus, and the sooner the better on both counts. The risk of being late in countering deflationary pressures is especially worrisome for postbubble economies like Japan and the United States. The trick is to move early enough while there is still policy traction.

The problems, of course, arise when you put the package together. That's because these remedies work at cross-purposes with one another. The conflict is most acute in the United States. The demand shortfall required to purge postbubble excesses clashes with the restoration of demand vigor needed to avoid deflation. The more successful any antideflationary measures are, the more likely it is that excesses will only intensify in a "revitalized" US economy—taking America further down the treacherous road of reduced saving, higher debt, and an import-led widening of already massive trade and current account deficits. In that critical respect, the policy stimulus required to avoid deflation will only exacerbate America's lingering postbubble excesses. Maybe the perils of deflation are so serious that it's worth taking just such a risk. That is basically my stance on the matter. At the same time, I would be the first to concede that in today's climate, the trade-off between avoiding deflation and the purging of postbubble excesses seems just about intractable. But those are precisely the tough choices that the authorities must now make.

The Perils of Deflation

In my opinion, two priorities should be uppermost in weighing the policy options that confront us today. The first is the avoidance of global deflation. This could well be the most serious issue we have faced in the world policy arena since the 1930s. Starting in Japan, deflation has spread throughout most of Asia, whose economies collectively account for about 30 percent of world GDP (figure 8.1). Of the major economies in the region, only Korea has managed to avoid deflation. Meanwhile in the United States, the GDP price index was increasing at a rate of just 0.8

Figure 8.1   Asian deflation at work (consumer price index, year on year)

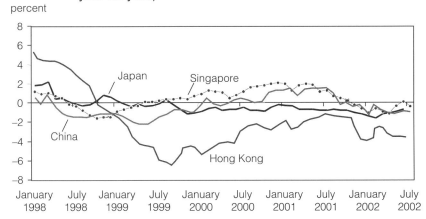

Source: Bloomberg.

Figure 8.2   Heading toward deflation? (US GDP chain-weighted price index, two-quarter moving average)

Source: US Department of Commerce.

percent in the third quarter of 2002—its slowest rate of rise in 48 years (see figure 8.2). Prices of goods and structures, combined—items that make up 47 percent of real GDP—are already contracting at an annual rate of −0.7 percent. Only in services, where price measurement is notoriously unreliable, is US inflation holding in positive territory. And deflationary concerns are mounting in Europe, where stabilization policies have suddenly become procyclical. Germany seems especially vulnerable in that regard.

For over 22 years disinflation has been the predominant macro theme shaping the global economy and world financial markets. From its peak of around 13 percent in 1980, industrial-world inflation has eased off to an estimated 1.6 percent in 2002. Yet the road to price stability has proved to be surprisingly treacherous. Most importantly, it has led to asset bubbles that now threaten to transform disinflation into deflation.

Two key complications may have biased the endgame toward deflation—the IT revolution and globalization. Both occurred in the latter half of the 1990s, after the regime shift in stabilization policies. The advent of the Internet gave rise to an extraordinary surge in the demand for information technology that led to a disproportionate expansion of aggregate supply. It also gave rise to a cyclical surge in productivity and the associated "new economy" mania that led to ever-greater monetary accommodation and the mother of all equity bubbles. At the same time, globalization took off, with the annualized expansion of world trade averaging 8.2 percent in the latter half of the 1990s—fully 50 percent faster than average gains of 5.5 percent in 1984-93. This reflected an equally important macro transformation—an IT-based integration of the global supply chain. The combination of the IT revolution and globalization tilted the balance toward deflation. Suddenly, toward the end of the 1990s—at the height of massive asset bubbles—the world was awash in excess supply, a classic setup for price destruction.

Then the music stopped. The equity bubble popped in early 2000, and a US-centric global economy slipped into mild recession in 2001. In retrospect, that may have been all it took to tip the scales toward deflation, in part because these shocks hit the world economy when it was operating at an exceedingly low inflation rate—a 0.8 percent increase in the industrialized world's GDP deflator in 1999. Initial conditions matter. If the world had been hit with a negative shock when the inflation rate was hovering around 3 to 4 percent, it would have been easier to absorb the jolt without unleashing deflation. But with inflation all but squeezed out of the system at the height of the mania, the popping of the bubble may well have been the straw that broke the back of price stability. At very low rates of inflation, there is little to cushion the world in the event of a shock. For that reason alone, the risk of deflation cannot be taken lightly. In retrospect, maybe we simply went too far down the road to price stability—eliminating the margin of error that surely would come in handy today.

In its ideal state, price stability represents perfect balance between aggregate supply and demand. The task for policymakers is to manage both sides of the macro equation in order to achieve this equilibrium. The so-called policy mix—trade-offs between monetary and fiscal actions—became central to the outcome. Not surprisingly, America led the way in using its policy mix in attempting to adhere to inflation targets. The first decade of US disinflation was characterized by tight money and easy fiscal policy. This mix was reversed in the 1990s, as a shift to fiscal austerity was countered by a more accommodative monetary policy. In my view, the problems arose from this shift in the policy mix. The transition from tight to easy money unleashed a massive asset bubble and concomitant

Figure 8.3 Domestic demand disparities

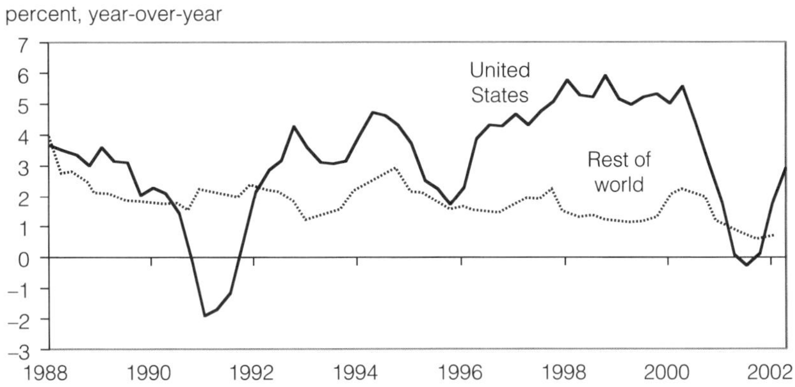

percent, year-over-year

Note: All data are for January of the year indicated.

Source: International Monetary Fund.

excesses in the real economy. Without a purging of these excesses, sustainable recovery in the US economy and in a US-centric global economy will be most difficult to achieve.

Global Rebalancing and the Dollar

The second priority for global policy is what I would call a rebalancing of a lopsided world economy (figure 8.3). In essence, this is all about shifting the mix of global demand away from the United States and toward the rest of the world. It is the imperative of global rebalancing that brings the dollar into play. Such a transformation boils down to a shift in relative prices. And the dollar is by far the world's most important relative price. As I see it, the time is now ripe for the United Sates to welcome a sharp decline in the dollar—a drop of 15 to 20 percent on a trade-weighted basis. It would serve three important purposes: First, it would be inflationary—putting an end to the unrelenting fall in import prices and thereby arresting the strain of "imported deflation" that is currently afflicting the United States (figure 8.4). Second, a weaker dollar is key to America's long overdue current account adjustment. It would shift purchases from foreign-produced to domestically produced products, but it would also reduce the growth of domestic demand; this latter development would stem from the higher real interest rates that typically accompany sharp currency corrections. Saving would probably increase as a result, also tempering the excesses of debt that weighs on consumer balance sheets.

Third, a weaker dollar, of course, also has important consequences for the rest of the world. Obviously, it would imply a strengthening of other major currencies—especially the euro and the yen—which would undoubtedly cause great consternation and angst overseas. Yet that might

Figure 8.4 Falling US import prices

index 2000 = 100

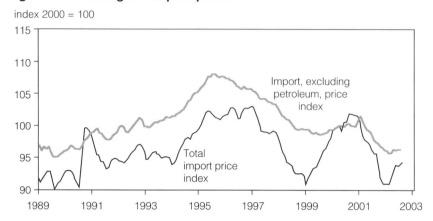

Note: All data are for January of the year indicated.

Source: US Department of Commerce.

be exactly the kick the rest of the world needs in order to embrace long overdue progrowth policy reforms. As a result, a weaker dollar could well intensify pressure on foreign authorities to shift the mix of their growth objectives away from relying on US-led external demand and toward stimulating long-deficient domestic demand. A failure of the rest of the world to embrace progrowth policy stimulus remains a major impediment to sustained global economic recovery, in my view. Japan, of course, has taken major steps in that direction. But they came too late—after the Japanese economy had already tumbled into a deflationary trap. To say that Europe is dragging its feet on this score would be a serious understatement. With fiscal policy stimulus closed off by the strictures of the Stability and Growth Pact, and with monetary easing occurring only reluctantly by a central bank still fighting inflation in a deflationary world, the very concept of progrowth policies has become an oxymoron in Europe.

A depreciation of the dollar would put considerable pressure on the rest of the world to see stabilization policy in a very different light. A strengthening of the yen may well be the final straw for a long-battered Japanese economy, forcing politicians and policymakers finally to come to grips with the imperatives of reform. A strengthening of the euro might have a comparable effect on European authorities, forcing a rethinking of procyclical fiscal policies and pushing the European Central Bank to rethink its battle against a long-vanquished inflation. Most importantly, a weaker dollar would go a long way toward putting the world on notice that it can no longer avoid the imperatives of global rebalancing. US-centric global growth can only work for so long. There comes a time when the rest of the world has to carry its own weight. Given the ominous buildup of America's postbubble excesses, that time is at hand.

Figure 8.5 Dollar risk

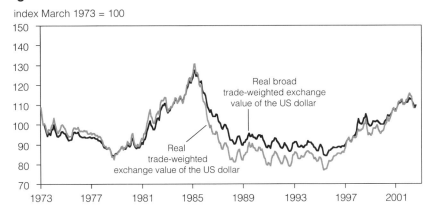

index March 1973 = 100

Note: Data for January of each year indicated.

Source: Federal Reserve.

What if the Dollar Doesn't Fall?

The Teflon-like US dollar, of course, seems largely unsympathetic to the urgency of the world's dilemma. After falling by about 6 percent in the first six months of 2002, the dollar retraced more than half its descent, as measured on a trade-weighted basis against the broadest possible basket of US trading partners (figure 8.5). The dollar currently (mid-December 2002) is only 3 percent below its late January highs, hardly enough to spur the global rebalancing that the world so desperately needs. (It has, however, weakened in the early days of 2003.) While a fundamentally overvalued dollar remains vulnerable to a sharp correction, trading action over the past year makes it abundantly clear that heightened global angst has the potential to put any such depreciation on hold. Needless to say, that's hardly a trivial consideration in light of intensified concerns over the possibility of a US double-dip recession and a war in Iraq. In a US-centric global economy, there is no "growth premium" for the rest of the world in the event of an American recessionary relapse. And a war in the Middle East and its concomitant threat to world oil supplies appears to have "safe haven" written all over it. For those reasons alone, the dollar may prove to be stubbornly resistant on the downside—thereby closing off the last option for an unbalanced global economy to find a new equilibrium.

Should the US dollar fail to correct, the noose can only tighten on a shaky global economy. Global rebalancing will then have to be vented by sharp corrections in other US assets, notably stocks and/or bonds. America will then find itself stuck between deflation and the unrelenting pressures of its postbubble excesses, and the rest of the world will find itself unduly dependent on the whims of an ever-fickle US growth dynamic. Nor will there be any realistic options for global policymakers to find a benign solution to this unrelenting buildup of global tensions. In the end, a long overdue rebalancing of a US-centric global economy is really the only way out. I continue to believe that a significant depreciation of the dollar offers the most realistic and least painful avenue for resolution. I remain convinced that, one way or another, the current disequilibrium in the global economy will eventually force a new equilibrium.

Gauging the Impacts

Martin Baily's paper in this volume confirms many of the conceptual points I have made above as far as the macro impact of a weaker dollar in concerned. I have to confess that I've never been too sympathetic to soft landings. Instead, I prefer the "fast dollar decline" scenario he describes as a more realistic assessment of what lies ahead. In that simulation, Baily finds that a 20 percent drop in the value of the dollar would reduce the level of real GDP by 1.2 percent by 2007, with personal consumption down over 5 percent and capital spending down nearly 12 percent over the same period. Higher interest rates would be the precipitating factor in this demand adjustment, with the federal funds rate going back to 10 percent over the next five years. One of his most important findings is that a sharp decline in the value of the dollar raises the CPI-based inflation rate by one full percentage point over each of the next five years. Such an outcome could well make a real difference in staving off deflationary pressures currently bearing down on the United States.

The one surprise in Baily's analysis is that the rest of the world doesn't do any better than the United States. However, a key assumption in this aspect of his research is that no meaningful policy actions are taken by foreign economies in order to stimulate their domestic demand. I remain hopeful that such actions will occur, as a dollar correction triggers the progrowth reforms noted above—in effect, sparking a global rebalancing that leads to a delinking of the rest of the world from the US economy. The good news is that, even if that's not the case, Baily estimates that the US current account deficit would be cut in half, thereby returning to 2.5 percent of GDP over the next five years. Needless to say, if I'm right and dollar weakness triggers progrowth policies elsewhere in the world, the US external deficit would undoubtedly shrink a good deal more.

Other Policy Actions

Of course I do not believe a weaker dollar is a panacea for all that ails the US or the global economies. Nor do I believe in competitive currency devaluation as a means toward any end. Yet an unbalanced world needs a realignment of relative prices, and a weaker dollar is the most sensible way to achieve this, in my opinion. It also happens to be the one option with the greatest potential to stave off America's deflationary endgame. But the dollar certainly can't do the job alone. Additional Fed policy stimulus may well be required to trigger this adjustment in the dollar. Such easing would reinforce the dollar-correction scenario I have in mind, but it would also be helpful in putting a floor on US domestic demand— yet another remedy to contain deflation. Nor would I shy away from another dose of fiscal stimulus in this climate, especially tax cuts aimed at middle-income workers.

The odds of outright deflation are now high enough, in my view, for policymakers to take extraordinary actions to prevent it. As the Fed's own research staff has duly noted, that's a key lesson from the Japanese experience that should not be lost on the United States or, for that matter, on any industrial economy.[1] There's always a risk that these actions might come too late to make a real difference for a postbubble economy. But at this point in time, the bigger risk comes from doing nothing. The time to act is now.

A lopsided world economy on the brink of deflation needs a major policy fix. Tensions on this order arise rarely. And they require a radical rethinking of policy options. In my view, a rethinking of America's strong-dollar policy is at the top of the list. The questions we ponder not only have academic interest: they could well hold the key to some of the most vexing problems the world has faced in 70 years.

---

1. See Alan Ahearne, Joseph Gagnon, Jane Haltmaier, Steve Kamin, et al., "Preventing Deflation: Lessons from Japan's Experience in the 1990s," Board of Governors of the Federal Reserve, International Finance Discussion Paper No. 729, Washington, June 2002.

9

The Impact of US External Adjustment on Japan

WILLIAM R. CLINE

In the late 1990s the United States entered once again into a period of large external current account deficits. By 2000 the deficit reached $410 billion, or 4.2 percent of GDP. This was even higher than the previous peak of 3.4 percent in 1987, at the end of a period when the overvaluation of the dollar and the external deficit were considered a sufficient threat to international economic stability that the G-7 had undertaken coordinated intervention beginning in 1985 to bring the dollar down from its high level.[1] In contrast, this time around US policy has been nonchalant about, or even welcoming of, the strong dollar and the large external deficit. In part this stance has reflected recognition that external resources were useful for meeting buoyant domestic demand without inflation in the late 1990s. In part it has reflected the policy view, especially in the Clinton administration, that a strong dollar is good for the US economy. Acceptance of large external deficits has also reflected recognition that in the late 1990s the US economy was providing a vital role as locomotive for the global economy, especially in view of weakness in Japan and emerging markets. Finally, in contrast to the 1980s, this time the draw on foreign resources has been associated with a boom in private domestic investment

William R. Cline is senior fellow jointly at the Institute for International Economics and the Center for Global Development in Washington, DC. During 1996-2001 while on leave from the Institute, he was deputy managing director and chief economist of the Institute of International Finance in Washington, DC. The author thanks Ceren Ozer for research assistance.

1. The US external deficit tends to respond to the exchange rate with a two-year lag (Cline 1989).

and consumption that overshadowed a move into fiscal surplus, and the absence of fiscal imbalance likely helped to depict the external imbalance as benign.

The premise of this conference, however, is that the large and potentially widening external deficit poses risks for the US economy, and that prudence requires thinking not only about what measures could narrow the deficit but also about what the ramifications will be for other key economies when adjustment does take place. One reason there is a limit to the external deficit is that there is a limit to the share of global capital flows and corresponding shares in foreigners' portfolios that the United States can plausibly command (Mann 2002). Another reason is that there is presumably a limit to the extent to which current policymakers should saddle future generations with external debt, defined broadly to refer to net liabilities in loans and bonds, portfolio equities, and direct investment. A third and related reason is the potential for a disruptive break in the dollar if the large external deficits and net liability buildup continue—a hard-landing scenario worth considering even if the 1980s fears of such an outcome proved exaggerated (Marris 1985). A fourth reason is that the strong dollar and the external deficit pose special problems for US manufacturing and agriculture, raising questions of long-term inefficiencies from distorted price signals for sectoral allocation of investment (even if macroeconomic policy can compensate in nontradable sectors to maintain full employment).

For all these reasons, it would seem reasonable to set as a goal of policy that the external deficit be curbed enough to stabilize the ratio of net external liabilities to GDP. It turns out that this target implies an aggressive reduction in the current account deficit. The US adjustment, in turn, implies that foreign trading partners will be faced with falling current account surpluses or rising current account deficits as the mirror image of the US deficit reduction. In this paper I examine the implications of this counterpart foreign adjustment for the case of Japan.

A focus on Japan is warranted for two principal reasons. First, as the largest surplus economy in terms of both current account and net international assets, Japan seems likely to be faced with picking up a major share of the surplus-reduction counterpart of the US deficit reduction. Second, because Japan's economy has been in extended stagnation or recession in recent years, there are reasons for concern about the impact on Japan's growth. A reduction in Japan's surplus resulting from a decline in exports and rise in imports unaccompanied by a rise in domestic demand would push the Japanese economy further into recession.

In this paper I first gauge the likely magnitudes of the US and Japanese external adjustments. I then consider the implications for Japanese economic performance and for the appropriate international policy approach to Japan's role in the global adjustment. First, however, it is necessary to review briefly the delicate position in which the Japanese economy currently stands.

The Japanese Economy at Risk

The prolonged weakness of the Japanese economy since the early 1990s has been examined in detail (see, e.g., Posen 1998 and Ahearne et al. 2002). There is a wide consensus about some of the causes, including collapse of the early 1990s asset price bubble, subsequent plunge in investment, failure to restore strength to the banking sector, and foreign pressures as the East Asian crisis affected a prime export market. There has been ample room for debate, however, on the proper policy remedies. As Japan has entered into deflation, and as nominal interest rates have approached zero, it could be argued that the conditions have come to resemble those of the Great Depression (Krugman 1998). Hence, some of the principles of Keynesian analysis might be thought to apply, including inefficacy of monetary policy and the need to adopt fiscal expansion to get the economy moving. At the same time, however, weak revenue and recurrent rounds of fiscal stimulus have brought a sharp escalation in the ratio of public debt to GDP, which from 1992 to 1999 rose from 65 percent to 120 percent in gross terms and from 40 percent to 85 percent on a net basis, excluding social security system assets (but also excluding potential liabilities from loan guarantees and bank support; International Monetary Fund 2001, 91).[2] This in turn has raised doubts about further fiscal expansionary measures, contributing to increased interest by many analysts in seeking further monetary expansion.[3]

The usual industrialized country policy dilemma of the 1970s and 1980s was the problem of stagflation: recessions triggered by oil shocks (for example) could not be easily addressed through monetary and fiscal expansion without risk of aggravating inflation. Japan has recently faced a different kind of policy dilemma, in which the fiscal stimulus desirable for recovery heightens uncertainty because of the public solvency concern, while policymakers are doubtful about monetary stimulus both because of the absence of the normal interest rate transmission mechanism and, apparently, a classic central-banker fear that too much monetary expansion could bring back excessive inflation.

---

2. In principle the net basis is more meaningful for fiscal solvency, but it is unclear to what extent the assets deducted in the Japanese public accounting are economically meaningful.

3. The usual manifestation of monetary ease, lower interest rates, would not result, as these are already close to zero, but several analysts consider that a firm commitment to expand the monetary base by central bank purchases of government bonds would bring about expectations of a return to mild inflation, in turn reversing the depressing effect of deflationary expectations on current consumption.

Whatever the merits of the official views and those of critics, there is little doubt that economic policy in Japan has faced and continues to face a quandary in which no solutions appear obvious and without risk. A resulting paralysis in macroeconomic policy has been accompanied by lethargic reform of the banking sector. As a result, despite repeated announcements of new forceful action, the ratio of nonperforming loans to bank capital (including unrealized capital gains) has continued to escalate from 69.3 percent in March 1999 to 146.9 percent in March 2002 (Bank of Japan 2002b). The plunge of the Nikkei 225 stock index (from 11,025 at the end of March 2002 to 9,619 at the end of August; Bank of Japan 2002b) has aggravated this weakness by virtually eliminating unrealized capital gains on the banking system's large holdings of equities. Indeed, the most recent, and perhaps most dramatic, manifestation of the dire condition of the Japanese economy is the decision of the Bank of Japan to purchase stocks held by Japanese banks to help ensure that their disposal of stocks does not further depress the stock market and push them below, or further below, international capital requirements.[4]

This brief review is intended simply to sharpen the context for this study by highlighting the serious challenges and uncertainties facing the Japanese economy and its policymakers. No remedy will be suggested here, but these circumstances do mean that at least the timing of the Japanese response to the US external correction should be such as to avoid, as far as possible, tipping the economy further into recession.

Finally, two additional points are warranted to provide perspective. First, the Japanese economy in the 1990s has disappointed primarily because of its sharp slowdown from excellent performance in previous decades. In absolute terms, the performance looks less devastating. Thus, between the decades 1980-90 and 1990-2000, growth of real GDP relative to available labor force accelerated from 1.7 percent to 2.2 percent in the United States but plunged from 2.8 percent to 0.6 percent in Japan.[5] Even so, Japan was only slightly behind the pace for Italy (0.8 percent in the 1990s), although significantly lower than the average for Germany and

---

4. Although unprecedented in the industrialized countries, central bank stock purchases from the market have a precedent in Hong Kong's monetary authority purchases in the late 1990s, although these were not from banks. Japan's proposal amounts to a specific way to increase the money supply that at the same time helps avoid further weakening of the banking system. The implicit potential subsidy to the banks, if the stock market falls further, is equivalent to a public-sector bailout, something the political system has been unprepared to do by the direct route of legislated subsidies. The usual inflationary risk of using central bank financing to support a weak banking system, instead of appropriated government expenditures, is absent in this case because the problem is not inflation but deflation.

5. This is perhaps the best gauge of economic performance. GDP growth alone does not reflect the fact that some countries have rapidly growing labor and others do not. Productivity per worker is not a satisfactory gauge because it considers only the employed.

France (1.4 percent).[6] Nonetheless, Japan's fall from the top to the bottom of the industrialized country growth league poses special concerns because of its large economic size and its important role in the market for exports from Asian emerging market economies in particular.

Second, it is worth underscoring that the by now long-standing failure of macroeconomic adjustment in Japan is centered on the proven inability to replace foreign demand with sustained growth in domestic demand as the engine of economic expansion. Thus, from 1990 to 2000, real domestic private consumption expanded by an amount equivalent to only 9 percent of 1990 real GDP (calculated from Economic and Social Research Institute 2002). Real gross private investment was actually lower at the end of the decade than at the beginning, falling by 5.6 percent, an amount equivalent to 1.4 percent of 1990 real GDP. In contrast, real net exports rose over this period by 114 percent, or by an amount equal to 1.5 percent of 1990 real GDP. As the United States enters into external adjustment, Japan will find it increasingly difficult to rely on foreign demand as the source of growth.

Relative Productivity Growth: Deus ex Machina?

Finally, before turning to the main estimates of this paper, it is important to consider the argument that the US external deficit can be justified by a rise in the gap between the rate of productivity growth in the United States and that abroad. Some have argued that the fundamental equilibrium exchange rate for the dollar has risen because of the rise in relative US productivity growth (see Michael Rosenberg's paper in this volume). Similarly, US officials have recently tended to cast doubt on the importance of a large deficit on the grounds that it reflects investment inflow in response to opportunities arising from more rapid productivity growth.[7]

While it is true in principle that increased relative productivity growth and hence relative return to capital should imply a period of increased capital inflows and thus larger current account deficits, there are several reasons to be skeptical that this argument justifies US external deficits on the current scale. First, it is no longer true that the deficit is mainly financing investment. The US investment boom of 1997-2000 has given way to an investment bust, yet the current account deficit has continued

---

6. Calculated from World Bank (2002, 2001).

7. In contrast, the International Monetary Fund (2002c) has become increasingly emphatic in raising concerns about the risks posed by the rising US current account deficit.

to rise.[8] Second, the productivity-gap argument implicitly requires a permanent relative shift, yet historically there have been alternating periods of rising and falling US productivity growth relative to Europe and Japan, and there is no assurance that the recent gap will persist. Third, the magnitudes involved are incommensurate. Few would argue that the gap between annual US productivity growth and that in Europe in particular has risen by more than, say, one percentage point. Yet if the net foreign liability position is to stabilize at about 25 percent of GDP for the United States, then an extra percentage point of growth warrants an increase of only 0.25 percent of GDP in the sustainable current account deficit—not an increase of some 3 to 4 percentage points, as has actually occurred since the early 1990s.[9]

Fourth, the classic economic argument on the issue is the "Balassa-Samuelson effect," whereby an increase in productivity growth of the export sector leads to a real appreciation of the exchange rate (Balassa 1964). But in this effect, the sequencing is the reverse: the increase in productivity growth first leads to a surge in exports and a rise in the trade surplus, which in turn bids up the currency. Recent US experience has been just the opposite, as the capital market has bid up the dollar despite a widening trade deficit. In sum, to the extent that rising US relative productivity growth has played a role, there are good reasons to think that the capital market has caused a temporary overshooting of both the real value of the dollar and the size of the US current account deficit beyond longer-term sustainable levels. Indeed, the "new economy" productivity argument helped disguise the unsustainability of what turned out to be a bubble in the US stock market, and the same argument may well have done the same thing for the dollar and the US current account deficit.

Gauging the US External Adjustment Task

Undertaking the objective of stabilizing the ratio of US net foreign liabilities to GDP would mean seeking to halt what has been a sharp rise over the past decade. At the end of 2001, gross US foreign assets stood at $6.86 trillion and gross foreign liabilities at $9.17 trillion, leaving the net liability position at $2.31 trillion, or 22.9 percent of GDP (Bureau of Economic Analysis 2002a, 2002b). This represents a major escalation from net foreign liabilities of only 4.4 percent of GDP in 1991. Correspondingly, at the end

---

8. From 1991 to 2000, private fixed investment rose from 13.4 percent of GDP to 17.9 percent. The rate fell to 15.7 percent in 2001, however, and to 15.2 percent in the first half of 2002 (Bureau of Economic Analysis 2002b).

9. The relationship between the ceiling current account deficit and the target net liability position relative to GDP is discussed below.

Figure 9.1 Net foreign asset position, 1991-2000

billions of US dollars

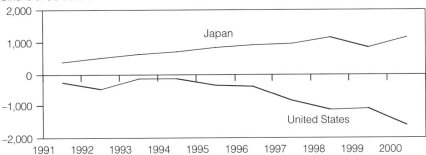

Sources: IMF (2002a); BEA (2002a).

of 2000, Japan's gross foreign assets stood at $3.0 trillion and gross foreign liabilities at $1.8 trillion, for a net international asset position of $1.2 trillion, or 24.3 percent of GDP (International Monetary Fund 2002a). This position was also a strong increase from 11.0 percent of GDP in 1991, although the upswing in the international balance sheet for Japan was a somewhat smaller share of GDP than the downswing for the United States (figure 9.1).

So far the eroding international asset position of the United States has shown up only mildly in the capital income accounts. Thus, net capital income in the US current account swung from +$27 billion in 1991 to −$8 billion in the first half of 2002 (annual rate), as Japan's net capital income rose from $26.0 billion in 1991 to $70.1 billion in 2001 (Bureau of Economic Analysis 2002a; International Monetary Fund 2002a). A total downswing of $35 billion in the US capital income account, compared to a total net foreign asset downswing of $2.1 trillion (from the end of 1990 to the end of 2001), implies a surprisingly low average rate of return of 1.6 percent. So far, then, the economic cost of rising international indebtedness for the United States has been muted, reflecting a higher implied rate of return on foreign assets than on foreign liabilities. This differential appears to have been declining, however, suggesting the potential for a rising implicit return on net foreign liabilities (and rising deficit on capital income relative to net foreign liabilities) in the future.[10]

---

10. For 1991-97, capital income averaged 5.72 percent on US gross foreign assets, and capital payments 4.46 percent on US gross foreign liabilities, for a differential of 1.26 percent. These rates moved closer by 2001-02 to 3.63 percent on assets and 2.78 percent on liabilities, for a differential of 0.85 percent. For its part, Japan had higher rates of return on both its foreign assets and liabilities through the period but without much differential (with returns of about 7 percent on both assets and liabilities). Note that in July 2002 the official US data series both for foreign assets and liabilities and for capital income receipts and payments were substantially revised, to show a much slower decline in net foreign assets and, especially, net foreign capital income than previously reported.

Figure 9.2 Current account and change in net foreign assets, 1992-2000

billions of US dollars

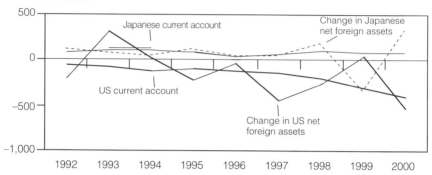

Sources: IMF (2002a); BEA (2002a).

The changes in the net foreign asset positions of both the United States and Japan have broadly tracked their respective current account balances, though with big swings year to year (figure 9.2). This means that the accounting in the external statistics is broadly consistent with the conceptual economic requirement that in order to arrest the buildup of net external liabilities the United States will need to curb its current account deficit correspondingly.

To stabilize net foreign liabilities at, say, 25 percent of GDP, then at the margin the rise in the net foreign debt should not exceed this fraction of the rise in nominal GDP. Suppose the latter is 3 percent real growth plus 2.5 percent inflation, or 5.5 percent. This means the annual current account deficit should not exceed $0.25 \times 5.5 = 1.37$ percent of GDP, or $143 billion at present-scale nominal US GDP. This is an ambitious target, considering that the deficit reached $410 billion in 2000, eased only modestly to $393 billion in recession year 2001, and by the second quarter of 2002 was running at an annual rate of $520 billion, or 5.0 percent of GDP (Bureau of Economic Analysis 2002a, 2002b).

To identify the size of the economic external adjustment, it is first necessary to separate out that portion of the deficit that merely represents statistical illusion. From 1995-97 to 2000 the world current account discrepancy rose from an average of $-$31 billion (0.23 percent of total world current account transactions) to $-$133 billion (0.9 percent; International Monetary Fund 2002c, 202). The United States accounted for 13 percent of world merchandise exports plus imports in 1996, rising to 16 percent in 2000 (International Monetary Fund 2002b). Applying a US world trade share of 15 percent to the $190 billion world current account discrepancy projected for 2002 by the International Monetary Fund (IMF) (table 9.1), the recorded US current account deficit is currently exaggerated by about $30 billion. At the same time, this allocation also indicates that only a

Table 9.1 Current account balances (billions of US dollars)

	1994	1995	1996	1997	1998	1999	2000	2001	2002f
United States	−118.2	−105.8	−117.8	−128.4	−203.8	−292.9	−410.3	−393.4	−479.6
European Union	10.1	48.3	79.0	108.6	68.5	13.7	−35.1	3.2	50.7
Japan	130.6	111.4	65.7	96.6	119.1	114.5	119.6	87.8	119.3
Other advanced economies[a]	−14.1	−5.8	10.5	5.7	−4.0	7.7	53.2	56.9	41.5
NIAE[b]	12.9	2.8	−3.5	10.8	67.4	60.9	45.5	57.1	57.9
Developing:	−84.6	−95.5	−74.7	−58.0	−85.1	−10.2	66.7	39.6	18.9
Africa	−11.1	−16.8	−6.4	−7.4	−20.1	−14.3	5.4	1.3	−7.2
China, India	6.0	−3.9	1.1	33.9	24.6	12.5	16.1	17.3	19.4
Other Asia	−25.0	−38.6	−40.0	−25.0	22.7	33.5	29.3	22.1	14.1
Latin America	−52.2	−36.5	−40.0	−67.2	−90.8	−56.7	−47.8	−52.9	−32.6
Middle East, Turkey	−2.3	0.2	10.6	7.7	−21.5	14.9	63.7	51.8	25.2
Transition	2.4	−2.3	−16.8	−24.1	−29.4	−1.9	27.1	11.8	1.4
Discrepancy	−61.1	−46.9	−57.6	11.2	−67.3	−108.0	−133.4	−136.9	−189.9
As percent of world current account transactions	−0.6	−0.4	−0.4	0.1	−0.5	−0.8	−0.9	−0.9	−1.2

f = forecast

a. Excluding NIAE.
b. NIAE = newly industrialized Asian economies: Korea, Taiwan, Hong Kong, Singapore.

Source: IMF, *World Economic Outlook*, September 2002.

Figure 9.3 Current account: US deficit and Japanese surplus, 1991-2001

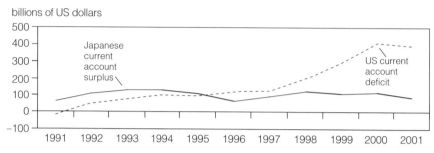

billions of US dollars

Sources: IMF (2002a); BEA (2002a).

small part of the increase in the US external deficit in recent years has been attributable to the widening global discrepancy. Thus, from the 1995-97 average to 2000, 15 percent of the increase in the global discrepancy represented only $24 billion, or only 8 percent of the increase in the US current account deficit from $117 billion to $410 billion in this period.

If we assume that the target current account deficit ceiling of one-fourth of nominal GDP growth should be attained by 2005, then the target that year is approximately $170 billion.[11] Adding the statistical overstatement, the corresponding target for the recorded deficit would be approximately $200 billion in 2005. Assuming a benchmark US current account deficit of around $480 billion for 2002,[12] attainment of a $200 billion deficit by 2005 would require a US current account adjustment amounting to about $280 billion, phased in over three years. This US adjustment, then, can serve as a benchmark for the implied effects for the Japanese economy.

Extent of Japan's Share in the Counterpart

The first step in gauging the magnitude of the corresponding counterpart adjustment in Japan's current account surplus is to ask what share would be appropriate under "normal" circumstances. Any appropriate departure in implied Japanese adjustment in view of Japan's prolonged recession can then be considered separately.

Somewhat surprisingly, over the past several years there has been anything but a lockstep pattern relating changes in Japan's current account surplus to changes in the US current account deficit (see figure 9.3).

---

11. Assuming 5 percent nominal GDP growth this year and 5.5 percent thereafter, nominal US GDP reaches $12.25 trillion in 2005.

12. For the first half, the cumulative total was $242.5 billion. If the second half returns to the first-quarter rate, the total for the year will stand at $467 billion. If it maintains the second-quarter rate, the total will be $502 billion.

Although the two moved broadly together in 1991-94 and again in 1996-98, since 1997 Japan's surplus has remained relatively flat at about $100 billion while the US deficit has mushroomed from $140 billion to about $400 billion in 2000-01.

Part of the lack of widening in Japan's surplus can be attributed to Japan's share in the growing overstatement of the global deficit. Even so, this effect is relatively small. Japan's share in global trade turnover in 2000 was 6.3 percent. Applied to the IMF's projected global discrepancy for 2002, Japan's surplus this year is likely to be understated by only $12 billion. The recorded current account surplus was running at an annual rate of about $120 billion in the first seven months of 2002 (Bank of Japan 2002a). The surprising stagnation of Japan's surplus in the face of the ballooning US deficit also likely reflects Japan's trade surplus erosion vis-à-vis East Asia following the regional currency crisis.

Going forward, it is implausible that Japan's surplus can remain unchanged while the US deficit declines by some $280 billion after adjustment for global statistical discrepancy. What is the right Japan share in the counterpart adjustment? Various benchmarks come to mind. The first is simply: where are the present current account surpluses to be found? Table 9.2 reports the major current account deficits and surpluses in 2000 for about 80 economies. Japan's surplus that year ($117 billion) amounted to 25 percent of the sum of surpluses for all surplus countries. (The US deficit of $410 billion was 65 percent of the sum of major deficits by country.)

The current account surplus benchmark, moreover, could point to an even higher Japanese share in the counterpart adjustment. Some important "surplus" countries are not in a particularly strong position to experience a reduction in their surpluses, because these are already being used to finance capital flight. Russia and Venezuela alone account for about $60 billion in surpluses that are likely already earmarked for financing capital flight. If these two countries are excluded, Japan's share of the global surplus of surplus economies rises to 26.7 percent.

Another benchmark is Japan's share in global trade turnover. As shown in figure 9.4, whereas the US share in global trade turnover rose from about 13 percent in 1991 to 16 percent by 2000, Japan's share fell from 7.2 percent to 5.8 percent, an indication of Japan's shrinking role in the world economy. (Over this same period, Japan's GDP fell from 58 percent of US GDP to 48 percent, and further to 41 percent in 2001.) Excluding the United States from the pool of trade for calibrating the counterparty adjustment, Japan's share in non-US global trade turnover (the white bar in the figure) stood at about 6 percent in 2001.

Still another gauge is Japan's share in bilateral US trade turnover, which was about 11 percent in 2000 (table 9.3). Unfortunately, a large block of US trade is with a relatively rigid dollar area. China and Hong Kong have

Table 9.2 Principal current account surplus and deficit countries
(billions of dollars, 2000)

Surplus		Deficit	
Colombia	0.4	United States	−410.4
Kazakhstan	0.4	United Kingdom	−28.8
Ecuador	0.9	Brazil	−24.6
Vietnam	1.0	Spain	−19.2
Syrian Arab Republic	1.1	Germany	−18.7
Ukraine	1.5	Mexico	−17.8
Yemen, Republic of	1.9	Australia	−15.4
Denmark	2.5	Portugal	−11.0
Oman	3.3	Poland	−10.0
Sweden	6.6	Greece	−9.8
Indonesia	8.0	Turkey	−9.8
Malaysia	8.4	Argentina	−9.0
Philippines	8.5	Italy	−5.8
Hong Kong	8.9	Austria	−4.9
Taiwan	8.9	India	−4.2
Finland	9.0	New Zealand	−2.7
Thailand	9.3	Czech Republic	−2.2
Netherlands	11.2	Peru	−1.6
Korea	12.2	Israel	−1.4
Iran	12.6	Romania	−1.4
Venezuela	13.1	Hungary	−1.3
Saudi Arabia	14.3	Guatemala	−1.0
Kuwait	14.7	Dominican Republic	−1.0
Canada	18.6	Chile	−1.0
France	20.4	Egypt	−1.0
China	20.5	Panama	−0.9
Singapore	21.8	Tunisia	−0.8
Norway	23.0	Mozambique	−0.8
Switzerland	32.5	Bulgaria	−0.7
Russia	46.4	Slovak Republic	−0.7
Japan	116.9	Lithuania	−0.7
Others	3.9	Uruguay	−0.6
Total	**462.8**	Zambia	−0.6
		South Africa	−0.6
		Sudan	−0.6
		Honduras	−0.5
		Nicaragua	−0.5
		Morocco	−0.5
		Latvia	−0.5
		Tanzania	−0.5
		Bolivia	−0.5
		El Salvador	−0.4
		Ghana	−0.4
		Estonia	−0.3
		Bangladesh	−0.3
		Jamaica	−0.3
		Kenya	−0.2
		Barbados	−0.1
		Paraguay	−0.1
		Pakistan	−0.1
		Total	**−626.3**

Source: IMF (2002a).

Figure 9.4 World trade turnover, 1991-2001 (percent)

percent

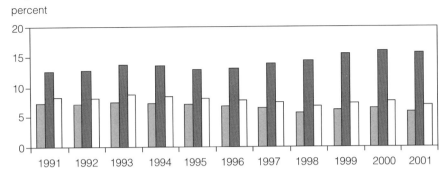

Note: Light gray bar represents Japan's share of world trade turnover. Dark gray bar represents US share of world trade turnover. White bar represents Japan's share of non-US world trade turnover.

Source: IMF (2002a).

Table 9.3 Trade shares in 2000 by partner (percent)

	United States			Japan		
	Exports	Imports	Turnover	Exports	Imports	Turnover
United States	0	0	0	30.1	19.1	25.2
Japan	8.4	12.1	10.6	0	0	0
European Union	21.3	18.0	19.3	16.4	12.3	14.6
Canada	22.6	18.5	20.1	1.6	2.3	1.9
Other industrialized economies	3.3	2.1	2.5	2.8	5.7	4.1
Mexico	14.1	10.9	12.1	1.1	0.6	0.9
China	2.1	8.6	6.1	6.3	14.5	10.0
Hong Kong	1.9	1.0	1.3	5.7	0.4	3.4
Korea	3.5	3.3	3.4	6.4	5.4	6.0
Other Asia	9.8	12.3	11.4	22.8	21.5	22.2
Other Latin America	7.6	6.1	6.7	2.8	2.2	2.5
Middle East	3.0	3.3	3.2	2.2	13.0	7.0
Rest of world	2.4	3.9	3.3	1.8	2.9	2.3
Total	100	100	100	100	100	100
Dollar area:	18.0	20.4	19.5	43.2	34.7	39.5
United States	0.0	0.0	0.0	30.1	19.1	25.2
China and Hong Kong	4.0	9.5	7.4	12.0	15.0	13.3
Mexico	14.1	10.9	12.1	1.1	0.6	0.9

Source: IMF (2002d).

a de facto peg to the dollar. Mexico's economy is in lockstep with that of the United States, and until recently its currency has been even stronger than the dollar. These three economies alone account for 20 percent of US trade turnover. Malaysia has a de jure peg, as do Ecuador and some others, boosting the share further. So whereas Japan accounts for 11 percent of total US trade turnover, it probably represents about 14 percent of US trade turnover excluding that with rigid dollar-area countries. Of course it might prove appropriate and even essential for some key economies, such as China, to participate in a general appreciation of

Table 9.4 Alternative benchmarks for Japan's prospective share in the US current account adjustment

Share	Percent
Share in current account change from 1995 to 2001	0
Share in sum of current account surpluses for surplus countries	24-27
Share in global non-US trade turnover	6
Share in US trade turnover	11
Share in US trade turnover excluding rigid dollar-area countries	14

Figure 9.5 Japan's exchange rate, 1981-2002

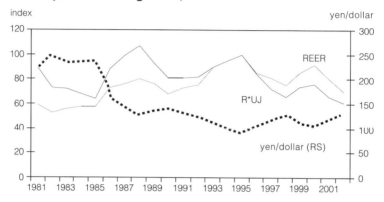

REER = real effective exchange rate; R*UJ = bilateral real exchange rate, yen/dollar (both 1995 = 100, left scale)

Sources: IMF (2002a)

foreign currencies against the dollar to permit US external adjustment. Even so, resistance can be expected from these governments.

Overall, the benchmarks seem to suggest a range of 10 to 25 percent for Japan's counterparty share in the US current account adjustment (table 9.4), when the latter is already calibrated to exclude any "free ride" from global discrepancy disappearance. On this basis, if we assume a $280 billion target reduction in the US current account deficit (after taking account of "water" in the reported magnitude from the global statistical discrepancy), and if 10 to 25 percent of the counterpart foreign adjustment is Japan's share, then Japan faces a current account adjustment ranging from $28 billion to $70 billion, before taking account of the special recessionary circumstances.

Implications for the Yen

In examining the implications of the Japanese external adjustment for the yen, it is useful first to recall where the yen stands and where it has come from (figure 9.5). In 1981 the yen was at 220 to the dollar. It weakened

Figure 9.6   Japan: Ratio of nonoil imports to exports, and lagged real exchange rate, 1980-2001 (percent and index)

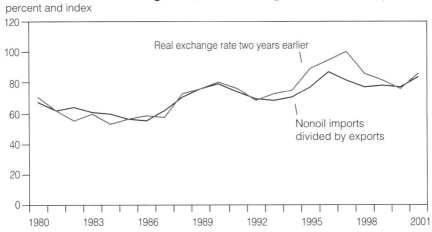

percent and index

Sources: IMF (2002a); Ministry of Public Management (2002); Statistics Canada (2002); and UNCTAD (2002).

to about 240 at the dollar's peak in 1985, then strengthened to 94 in 1995 before weakening during the 1996-2002 period of the Rubin-Summers strong-dollar policy (which was buttressed, from the exchange rate standpoint, by the US equity bubble and the corresponding inducement to capital inflows). The yen reached 130 (year average) in 1998, then strengthened to 108 in 2000 (the one recent year of nonrecession Japanese growth) before weakening again to an average of 132 in the first quarter of 2002 as the markets reacted to Japan's renewed recession. Since then (not shown) it has risen to an average of about 124 in the second quarter and 120 in the third as part of the retreat of the dollar and in response to some improvement in growth expectations from rising Japanese exports.

Japan's inflation has systematically been less than that of the United States, so the secular real appreciation of the yen is less than the nominal rate might imply. Figure 9.5 reports the IMF's real effective exchange rate (REER) for Japan (1995 = 100), based on relative unit labor costs, and a corresponding bilateral real exchange rate against the dollar deflating by consumer price indices. There are obvious cycles associated with the dollar cycle (Japan's REER was at a trough in 1985, rising sharply through 1988 after the dollar adjustment, rising to a new high by 1995, and then broadly falling with the late 1990s US boom).

Despite the swings, there has been a secular appreciation. A simple regression of the REER on time for 1981 through the first quarter of 2002 yields: REER = 59.3 (13.8) + 1.40T (4.3), in which the t-statistics are shown in parentheses. By this equation, the historical-trend real exchange rate for 2002 should average 90.1. That corresponds to a nominal yen of 103 per dollar for 2002 on average. So the yen remains undervalued compared to its historical trend of two decades. The trend also means that on average the REER for Japan appreciates 1 to 2 percent annually.

The relevance of the yen to Japan's external surplus depends, of course, on whether the exchange rate influences trade. The evidence suggests that it does. As shown in figure 9.6, there has been a close relationship between the ratio of non-oil merchandise imports relative to exports in a given year, on the one hand, and the level of the real exchange rate two years before, on the other.

In previous work I have presented econometric models for forecasting Japan's current account (Cline 1995, 1989).[13] These models are in the tradition of what Krugman (1991) has called the "Massachusetts Avenue" model (after the addresses of institutions in Cambridge, Massachusetts, and Washington, DC). This approach relates exports and imports to the relative price between home and foreign goods as affected by the exchange rate; exports are further related to foreign demand growth and imports to domestic demand growth. A key element in this approach is the assumption that a change in the nominal exchange rate tends to move the real exchange rate (in the same direction) rather than being largely or fully neutralized by a compensating change in domestic prices (contrary to the "law of one price" view). Krugman documents the close relationship of real to nominal exchange rate changes from the early 1980s through 1991 period.[14]

The appendix sets forth the structure of the reduced form model (RFM) and reports results of reestimation of the model through the second quarter of 2000. It also considers what values the model's parameters would take if instead "stylized" parameters from the literature were applied for the price and income elasticities and pass-through ratios. Table 9.5 translates the estimates of the reestimated and stylized models into impact parameters measuring the change in Japan's current account for a 1 percent change in the real exchange rate, in domestic growth, and in foreign growth. These parameters refer to the full effects after the two-year lags

---

13. Cline (1995) estimates the reduced form model (RFM), and Cline (1989) estimates the external adjustment with growth (EAG) model.

14. Obstfeld (2002) has noted that there have been historical rounds of "pessimism over the gross benefits of flexible exchange rate" dating back to the 1950s, when "elasticity pessimism" was used as one factor in supporting the Bretton Woods fixed exchange rate regime. He suggests that a recent round of pessimism, based on "extremely low and slow pass-through of exchange rates to consumer prices . . . stems from oversimplified modeling strategies" and concludes that the simplest models may remain relatively reliable as policy guides. He notes, however, that the transmission mechanism from exchange rate change to trade change may be different from the traditional model. He emphasizes that it may be firms, especially multinational firms allocating production geographically, whose decisions are central rather than consumers, and firms respond to the real exchange rate measured by relative unit costs. He also emphasizes that import prices paid at the point of entry may behave very differently from CPI prices of imported goods.

Table 9.5 Japan's current account impact parameters
(billions of US dollars)

	Model			
Impact of:	EAG89R	RFM95R	RFM02ES	RFM02ST
1 percent increase in real exchange rate	−4.4	−2.5	−1.3	−2.2
1 percent increase in growth rate sustained for one year:				
Domestic	−6.3	−3.4	−5.0	−3.8
Foreign	n.a.	3.5	1.3	3.1

EAG = Economic Adjustment with Growth Model
ES = estimated
n.a. = not applicable
R = rescaled
RFM = Reduced Form Model
ST = stylized

are completed (in the initial year there can instead be J-curve effects going the opposite direction, for exchange rate change). The table also reports the corresponding impact parameters from Cline (1995) after appropriate scaling up to levels consistent with the change in the trade base from the earlier model (1994 levels) to the average of 2000-01.[15]

One important feature of the rescaled estimates is that they are little changed from the 1994 base used in the 1995 model. This reflects the minimal export growth and modest import growth in dollar terms from 1994 to 2000-01.[16] This is another manifestation of the relative shrinkage of Japan in the world economy.

A provocative pattern of the estimated impact parameters scaled to 2000-01 is that they have shown a successive decline for the real exchange rate impact from the 1989 model to the 1995 model and now the 2002 model. The decline in the first period may reflect model differences, but in the second period the model structure is the same. At the least this trend suggests mild evidence on the side of increasing "elasticity pessimism" rather than of increasing elasticity optimism.[17]

---

15. Scale factors are from 1994 base to average 2000-01 base, as follows. For the exchange rate impact, sum of exports and nonoil imports, goods and nonfactor services; for domestic growth, imports of goods and nonfactor services; for foreign growth, exports of goods and nonfactor services.

16. Thus, whereas for the United States the dollar value of imports (goods and nonfactor services) rose 68.9 percent and exports 46.2 percent over this period, for Japan the respective increases were 21.2 percent and 2.8 percent. The scale factors from 1994 to 2000-01 are: exchange rate effect, 1.2; domestic growth, 1.17; foreign growth, 1.24.

17. What amounts to the excess of the sum of the import and export price elasticities above the Marshall-Lerner threshold of unity (after taking account of pass-through; see the appendix) has fallen from about 0.6 to about 0.3 in the RFM95 and RFM02 estimates.

Table 9.6 Alternative scenarios for Japan's external adjustment

	A	B	C	D	E
US adjustment target (billions of US dollars)	280	280	280	280	200
Japan's share:					
Percent change	15	15	15	25	10
Amount (billions of US dollars)	42	42	42	70	20
Accomplished by:					
Real exchange rate					
Percent change	18.0	11.9	5.9	29.9	−3.5
Amount (billions of US dollars)	42.0	27.9	13.8	70.0	−8.2
Domestic growth change:					
Year-percentage points	0	3	6	0	6
Amount (billions of US dollars)	0	14.1	28.2	0	28.2

Conversely, the 2002 version of the RFM shows a higher impact for domestic growth (where the elasticity has risen from 0.92 to 1.3). This is consistent with the broad image of Japan as a more open economy today than in the past. In contrast, the impact of a percent change in foreign growth has fallen, though this is likely because a sharp reduction in the elasticity (from 0.99 to 0.33) primarily reflects a shift toward greater inclusion of rapidly growing developing countries (especially China and Korea) in the 2002 version of the model estimates. Ironically, the new estimates seem to suggest a Houthakker-Magee elasticity asymmetry for Japan like that traditionally seen for the United States (exports grow more slowly in response to foreign income growth than imports in response to domestic growth), although the likelihood is that the new estimates reported in the appendix understate the export elasticity.

Taking a weighted average of the estimates in table 9.5 giving greater weight to the 2002 estimated RFM, the central estimates for Japan's current account impact parameters may be placed at $2.3 billion for a 1 percent change in the real exchange rate; $4.7 billion for 1 percent additional domestic growth for one year; and $2.3 billion for 1 percent additional foreign growth for one year.[18]

Using these impact parameters, it is possible to consider several broad alternative scenarios for external adjustment as Japan's counterpart to US external adjustment. Table 9.6 reports five scenarios. The first three are the principal cases for consideration, and the fourth and fifth are more in the nature of sensitivity analysis. The central target for US adjustment is to reduce the annual current account deficit by $280 billion by three

---

18. The weights are 0.4 for RFM02ES and 0.2 for each of the others, for the exchange rate and domestic growth effects; and 0.5 for RFM02ES and 0.25 for each of the others, for foreign growth effects (where there is no EAG89R estimate available).

years from now, as discussed above. The first three scenarios all assume that Japan's share of this adjustment is 15 percent ($42 billion), in the middle of the ranges identified in table 9.4. In comparison, in the first seven months of 2002 the actual current account surplus has been running at a rate of $120 billion annually, so this target would shrink the surplus by about one-third.

In variant A, there is no change from Japan's baseline growth, which is probably on the order of -0.5 percent in 2002 and 1.5 to 2 percent thereafter (year over year; see, e.g., Mussa 2002). With no acceleration of the growth baseline, all adjustment must be carried out by real appreciation of the yen on a trade-weighted basis. Applying the impact parameter, the yen must rise in real terms by 18 percent. The required adjustment on the exchange rate side is successively reduced in scenarios B and C by more ambitious targets for acceleration of Japanese domestic growth. In variant C, over a three-year period growth is sustained at 2 percentage points annually higher than the baseline (or at an annual average of about 3.5 to 4 percent). The 6 year-percentage points applied to the impact parameter contribute a $28 billion reduction in the surplus, leaving only $14 billion to be accomplished by real appreciation, which in turn can be accomplished by a rise of only about 6 percent in the real yen.

Scenario D considers an extreme variant in which Japan must take on 25 percent of the share in the US external adjustment, calling for a reduction in Japan's current account surplus by $70 billion (about 60 percent of the current level). Japan's economy remains stuck at low growth in this variant, so there is no contribution from domestic growth acceleration. The result is that real appreciation must reach 30 percent to attain the target adjustment. Scenario E considers the opposite extreme of easy adjustment. The US current account target is much less ambitious, at a $200 billion reduction. Japan's share is at the low end of the reasonable range, at only 10 percent. Japanese growth rises by the two percentage points over the full three years (as in scenario C). Under these circumstances, the yen does not need to decline at all, but instead can appreciate by 3.5 percent while still meeting the target of reducing Japan's current account deficit by $20 billion.

The most realistic of these scenarios would seem to be A and B. It should be pointed out that the implied rise of the yen against the dollar is larger than the rise in the real effective exchange rate. The United States accounts for almost half of Japan's exports. So if all other countries appreciate against the dollar in real terms by v percent and Japan does not appreciate at all against the dollar, Japan's real exchange rate falls by about $0.5v$ percent. Suppose that in the international adjustment process it will require a trade-weighted real depreciation of the dollar by about 15 percent.[19] If y is the appreciation of the yen against the dollar and z is

---

19. A rescaling of the RFM95 model for the United States, similar to that here for Japan, generates a real exchange rate impact parameter of a $17 billion adjustment for each percentage point real appreciation, yielding a required depreciation of 16 percent for a target adjustment of $280 billion. Note, however, that this impact estimate is probably on the high end of the range of international estimates.

the yen's appreciation against the rest of the world, then in scenario A, Japan's 18 percent effective appreciation would comprise: $x = 18 = 0.5y + 0.5(3)$; $y = 33$. Here, Japan's 18 percent appreciation in comparison with 15 percent by non-US rest of world means a 3 percent appreciation against these other countries ($z = 3$), so the real appreciation against the dollar must be 33 percent. For example, an appreciation of this magnitude would take the yen from its current rate of 122 to the dollar to 92 to the dollar. The corresponding calculation for scenario B generates a yen at 101 to the dollar.[20] The latter outcome turns out to place the yen at close to the level that would be consistent with its historical trend in real terms over the past two decades (as discussed above).

Taking Japan's Recession into Account

Many would argue, however, that the last thing Japan needs now is an appreciation of the yen, as the export sector seems to be the one source of recent buoyancy in a precarious economy. The converse of the special-exemption argument is the view that Japan cannot indefinitely be given a free ride in the process of international adjustment and be allowed chronically to "export its unemployment" to the rest of the world.

Cyclical Adjustment in Exchange Rate Policy

Treatment of divergent points in the business cycle within the framework of fundamental equilibrium exchange rates (FEERs), as proposed by Williamson (1983), allows for tailoring the adjustment to the circumstances. In particular, for an undervalued exchange rate in an economy in recession, the proper adjustment would be to expand fiscal stimulus, as this would tend to obtain internal adjustment while boosting interest rates and the currency and hence also contributing to external adjustment. In Japan's present circumstances, however, the problem is that the markets are concerned about the high ratio of public debt to GDP. Raising the fiscal deficit could raise the government default risk premium, partially offsetting the stimulus.

FEER adjustment also can be thought of as appropriately calibrated in terms of structural—or full-employment—exchange rates. In this approach, for a country in recession, undervaluation of the exchange rate relative to the FEER would be permitted until the economy has recovered. In one version of this formulation, where there is a wide band (e.g., ± 15 percent) around the FEER, a country in recession would be expected to

---

20. Or: $0.5y + 0.5(3) = 11.9$; $y = 20.8$ percent increase in the yen against the dollar.

be near the lower (depreciated) edge of the band, whereas a country in over-full employment would be expected to be toward the upper edge.

Financial Market Effects?

A key related question is whether the strength of the yen acts as a major signal affecting financial markets in Japan. The weakness of Japan's stock market in particular is of concern, considering not only that it likely affects consumer expectations and business investment plans but also that stock valuations affect bank capital because of the large stock holdings of Japanese banks (recently estimated at about ¥40 trillion, or $328 billion; *Financial Times,* September 18, 2002). Stock holdings are about the same in magnitude as the officially estimated nonperforming loans of the system (¥43 trillion). The Japanese banking system has continued to remain under severe pressure. Total bank capital has fallen from ¥35.1 trillion in March 1999 to ¥29.1 trillion in March 2002, while unrealized capital gains on stocks and other securities have fallen from ¥10.8 trillion to ¥0.3 trillion over this period (Bank of Japan 2002b). At the end of March 2002 the Nikkei 225 index stood at 11,204 (Bank of Japan 2002a); on September 17, 2002, it stood at 9,472, strongly suggesting that the unrealized capital gains have turned into sizable unrealized capital losses (prompting the Bank of Japan on that date to propose purchasing stocks directly from banks to prop up their balance sheets for the close of the quarter at the end of September). In short, if a significant appreciation of the yen were to depress the stock market further, it could impose through the financial markets channel an adverse impact on the Japanese economy that would magnify the direct trade effects of the external sector adjustment.

Some analysts have increasingly questioned whether the exchange rate is a dominant factor in determining growth and investment expectations and equity market prospects in Japan, however.[21] Moreover, the statistical evidence does not support a systematic influence of the yen exchange rate on stock prices. Trends in stock prices in the United States and Japan in recent years do not show a relationship of Japanese share prices to the value of the yen against the dollar. They do show a sympathetic response of Japanese share prices to US share prices, however, at least after late 1998 (figure 9.7).

For the period 1992 through August 2002, a simple regression of the monthly percent change in the Nikkei 225 index (dN) on the percent change in the exchange rate (dR) lagged one month (yen per dollar) and on the percent change in the S&P 500 index (dS) shows the following

---

21. One recent study (Matsuoka and Adachi 2002) judges that "the effects from the movement of the exchange rate, compared with 10 or 20 years ago, have become much less profound. . . . Positive effects on economic activity through yen depreciation and accompanying improvement in corporate profits may be smaller than had been thought."

Figure 9.7   Stock prices in the United States (S&P 500) and Japan (Nikkei 225) and yen exchange rate against the dollar

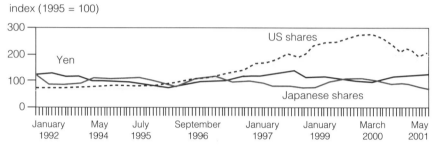

index (1995 = 100)

Sources: Yahoo Finance (2002).

relationship: $dN = -0.72 - 0.049dR + 0.582dS$. This result has the wrong sign for the supposed adverse impact of yen appreciation on the Japanese stock market, but this variable is not statistically significant in any event ($t = -0.36$). In contrast, the constant term showing a monthly decline of 0.72 percent is relatively significant ($t = 1.8$), and the US stock price term is highly significant ($t = 5.0$). A 1 percent rise in US stock prices over this period was associated with a 0.58 percent rise in Japanese stock prices.[22]

In short, the evidence does not support concerns that yen appreciation would cause a serious decline in the Japanese stock market. This finding suggests that the principal focus of concern about the impact of Japan's external adjustment should be on the real activity effects rather than the possible effects through stock prices and the financial markets.

Real Activity Effects

It is possible to consider the real growth effects of the external adjustment by going directly from the target current account surplus reduction to the implied impact on real net exports in the national accounts. The first step is to consider the magnitude of the adjustment relative to GDP. If we use a 15 percent share as Japan's target counterpart of the US adjustment, the resulting $42 billion (table 9.6) is equivalent to 0.94 percent of average 2000-01 GDP in dollar terms (IMF 2002a). If this were phased in over three years, the implication would be an adjustment magnitude equivalent to 0.31 percent of GDP annually.

The next step is to consider the relationship between the real external adjustment and the nominal adjustment. Appreciation of the currency makes exports more expensive in foreign currency (dollar) terms, while

---

22. A regression restricted to the period October 1998 through August 2002 boosts this coefficient to 0.69.

imports priced in foreign currency become cheaper in domestic currency terms (yen). Thus it will require a smaller physical volume of exports and a larger physical volume of imports to generate the same foreign-currency nominal value trade surplus. This means that the real trade balance adjustment is larger than the nominal trade balance adjustment.

With import and export price elasticities both in the vicinity of unity, and with import and export pass-through ratios in the range 0.7 to 0.9, the ratio of the real trade balance change to the nominal trade balance change is about 2 to 1 (Cline 1989, p. 360). Applying this ratio, the target adjustment for Japan would amount to a total of about 1.9 percent of GDP, or 0.63 percent annually over three years. This direct effect is substantial, gauged against a baseline growth rate of 1.5 to 2 percent.

Conclusion

Although the principle of cyclical adjustment suggests that some delay would be appropriate, eventually Japan should likely not be exempt from the international decrease in current account surpluses (or increase in deficits) that will be required as the counterpart of US reduction of its outsized current account deficit. The range of targets considered in this paper for the US adjustment and Japan's share suggests that in a relatively favorable outcome (such as that in variant B of table 9.6), by 2005 Japan could reduce its current account surplus by perhaps some $40 billion (compared to the current pace of $120 billion annual surplus) as its share in a $280 billion US current account deficit reduction. This would involve achieving domestic growth on the order of about 2.5 to 3 percent annually over this period, or 1 percent above baseline.

This outcome would require policies capable not only of securing the extra growth above baseline but also of compensating for about 0.6 percent of GDP annually that would be lost in real demand from the decline in real net exports associated with the adjustment. It would also likely require a real effective exchange rate appreciation of about 12 percent, which in turn would likely imply a real appreciation against the dollar of about 21 percent. This would take the yen from its current level of about 122 per dollar to 101 per dollar, which is also about the level that is consistent with the historical trend in the real value of the yen over the past two decades.

The policy implications of these findings would seem to include the following. First, once Japan begins to show sustained recovery, it would seem inappropriate for Japanese (or international) authorities to seek to block the gradual appreciation of the currency toward this range.[23] Second,

---

23. Note that, in contrast, Ito (2002) identifies 115 yen per dollar as a revealed intervention rate at which the Bank of Japan has sought to halt the rise of the yen in recent years.

the need for the United States to curb its external deficit and for Japan sooner or later to absorb some portion of the counterpart surplus reduction will likely be an additional reason—beyond the already challenging domestic difficulties, including banking sector fragility—for the Japanese authorities to pursue aggressive measures for economic stimulus for some time. Their task is a daunting one for which there are no easy recipes, in view of the Japanese economy's unusual combination of circumstances— recession and deflation despite near-zero interest rates; high government debt ratio; banking sector balance sheet problems; and a weak stock market.

Appendix 9.1
Modeling Japan's Current Account Balance

In a previous publication (Cline 1995) I set forth a forecasting model for Japan's current account balance, centered on the following relationship:

$$(1) \ \ln z_t = \ln \frac{p_f}{p_d} + \alpha + [\phi - \beta]\ln R^*_{Lt} - [\phi(1 + \rho) + \beta\epsilon]\ln R_{Lt}$$

$$+ \ \theta \ln Y_d - \gamma \ln Y_f + [\rho - \epsilon]\ln R_t$$

where z_t is the ratio of nonoil imports of goods and services to exports of goods and services; p_f is the foreign price of the imported goods in foreign currency; p_d is the domestic price of the exported goods in domestic currency; ϕ is the absolute value of the price elasticity of imports; β is the price elasticity (< 0) of exports; R is the nominal effective exchange rate; R^* is the real effective exchange rate; subscript t refers to the current period; operator L in the subscript refers to a weighted average of the previous eight quarters; θ is the income elasticity of imports; γ is the elasticity of exports with respect to foreign income; ρ is the pass-through parameter from the exchange rate to import prices; and ϵ is the pass-through parameter from the exchange rate to export prices.[24] When pass-through from exchange rate change to trade price change is complete, the pass-through parameters take the values $\beta = -1$ and $\epsilon = 0$. If instead pass-through is only 85 percent (for example), then $\beta = -0.85$ and $\epsilon = -0.15$.

This appendix reports new estimates of this model, using quarterly data from 1980 through the second quarter of 2000. The International Monetary Fund's index of nominal effective exchange rate (NEER, based on relative unit labor values) is used for R; its corresponding index for

---

24. See Cline (1995, 14). Note that the lag operator has the following weights on prior quarters beginning with the quarter prior to the present: 0.067, 0.117, 0.15, 0.167, 0.167, 0.15, 0.117, 0.067.

the real effective exchange rate (REER) is used for R^*; and p_f/p_d is calculated as NEER/REER (Cline 1995, 20). Weighted foreign GDP growth is based on the IMF's reported quarterly real GDP data for Japan's eight largest trading partners, weighted by 1990-95 shares in Japan's exports.[25] Japan's quarterly real GDP is also as reported by the IMF (2002a). Quarterly imports and exports of goods and nonfactor services are from the same source. The series on oil imports refers to Standard International Trade Classification (SITC) 33, and data are from the Ministry of Public Management (2002).

The regression estimated is:

$$(1') \ \ln z_t - \ln \frac{p_f}{p_d} = \alpha + \pi_1 \ln R^*_{Lt} + \pi_2 \ln R_{Lt} + \pi_3 \ln Y_d + \pi_4 Y_f$$

$$+ \ \pi_5 \ln R_t + \sum_i d_i D_i$$

where $\pi_1 = [\phi - \beta]$, $\pi_2 = -[\phi(1 + \rho) + \beta\epsilon]$, $\pi_3 = \theta$, $\pi_4 = -\gamma$, $\pi_5 = [\rho - \epsilon]$, and D_i are dummy variables for the quarter in question. The equation is estimated using Cochran-Orcutt correction for autocorrelation. The resulting estimated parameters are as follows, with t-statistic in parentheses:

$$\alpha = -6.28 \ (-6.9);$$
$$\pi_1 = 2.056 \ (7.8);$$
$$\pi_2 = -1.471 \ (-5.1);$$
$$\pi_3 = 1.297 \ (4.4);$$
$$\pi_4 = -0.331 \ (-2.4);$$
$$\pi_5 = -0.256 \ (-3.2);$$
$$d_1 = 0.0324 \ (2.2);$$
$$d_2 = 0.0128 \ (0.8);$$
$$d_3 = -0.0132 \ (-0.9);$$
$$rho = 0.242;$$
$$Adjusted \ R^2 = 0.5971.$$

Figure 9A.1 displays the fit between the predicted and actual ratio "z" of nonoil imports of goods and services to exports of goods and services for 1980Q1 through 2000Q2. The figure suggests a reasonably close fit, as does the adjusted R^2.

---

25. The countries and shares are: China, 0.064; Germany, 0.087; Hong Kong, 0.095; Korea, 0.098; Singapore, 0.072; Thailand, 0.057; United States, 0.47; and United Kingdom, 0.064.

Figure 9A.1 Predicted and actual ratio "z" of Japanese nonoil imports of goods and services to exports of goods and services, 1980Q1-2000Q2.

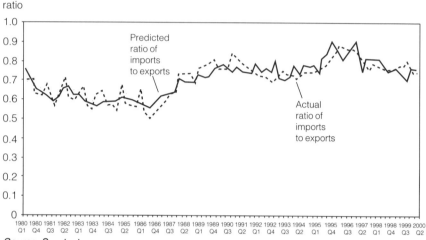

Source: See text.

These estimates place the sum of export and import price elasticities (π_1) at a relatively high value of 2. However, they also place leakage associated with pass-through ratios (captured in regression coefficients π_2 and π_5) relatively high. As shown in Cline (1995), the elasticity of the ratio of the value of nonoil imports of goods and services to exports of goods and services with respect to the real exchange rate is: $\pi_1 + \pi_2 + \pi_5$. This expression is analogous to the excess of the sum of export and import price elasticities over the threshold of unity in the Marshall-Lerner condition for devaluation to help correct the external deficit. In this estimate, this magnitude has shrunk to -0.33, from an estimate of -0.58 in Cline (1995), suggesting a deterioration in pass-through ratios in recent years from the standpoint of efficacy of adjustment through exchange rate changes.

As indicated in Cline (1995), the current account impact parameters showing the effect of a 1 percent change in real exchange rate (after completion of lags) or a one percentage point change in growth are estimated as:

2) $\Delta B_{R^*} = -X_0 z_0 [\pi_1 + \pi_2 + \pi_5][.01]$

for the real exchange rate;

3) $\Delta B_{gd} = -X_0 z_0 \pi_3 [.01]$

for domestic growth; and

4) $\Delta B_{gf} = -X_0 z_0 \pi_4 [.01]$

for foreign growth, where z_0 is the ratio of imports of nonoil goods and services to exports of goods and services in the base period and X_0 is the value of exports of goods and services in the base period. The main text uses the empirical estimates of this appendix for the parameters π_i and the average of 2000 and 2001 values for X_0 and z_0 to obtain the impact estimates reported in table 9.5.

An alternative approach is to use stylized parameters from the literature for the underlying elasticities and pass-through ratios that comprise the model coefficients of equations 1) through 4). Hooper and Marquez (1995) place pass-through parameters as: $\rho = -1$ (complete pass-through for import prices) and $\epsilon = -0.15$ (85 percent pass-through for export prices; see Cline 1995, 77). Obstfeld (2002, 6) suggests that recent estimates for international experience more generally might place both pass-through ratios at only about 0.5 for a one-year time frame but at complete pass-through over time. Hooper and Marquez place both the import and export income elasticities at unity ($\theta = \gamma = 1$), a result confirmed in Cline (1995, 22-25). Hooper, Johnson, and Marquez (1998, 3) estimate the long-run price elasticity at -1.0 for Japanese exports (β) but only -0.3 for Japanese imports ($-\phi$). The same study places the income elasticity of Japanese exports at 1.1 and imports at 0.9.

Consideration of these various estimates suggests the following. First, in decomposing the sum of import and export price elasticities (π_1) into their two respective components, a larger (absolute) value may be appropriate for the export price elasticity than for the import price elasticity. Second, somewhat less than complete pass-through seems appropriate on both the import and export sides for the time frame of two to three years.

Experimentation with stylized parameter values, moreover, shows that when the sum of price elasticities is as high as 2 (as in both the RFM95 and RFM02 models), when the pass-through parameters are raised above their low levels implied by these regression estimates toward high but below-complete pass-through, the result is to overpredict swings in the import/export ratio associated with swings in the real exchange rate. On this basis, some narrowing of the sum of price elasticities toward the relatively low 1.3 found by Hooper, Johnson, and Marquez (1998) seems appropriate.

Finally, the low export income elasticity estimated in the new results above likely reflects the shift of the foreign income variable to include such rapidly growing economies as China and Korea. For use with this foreign income series, somewhat below unity seems appropriate for the export income elasticity.

Table 9A.1 Stylized parameter values

Parameter	Concept	Value
ϕ	Import price elasticity (absolute value)	0.55
β	Export price elasticity	-0.95
θ	Import income elasticity	1.0
γ	Export income elasticity	0.8
ρ	Import price pass-through	-0.85
ϵ	Export price pass-through minus unity	-0.2
π_1	$= \phi\text{-}\beta$	1.5
π_2	$= -[\phi(1+\rho) + \beta\epsilon]$	-0.27
π_3	$= \theta$	1.0
π_4	$= \text{-}\gamma$	-0.8
π_5	$= [\rho-\epsilon]$	-0.65

Table 9A.1 presents a resulting set of "stylized" parameter values.

References

Ahearne, Alan, Joseph Gagnon, Jane Haltmaier, and Steve Kamin. 2002. Preventing Deflation: Lessons from Japan's Experience in the 1990s. Federal Reserve Board of Governors, International Finance Discussion Papers No. 2002-729. Washington: Federal Reserve Board of Governors.

Balassa, Bela. 1964. The Purchasing-Power Parity Doctrine: A Reappraisal. *Journal of Political Economy* 72 (December): 584-96.

Bank of Japan. 2002a. *Bank of Japan Statistics and Other Key Statistics.* Tokyo: Bank of Japan. http://www.boj.or.jp.

Bank of Japan. 2002b. Developments in Profits and Balance Sheets of Japanese Banks in Fiscal 2001 (Summary). Tokyo: Bank of Japan. http://www.boj.or.jp/en/ronbun/ron0208b.htm.

Bureau of Economic Analysis. 2002a. US International Transactions: Second Quarter 2002. Bureau of Economic Analysis, US Department of Commerce, September 12. http://www.bea.doc.gov.

Bureau of Economic Analysis. 2002b. Gross Domestic Product: Second Quarter 2002 (Final). Bureau of Economic Analysis, US Department of Commerce, September 27. http://www.bea.doc.gov.

Cline, William R. 1989. *United States External Adjustment and the World Economy.* Washington: Institute for International Economics.

Cline, William R. 1995. Predicting External Imbalances for the United States and Japan. POLICY ANALYSES IN INTERNATIONAL ECONOMICS 41. Washington: Institute for International Economics.

Economic and Social Research Institute. 2002. Annual Report on National Accounts for 2002. Tokyo: Economic and Social Research Institute Cabinet Office, Government of Japan. http://www.esri.cao.go.jp/index-e.html.

Hooper, Peter, and Jaime Marquez. 1995. Exchange Rates, Prices, and External Adjustment. In Peter B. Kenen, *Understanding Interdependence: The Macroeconomics of the Open Economy.* Princeton, NJ: Princeton University Press.

Hooper, Peter, Karen Johnson, and Jaime Marquez. 1998. Trade Elasticities for G-7 Countries. Federal Reserve Board of Governors, International Finance Discussion Papers No. 1998-609. Washington: Federal Reserve Board of Governors.

International Monetary Fund. 2001. *World Economic Outlook, May 2001: Fiscal Policy and Macroeconomic Stability*. Washington: International Monetary Fund.

International Monetary Fund. 2002a. *International Financial Statistics*. CD-ROM. Washington: International Monetary Fund, August.

International Monetary Fund. 2002b. *World Economic Outlook*. Washington: International Monetary Fund, April.

International Monetary Fund. 2002c. *World Economic Outlook: Trade and Finance*. Washington: International Monetary Fund, September.

International Monetary Fund. 2002d. Direction of Trade Statistics (CD-ROM). Washington: International Monetary Fund, April.

Ito, Takatoshi. 2002. Is Foreign Exchange Intervention Effective? The Japanese Experiences in the 1990s. NBER Working Paper No. 8914. Cambridge, MA: National Bureau of Economic Research.

Krugman, Paul. 1991. *Has the Adjustment Process Worked?* POLICY ANALYSES IN INTERNATIONAL ECONOMICS 34. Washington: Institute for International Economics.

Krugman, Paul. 1998. It's Baaack: Japan's Slump and the Return of the Liquidity Trap. *Brookings Papers on Economic Activity*, 1998:2: 137-87.

Mann, Catherine. 2002. Perspectives on the US Current Account Deficit and Sustainability. *Journal of Economic Perspectives* 16, no. 3 (Summer).

Marris, Stephen. 1985. *Deficits and the Dollar: The World Economy at Risk*. POLICY ANALYSES IN INTERNATIONAL ECONOMICS 14. Washington: Institute for International Economics.

Matsuoka, Mikihiro, and Kanou Adachi. 2002. Is Yen Depreciation a Panacea? Evidence of Declining Support to Corporate Profits. Deutsche Bank Group, Global Markets Research, 25 February.

Ministry of Public Management. 2002. Ministry of Public Management, Home Affairs, Post and Telecommunications (Japan), Statistics Bureau and Statistics Center Web site. http://www.stat.go.jp.

Mussa, Michael. 2002. Global Economic Prospects. Paper presented at the Institute for International Economics. Washington, September.

Obstfeld, Maurice. 2002. Exchange Rates and Adjustment: Perspectives from the New Open Economy Macroeconomics. NBER Working Paper 9118. Cambridge, MA: National Bureau of Economic Research.

Posen, Adam. 1998. *Restoring Japan's Economic Growth*. Washington: Institute for International Economics.

Statistics Canada. 2002. World Trade Analyzer. http://www.statcan.ca.

UNCTAD. 2002. Handbook of Statistics Online. http://stats.unctad.org.

Williamson, John. 1983. *The Exchange Rate System*, 2nd edition. POLICY ANALYSES IN INTERNATIONAL ECONOMICS 5. Washington: Institute for International Economics.

World Bank. 2001. *World Development Report 2000/2001: Attacking Poverty*. Washington: World Bank.

World Bank. 2002. *World Development Report 2002: Building Institutions for Markets*. Washington: World Bank.

Yahoo Finance. 2002. Yahoo Finance Historical Prices. http://finance.yahoo.com.

10

The Dollar and the European Economy

DANIEL GROS

In order to consider what impact the strong dollar has had on the European economy, and what would be the consequences of a weak dollar, it is convenient to start with a brief discussion of some salient characteristics of the current Euroland economy. The headline figures are well known: the euro has depreciated, even after the rally of the spring of 2002, by roughly 15 percent against the dollar since the start of the European Monetary Union (EMU) at the turn of 1998/1999. The first impression one has on looking at the euro's nearly four years of life is certainly not that the strong dollar has had a large impact on Euroland's economy. Growth is flagging, and the current account balance has not greatly improved.

Can this be explained by simply stating that the dollar cannot have a strong impact on the European economy anyway, because the Euroland economy is a closed one? In the second section of this paper I show that, on the contrary, Euroland is a fairly open economy. Another explanation seems more promising, namely, that the dollar is not "the" exchange rate for Euroland. On a real effective exchange rate basis, the euro has actually depreciated little since 1998-99, as I show in the third section. In the fourth section I turn to macroeconomic models for further guidance. The value of the output from these models depends, of course, on the accuracy of

Daniel Gros is director of the Centre for European Policy Studies in Brussels. He was an economist at the European and research departments of the International Monetary Fund (1983-86) and economic adviser at the Directorate General II of the European Commission (1988-90). This paper draws in part on joint work with Ansgar Belke and research undertaken for a project on EU-US transatlantic monetary relations financed by DGRELEX.

the input. The essence of the results from these models seems to be that an exogenous appreciation of the dollar can provide a sizable but strictly temporary boost to Euroland's economy. Most discussions about the dollar focus exclusively on its level, and whether it is too high, sustainable, or appropriate. However, for Europe its stability also matters. In the final section of the paper I report on some research that suggests that a high variability of the dollar/euro rate or the euro's effective exchange rate is usually associated with higher unemployment in Euroland.

European Stagflation

In contrast with the discussion of deflation in several of the papers in this conference, the hot topic in Europe is the status of inflation. Yet growth is low; many people believe it is below its potential, but perhaps its potential has decreased. At the same time, inflation remains stubborn.

For Euroland as a whole, core inflation has been running at 2.5 percent or so over recent months. That is not a very high rate, but it is above the target of 0 to 2 percent that the European Central Bank (ECB) has set itself. In fact, inflation has been running above this ceiling for almost three years now, which leads some to ask whether we should not start tightening. At least it suggests that there is likely to be resistance to all the demands for loosening that come from those who look at the weak state of the European economy. Last year the ECB actually loosened policy while headline inflation was still about 3 percent, though at that time you could point to core inflation, which was rather well behaved. But, in my view, it is becoming more and more difficult for the ECB to justify cutting rates now, when the one indicator that is more forward looking and therefore a bit more stable—namely, core inflation—is still running well above 2 percent. Most observers from both the private and official sectors had expected that, at least by early 2002, inflation would no longer be a problem and core inflation would fall rather quickly. Yet every month the inflation figures have surprised us, which makes it more difficult for the ECB to act to lower interest rates.

Europe seems to be stuck with a combination of relatively low growth and relatively high inflation. Why this combination? One explanation is that productivity growth in Euroland has collapsed. There has been a clear deterioration of the productivity performance of Europe vis-à-vis the United States; it has been going on for a long time, but 2001 was particularly dismal, with productivity growth of essentially zero. Of course productivity is a longer-term phenomenon, and the numbers fluctuate a good bit. That is because actual growth has fluctuated a good bit. We therefore did a simple regression analysis relating the year-to-year

Table 10.1 Regression analysis of the rate of growth of GDP/employee on GDP growth

Output per employee	Coefficient	Standard error	t-statistic	p value
Intercept	−0.12	0.28	−0.41	0.68
Lagged dependent	0.33	0.10	3.47	<0.001
GDP growth	0.62	0.09	6.63	<0.001

Note: Adjusted R^2, 0.76; standard error, 0.77; observations, 39.

Source: Author's calculations.

Table 10.2 Productivity performance and the business cycle

	United States		European Union	
	Predicted	Forecast error	Predicted	Forecast error
1999	1.85	0.35	1.93	−0.93
2000	1.88	0.22	2.41	−1.01
2001	0.75	0.55	1.39	−1.19

Source: Author's calculations.

productivity numbers to the overall growth rate (table 10.1). The results confirm that productivity is strongly related to the business cycle, implying that labor is almost a fixed cost.

We then took the resulting equation and examined what it has predicted for recent years, and compared that with actual outcomes. The final column in table 10.2 shows consistently large, and negative, forecasting errors for Euroland. Over the last three years productivity growth in Euroland has been about one percentage point lower than would have been expected given the state of the business cycle and the relationship between productivity and the business cycle that has held up pretty well over the past thirty years. This confirms that although a trend had already been under way for some time, it seems to have gone from bad to worse in the recent past.

The big question is: Will it last? That is a difficult question to answer, because we don't really know what is causing the deterioration of European performance. Nevertheless, I see little reason to expect productivity growth to accelerate quickly. There is no sign of any policy action that might lead to that, such as labor market reforms. The only hope might come from the prospect of enlargement, meaning that the size of the market will increase, and perhaps the pressure for reforms in some existing member countries will become stronger. But my bet would be that, for the time being at least, we are stuck with a situation in which reforms are difficult to undertake, and it is therefore unlikely that productivity will increase quickly again.

Table 10.3 Standard indicators of openness and size, 2000

	Euro zone	United States	Japan	Germany
Exports as percent of GDP	15.3	7.8	9.7	29.3
Exports as percent of world total	14.3	12.2	7.3	8.7
Average of exports and imports as percent of GDP	15.1	10.1	8.4	27.8
Average of exports and imports as percent of world total	14.1	15.8	6.3	8.2

Note: Exports and imports of goods only.

Source: International Monetary Fund.

How Open Is Euroland?

In Europe, in both official and public discussion of economic issues, the exchange rate plays a much more important role than it does in the United States. This is a natural consequence of the simple fact that Euroland is actually quite an open economy. Indeed, it may well be the only case of a large open economy that we have in economics.

To gain insight into the exposure of Euroland to external shocks, one needs a measure of the openness of the economic system. This openness can be measured in many ways. One standard measure looks at the share of trade to national income. The more important trade is in national income, the more open the economy is. In this regard, many have suggested that Euroland will be radically less open than the individual economies of Euroland. In fact, many of the Euroland economies are substantially open. Taken individually, the openness of the Eurozone countries, as measured by the share of exports of goods and services to domestic income, ranges from about 25 percent in Greece to over 90 percent in Luxembourg, and averages around 35 percent.

However, since a large percentage of trade within Euroland occurs among the 12 members, it is necessary to examine only external trade to gain a true picture of openness. Under this measure, which is net of internal exports of goods and services among the 12, the degree of openness for the EU-12 is only 19.7 percent.

This fact does not, by itself, mean that Euroland is a closed economy, however. To make this judgment, it is useful to compare the degree of openness of the G-3—the United States, the euro zone, and Japan. As shown in table 10.3, even when looking solely at trade with third countries, the euro zone is substantially more open than either the United States or Japan. In both of these economies, exports (of goods only) account for less than 10 percent of national income. The difference between Euroland and the United States narrows when both exports and imports are exam-

Table 10.4 Different openness indicators in 1998, as a share of GDP

Exports of:	Euro zone	United States	Japan	Germany
Goods only	15.3	7.8	9.7	29.3
Goods and services	19.7	10.8	11.1	33.8
All current account credits	23.9	14.5	15.6	39.8

Source: International Monetary Fund.

ined because of the current account deficit in the United States. For the United States, imports of goods and services are about 4 percentage points of GDP larger than exports, whereas Euroland has a small current account surplus.

These raw data thus suggest that Euroland is substantially more open than the United States. The difference between export-oriented Germany and Euroland is (proportionally) about as large as the difference between the United States and Euroland.

If openness is measured by including all current account transactions (trade in goods and services, plus capital income, plus unilateral transfers), the euro zone becomes even more open, with the measure rising to about 24 percent (2000). This figure is about 50 percent higher than the 14.5 percent share for the United States (and the 15.6 percent share for Japan— see table 10.4). Again the difference between Germany and Euroland is proportionally as important as the difference between the United States and Euroland.

In summary, the raw data suggest that while Euroland is in the aggregate less open than its constituent members, it is substantially more open than the United States. This fact alone suggests that the exchange rate should play a more important role for Euroland than for the United States.

Is the Dollar "the" Exchange Rate for Euroland?

Despite the relative importance of EU-US bilateral trade links, the dollar/ euro rate is not necessarily the most important single exchange rate for Euroland. For the euro zone, trade with the United Kingdom is slightly more important than trade with the United States (see the appendix, table 10A.1, for the regional distribution of G-3 trade). Likewise, for the United States, trade with Canada alone is more important than trade with Euroland.

In general one would expect that it is not the "dollar" (the bilateral dollar/euro rate) that matters for Euroland, but the "euro" (the effective exchange rate of the euro). Do these two move together in reality? The answer is not straightforward; the "dollar" and the "euro" have a strong

Table 10.5 Correlations of exchange rates

Correlation coefficient of US and euro area effective exchange rates

NEER	−52.2
REER	−48.0

Correlation coefficient of bilateral dollar/euro exchange rate with:

	NEER	REER
Euro area	83.5	81.0
United States	−84.9	−81.5

REER = real effective exchange rate
NEER = nominal effective exchange rate

Notes: Correlations are computed as a correlation coefficient of differences of logarithms of the monthly exchange rate levels (1990-2001).

Source: Author's calculations.

Table 10.6 Ordinary-least-squares regression of monthly percentage changes of the real effective exchange rate of the euro area

Regression statistics

Adjusted R^2	0.65
Standard error	0.01
Observations	143

	Coefficients	Standard error	t-statistics
Intercept	0.00	0.00	−1.42
Dollar/euro exchange rate	0.45	0.03	16.40

Source: Author's calculations.

tendency to move in tandem, but they are not at all the same variable (table 10.5).

The correlation between the bilateral dollar/euro exchange rate and measures of the effective exchange rate of Euroland is rather high at over 80 percent (the precise value depends on the exact measure of the effective exchange rate chosen). This suggests that the two almost always move in a similar direction. But by how much? An ordinary-least-squares regression of the monthly percentage changes can give a tentative answer (table 10.6). It turns out that only about one-half of any change in the bilateral dollar/euro rate has in the past translated into a change of the effective exchange rate of the euro area (whether in nominal or real terms does not really matter in this context, as price levels move much more slowly than exchange rates).

A similar, but more complicated, story emerges if one looks at the changes in the dollar/euro rate over the past decade and compares them with changes in the effective exchange rate of the euro (table 10.7). Over longer time periods price levels can move to offset changes in nominal exchange rates. Hence in this case one should look instead at the measures of the real (effective) exchange rate. As any cognoscente of this area knows, "the" real exchange rate does not exist. Table 10.7 thus reports a number of different measures of the real exchange rate of the euro area. The most recent numbers are reported in the final column, which shows that between the beginning of 1999 and July 2002 the real effective exchange of the euro (as measured by the ECB) declined less than 6 percent (less than one-half of the decline in the dollar price of the euro, which was approximately 15 percent).

In this sense one could say that the dollar is only half of the story as far as the euro is concerned.

What Do the Models Tell Us?

The major macroeconomic models used by international organizations predict that changes in the dollar/euro rate can have strong effects on the economies on both sides of the Atlantic. However, when one turns to these models for an answer to the question of what impact the strong dollar might have had on Europe, one first receives a question in return, namely, "What was the reason for the strong dollar?"

A convincing answer to this more fundamental question has not yet been found. It is apparent that the strong dollar would have a quite different impact on the European economy depending on whether dollar strength was a by-product, for example, of higher US productivity or of a lax monetary policy in Euroland (see European Commission 2002).

For example, the International Monetary Fund (1998) reports that a 15 percent appreciation of the dollar, induced by a shift in portfolio preferences toward US (or, rather, dollar-denominated) securities, would lead to an increase in European GDP of close to one full percentage point and would have a negative impact on the United States of a similar size. Most of the impact on the level of demand would disappear after two years, so that the effect would become strongly negative in terms of growth rates starting in year two.

More recent simulations (see in't Veld 2002 for more details) with other, similar models yield qualitatively similar results regarding demand, and usually find somewhat stronger effects because the more recent simulations are based on Euroland aggregates, whereas older simulations looked at the entire EU-15 (which is less open than Euroland alone). Taken at face value, the models thus suggest that the shift in portfolio preferences toward the dollar and away from the euro would considerably enhance growth in Euroland for two years and have a dampening impact on the United States.

Table 10.7 Percentage rate of depreciation of the euro using alternative measures

		NEER			REER		
		2001/1990	2001/1999	2001/1990	2001/1999	July 2002/ January 1999
ECB data	Narrow group	n.a.	−13.1	n.a.	−10.6	−5.3
	Broad group	n.a.	−8.4	n.a.	−12.2	−5.9
IMF data	19 industrialized economies	−19.0	−13.0	−27.0	−17.1	n.a.
	Memorandum: United States	17.6	16.1	15.1	24.6	n.a.
	Memorandum: Bilateral	Nominal	Nominal	n.a.	n.a.	Nominal
	exchange rate	−27.3	−19.7			−15.7

n.a. = not available
NEER = nominal effective exchange rate
REER = real effective exchange rate

Note: Deflator: Consumer Price Index for ECB and Unit Labor Costs for IMF.

Sources: International Monetary Fund and European Central Bank.

The perspective for the Euroland economy appears quite grim in the light of these simulation results. One could thus argue that a substantial part of the acceleration of growth in Euroland until 2001 was due to the weakness of the euro over the period 1998-2000. Furthermore, should the euro stabilize at the current, somewhat higher level, the impact on demand should become negative during 2002-03 under the joint influence of the slight dollar weakness in the spring of 2002 and the reversal of the previous expansionary effect predicted by the models.

A return of the dollar to the 1998-99 level could thus detract much more than one full percentage point from Euroland growth over the next two years, possibly aborting the tepid recovery that is still expected for 2003. This result depends of course on the ceteris paribus assumption for monetary policy in Euroland. An "enlightened" response by the ECB should reduce the loss in output considerably.

Unfortunately, the models are of no help in predicting what part of any dollar strength (or weakness) would translate into a change in the effective exchange rate of the euro. If one assumes a shock to the demand for euro assets, the model would show that the bilateral dollar/euro rate and the effective rate of the euro move in tandem. If, as usually assumed in the past, the shock is to dollar assets, then nondollar currencies would remain stable against the euro and the bilateral dollar/euro rate would move by much more than the effective rate. From the data presented above it appears that reality has been situated between these two extremes.

Not Only the Level Counts

The most frequently asked question about the dollar is what impact its level has on other economies, such as Euroland. However, one should not forget that it is not only the level that counts, but also the variability.

Why should transatlantic exchange rate variability be important? The obvious answer has usually been that exchange rate variability discourages trade. Unfortunately, a large empirical literature on this issue has not been able to document a strong link between exchange rate variability and the volume of trade.[1] But a bit of reflection shows that the volume of trade is not an important variable in itself. It is other variables that policymakers should care about, such as (un)employment and investment.

Recently it has become fashionable to argue that exchange rate variability might not have any immediate impact (on anything) because of "pricing to market," that is, the practice of keeping local prices fixed even in the face of large exchange rate changes.[2] This implies, for example, that

---

1. See Belke and Gros (2002) for references.

2. See Obstfeld (2002) for a recent survey and criticism.

foreign sales should react little to exchange rates. Firms simply keep producing and export more or less the same amount, but their domestic currency earnings become variable, whereas their domestic costs remain stable. But a key consequence is that exchange rate variability can thus certainly influence the variability of profits, even if quantities react little. Firms might thus react to an increase in exchange rate (and hence profit) variability in the first instance by reducing investment in trade-related activities.

Exchange rate variability might thus have mainly a significant short-run impact on investment and on (un)employment because investment is an important component of demand. Moreover, in most continental European countries, hiring workers also represents an investment in the sense that there are high costs to reversing this decision. This is an additional reason (independent of the demand effect) why exchange rate variability should affect (un)employment. Moreover, if labor is de facto a semifixed factor of production, the short-run marginal costs of changing the volume of production must be very high. Firms will typically be reluctant to engage new labor (which involves a heavy sunk cost in most European countries) if the variability of the exchange rate is so high that the probability that this labor will not be used after all is also high. However, this does not apply to the United States, and so one would expect the link between exchange rate variability and US labor market performance to be less strong.

This is confirmed by the data. As shown in Belke and Gros (2002), the variability of the euro seems to have a statistically significant and economically small, but nonnegligible, impact on labor markets in Euroland. Unemployment tends to increase and employment growth tends to fall whenever the effective exchange rate of the euro or the bilateral dollar/euro exchange rate becomes more variable. In the United States a similar effect, though statistically weaker, seems to be operating, especially concerning employment growth, which seems largely insulated from exchange rate variability. These results fit the general observations that US labor markets are more flexible and that the euro zone is considerably more open than the United States.

The potential effects of lower (or higher) exchange rate variability on Euroland's labor markets, as estimated by Belke and Gros (2002), could be significant. A doubling of the variability (standard deviation) of the dollar rate of the euro could increase unemployment by over one full percentage point in Euroland.

Concluding Remarks

Just by looking at the data for openness, one would expect the exchange rate to be more important for Euroland than for the United States. But what exchange rate? Almost four years since the start of EMU the euro is still 15 percent lower against the dollar, but on an effective real exchange rate basis, the depreciation has been much less, only around 5 to 6 percent. It is thus not surprising that the weakness of the euro has not had a strong impact on the Euroland economy, whether in terms of growth or of the current account.

Euroland tends to benefit from lower exchange rate variability because of its greater openness and its less flexible labor markets. The worst combination would thus be for Europe to face a weaker and at the same time less stable dollar. A weaker dollar is a big worry for Europe only if it translates into a stronger euro, in the sense that movements in the bilateral dollar/euro rate translate into movements in the effective exchange rate of the euro. Historically this has not always been the case. Hence Euroland should not suffer too much from renewed dollar weakness.

Appendix 10.1

Table 10A.1 Indicators of openness (exports and imports of goods only, billions of US dollars and as a share of GDP, 1996)

	Exports	Share of GDP (percent)	Imports	Share of GDP (percent)
US total	623.0	8.2	817.8	10.7
To Canada	132.6	1.7	159.7	2.1
To Mexico	56.8	0.7	74.1	1.0
Outside NAFTA	433.6	5.7	583.9	7.6
Memorandum item:				
To European Union	127.5	1.7	147.5	1.9
Euro zone total	818.0	11.9	749	10.9
To non-euro zone	209.0	3.0	177.8	2.6
To European Free Trade Association and Switzerland	64.9	0.9	67	1.0
Outside European Economic Area	544.1	7.9	504.2	7.3
Memorandum item:				
To United States	104.0	1.5	109.9	1.6
Memorandum items:				
EU-15	792.6	9.2	770.7	10.1
To non-euro zone	209.0	2.4	177.8	2.3
To European Free Trade Association and Switzerland	90.4	1.0	93.9	1.2
Outside European Economic Area	493.2	5.7	499.0	6.5
To United States	144.9	1.7	152.2	2.0

Source: International Monetary Fund, Direction of Trade Statistics.

References

Belke, Ansgar, and Daniel Gros. 2002. Designing EU-US Transatlantic Monetary Relations. *World Economy* 25, no. 6: 789-813.

European Commission, ECOFIN. 2002. Economic Implications of the Depreciation in the Euro Exchange Rate. Photocopy, Brussels.

International Monetary Fund. 1998 *World Economic Outlook.* Washington, May.

in't Veld, Jan. 2002. Exchange Rate Changes and Monetary Policy: Simulations with the QUEST Model. *European Economy* 71: *The EU Economy: 2000 Review*, 56-66.

Obstfeld, Maurice. 2002. Exchange Rates and Adjustment: Perspectives from the New Open Economics Macroeconomics. NBER Working Paper No. 9118. Cambridge, MA: National Bureau of Economic Research.

11

Foreign Exchange Intervention: Did It Work in the 1990s?

KATHRYN M. DOMINGUEZ

For as long as there have been exchange rates, there have been individuals and governments who have sought to manipulate them. Although there is anecdotal evidence that some individuals have been highly successful at influencing markets (such as George Soros in 1992), theory suggests that as markets develop and deepen they should become less vulnerable to manipulation. This, in turn, may imply that over time interventions by central banks in well-developed foreign exchange markets may be less and less likely to be successful.[1] Dominguez and Frankel (1993b) find strong evidence that interventions implemented by the US Federal Reserve (Fed), the German Bundesbank, and the Bank of Japan (BOJ) in the 1980s influenced dollar exchange rates. Other studies come to similar conclusions.[2] Does intervention policy continue to work? Or, as theory would predict, has dollar intervention policy become less effective?

Kathryn M. Dominguez is associate professor of public policy and economics at the University of Michigan and research associate at the National Bureau of Economic Research. The author is grateful to Ted Truman for his many helpful comments and suggestions.

1. Here I am implicitly assuming that a transaction in the foreign exchange market by a central bank is no different from one made by an individual investor or nongovernmental institution. It may be that because central banks have the ability to support interventions with current or future changes in monetary policy, interventions are likely to influence exchange rates whether or not markets are developed. This study tests whether interventions influence exchange rates, but not why this is the case. See Dominguez (1992, 1998), Dominguez and Frankel (1993a,b,c), Evans and Lyons (2001), Lyons (2001), Montgomery and Popper (2001), Mussa (1980), and Naranjo and Nimalendran (2000) for discussions of why interventions might influence exchange rates.

2. See Edison (1993) and Sarno and Taylor (2001) for excellent surveys of the intervention literature. Also see Dominguez (1990, 1992, 1997, 1998), Dominguez and Frankel (1993a,b,c), Henderson (1984), Kenen (1987), Lewis (1995), and Obstfeld (1990).

There are at least four reasons to think that effects of foreign exchange intervention in the 1990s might differ from the effects of earlier interventions. First, economic conditions in the G-3 countries changed dramatically in the 1990s. The United States experienced its longest-lasting economic expansion over this period, while economic growth in Germany and Europe was largely stalled, and the Japanese economy was often in recession. Second, the US current account deficit grew dramatically over this period, in large part as a result of the strong relative position of the US economy over the decade. Gross portfolio and foreign direct investment flows also rose dramatically in the 1990s, suggesting that global capital flows were higher and financial markets were more globalized. Third, in a process culminating in the establishment of the European Central Bank (ECB) in 1999, the European countries achieved monetary union in the 1990s, and the ECB took over jurisdiction of intervention policy for Germany and the other European countries. Fourth, interest rates in Japan were so low over this period that monetary policy was thought to be largely ineffective.

Researchers examining recent data continue to find evidence that intervention operations are effective, although estimates of the magnitude of the effects vary, as do views on whether intervention is a useful policy tool.[3] Part of the explanation for the differing results is that studies focus on different central banks, different exchange rates, and different time periods, all leading to difficult comparisons. But, in large part, the differences in results across studies and in views regarding the efficacy of intervention are consequences of the way in which researchers define the success of an intervention.

Central bankers, market participants, and researchers are all likely to agree that a successful intervention is one that significantly influences either the relative price or the volatility of a currency in the appropriate direction.[4] Where disagreement about success is likely to arise is in the definition of "significant influence," which in turn depends on the size and persistence of the influence intervention has on exchange rates. One of the reasons this is difficult to resolve is that there is no consensus model of exchange rate determination, so it is difficult to compare actual behavior and what exchange rates would have been in the absence of intervention.[5] There is also the problem of defining temporal correlations.

---

3. See, for example, Fatum and Hutchison (2002a,b,c), Galati, Melick, and Micu (2002), Humpage (1999), Ito (2002), Neely (2002), and Ramaswamy and Hossein (2000).

4. For an overview of studies that focus on the influence of interventions on the volatility of exchange rates, see Dominguez (1998) and Galati, Melick, and Micu (2002). The empirical work in this paper focuses exclusively on the influence of intervention on the level of the exchange rate.

5. Meese and Rogoff (1983) were the first to show that a random-walk model outperforms standard exchange rate determination models in predicting exchange rate behavior out of sample.

Should there be a direct correlation between intervention operations and the immediate movement of the exchange rate in order to make the case that intervention caused the change in the exchange rate? Or is it possible to claim causality when, after days of interventions with no discernible contemporaneous changes in the exchange rate, there eventually is a movement of the exchange rate in the desired direction?

This study examines the intervention operations of the G-3 countries—the United States, Japan, and Germany—over the period 1990-2002. I analyze the very short-term (four-hour) effects of G-3 intervention operations on dollar exchange rates as well as the longer-term correlations between episodes of intervention and subsequent currency movements. The more recent G-3 intervention data suggest that intervention policy is both alive and well—G-3 central banks continue to intervene to influence currency values—and these interventions were often successful in influencing short-term and longer-term exchange rate movements.

Dollar Exchange Rate Movements and G-3 Interventions in the 1990s Compared to Those in the 1980s

In the 1980s we saw dramatic long-run movements in the yen/dollar and deutsche mark/dollar exchange rates. The dollar was strong against most currencies in the early 1980s and then depreciated by over 40 percent relative to the yen and the mark over the course of about a year, starting in 1985 (coincident with the famous Plaza Accord intervention operations that took place in September 1985).[6] Figures 11.1 and 11.2 show the yen/dollar and mark/dollar exchange rates over the period 1977-2002. Although day-to-day volatility in both rates remained fairly constant over the 25-year span, the longer-term movements were less dramatic in the 1990s.

The yen/dollar rate reached historic lows in 1995, although from its peak of 159.7 in April 1990 to its lowest point of 80.6 on April 18, 1995, the decline in the dollar was relatively gradual. And for most of the 1990s the yen/dollar rate stayed within the relatively narrow bounds of 135 and 105.

The mark/dollar rate was even more stable than the yen/dollar rate in the 1990s, reaching its low point of 1.35 in April 1995 and peaking at 1.88 in August 1997. (After the introduction of the euro in January 1999, the mark/dollar rate climbed to 2.36 in October 2000.) Over most of the 1990s the mark/dollar rate stayed within a narrow band of 1.75 to 1.40.

---

6. See Dominguez and Frankel (1993b), Funabashi (1988), Henning (1994), and Klein and Rosengren (1991) for a detailed account of the politics and economics of the Plaza Accord and other intervention episodes in the 1980s.

Figure 11.1 Yen/US dollar exchange rate, 1977-2002

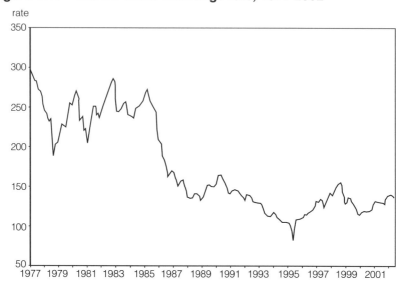

Note: All data are for January of the year indicated.

Sources: New York Federal Reserve (daily data were collected at the close of New York trading).

Figure 11.2 Deutsche mark/US dollar exchange rate, 1977-2002

Note: All data are for January of the year indicated.

Sources: New York Federal Reserve (daily data were collected at the close of New York trading).

Figure 11.3   US intervention operations, 1977-2002

millions of US dollars

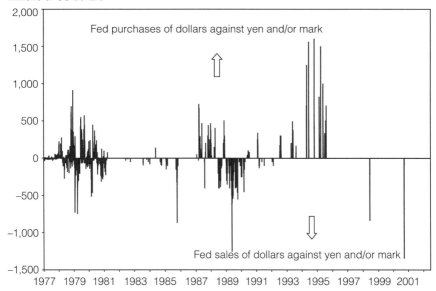

Sources: Treasury and Federal Reserve Foreign Exchange Operations, New York Federal Reserve Quarterly Review.

Although the G-3 central banks continued to intervene in foreign exchange markets in the 1990s, they did so much less frequently than in the 1980s. Figure 11.3 shows US dollar intervention operations in the yen and mark markets over the period 1977-2002.[7] The two most active periods of US intervention were in the late 1970s and early 1980s and again in the mid- to late 1980s. Although the total number of Fed operations fell in the 1990s, the size of daily operations was generally much larger. The largest single-day US purchase of $1.6 billion occurred on November 2, 1994 (and involved a sale of $800 million of yen and $800 million of marks). The largest single-day US dollar sale, involving $1.34 billion (for euros) occurred on September 22, 2000. Figure 11.3 also shows that the last two US interventions involved operations over only one day. In the 1980s US intervention episodes typically continued for weeks and sometimes months.

---

7. In the United States the US Treasury Department and the Federal Reserve have independent legal authority to intervene in foreign exchange markets. In practice, the Treasury and the Fed typically act jointly and split the costs of intervention equally against their separate accounts. The New York Fed implements intervention policy for the United States, and for this reason I follow the convention of associating US intervention operations with the Fed in this paper.

Figure 11.4 Japanese intervention operations, 1977-2002

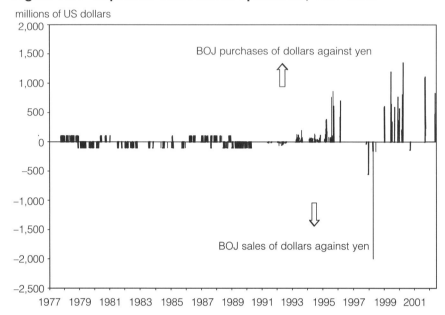

Notes: Pre-1991 BOJ intervention data are unofficial (based on reports in the financial press) and are dollar purchase/sale dummy variables (arbitrarily drawn here as [1,000, 0, −1,000] for better visibility).

Sources: Dominguez and Frankel (1993b), and Ministry of Finance, Japan.

The Japanese Ministry of Finance recently released its official daily intervention series going back to 1991.[8] In the past, researchers were forced to rely on financial press reports of BOJ interventions to compile a daily series, and these reports rarely included intervention magnitudes. Figure 11.4 includes the pre-1991 unofficial BOJ intervention series (used in Dominguez and Frankel 1993a, b, c), shown arbitrarily (1,000, 0, −1,000) for better visibility on the graph (positive observations denote BOJ purchases of dollars and negative observations denote BOJ sales of dollars). Without information on the size of BOJ interventions before 1991, it is difficult to make a direct comparison of the operations in the 1980s relative to the 1990s, although a visual scan of figure 11.4 suggests that the BOJ was probably more active in the earlier period. If we focus only on the operations after 1991, the BOJ was much more likely to purchase dollars than to sell them, although the largest operation on one day involved a sale of just under $20 billion against yen on April 10, 1998. The largest daily

8. In Japan intervention decisions are made by the Ministry of Finance and implemented by the Bank of Japan (BOJ). The ministry discloses BOJ interventions four times a year at http://www.mof.go.jp/english/e1c021.htm and provides historical data starting in 1991.

Figure 11.5 German intervention operations, 1977-98

millions of US dollars

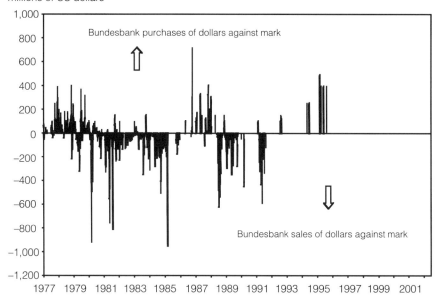

Notes: Pre-1991 BOJ intervention data are unofficial (based on reports in the financial press) and are dollar purchase/sale dummy variables (arbitrarily drawn here as [1,000, 0, −1,000] for better visibility).

Source: Deutsche Bundesbank.

BOJ purchase of dollars ($13.5 billion) occurred on April 3, 2000. Unlike the Fed, the BOJ has continued to intervene in the past few years, and episodes have generally continued to involve operations across multiple days.

The German Bundesbank continued to intervene actively in the mark/dollar market through 1992, although after that, the few remaining interventions involved only dollar purchases against the mark (figure 11.5).[9] In contrast to the Fed, Bundesbank operations in the 1990s were generally smaller on a daily basis than had been the case in the 1980s. The largest Bundesbank dollar purchase after 1990 involved $492 million on March 3, 1995, and the largest dollar sale involved $592 million.

The next section focuses exclusively on the efficacy of the G-3 interventions in the 1990s. However, it would be instructive to keep in mind the historical context of these interventions. Long-run movements in the two main dollar exchange rates were less volatile than was the case in the

---

9. The Bundesbank had sole jurisdiction over intervention decisions and implemented intervention operations prior to 1999.

Table 11.1 Typical timing of G-3 interventions during the 24-hour clock, and timing of available exchange rate data

	GMT22 (t − 1)	GMT6	GMT8	GMT10	GMT14	GMT17	GMT22
Tokyo	BOJ interventions						
	7 A.M.	3 P.M.	5 P.M.				
Frankfurt				Bundesbank interventions			
			9 A.M.	11 A.M.	3 P.M.	6 P.M.	
New York					Fed interventions		
					9 A.M.	Noon	5 P.M.

GMT = Greenwich Mean Time

Source: Author's calculations.

1980s, although the daily volatilities did not change much over the two decades. Perhaps as a consequence of the less dramatic long-run movements in currency values, the G-3 central banks were generally less active interveners in the 1990s. The Bundesbank operations were the smallest and the least frequent of the three. The United States intervened less frequently in the 1990s than in the 1980s, although the average size of daily Fed operations was much larger, especially after 1994. The BOJ was by a wide margin the most active intervener of the G-3 in the 1990s, and the size of the largest BOJ interventions was almost three times larger than Bundesbank operations and twice the size of the largest Fed operations.

Analysis of G-3 Interventions in the 1990s

Timing of Interventions

The foreign exchange market is open 24 hours, though the most active trading periods in the market occur during business hours in Asia, Europe, and New York. In Dominguez (2003) I analyze Reuters reports of G-3 interventions from 1989 to 1993. The reports indicate that central banks typically intervene during business hours in their respective markets.[10] Frequency distributions of the times of G-3 intervention suggest that the BOJ is most likely to intervene at 3:56:36 GMT (or around 1:00 p.m. in Tokyo). The Bundesbank is most likely to intervene at 11:31:16 GMT (or at 12:30 p.m. in Frankfurt). And the Fed is most likely to intervene at 14:57:10 GMT (or 10:00 a.m. EST). Table 11.1 shows the relative timing

10. Neely (2000) provides detailed information based on survey data about the practice of central bank intervention. Beattie and Fillion (1999), Chang and Taylor (1998), Dominguez (2003), Fischer and Zurlinden (1999), Goodhart and Hesse (1993), Neely (2002), Payne and Vitale (forthcoming), and Peiers (1997) examine the intraday efficacy of central bank interventions.

of the Tokyo, Frankfurt, and New York markets using the GMT scale and indicates the times when each central bank is likely to be in the market. Table 11.1 also includes the times during the 24-hour clock when exchange rate data series are available. (These data series are used in the subsequent empirical tests.)[11] It is worth noting that Tokyo business hours end just as the Frankfurt market opens, and the New York market overlaps the Frankfurt market for two hours. The New York market closes two hours before the Tokyo financial market opens.

The G-3 central banks all currently make public historical daily intervention data. Unfortunately, they do not provide the exact timing of interventions, nor do they disclose how many operations occurred over the course of the day. Therefore, in order to measure the influence of interventions on foreign exchange markets it is important to take into account the timing of when interventions are likely to take place. For example, if we want to know whether an intervention by the BOJ on day t influenced the yen/dollar rate on the same day, we would want to look at the change in the yen/dollar rate before the Tokyo market opens relative to the exchange rate at the close of the Tokyo market. However, if the Fed or the Bundesbank intervened on the same day, it would be inappropriate to look for the effects of those interventions on the yen/dollar rate during the Tokyo market hours, because neither bank would likely have intervened until well after the Tokyo market was closed. In this study I use seven hourly observations (listed in table 11.1 and spaced approximately every four hours) of the yen/dollar and mark/dollar exchange rates in order to be able to measure the contemporaneous impact of the interventions during the relevant business hours and to measure the persistence of these effects.[12]

The Efficacy of Japanese Intervention Operations

The BOJ was the most active intervener of the G-3 in the foreign exchange market during the 1990s. The total volume of BOJ interventions exceeded those by both the Fed and the Bundesbank by over 13 times. The BOJ was also much more likely to intervene unilaterally than the other two.

11. Because mark/dollar data are not available at 5:00 p.m. Frankfurt time (GMT16), data from 6:00 p.m. (GMT17) are used as a proxy for Frankfurt closing in the regression analysis. Likewise, yen/dollar data are not available at 9:00 a.m. Tokyo (GMT1), so data observed at GMT22(t-1) are used in the analysis as a proxy for the Tokyo open price.

12. The GMT6 exchange rate data are from the Reserve Bank of Australia, GMT8 data are from the Bank of Japan, GMT10 data are from the Swiss National Bank, and GMT14,17,22 data are from the New York Fed. I am grateful to Carol Osler, Andres Fischer, Masashi Nakajima, and especially Chris Neely for their assistance in acquiring these data.

Figure 11.6 Japanese interventions and the yen/US dollar exchange rate, 1990-June 2002

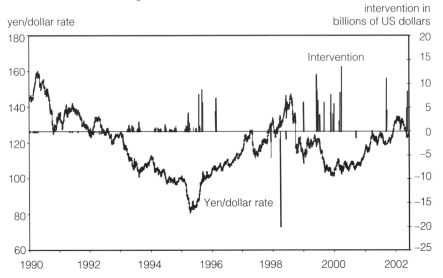

Note: All data are for January of the year indicated.
Source: Japanese Ministry of Finance.

Only 47 percent of BOJ interventions were coordinated with another central bank. Figure 11.6 shows the yen/dollar exchange rate together with BOJ interventions over the period 1991 through June 2002. The BOJ intervened on a total of 219 days over the 12-year period, spending a total of nearly $300 billion.[13] These interventions generally involved purchases of US dollars (and sales of yen), indicating that the BOJ was generally attempting to weaken the yen relative to the dollar over this period. BOJ operations were episodic, with long spells of no intervention activity and then weeks, and sometimes months, of periodic operations. Table 11.2 indicates that there were two episodes during this period in which the BOJ sold dollars (and purchased yen)—in 1991-92 and again in 1997-98; in both of these periods the yen/dollar rate generally exceeded 125 and the BOJ's stated objective was to strengthen the yen relative to the dollar.[14] In the three episodes when the BOJ purchased dollars, the yen/dollar rate was always well below 125, implicitly suggesting that 125

13. One of these interventions, on September 22, 2000, was in support of the euro against the yen (all other operations were against the dollar).

14. The exceptions are three BOJ dollar sales operations on November 3, 5, and 6, 1997, that occurred when the yen/dollar rate was between 120.3 and 123.1. The yen/dollar rate reached 125 on November 11, 1997.

Table 11.2 The influence of BOJ interventions on the yen/dollar rate during Tokyo business hours, 1991-2002

	1991-2002 (full period)	May 1991-August 1992 (dollar sales)	April 1993-February 1996 (dollar buy)	November 1997-June 1998 (dollar sales)	January 1999-April 2000 (dollar buy)	September 2001-June 2002 (dollar buy)
Number of interventions	218	27	152	11	17	11
Average daily size (millions of US dollars)	$1,357	−$223	$747	−$2,894	$5,706	$4,321
Total amount (millions of US dollars)[a]	$297,249.7	−$6,017.60	$113,524.1	−$31,834.2	$97,001.2	$47,527.0
Percent daily returns with correct sign[a]	47	48	42	27	75	82
Percent coordinated with Fed[b]	10	11	12	9	0	0
4-hour impact of BOJ intervention[c]	1.027	−0.527	1.014	1.027	1.006	0.533
T-statistic[d]	4.244	−0.207	2.261	0.544	2.314	2.728
8-hour impact of BOJ intervention[c]	0.004	−4.033	0.326	0.717	0.429	0.341
T-statistic[d]	0.354	−1.44	1.114	1.807	2.187	3.397
48-hour persistence?[e]	No	No	No	Yes	Yes	Yes
Yen/dollar rate[f]						
Before interventions	138.73	138.73	114.03	120.33	108.78	117.29
After interventions	124.15	127.98	104.26	136.54	104.80	124.15
1 month after interventions		124.30	106.50	139.50	109	120.20
2 months after interventions		121.10	105.70	145.80	108	121.10
3 months after interventions		123.90	107.90	132.60	105	118.00
Success during intervention?[g]	No	Yes	No	No	No	Yes
Long-run success?[h]	No	Yes	10 months	4 months	Yes	Yes

(table continues next page)

Table 11.2 The influence of BOJ interventions on the yen/dollar rate during Tokyo business hours, 1991-2002 *(continued)*

a. Indicates percentage of intervention days when the daily yen/dollar rate moved in the appropriate direction (so that a dollar-strengthening operation led to an increase in the yen/dollar rate) during Tokyo trading hours.

b. Indicates the percentage of BOJ intervention days when the Fed also intervened.

c. The entries for 4-hour and 8-hour impact indicate the coefficient on BOJ intervention in a regression of 4-hour and 8-hour yen/dollar returns on constant, BOJ, Fed, and Bundesbank dollar intervention magnitudes (with each central bank's intervention assumed to occur during the 4-hour morning period or the 8-hour trading period, 9 A.M. to 5 P.M., in each of the respective markets).

d. The t-statistics are based on robust standard errors for the corresponding regression coefficient.

e. Indicates whether 48-hour lags of BOJ intervention operations are statistically significant.

f. The exchange rate before interventions is the rate just before the opening of the Tokyo market (GMT22[t − 1]) on the first day of BOJ interventions in the episode. The yen/dollar rate after interventions is the rate at the close of the New York market (GMT22) on the last day of BOJ interventions in the episode.

g. Indicates whether the yen/dollar rate moved in the appropriate direction over the period in which intervention operations took place (measured at the close of the New York market on the day before intervention operations started relative to the close of the New York market on the last day of intervention).

h. Indicates whether the yen/dollar rate moved in the appropriate direction within three months of the last intervention operation in the episode. If the yen/dollar rate moved in the appropriate direction more than 3 months later, the number of months is listed.

Note: The BOJ intervention in support of the euro on September 22, 2000, is excluded because it was not intended to directly impact the yen/dollar rate.

Source: Japanese Ministry of Finance.

was a target or threshold value of the yen/dollar exchange rate over this period.

From 1991[15] through August 1992, the BOJ intervened on 27 days, selling a total of $6 billion in an attempt to increase the value of the yen relative to the dollar. Over the same period, the yen/dollar rate fell from a high of 138.7 yen to the dollar on May 13, 1991 (on the morning of the first day on which the BOJ intervened) to 127.9 yen to the dollar at the end of the last day of intervention on August 11, 1992. Although the movement of the yen over the two-year period is consistent with BOJ (and Fed) interventions, the daily correlation of interventions and exchange rate movements is negative (and statistically insignificant) over this period, indicating that on the days when the BOJ sold dollars, the dollar typically rose in value. Overall, the objective of the BOJ (to strengthen the yen) succeeded over the period of intervention operations. Furthermore, the yen/dollar rate remained below 125 three months after the last BOJ intervention operation in this episode. On the other hand, analysis of the daily data does not provide direct evidence to indicate that it was the intervention operations that led to the rise in the relative value of the yen over this period.

The second episode of BOJ intervention started in April 1993 and continued through February 1996. Over the four-year period the BOJ intervened on 152 days, purchasing a total of $113 billion in an attempt to weaken the yen relative to the dollar. As can be seen in figure 11.6, the yen/dollar rate hovered around 124 in January 1993, hit a low of 81 in April 1995, and rose back to 126 by April 1997. The BOJ began its intervention operations when the yen/dollar exchange rate was 114 in April 1993 and ended its interventions when the rate reached 104 in February 1996, with the largest dollar purchases occurring in August and September 1995. If we look at this period as one long intervention episode, the BOJ objective of weakening the yen was unsuccessful in the sense that the yen/dollar rate ended lower after the interventions than before. It is impossible, however, to know how the yen/dollar rate might have moved had the BOJ not intervened. On the other hand, if we look only at the interventions that occurred starting in August 1995 (after the yen/dollar rate had bottomed out) the operations appear to have been highly successful. An analysis of the daily data over the full four-year period indicates that interventions did affect 4-hour returns both significantly and in the right direction—but this effect does not show up in the 8-hour returns, suggesting that the efficacy of the operations was extremely short-lived. If we examine

15. Official Japanese intervention data are available starting in January 1991. Reports in the financial press indicate that the BOJ was also very active in foreign exchange markets in 1990, but since these data may contain type I and type II errors—that is, they may include days when no intervention actually took place and may exclude days when intervention did take place—the analysis of BOJ operations in this paper starts in 1991.

Table 11.3 BOJ interventions with the largest daily impact, 1991-2002

Date	Percent increase in yen/ dollar rate	BOJ dollar amount (millions of US dollars)	Coordinated with G-2?
BOJ's three most effective US dollar-strengthening interventions			
August 19, 1993	4.21	$167	Fed
August 15, 1995	3.37	$515	Fed and Bundesbank
August 2, 1995	3.26	$7,672	Fed
BOJ's three most effective yen-strengthening interventions			
June 17, 1998	−4.87	−$1,613	Fed
December 17, 1997	−2.91	−$2,144	No
January 17, 1992	−2.91	−$49.1	Fed

Note: Yen/dollar returns are measured over a 24-hour period, starting two hours before the Tokyo market opens and ending with the close of New York trading.

Source: Japanese Ministry of Finance.

the 11 interventions that occurred between August 1995 and February 1996 separately, we find both a 4-hour impact effect and strong evidence of persistence.[16]

The third episode of BOJ intervention involved sales of dollars (and purchases of yen) starting in November 1997 and ending in June 1998. This is another case where the yen/dollar rate over the period actually rose initially and subsequently fell, so the connection between the interventions and the currency movements is not unidirectional. On a daily basis, interventions are found to affect the exchange rate in the right direction (though the effect becomes more significant, although smaller, after 8 hours), and there is evidence of persistence beyond 48 hours. The largest daily intervention operation by the BOJ occurred in this period, on April 10, 1998, with a sale of $19.9 billion resulting in a 1.9 percent fall in the yen/dollar rate by the close of the New York market. Interestingly, as shown in table 11.3, the BOJ's next dollar sale, on June 17, 1998, involved sales of $1.6 billion (coordinated with an $833 million Fed operation), but it had a much larger effect (4.87 percent) on the yen/dollar rate.

The BOJ returned to purchasing dollars (and selling yen) between January 1999 and March 2000 and then, after a year's hiatus, it bought dollars again between September 2001 and June 2002. In the first of these dollar-

---

16. The 11 BOJ dollar purchases from August 1995 through February 1996 totaled $41.6 billion and averaged $3.5 billion per day. The 4-hour impact of BOJ interventions on returns was 1.701 with a t-statistic of 3.444; after 8 hours the effect falls to 0.219 and continues to have a statistically significant effect after 48 hours. The yen/dollar rate on the first day of these operations was 88.07, and at the end of the period it was 104.26.

Figure 11.7   German interventions and the deutsche mark/US dollar exchange rate, 1990-98

deutsche mark/dollar rate

millions of US dollars

Note: All data are for January of the year indicated.

Source: Deutsche Bundesbank.

buying episodes the yen/dollar rate fell from 108.8 to 104.8, suggesting that the BOJ was not successful at weakening the yen. The analysis of the daily impact of these operations suggests, however, that they were both statistically significant and persistent. To borrow a battlefield analogy, the BOJ seems to have won many daily battles with the foreign exchange market in this period, yet it lost the war. Dollar buying resumed again in September 2001 and from May through June 2002. Over this period the yen/dollar rate rose from 117 to 124, and the daily analysis suggests that on average these operations had a statistically significant and persistent influence.

The Efficacy of German Intervention Operations

The Bundesbank had jurisdiction over mark intervention policy through 1998, although its last operation took place on August 15, 1995. Sixty percent of Bundesbank interventions over this period were coordinated with the Fed, and all interventions after 1991 were coordinated. Figure 11.7 shows Bundesbank intervention operations and the mark/dollar exchange rate over the period 1990-1998. The information in table 11.4 indicates that the Bundesbank intervened on 36 days during this period, for a total of just over $7 billion, with the bulk of operations occurring before 1992. Bundesbank daily interventions were generally much smaller than BOJ operations in magnitude, and in most instances the Bundesbank intervened over much shorter episodes. The majority of Bundesbank interven-

Table 11.4 The influence of Bundesbank interventions on the deutsche mark/dollar rate during Frankfurt business hours, 1990-98

	1990-98 (full period)	January-March 1990 (dollar sales)	February 1991 (dollar buy)	March-August 1991 (dollar sales)	July-August 1992 (dollar buy)	May-June 1994 (dollar buy)	March-August 1995 (dollar buy)
Number of interventions	36	5	4	17	4	2	4
Average daily size (millions of US dollars)	$202	−$148	$68	−$207	$128	$253	$422
Total amount (millions of US dollars)	$7,261	−$739	$270	−$3,546	$513	$506	$1,687
Percent daily returns with correct sign	47	80	50	35	50	50	50
Percent coordinated with Fed	61	40	100	29	100	100	100
4-hour impact of Bundesbank intervention	2.106	1.432	17.085	3.042	1.218	10.485	1.125
T-statistic	0.816	1.038	1.584	0.810	0.191	1.033	0.203
8-hour impact of Bundesbank intervention	9.777	16.570	17.181	1.734	7.717	23.939	20.650
T-statistic	1.906	4.147	1.879	0.259	0.454	2.195	1.638
48-hour persistence?	No	Yes	No	No	No	No	No
Deutsche mark/US dollar rate							
Before interventions	1.727	1.727	1.468	1.569	1.458	1.636	1.443
After interventions	1.476	1.698	1.454	1.824	1.403	1.584	1.476
1 month after interventions		1.693	1.569	1.688	1.485	1.589	1.488
2 months after interventions		1.636	1.683	1.693	1.53	1.546	1.422
3 months after interventions		1.697	1.713	1.616	1.595	1.548	1.410
Success during intervention?		Yes	No	No	No	No	Yes
Long-run success?		Yes	Yes	4 months	Yes	No	Yes

Note: See table 11.2.

Source: Deutsche Bundesbank.

tion operations involved sales of dollars for marks in early 1990 and late 1991. In both episodes of dollar sales the mark/dollar rate was well above 1.6. And in three of the four episodes of dollar purchases the mark-dollar rate was well below 1.5, suggesting that 1.55 was the relevant pivot rate for the Bundesbank over this period. The one episode that is a bit puzzling occurred in May and June 1994 when the Bundesbank purchased dollars on two occasions when the mark/dollar rate was above 1.55, although both of these operations were coordinated with the Fed and the BOJ, suggesting that these may have been intended to strengthen the dollar relative to the yen, rather than to weaken the mark.

Over the six episodes of Bundesbank intervention, only the 1990 operations had persistent effects—that is, lasting more than 48 hours—on the mark/dollar rate. That said, figure 11.7 shows that in all but the 1994 episode, the mark/dollar rate eventually moved in the direction of the Bundesbank interventions. Indeed, table 11.4 indicates that only in the case of the two interventions in 1994 did the mark/dollar rate not move in the appropriate direction within three months of the last Bundesbank intervention operation. So again, an evaluation of the overall efficacy of Bundesbank operations depends critically on whether one expects to see effects of interventions on the exchange rate immediately or over a longer horizon. It obviously becomes more difficult to make the case that interventions "caused" the subsequent changes in the mark/dollar rate when the two series are not closely linked temporally. In all of the episodes the sign on the coefficient of Bundesbank interventions is positive, suggesting that, on average, the mark/dollar rate moved in the appropriate direction on the day of intervention. And in four of the six episodes (including the 1994 operations), and in the full sample period, Bundesbank interventions had a statistically significant effect on the mark/dollar rate over an 8-hour period. Table 11.5 shows that the largest percentage change in the mark/dollar rate on an intervention day occurred on August 15, 1995, when the Bundesbank purchased $398.1 million (together with the Fed and the BOJ).

The Efficacy of European Intervention Operations

In January 1999 the euro replaced the mark and became the European currency. The European Central Bank (ECB) implements euro intervention policy, and, after much speculation in the financial press over whether it would ever intervene, the ECB intervened on four occasions in September and November 2000.[17] Figure 11.8 shows the euro/US dollar exchange rate together with the four ECB interventions in the fall of 2000. The dollar

---

17. Intervention decisions involving the euro are made by the ECB in consultation with the ECOFIN council. The dates of the ECB interventions in 2000 are September 22 and November 3, 6, and 9.

Table 11.5 Bundesbank interventions with the largest daily impact, 1990-98

Date	Percent increase in deutsche mark/ dollar rate	Bundesbank dollar amount (millions of US dollars)	Coordinated with G-2?
Bundesbank's three largest US dollar-strengthening interventions			
August 15, 1995	2.823	398.1	Fed and BOJ
July 20, 1992	2.371	100.9	Fed
May 31, 1995	1.015	395.6	Fed and BOJ
Bundesbank's three largest deutsche mark-strengthening interventions			
July 12, 1991	−2.528	−339.5	Fed
January 4, 1990	−2.401	−50.4	BOJ
April 23, 1991	−1.255	−430.3	No

Note: Deutsche mark/dollar returns are measured over a 24-hour period, starting two hours before the Tokyo market opens and ending with the close of New York trading.

Source: Deutsche Bundesbank.

Figure 11.8 European interventions and the euro/US dollar exchange rate, 1999-June 2002

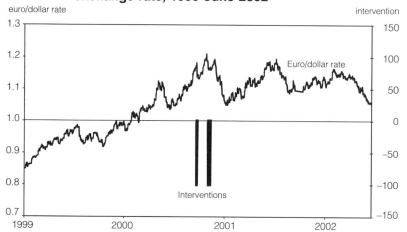

Notes: ECB interventions are based on reports in the financial press and are arbitrarily drawn here as (0, −100). All data are for January of the year indicated.

Source: European Central Bank.

magnitudes of the ECB operations have not been made public, so they are shown on the graph (arbitrarily) as interventions of equal size (100 million). The ECB operations came as the euro was at its weakest against the dollar, and the operations coincided with a substantial (although relatively short-lived) strengthening of the euro. The first ECB operation was coordinated with the Fed and the BOJ, along with other central banks.

Table 11.6 The influence of ECB interventions on the euro/US dollar rate during Frankfurt business hours

	September-November 2000 dollar sales
Number of interventions	4
Percent with correct sign	75
Percent coordinated	25
4-hour impact of ECB intervention	2.649
T-statistic	2.655
8-hour impact of ECB intervention	7.920
T-statistic	1.337
Persistence?	No
Euro/US dollar rate	
Before interventions	1.164
After interventions	1.152
1 month after interventions	1.124
2 months after interventions	1.059
3 months after interventions	1.081
Success during intervention?	Yes
Long-run success?	Yes

ECB = European Central Bank

Note: See table 11.2.

Source: European Central Bank.

Table 11.6 shows that ECB operations had statistically significant effects at 4 hours, though the effects had largely died out by the end of 8 hours. Again, if we consider the longer-term (but not long-term) movement of the euro relative to the dollar, there continues to be evidence of persistence (with the euro/US dollar rate continuing to fall) three months after the last ECB intervention operation.

The Efficacy of US Intervention Operations

Over the period 1990-2002 the Fed intervened on 74 days, with 39 daily operations in the yen/dollar market, 48 daily operations in the mark/dollar market, and one operation in the euro/dollar market.[18] Figures 11.9 and 11.10 depict Fed operations in each of the currency markets together with the relevant exchange rate. Just as was the case for the BOJ and Bundesbank, the Fed intervened episodically in both markets. Tables 11.7 through 11.10 summarize the daily effects of these interventions.

Fed interventions in the yen/dollar market can be grouped into four episodes, many of which overlap with the episodes examined earlier for the BOJ. Indeed, on 94 percent of the US intervention days in the yen/

18. There were 14 days on which the Fed intervened in both the yen/dollar and mark/dollar (or euro/dollar) markets over this period.

Figure 11.9 US intervention and the yen/US dollar exchange rate

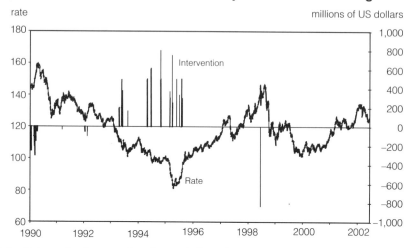

Note: Data are for January of each year indicated.
Source: Federal Reserve.

Figure 11.10 US intervention and the deutsche mark/US dollar exchange rate

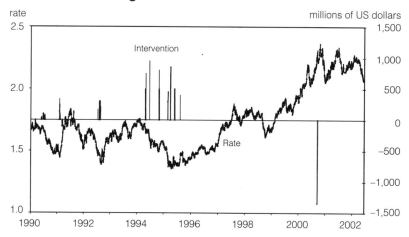

Note: Data are for January of each year indicated.
Source: Federal Reserve.

dollar market, the Fed coordinated its operations with the BOJ (and all operations after July 1992 were coordinated with the BOJ).

All the US operations before July 1992 involved sales of dollars for yen in an attempt to lower the yen/dollar rate. These operations were relatively small in magnitude. The operations in 1990 exerted a statistically signifi-

Table 11.7 The influence of Fed intervention on the yen/dollar rate during New York business hours

	1990-2002 (full period)	January-April 1990 (dollar sale)	March 1991-February 1992 (dollar sale)	April 1993-August 1995 (dollar buy)	June 1998 (dollar sale)
Number of interventions	39	16	4	18	1
Average daily size (millions of US dollars)	$272	−$136	−$58	$408	−$833
Total amount (millions of US dollars)	$10,595.30	−$2,180	−$238	$7,344	−$833
Percent daily returns with correct sign	35	7	50	55	100
Percent coordinated with BOJ	94	94	75	100	100
4-hour impact of Fed intervention	2.231	−15.106	15.557	2.788	9.439
T-statistic	0.952	−2.451	0.332	1.093	15.743
8-hour impact of Fed intervention	2.151	0.058	16.931	0.063	10.084
T-statistic	1.104	0.104	1.130	0.319	16.818
48-hour persistence?	No	No	No	No	Yes
Yen/US dollar rate					
Before interventions	144.52	144.52	136.11	110.59	143.35
After interventions	136.53	158.33	128.63	96.81	136.53
1 month after interventions		156.50	133.80	104.10	139.50
2 months after interventions		153.50	134.30	100.60	145.90
3 months after interventions		151.20	129.50	101.50	133.90
Success during interventions?	No	No	Yes	No	Yes
Long-run success?		4 months	Yes	13 months	Yes

Note: See table 11.2.

Source: Federal Reserve.

Table 11.8 Fed interventions with the largest daily impact on the yen/US dollar rate, 1990-2002

Date	Percent increase in yen/ dollar rate	Fed $ amount (millions of dollars)	Coordinated with G-2?
Fed's three largest US dollar-strengthening interventions			
August 19, 1993	4.21	$165	BOJ
August 15, 1995	3.37	$300	BOJ and Bundesbank
August 2, 1995	3.26	$500	BOJ
Fed's three largest yen-strengthening interventions			
June 17, 1998	−4.87	−$833	BOJ
January 17, 1992	−2.91	−$50	BOJ
March 2, 1995	−1.58	−$150	BOJ and Bundesbank

Note: Yen/dollar returns are measured over a 24-hour period, starting two hours before the Tokyo market opens and ending with the close of New York trading.

Source: Federal Reserve.

cant influence on the yen/dollar rate on impact, although the negative coefficient on Fed intervention suggests that, on average, the dollar rose rather than fell in value during the morning hours in New York. There is no evidence of intervention's influence, however, beyond those few hours. (Four months after the last Fed intervention in this episode, the yen/dollar rate fell below 144, the rate on the day before the interventions in this episode started.)

The longest period over which the United States intervened in the same direction involved 18 days of purchasing dollars for yen over the period 1992-95. Over this period the yen/dollar rate fell from 110 to just above 80 and then eventually reached 96.81 at the end of the last day of Fed intervention. Recall that over this same period the BOJ intervened on 152 days. Dividing the Fed interventions over this period by year, it is only in 1994 that the interventions have a statistically significant influence on the yen/dollar rate, this time in the correct direction. The effect does not last beyond the New York morning hours in the 48-hour-persistence tests. And it was only 13 months after the last US intervention that the yen/dollar rate exceeded 110 (the rate on the day of the first Fed operation in this episode).

The most successful Fed operation, in terms of immediate impact and 48-hour persistence, occurred on the Fed's last day of intervention in the yen/dollar market, on June 17, 1998. On this day the Fed sold $833 million in an effort to strengthen the yen in coordination with the BOJ. As shown in table 11.8, the Fed and BOJ interventions on this day led to a 4.87 percent decrease in the yen/dollar exchange rate between the Tokyo morning hours and the close of the New York market.

Table 11.9 The influence of Fed interventions on the deutsche mark/US dollar rate during New York business hours, 1990-2002

	1990-2002 (full period)	Jauary-March 1990 (dollar sale)	May–July 1990 (dollar buy)	February 1991 (dollar buy)	March–July 1991 (dollar sale)	July 1992-August 1995 (dollar buy)	September 2000 (dollar sale)
Number of interventions	49	2	17	7	6	16	1
Average daily size (millions of US dollars)	$253	−$100	$59	$191	−$87	$501	−$1,340
Total amount (millions of US dollars)	$12,416	−$200	$1,000	$1,336	−$520	$8,020	−$1,340
Percent daily returns with correct sign	47	100	57	42	17	44	100
Percent coordinated with Bundesbank	57	100	0	57	83	63	0
4-hour impact of Fed intervention	−4.796	11.819	−12.634	−13.357	−20.763	−2.634	7.109
T-statistic	−2.693	2.926	−1.375	−2.914	−0.557	−1.055	4.588
8-hour impact of Fed intervention	0.543	3.593	−0.742	−3.039	−0.769	−1.487	1.495
T-statistic	0.329	6.216	−0.071	−0.751	−0.047	−0.580	9.377
48-hour persistence?	No	Yes	No	No	No	No	Yes
Deutsche mark/dollar rate							
Before interventions	1.715	1.715	1.672	1.468	1.569	1.458	2.275
After interventions	2.231	1.698	1.644	1.454	1.789	1.476	2.231
1 month after interventions		1.693	1.546	1.569	1.724	1.488	2.339
2 months after interventions		1.655	1.548	1.683	1.684	1.422	2.314
3 months after interventions		1.692	1.562	1.713	1.691	1.406	2.110
Success during intervention?	No	Yes	No	No	No	Yes	Yes
Long-run success?		Yes	No	Yes	5 months	Yes	Yes

Note: See table 11.2.

Source: Federal Reserve.

239

Table 11.10 Fed interventions with the largest daily impact on the deutsche mark/dollar rate, 1990-2002

Date	Percent increase in deutsche mark/ dollar rate	Fed dollar amount (millions of US dollars)	Coordinated with G-2?
Fed's three largest US dollar-strengthening interventions			
August 15, 1992	2.822	$400	BOJ and Bundesbank
July 20, 1992	2.371	$170	Bundesbank
May 31, 1995	2.015	$500	BOJ and Bundesbank
Fed's three largest deutsche mark-strengthening interventions			
July 12, 1991	−2.528	−$100	Bundesbank
September 22, 2000	−1.993	−$1,340	BOJ
March 5, 1990	−1.058	−$50	BOJ and Bundesbank

Note: Deutsche mark/dollar returns are measured over a 24-hour period, starting two hours before the Tokyo market opens and ending with the close of New York trading.

Source: Federal Reserve.

Figure 11.10 shows the Fed interventions that were intended to influence the mark/dollar exchange rate. Table 11.9 provides a summary of the results of analyzing the six main episodes of Fed intervention over this period. With the exception of two short episodes of dollar sales in early 1990 and mid-1991, the bulk of the interventions in this market were aimed at strengthening the dollar relative to the mark.

The first intervention episode involving dollar sales in early 1990 was extremely successful both in terms of daily and longer-term movements of the mark/dollar exchange rate. The coefficient on Fed intervention is statistically significant, has the correct sign, and is large in magnitude, indicating that the two dollar interventions in March 1990 led to an average 1.18 percent decline in the mark/dollar rate in the New York morning hours. The interventions led to an additional 0.3 percent decline in the New York afternoon hours, with further evidence of statistically significant persistence for 48 hours. It is interesting to note that both Fed interventions in this episode were coordinated with the Bundesbank.

In May 1990 the Fed switched to buying dollars in an effort to strengthen the dollar relative to the mark, and although the Fed intervened on 17 occasions and spent $1 billion dollars, the interventions were unsuccessful both on a daily basis and over a longer-term horizon.

In February 1991 the Fed again purchased dollars, and this time (as shown in table 11.9) there is evidence that the interventions significantly influenced the mark/dollar rate in the New York morning hours. The negative sign on the coefficient on Fed intervention suggests, however, that the dollar fell rather than rose on impact. There is no evidence of persistence in the 48-hour period beyond the New York morning hours.

Although the mark/dollar rate rose within a month of the last intervention in this episode, the Fed had already started selling dollars in March 1991, suggesting that the February operations were unlikely to have been causal.

In March 1991 through July 1991 the Fed sold dollars on six occasions. The operations in this period were relatively small ($87 million on average), and 83 percent of the operations were coordinated with the Bundesbank. There is no evidence that these Fed interventions affected the mark/dollar rate in the short term—and it was not until five months after the last Fed intervention that the rate fell below its level at the start of the intervention episode.

The long string of Fed dollar purchases between 1992 and 1995 generally resulted in the mark/dollar rate falling rather than rising on a daily basis. Over the longer term the dollar did eventually rise both in the aftermath of the interventions in July and August 1992 and in the period after the last Fed intervention episode in August 1995.

The final Fed intervention over this period was (again) the most successful. On September 22, 2000, the Fed sold $1.34 billion and purchased euros together with the ECB and the BOJ in an effort to raise the relative value of the euro. On the day of the joint intervention, the euro rose 2 percent from before the Tokyo market opened to the close of New York trading. The evidence indicates that the influence of the interventions continued through 48 hours. Furthermore, the euro/US dollar rate continued to decline three months after the joint intervention operation.

Conclusions

Empirical evidence from the 1990s suggests that intervention can effectively influence exchange rates. The G-3 central banks were less active interveners in the dollar market in the 1990s, and long-run movements in the dollar exchange rate were less dramatic than had been the case in the 1980s, but intervention operations were nevertheless often effective. Dominguez and Frankel (1993b) challenged the conventional view that intervention could only be effective if combined with contemporaneous changes in money supply (or, in other words, only if interventions were unsterilized). That study concluded that foreign exchange intervention could continue to work, especially if it is "properly conceived and executed." More specifically, we argued that intervention was least likely to be effective if it was inconsistent with either future monetary policy intentions or future exchange rate fundamentals. The interventions in the 1980s that had the largest and most sustained influence were the dollar sales in 1985 that helped bring down the relative value of the dollar, which was viewed both at the time and with hindsight as massively overvalued. The closest analogy to 1985 in the 1990s was the appreciation of the yen in April 1995. The yen/dollar rate at 80 was widely thought to be inconsistent with fundamentals.[19] As was the case a decade earlier, the BOJ and Fed intervention operations in this period eventually led to a rise in the yen/dollar rate, returning it to a more appropriate level.

Dominguez and Frankel (1993b) also made some specific recommendations regarding the execution of intervention policy. Interventions that were unanticipated, publicly announced, and coordinated were the most effective. Behavior of the G-3 central banks since 1990 has been largely consistent with these recommendations. Ito (2002) notes that Eisuke Sakakibara, the director-general of the International Finance Bureau and the person in charge of intervention policy for Japan starting in June 1995, felt that the market had become too accustomed to BOJ interventions. Under his jurisdiction BOJ intervention policy became less predictable and less frequent, and daily intervention magnitudes increased. Fed interventions over this period were also larger, less frequent, and unpredictable. Although the size of the ECB interventions have not been made public, since 1999 the ECB has only intervened on four occasions, and financial reports suggest that these operations caught the market by surprise. In the 1970s and 1980s central banks rarely acknowledged their own intervention operations. This is no longer the case. The US Treasury started to routinely release information to the press after Fed interventions in the mid-1990s. The BOJ is also much more forthcoming about its presence in the market after intervention operations have taken place. The Ministry of Finance in Japan has gone so far as to publish its daily intervention data on its home page on a quarterly basis. Central banks were also much more likely to coordinate intervention operations in the 1990s. Ninety-four percent of all Fed interventions were coordinated in the full period, and all interventions after July 1992 were coordinated. The Bundesbank also coordinated all of its interventions after July 1992. The bulk of BOJ interventions in the 1990s continued to be unilateral, although some of the largest and most successful one-day operations were coordinated with the Fed.

This examination of the intervention operations by the G-3 central banks in the 1990s suggests that even as financial markets became more globalized and economic conditions across the countries diverged, interventions in the foreign exchange market continued to serve as a useful policy tool. Although there were plenty of intervention days when exchange rates either did not move or moved in the opposite direction from where central banks hoped they would, the longer-term movements

---

19. Ito (2002) suggests two possible reasons for the yen/dollar movement to 80: technical factors such as knock-out options and delta hedge strategies, and trade conflicts over the US-Japan auto talks that may have led the Office of the US Trade Representative to put pressure on Japan by creating a yen appreciation.

in the dollar rates largely conformed to central bank objectives.[20] The deeper questions of why and how the intervention operations in the 1990s influenced exchange rates remain for further study.

References

Beattie, N., and J. Fillion. 1999. An Intraday Analysis of the Effectiveness of Foreign Exchange Intervention. Bank of Canada Working Paper 99-4. Ottawa, Ontario, Canada: Bank of Canada.

Chang, Y., and S. Taylor. 1998. Intraday Effects of Foreign Exchange Intervention by the Bank of Japan. *Journal of International Money and Finance* 18, 191-210.

Deutsche Bundesbank. Daily German Intervention Data 1977-98. Frankfurt, Germany.

Dominguez, K. 1990. Market Responses to Coordinated Central Bank Intervention. Carnegie-Rochester Series on Public Policy, vol. 32 (Spring). North Holland, Amsterdam.

Dominguez, K. 1992. The Informational Role of Official Foreign Exchange Intervention Operations: The Signalling Hypothesis. In *Exchange Rate Efficiency and the Behavior of International Asset Markets,* by K. Dominguez, 41-80. New York: Garland Publishing Company.

Dominguez, K. 1997. The International Evidence: An Assessment of Experience with Foreign Exchange Intervention in the G-3. In *Exchange Rates and Monetary Policy,* edited by P. Fenton and J. Murray. Ottawa: Bank of Canada.

Dominguez, K. 1998. Central Bank Intervention and Exchange Rate Volatility. *Journal of International Money and Finance* 18: 161-90.

Dominguez, K. 2003. The Market Microstructure of Central Bank Intervention. *Journal of International Economics*, vol. 59/1: 25-45.

Dominguez, K., and J. Frankel. 1993a. Does Foreign Exchange Intervention Matter? The Portfolio Effect. *American Economic Review* 83: 1356-369.

Dominguez, K., and J. Frankel. 1993b. *Does Foreign Exchange Intervention Work?* Washington: Institute for International Economics.

Dominguez, K., and J. Frankel. 1993c. Foreign Exchange Intervention: An Empirical Analysis. In *On Exchange Rates,* edited by J. Frankel. Cambridge, MA: MIT Press.

Edison, H. 1993. The Effectiveness of Central Bank Intervention: A Survey of the Literature After 1982. *Special Papers in International Economics*, no. 18. Princeton, NJ: Princeton University Press.

Evans, M., and R. Lyons. 2001. Portfolio Balance, Price Impact, and Secret Intervention. NBER Working Paper No. 8356. Cambridge, MA: National Bureau of Economic Research.

Fatum, R., and M. Hutchison. 2002a. Is Foreign Exchange Market Intervention an Alternative to Monetary Policy? Evidence from Japan. University of California, Santa Cruz, working paper.

---

20. In the 22 (sometimes overlapping) episodes of intervention studied in this paper (five for the BOJ, six for the Bundesbank, one for the ECB, four for the Fed in the yen/dollar market, and six for the Fed in the mark/dollar market) there were seven (32 percent) episodes when interventions had a correctly signed and statistically significant 4-hour impact on the relevant exchange rate and 10 (45 percent) episodes when interventions had a correctly signed and statistically significant 8-hour impact on the relevant exchange rate. In 45 percent of the 22 episodes, the relevant exchange rate moved in the appropriate direction by the end of the intervention episode (noted in the row "Success during intervention?" in the tables), and in 64 percent of the episodes (14 out of 22) the relevant exchange rate moved in the appropriate direction within three months of the final intervention operation of the episode (noted in the row "Long-run success?" in the tables).

Fatum, R., and M. Hutchison. 2002b. Is Sterilized Foreign Exchange Intervention Effective After All? An Event Study Approach. *Economic Journal,* forthcoming.

Fatum, R., and M. Hutchison. 2002c. ECB Foreign Exchange Intervention and the Euro: Institutional Framework, News, and Intervention. *Open Economies Review* 13: 413-25.

Fischer, A. M., and M. Zurlinden. 1999. Exchange Rate Effects of Central Bank Interventions: An Analysis of Transaction Prices. *Economic Journal* 109, 662-76.

Funabashi, Y. 1988. *Managing the Dollar: From the Plaza to the Louvre.* Washington: Institute for International Economics.

Galati, G., W. Melick, and M. Micu. 2002. Foreign Exchange Market Intervention and Expectations: An Empirical Study of the Dollar/Yen Exchange Rate. Photocopy, August. Kenyon College, Ohio.

Goodhart, C., and T. Hesse. 1993. Central Bank Forex Intervention Assessed in Continuous Time. *Journal of International Money and Finance* 12: 368-89.

Henderson, D. 1984. Exchange Market Intervention Operations: Their Role in Financial Policy and Their Effects. In *Exchange Rate Theory and Practice,* NBER Conference Report, edited by J. Bilson and R. Marston, 359-98. Chicago: University of Chicago Press.

Henning, C. Randall. 1994. Currencies and Politics in the United States, Germany, and Japan. Washington: Institute for International Economics.

Humpage, O. 1999. US Intervention: Assessing the Probability of Success. *Journal of Money, Credit, and Banking* 31, no. 4 (November): 731-47.

Ito, T. 2002. Is Foreign Exchange Intervention Effective? The Japanese Experiences in the 1990s. NBER Working Papers 8914. Cambridge, MA: National Bureau of Economic Research.

Kenen, P. B. 1987. Exchange Rate Management: What Role for Intervention? *American Economic Review* 77, no. 2: 194-99.

Klein, M., and E. Rosengren. 1991. Foreign Exchange Intervention as a Signal of Monetary Policy. *New England Economic Review* (May/June): 39-50.

Lewis, K. 1995. Are Foreign Exchange Intervention and Monetary Policy Related, and Does It Really Matter? *Journal of Business* 68, no. 2: 185-214.

Lyons, R. 2001. *The Microstructure Approach to Exchange Rates.* Cambridge, MA: MIT Press.

Meese, R., and K. Rogoff. 1983. Empirical Exchange Rate Models of the Seventies: Do They Fit Out of Sample? *Journal of International Economics* 14 (1-2): 3-24.

Ministry of Finance, Japan. Daily Japanese Intervention Data, 1991-2002. Tokyo, Japan.

Montgomery, J., and H. Popper. 2001. Information Sharing and Central Bank Intervention in the Foreign Exchange Market. *Journal of International Economics* 55, no. 2: 295-316.

Mussa, M. 1980. *The Role of Official Intervention.* New York: Group of Thirty.

Naranjo, A., and M. Nimalendran. 2000. Government Intervention and Adverse Selection Costs in Foreign Exchange Markets. *Review of Financial Studies* 13: 453-77.

Neely, C. 2000. The Practice of Central Bank Intervention: Looking Under the Hood. *Central Banking* 11, no. 2: 24-37.

Neely, C. 2002. The Temporal Pattern of Trading Rule Returns and Central Bank Intervention: Intervention Does Not Generate Technical Trading Rule Profits. *Journal of International Economics* 58: 211-32.

Obstfeld, M. 1990. The Effectiveness of Foreign-Exchange Intervention: Recent Experience: 1985-1988. In *International Policy Coordination and Exchange Rate Fluctuations,* NBER Conference Report, edited by W. Branson, J. Frenkel, and M. Goldstein, 197-237. Chicago: University of Chicago Press.

Payne, R., and P. Vitale. Forthcoming. A Transaction Level Study of the Effects of Central Bank Intervention on Exchange Rates. *Journal of International Economics.*

Peiers, B. 1997. Informed Traders, Intervention, and Price Leadership: A Deeper View of the Microstructure of the Foreign Exchange Market. *Journal of Finance* 52, no. 4: 1589-614.

Ramaswamy, R., and S. Hossein. 2000. The Yen-Dollar Rate: Have Interventions Mattered? IMF Working Paper WP/00/95. Washington: International Monetary Fund.

Sarno, L., and M. Taylor. 2001. Official Intervention in the Foreign Exchange Market: Is It Effective and, If So, How Does It Work? *Journal of Economic Literature* 39 (September): 839-68.

US Department of the Treasury. Daily US Intervention Data 1977-2002. Washington, DC.

12

The Limits of Exchange Market Intervention

EDWIN M. TRUMAN

On April 29, 1983, the Summit finance ministers, central bank governors, and representatives of the European Community (1983) issued a Statement on the Intervention Study, which had been commissioned at the Versailles Economic Summit in June 1982. The final paragraph read:

> Under present circumstances, the role of intervention can only be limited. Intervention can be useful to counter disorderly market conditions and to reduce short-term volatility. Intervention may also on occasion express an attitude toward exchange markets. Intervention normally will be useful only when complementing and supporting other policies. We are agreed on the need for closer consultations on policies and market conditions; and, while retaining our freedom to operate independently, are willing to undertake coordinated intervention in instances where it is agreed that such interventions would be helpful.

I would submit that finance ministry and central bank attitudes in the major industrialized countries toward sterilized exchange market intervention have not changed substantially in the intervening 20 years. If anything, officials have become more skeptical about the usefulness of the instrument. They are more reluctant to intervene to counter disorderly market conditions or to reduce volatility that is short-term in nature.[1] They are

Edwin M. Truman, senior fellow at the Institute for International Economics, served as assistant secretary of the US Treasury for international affairs from December 1998 to January 2001. This paper has benefited from comments by Kathryn Dominguez, Hali Edison, and Will Melick as well as from excellent research assistance provided by Frank Gaenssmantel.

1. The Japanese authorities are the least reluctant, and Ministry of Finance officials are the most likely to be quoted as expressing concern about short-term volatility, leading to more frequent intervention operations. However, as detailed by Ito (2002), since the mid-1990s the Japanese approach has changed substantially, moving away from repeated operations day after day toward larger, tactical operations.

prepared to express an attitude toward exchange market developments when their "close consultations" lead them to a consensus. If they can agree that coordinated intervention would be helpful, they are willing to do it. However, they continue to think that intervention is not a separate instrument of policy and that normally it will be effective only when it is seen to be complementary with and supported by other policies. Those are demanding conditions indeed.

As a Federal Reserve official, I spent much of my career leaning against the current US official fashion with respect to the effectiveness of foreign exchange market intervention. Because during much of that period, including the early 1980s, US official fashion was anti-intervention, I was involved in efforts to demonstrate the effectiveness of the instrument, including service as the Federal Reserve's representative on the Working Group on Exchange Market Intervention that was chaired by Philippe Jurgensen (1983) (Jurgensen Report). During other periods, such as the late 1970s, when US Treasury officials felt that the inflation problem in the US economy did not require tighter US monetary policy and could be successfully addressed by exchange market intervention, or the late 1980s, when the US authorities intervened in exchange markets heavily, including on 97 days in 1989, with little or no effect, I leaned equally heavily to the other side of the ongoing debate.

The evidence on the short-run effectiveness of exchange market intervention is sufficient in my view to support the judicious use of intervention by the United States as a supplementary policy instrument as long as it generally is used in a manner consistent with other economic policies; however, that same evidence falls substantially short of demonstrating that intervention is a separate policy instrument that can be used to manage exchange rates with any lasting effect. Even in the short run, the evidence is that the probability of the effectiveness of intervention on the spot exchange rate is at best equal to the flip of a fair coin. Moreover, most of the evidence comes from studies in which the test is correlation not causation, in the sense that there is no underlying structural model. Therefore, one cannot dismiss the possibility that the correlations are due to randomness.

What harm is there in using an instrument that may or may not be at all effective but at least is associated about half the time with success? The harm lies in the potential for collateral damage by, for example, distracting the authorities from correcting fundamental economic policies, sending incorrect signals about those policies, or potentially moving exchange rates in directions inconsistent with those policies. These considerations suggest some of the limits on intervention as a policy tool; it may not be effective and it may not be a benign instrument. Moreover, according to the advocates, the effectiveness of intervention is enhanced not only by a need for consistency with fundamental economic policies but also by a need for an international consensus to support coordinated intervention.

The remainder of this paper is divided into two parts. The first addresses the technical question of the effectiveness of exchange market intervention by the major industrialized countries. The second addresses policy considerations from a US or national perspective and from an international perspective.

The Effectiveness of Intervention

The literature on the effectiveness of exchange market intervention on spot exchange rates has blossomed since the early 1980s, aided in large part by the studies that were produced at the Federal Reserve and elsewhere as background for the Jurgensen Report.[2] Neither the research that was done as background for the Jurgensen Report nor any of the subsequent research justifies the opinion expressed by Kathryn Dominguez in her paper for this conference that the conventional view as of the early 1990s was that "intervention could only be effective if combined with contemporaneous changes in money supply (or, in other words, only if interventions were unsterilized)." Sterilized intervention never has been dead as a policy instrument even for the major economies with large open capital markets; the issue always has been how effective it is and to what extent it can be relied on as an instrument of policy.

Research on the effectiveness of intervention has been aided by the gradual relaxation of prohibitions on access to intervention data, but the availability of those data has proven to be less helpful than many had hoped in resolving the basic issues surrounding the effectiveness of intervention. One reason is the lack of a robust model explaining exchange rate determination.

Dominguez, working alone (1987) and also collaborating with Jeffrey A. Frankel (1993), has been one of the major contributors to this literature. In the paper she presented at this conference, Dominguez continues in that tradition of careful and rich analysis. In part she uses statistical techniques to examine intervention episodes that are as short as a single day and as long as several years.[3] She examines intervention by G-3 (Japanese, German/European, and US) monetary authorities. She presents the results of a range of tests from four-hour effects to 48-hour effects and beyond. Averaging across those tests for the G-3, the results are significant and with the correct sign, on a generous interpretation, in about half the cases. The results are similarly uneven for each monetary

---

2. For a summary of the ten studies produced primarily at the Federal Reserve, see Henderson and Sampson (1983).

3. In the former episodes, she embeds the day of intervention in a month's worth of data to derive her results.

authority's operations and regardless of whether they are buying or selling.

Dominguez chooses to highlight four tests: four-hour impacts, eight-hour impacts, success during the intervention episode (exchange rate movement in the appropriate direction from start to finish), and long-run success (exchange-rate movement in the appropriate direction within three months of the final intervention). The mean score for the 22 (sometimes overlapping) episodes was a success rate of 46 percent. In only four (18 percent) of the episodes were all four principal tests satisfied. This illustrates what Dominguez calls the "problem of temporal correlations" in this literature: the time frame for your measure of effectiveness. She does not highlight what on this basis might be considered the most relevant of her tests, the "48-hour persistence" of the effects of intervention with the correct sign and significance. Only six of the episodes pass this test.

The evidence presented on the long-run success of the intervention is particularly problematic. Not only is it biased because the authorities were free to continue operating until they could declare victory regardless of the effects of their operation, but also she is selective in her interpretation of what she calls a three-month success. For example, the US-Japanese operation in June 1998 purchasing yen passes all four of Dominguez's major tests, but it passes the test of long-run success (the yen stronger after three months than at the start of the intervention) even though two months after the intervention the yen rate was weaker than at the start of the intervention. The basic message of Dominguez's new research is that sometimes intervention appears to have an effect on exchange rates, but long-term or lasting effects are very difficult to prove, and the effects over any time horizon are imprecise and unpredictable.

Conclusions from surveys of the intervention literature range from sympathetic to skeptical. Among the more sympathetic surveys are Sarno and Taylor (2001) and Hutchison (2002). Sarno and Taylor conclude, "Overall, the evidence on the effectiveness of official intervention, through either the portfolio balance channel or the signaling channel, is still mixed on balance, although the more recent literature does suggest a significant effect of official intervention on both the level and the change of exchange rates" (2001, 862). Dominguez concludes on the basis of her study of the 1990s that "intervention policy is both alive and well." This is a somewhat surprising statement in light of the paucity of G-3 interventions since 1995; even the Japanese have sharply cut back on the frequency of their operations.[4]

---

4. Since February 1996 (and through June 2002), the Japanese authorities operated on only 39 days or about once every other month. In contrast, from the start of 1991 through February 1996, the Japanese operated 179 days, or on average about three days every month. Over the seven years since August 1995, the US authorities have operated on only two days and the European (Bundesbank or ECB) authorities on only four days.

Much of the recent evidence on the effectiveness of intervention has been based on so-called event studies or case studies. The former are more statistically sophisticated than the latter, and in practice either approach often involves the application of a range of statistical techniques, but the more they resemble event studies, narrowly defined, the more likely it is that they discard a good deal of the context found in broader descriptive case studies. See, for example, Fatum (2000), Galati, Melick, and Micu (2002), Hutchison (2002), Ito (2002), and Catte, Galli, and Rebecchini (1994).[5]

Hutchison (2002) concludes, "Empirical work based on event study methodologies is much more supportive of the effectiveness of sterilized intervention than most work based on time-series methodologies." His policy conclusion is that there is "a limited role for sterilized intervention and that it should play a role in short-run stabilization policy." Similarly, Fatum (2000, 18) concludes in his study of US and German intervention, "The results clearly suggested that intervention is indeed effective in terms of influencing the evolution of exchange rates over the short run, thereby questioning the view that sterilized intervention is central bank force of habit rather than rational policy conduct." However, he immediately qualifies his conclusion: "The potency of sterilized intervention on its own should not be exaggerated. Although potentially effective in the short run, sterilized intervention is unlikely to have lasting effects on its own."

The case study and event study literature is not without its critics. One of the most trenchant criticisms is that the selection of events is biased in the direction of a finding of success because in many cases the authorities clearly continued to operate over many days until they could declare victory, but the evidence that such victories were associated with the intervention, as opposed to the other market forces just exhausting themselves, is questionable.[6]

---

5. Galati, Melick, and Micu are an exception to this generalization. They do provide some context for the episodes they examine. They also apply very sophisticated techniques looking at the effects of intervention on four moments of estimated probability density functions. On balance, they find (using event study methods) that intervention often is associated with the movement of expectations in the intended direction, but impacts vary considerably across episodes, and those movements generally are not statistically significant.

The Ito (2002) paper is of particular interest because, like Dominguez's paper for the conference, it covers Japanese experience in the 1990s. A careful reading of Ito's results points to a similar conclusion: Japanese intervention was effective in the very short run about half the time.

6. One of the first such studies was that by Catte et al. (1994), which I criticized on these grounds when it was first presented (Truman 1994). (Obstfeld (1995) reached a similar conclusion.) The basic problem is illustrated by Dominguez in her conference paper when she cites Japanese and US efforts to turn around the weakness of the dollar in 1995; there was a substantial amount of intervention, including intervention when the dollar was moving up, and eventually the dollar turned in August, but whether, after months of apparently fruitless efforts, the intervention caused the turn is debatable.

Edison (1998) conducts a careful study of US intervention in support of the dollar through sales of deutsche marks and yen from 1993 to 1995 using an event study methodology. However, in her study, the length of the events was limited to a few days at most. With respect to the deutsche mark, in eight episodes she finds that three were complete failures; they neither reversed the movement of the currency of the previous day nor reversed it after a month. Two were definite successes, in that they were associated with favorable movements on the day of the intervention as well as over the next month. Two episodes involved only short-run success, and one involved only longer-run success. With respect to the yen, out of 14 episodes, five were failures, five were definite successes, one was a short-run success, and three were longer-run successes.

Edison also reexamines the Catte et al. episodes for the period January 1985 to March 1991. Their episodes generally involved long periods of intervention. She examines the data on an objective, statistical basis in terms of the results over the month following the end of the operation in place of the subjective judgments by Catte et al. She finds success in about one-third of the episodes, failure in about one-third, and temporary success in about one-third.[7] Edison (1998) reaches a conclusion that is similar to hers in Edison (1993): "It is possible to show that intervention can have short-lived effects. Thus, this explains why central bankers might want to keep intervention in their toolkit. However, it remains to be shown that intervention can have a long-lasting, quantitatively significant effect."

One of the principal drawbacks of the case or event study approach is that the studies are not based on structural models and therefore can shed no light on the channels through which intervention may be effective. Sarno and Taylor (2001) suggest that we should expand the list of channels beyond the traditional portfolio balance channel, for which there is limited support to date and which may in any case be losing relevance for the major currencies, and the signaling channel, for which there is greater support, to include what they call a "coordination channel" aimed at overcoming a coordination failure in the market when almost all participants know that an exchange rate has gone too far, but no individual actor has the power or resources to buck the trend.[8] They motivate their discussion of the coordination channel by an appeal to the literature

---

7. Temporary success occurs when the postintervention exchange rate move is in the intended direction, but the next intervention episode is in the same direction.

8. The Jurgensen Report put forward 14 possible, not mutually exclusive objectives of intervention. It also discussed sending a signal to the market (paragraph 25)—the coordination channel—and (paragraph 66) the "demonstration effect" of intervention influencing "expectations about future underlying economic conditions or policies"—the signaling channel. The signaling channel also has been associated with Mussa (1981).

on second-generation speculative attacks and the avoidance of a bad equilibrium.

For the policymaker, it is a disappointment that the portfolio balance channel has not been supported by the empirical studies; the supply-and-demand framework of the portfolio balance model is inherently appealing when thinking about intervention operations. The signaling channel, on the other hand, is problematic for the policymaker, because if it is a signal about future policy, in the absence of that policy, the intervention should lose its effectiveness, and in the presence of that policy, it is the policy, not the intervention, that has been effective.

In a significant number of the important episodes of intervention, the crux of the issue is the nature of the signal. For example, in the 1992 phase of the European Exchange Rate Mechanism (ERM) crisis, the United States sold deutsche marks in July and August to signal that the United States was not practicing benign neglect toward the dollar's weakness, but the intention was definitely not to signal that the Federal Reserve's trend of easing interest rates was about to be reversed. For the European participants in this drama, the central issue was the signal conveyed by their massive intervention operations about their economic policies—in particular monetary policy, but also other policies—and whether those policies were going to be addressed solely toward defending existing exchange rate pegs or were going to be addressed toward the needs of the underlying economy. (See Truman 2002.) Obstfeld (1995, 18) concludes with respect to signaling: "Intervention can be used in providing a costly and therefore informative signal of official intentions when markets are confused about policy. . . . But intervention, acting alone, cannot halt market trends for long, let alone reverse them."

The attraction of the coordination channel for the effectiveness of intervention is that it focuses on market dynamics without implicating policy.[9] One reason for the apparent effectiveness of intervention that is implemented within such a conceptual framework is that by its nature it is designed to catch the market off-guard, forcing short-term traders to absorb losses as they close their open positions and, at least for a period of a few hours, contributing to a market dynamic that differs from one that may have prevailed over the previous days, weeks, or months. Market participants may be led to "think" about whether the rate has moved "too far."

Two implications flow from the conceptual framework of a coordinating channel. First, intervention operations that are repeated or reactive are not likely to be effective. The authorities have a few chances, perhaps,

---

9. As noted earlier, Galati, Melick, and Micu (2002) look in their research at the behavior of four moments of estimated probability density functions for exchange rates in the context of intervention; this approach is in the spirit of the coordination channel.

extending over a period of at most a few days, to make their point and alter market psychology.[10] If they are not successful, they risk becoming victims of the "tar-baby phenomenon,"[11] seeking to extricate themselves from the market without admitting to failure. As a consequence, operations have become larger to ensure that some damage is inflicted on the traders' positions, and they have become more infrequent. Some call the approach guerrilla tactics.

The second implication of the conceptual framework of a coordination channel is that the authorities have been induced to abandon strategies that seek regularly to counter disorderly market conditions, that is, they no longer try to smooth day-to-day fluctuations in rates, while remaining free to deal with disorder that might be associated with isolated events like the failure of a large financial institution or a political shock. Furthermore, to the extent that intervention is directed at defending a soft or hard exchange rate band, it must rely on another framework for its effectiveness—the portfolio balance or policy signaling channels—because sporadic operations cannot be counted on to have long-term effects, and repeated operations face diminishing returns. On the other hand, to the extent that intervention is a policy tool that is used in the context of a loose notion about the rate that is consistent with long-term economic and financial trends, it would be compatible with a framework for exchange market intervention that relied on the coordination channel and sporadic operations for its effects.

To summarize, my reading of both the economics literature on the effectiveness of intervention and my assessment of the actual use of the instrument by G-3 authorities in recent years is essentially the same as it was a decade ago (Truman 1994, 249): the evidence is sufficient "to support the continued judicious use of intervention as a supplementary policy instrument."[12] Even Sarno and Taylor (2001, 862), who, as noted earlier, are in the camp of those who are positive about intervention's effectiveness, state that the studies "allow us to conclude cautiously that official intervention can be effective, especially if it is publicly announced and

---

10. Many consider the August 15, 1995, joint Japan-US operation as a classic example of such opportunism, going with the flow of the market (Bank for International Settlements 1996, 101).

11. This term, drawn from American literature, was often used by Sam Y. Cross, a former US Treasury official, who was manager of foreign operations for the Federal Reserve System Open Market Account from the early 1980s through 1991, to warn against the risk of entering the market without an exit strategy.

12. To emphasize here a point that has applied throughout this paper, the issue is intervention involving the G-3 currencies. Exchange rates involving less international currencies may be more responsive to intervention, or may be responsive for a longer run, because of either capital controls or other aspects that make them much less perfect substitutes.

concerted and provided that it is consistent with the underlying stance of monetary policy."[13]

Two aspects of this statement deserve emphasis: First, they conclude that intervention "can" be effective, which is not the same as saying that it is always effective. Second, they lay down three conditions in which it is more likely to be effective: public announcement, multilateral engagement, and policy consistency.[14] While public announcement is simple and now common practice among the G-3 authorities, the other two conditions are more demanding. They are discussed further in the second part of this paper. Reaching international agreement that now is the time to operate in the foreign exchange market is a tedious process, in part because the interests of two or more sets of authorities may differ, and in part because their views may differ on the effectiveness of the instrument and the costs of its overuse. Moreover, frequently there is a lack of consensus that an intervention operation would be consistent with underlying macroeconomic policies. One consequence is that attempts to establish guidelines for G-3 intervention operations such as in the 1987 Louvre Accord are destined to fail within a few days or weeks as soon as conditions and attitudes change to destroy the consensus.

Exchange Market Intervention: Policy Considerations

From a US or national perspective, the overriding objective of macroeconomic policies is to achieve maximum sustainable noninflationary growth. In this context, the foreign exchange value of the dollar and the US current account and international investment position are not policy objectives. Those variables also do not systematically affect the achievement of the primary policy objective using the instruments of monetary and fiscal policy. Policymakers, reflecting the views of the general public, may have preferences about the allocation of fully employed resources between sectors producing traded (manufactured) goods and services and sectors producing nontraded (primarily nonmanufactured) goods and services. They also may have concerns about the sustainability of the US current account balance or international investment position. However, the evi-

---

13. Ito (2002) as well as other researchers have interpreted their results as consistent with the view that coordinated intervention is more effective, or more likely to be effective. Galati, Melick, and Micu (2002) test this proposition directly and find that coordinated operations do not add to the significance of the intervention.

14. Dominguez and Frankel (1993) also recommended that intervention should be unanticipated, publicly announced, and coordinated. They also argued, as Dominguez recounts in her conference paper, that "intervention was least likely to be effective if it was inconsistent with either future monetary policy intentions or future exchange rate fundamentals."

Figure 12.1   US output gap, monetary policy stance, and real exchange rate index, 1981-2002

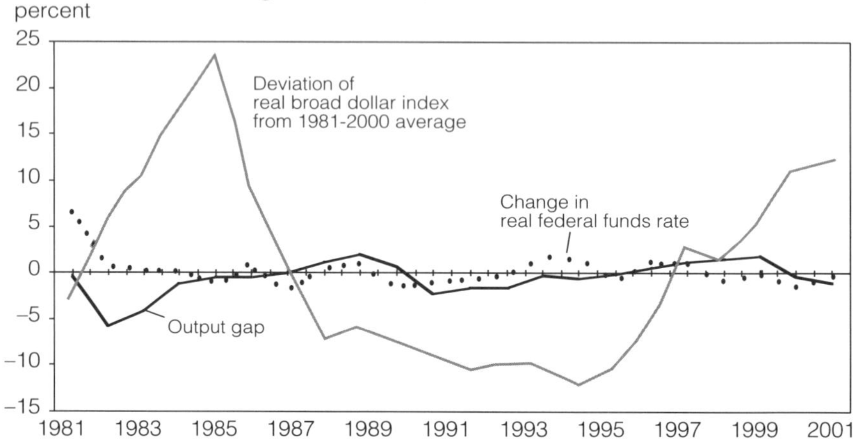

percent

Sources: Output gap: OECD *Economic Outlook*, Nos. 65, 67, and 71; real broad dollar index: Federal Reserve Board statistics; inflation data (to compute real federal funds rate): Bureau of Labor Statistics.

dence from empirical studies, as discussed above, is that they lack an instrument independent of the settings of monetary and fiscal policies to achieve, with any reliability or consistency, the desired allocation of production across sectors or to alter the external accounts.

Policymakers, of course, do take account of actual and potential developments in exchange rates and external accounts when making policy and balancing risks. For example, they try to anticipate the effects of exchange rate depreciation on the real economy and thereby on inflation, they try to anticipate the tendency of exchange rate appreciation to dampen the real economy, and generally they are alert to the possibility that an unsustainable position in the external accounts will eventually be corrected. That amounts to good analysis, but it is not the same thing as directing economic policy at an exchange rate target or at the current account.

Under some circumstances, economic conditions and the orientation of monetary and fiscal policy may be consistent with the judicious use of exchange market intervention in an effort to influence exchange market behavior in a manner that supports those objectives. However, conflicts are common.

Figure 12.1 depicts annual data from 1981 to 2002 for the US output gap (a summary measure of the condition of the domestic economy), the stance of US monetary policy (indexed by the change in the real federal funds rate), and the foreign exchange value of the dollar (as measured

Figure 12.2 Consistency of US monetary policy with the needs of the real economy and the real exchange rate index

		Monetary policy consistent with moving exchange rate index toward average	
		Yes	No
Monetary policy consistent with needs of real economy	Yes	1984 1985 1988 1989 1997 2001 2002	1987 1991 1992 1993 1996 1998 2000
	No	1981 1994 1995 1999	1982 1983* 1986 1990

*Monetary policy unchanged.

Notes: *US monetary policy* indicates change in real federal funds rate.
    Needs of real economy indicates sign of output gap.
    Exchange rate indicates deviation of real broad dollar index from 1981-2002 average (Federal Reserve).

Source: Author's calculations.

by the broad real exchange rate index developed by the staff of the Federal Reserve Board).[15] The figure illustrates several points.

First, even using these crude indicators, in two-thirds (14 of the 22) of the years the stance of monetary policy was consistent with the needs of the macroeconomy; the direction of monetary policy was toward easing when the output gap was negative and vice versa (see figure 12.2).[16]

---

15. The data for 2002 on the output gap are the latest estimates from the Organization for Economic Cooperation and Development; the 2002 data for the stance of monetary policy and the exchange rate index treat the average through August 2002 as the average for the year.

16. The eight years where this relationship did not hold are three years in the early 1980s (1981-83), when monetary policy continued to tighten in order to stamp out the high inflation and attendant inflation expectations of the late 1970s, and the economy experienced two recessions; 1986 and 1990, when the measure of the stance of monetary policy is distorted by the impact of oil prices (lower in 1986 and higher in 1990) on the consumer price index that is used to deflate the federal funds rate; 1994 and 1995, when the Federal Reserve took preemptive action to tighten monetary policy when the output gap (as measured) was still negative; and 1999 when monetary policy was eased when global financial conditions tightened in the wake of the Russian default although the output gap suggested that policy should be tightened.

Second, in half the years, the stance of monetary policy was inconsistent with bringing the foreign exchange value of the dollar back toward its average value for the entire period, which is presented as a reasonable norm, on the assumption that easier policy would tend to depreciate the dollar and vice versa. In other words, in half the years (11 of 22), there was a potential conflict between the use of intervention to influence the dollar's value and the stance of monetary policy.[17] Restricting attention to the 14 years when the stance of policy was clearly consistent with the needs of the macroeconomy, in half the years, again, there was a potential conflict between the use of intervention and the stance of monetary policy: 1987, 1991, 1992, 1993, 1996, 1998, and 2000. In the last two years, monetary policy was tightening when the dollar was above the average for the period; in the other five years, monetary policy was easing when the dollar was below the average.[18]

Third, in six of the seven years in which there was a potential conflict between the use of exchange market intervention to move the dollar toward its average value and the stance of monetary policy, the US monetary authorities did operate in the exchange market. The exception was 1996. In five of those six years, the direction of the operation was consistent with trying to move the dollar toward the average. The sixth year was 1991, when the dollar was below the average and the US authorities sold dollars against yen and both bought and sold dollars against deutsche marks; total dollar purchases did exceed total dollar sales.

Excluding 1991, a judgmental assessment of the success or failure of US foreign exchange market operations in the remaining five years suggests that they failed in their objectives in 1987 (when the dollar continued to fall despite the Louvre Accord) and 1992 (when the dollar also continued to fall). In 1992, the dollar was caught for much of the year in the backwash of the unfolding events of the first year of the 1992-93 ERM crisis. That year also posed the most severe conflict between the needs of the domestic economy and the associated stance of monetary policy and the dollar's external value; the negative output gap was 175 basis points, the real funds rate was reduced by 92 basis points, and the dollar was more than 10 percentage points below its average for the period as a whole.

---

17. If leaning against *changes* in the real broad dollar index from the previous year is used as an indicator of the direction in which monetary policy should move, again half the years were conflict situations, although, of course, the years are not all the same.

18. For 11 years in which the stance of monetary policy was inconsistent with moving the dollar back toward the average for the period, in six years policy was easing when the dollar was below the average, in four years policy was tightening when the dollar was above the average, and in one year policy was unchanged when the dollar was below the average.

In 1993, 1998, and 2000, results of US intervention operations were mixed. In 1993, the dollar rose based on the broad index of the dollar's value in real terms, and also rose against the deutsche mark, but the dollar fell against the yen. In 1998 and 2000, in which there were one-day US intervention operations, buying yen in June 1998 and buying euros in September 2000, the intervention apparently produced the desired short-run effect of temporarily weakening the dollar against those two currencies, but in both years the dollar later appreciated further against these currencies and appreciated on average for the year in terms of the broad index of its real value.[19]

As is generally the case in this area, different observers may choose to interpret differently the evidence just presented. I conclude that it points to the limits of exchange market intervention when it is inconsistent with underlying policies and to the consequent risk of failure that would further discredit the use of the instrument.

The risks associated with exchange market intervention are not limited to the risk of failure, however. Aside from the possibility of failure, four possible risks can be identified. First is distraction risk: intervention may distract the authorities from the use of other policies to address the fundamental problems of the economy. For example, in 1978-79, after the failed attempt of the Carter administration to devalue the dollar to restore US economic prosperity, exchange market intervention was used heavily as an alternative to tightening monetary policy in the face of rising inflation. As I commented to the Federal Open Market Committee (FOMC) during its 1990 discussion of US foreign exchange operations, "Treasury officials [in 1989 and 1990] certainly are on the side that say intervention is and has been and should be—certainly should be—effective. . . . They were in exactly the same situation in the 1978-79 period" (Board of Governors of the Federal Reserve System 1990, 66). The delay in 1978-79 caused by the distraction of exchange market intervention in trying unsuccessfully to deal with the symptoms of a weak dollar led to the highest rate of US

---

19. For completeness, with respect to the seven years in the yes-yes box of figure 12.2, no intervention occurred in years 1997, 2001, and 2002 to date. In 1984, there were about $450 million in sales of deutsche marks spread through the year, despite the fact that the folklore is that this was a nonintervention period for the United States; the operations were not successful but were consistent with the thrust of monetary policy and the needs of the macroeconomy as well as with the level of the dollar relative to the longer-term average. In 1985, US sales of dollars were associated with what is generally viewed as successful intervention and consistent with the thrust of monetary policy as well as the needs of the macro economy. In 1988, the US authorities bought dollars early in the year (in what is often considered a successful operation), sold dollars in the middle of the year, and bought dollars again at the end of the year, but sales exceeded purchases, and the net sales were inconsistent with monetary policy and the level of the dollar on average during the year relative to its longer-run average. In 1989, the US authorities engaged in massive dollar sales in conflict with the thrust of monetary policy (see below) and the dollar's level at the time, to little apparent effect.

inflation recorded in the post-World War II period and to the need to adopt draconian measures to bring inflation under control, which in turn were associated with one of the deepest recessions of the postwar period.

Second is signal risk: intervention may send the wrong signal about policy. That was the case in 1989-90, when US monetary policy was tightening and the US intervention operations were oriented toward weakening the dollar. This was a period of conflict between the Federal Reserve and the US Treasury over intervention operations. The FOMC held an extended discussion of the Federal Reserve's involvement in US intervention operations on the basis of a report from a staff Task Force on System Foreign Exchange Operations and against the background of US intervention operations in 1989 on a record 97 days designed to weaken the dollar, or resist its strengthening, at a time when the Federal Reserve was tightening policy.[20] Manley Johnson succinctly summarized the policy conflict: "If I were a market participant and I were sitting out there seeing the Federal Reserve talking about price stability and yet selling massive amounts of dollars, I think eventually I'd decide that was a joke as a policy" (Board of Governors of the Federal Reserve System 1990, 55). Gerald Corrigan echoed Johnson's concerns: "As I see it, the biggest danger with intervention—whether or not it's done by the Federal Reserve or the Treasury or both—is the danger that it can ultimately co-opt monetary policy" (Board of Governors of the Federal Reserve System 1990, 58).[21]

Third is exacerbation risk: intervention, if it is successful, may exacerbate problems in the domestic economy. For example, if foreign exchange market intervention had been used extensively in 1999 to lower the foreign exchange value of the dollar when the economy was already booming and the output gap was positive and that intervention had been successful

---

20. Kaminsky and Lewis (1996) look at this period in some detail, stopping their analysis in February 1990 in the mistaken belief that the Federal Reserve withdrew from joint operations with the Treasury for the remainder of the year rather than just in one or two operations in March. The inconsistency between the stance of monetary policy and the direction of foreign exchange operations, which were also counter to what is depicted in figure 12.1 as a need to strengthen the dollar, contributed to their finding that there was a significant signaling effect in US intervention in the 1985-89 period, but it had the wrong sign, that is, it signaled easing when policy was tightening.

21. Let me be clear—intervention may be justified even when it may appear to be inconsistent with the stance of other policies, but then it must satisfy tougher conditions. In the build-up to the ERM crisis of 1992, the US authorities intervened in the summer of 1992 to support the dollar even as the Federal Reserve was easing in order to demonstrate an absence of US indifference to the dollar's weakness. However, the operations were unsuccessful (Truman 2002). Sushil Wadhwani (2000) advocated consideration of intervention by the Bank of England in mid-2000 when he felt the pound sterling was overvalued, despite the fact that the UK economy was operating at or near full capacity. He said foreign exchange market "intervention could potentially be useful in terms of achieving our overall monetary policy objectives, though it is no panacea." However, he added, "it would be important to only use it when the pre-conditions for likely success were in place."

in reducing the dollar's value substantially, the domestic economy could have suffered extensive damage.

The simulations presented in this conference by Martin Baily illustrate this point. If the dollar somehow had been held constant at its 1991 level during the 1990s, the trade deficit would have been substantially reduced in the late 1990s, but consumption would have been lower, investment would have been lower, inflation would have been higher (even under the assumption that the Federal Reserve would have reacted to the higher growth and inflation), and growth in 2000 and 2001 would have been significantly reduced. It is worth noting that if the Federal Reserve had eased monetary policy in order to reduce the attractiveness of the dollar in the late 1990s, it would have risked overheating the economy. In retrospect, there is now a hot debate about the actual easing of Federal Reserve policy in the fall of 1998, in the wake of the Russian default and the widening of spread in credit markets that brought down Long Term Capital Management (LTCM). The easing carried over into 1999 and produced a reduction in the real federal funds rate of almost one percentage point on average in 1999, and some argue the easing was a mistake because it allowed the stock market bubble to persist for another year and subsequently damaged the economy.

Fourth is success risk: intervention may be too successful.[22] In 2000, for example, the US economy appeared to be operating above potential, and monetary policy had shifted toward restraint, although, based on the indicator shown in figure 12.1, the shift amounted to only a few basis points because much of the rise in the nominal federal funds rate was offset by a rise in consumer prices in part associated with higher petroleum prices caused by tight conditions in global oil markets because of rising demand. The risk, as perceived by some policymakers at the time, was that the US economy would slow down, equity markets would collapse, and the foreign exchange value of the dollar would reverse sharply its levitation of the late 1990s. Successful exchange market intervention might have precipitated, in perception if not in causality, precisely the scenario that policymakers wanted to avoid, broad-based turbulence in a wide range of financial markets.

Thus, from a national policy perspective, there may be occasions, such as June 1998 and September 2000, when judicious use of foreign exchange market intervention may be effective even if not fully consistent with the stance of US macroeconomic policies, but those occasions are not likely to be frequent, and each involves a number of potential risks.

Bringing in the international perspective, policy considerations surrounding exchange market intervention are even more complex because all the considerations that have just been outlined from a national perspec-

---

22. As a senior colleague commented to me in 1985, when a country intervenes to depress its currency it does so at its own peril. In the US case, the peril materialized two years later in a decline in the dollar that was unwelcome and could not be stopped via intervention.

tive are replicated in one or more economies elsewhere in the world. These considerations are relevant because exchange rates are two-sided, by definition, and because of the general perception that coordinated operations have a greater chance of being effective.

Even if the US authorities reach a judgment that the balance is tilted in the direction of operating in exchange markets, views elsewhere may differ. Authorities in other countries have differences in view about the effectiveness of intervention. Views in other countries may also differ because of different economic circumstances; for example, today neither the Japanese nor the European authorities are anxious to see their currencies appreciate because that would be inconsistent with the needs of their domestic economies, which they see as benefiting, in the case of Japan, from export-led growth or being hurt, in the case of Europe, from a withdrawal of external stimulus. Finally, views in other countries may differ on the appropriateness of intervention given the risks of collateral damage as outlined above.

As in the United States, reaching a favorable judgment in other economies that foreign exchange market intervention is appropriate usually involves alignment of the views in the finance ministry and those in the central bank. It may be that one or the other institution has the final say or that one or the other institution is very much a junior partner in such operations, but rarely does intervention occur on any substantial scale over the active opposition of one of the two institutions.[23]

In addition to these policy and institutional considerations, coordinated exchange market intervention often involves a host of technical and tactical considerations. Given how rare intervention is these days, time is required to conduct the necessary consultations to crank up the machinery. Tactical considerations include such matters as agreeing on what is to be said before, during, and after the operation. Moreover, it is often important to some participants, as it was to the United States in 1998 and 2000, that it be known who initiated any coordinated foreign exchange market operation.

Conclusion

Exchange market intervention has definite limits as a policy instrument. Its effectiveness is uncertain and imprecise, and therefore it is at best a

---

23. Each of the G-3 economies operates under different institutional arrangements. In the United States, both the US Treasury and the Federal Reserve have independent legal authority to operate in the foreign exchange market, and they normally act jointly for their separate accounts, unless one or the other party does not agree, which occasionally occurs. In Japan the intervention decisions are made by the Ministry of Finance, which also holds the bulk of Japan's foreign exchange reserves. In Germany, the Bundesbank made intervention decisions. With the birth of the euro, the European Central Bank makes the tactical decisions, but the euro area finance ministries are involved in strategic decisions. In this context, it is somewhat unfortunate that Dominguez, in her paper for this conference, follows the normal convention of associating intervention with the central bank conducting the operation rather than the monetary authority (central bank or finance ministry) that makes the decision.

blunt or a blunted instrument. It is advisable that it be used as a supplement to and consistent with fundamental economic policies, as suggested by the empirical research on the effectiveness of intervention. The US experience over the past 20 years suggests that roughly half the time the potential use of intervention would be in conflict with those policies. The possibility of collateral damage further limits the scope to use the instrument. Finally, it is a challenge to align official attitudes about foreign exchange operations in other countries with the prevailing attitude in the United States because views about these issues, in light of their own experience and circumstances, necessarily differ.

Where does this leave intervention as a policy tool? First, intervention is not a separate instrument of policy that can be used regardless of the stance of other economic and financial policies; it is not effective in achieving discrete adjustments in exchange rates, moving them from one level to another and holding them there. Second, intervention is not an available instrument to manage G-3 exchange rates within target zones or to fine-tune exchange rate movements.

Foreign exchange market intervention is analogous to a drug that has not received, and is not likely to receive, FDA approval for general use. We know it works sometimes, but we do not know why it works. We also know it can have adverse effects, for example, adding generally to financial market turbulence or distracting the authorities from focusing on economic fundamentals. The consequences of using the instrument are decidedly imprecise. As a result, it is dangerous to prescribe the use of intervention except in extreme situations, and it is certainly not recommended for everyday use. This suggests that the instrument should be used sparingly and cannot be counted upon to address satisfactorily actual or perceived misalignments of exchange rates.

It follows that it is appropriate to be modest in any claims about the effectiveness of exchange market intervention. For example, when addressing the legitimate concerns of US manufacturing industries, it is fraudulent and irresponsible to claim that exchange market intervention can be used with any confidence or precision to improve their competitiveness, in particular without requiring any other complementary policy adjustments, such as increases in interest rates or strengthening of fiscal positions, in particular when the economy is at or near full employment.

On the other hand, in the context of a broad consensus that the dollar is misaligned, if such a consensus is shared by the other G-3 authorities, and under conditions in which the principal (monetary and fiscal) instruments of macroeconomic policy are pointed in a consistent direction in all three economies, it is reasonable to consider coordinated intervention operations. I submit that those conditions do not prevail today. The G-3 authorities have not reached a consensus that the dollar is seriously misaligned. US monetary policy may be consistent with a weaker dollar, but US fiscal policy is not, because of the renewed prospect of ever-widening fiscal deficits.

References

Bank for International Settlements. 1996. *Annual Report.* Basel: Bank for International Settlements.

Board of Governors of the Federal Reserve System. 1990. Transcript of Meeting of the Federal Open Market Committee: March 27, 1990. Washington: Board of Governors of the Federal Reserve System.

Catte, Pietro, Giampaolo Galli, and Salvatore Rebecchini. 1994. Concerted Interventions and the Dollar: An Analysis of Daily Data. In *The International Monetary System,* edited by Peter B. Kenen, Francesco Papdia, and Fabrizio Saccomanni. Cambridge, England: Cambridge University Press.

Dominguez, Kathryn M. 1987. Exchange Rate Efficiency and the Behavior of International Asset Markets. Yale University, Ph.D. dissertation.

Dominguez, Kathryn M., and Jeffrey A. Frankel. 1993. *Does Foreign Exchange Market Intervention Work?* Washington: Institute for International Economics.

Edison, Hali J. 1993. *The Effectiveness of Central Bank Intervention: A Survey of the Literature After 1982.* Special Papers in International Economics No. 18. Princeton, NJ: Princeton University, International Finance Section, July.

Edison, Hali J. 1998. On Foreign Exchange Intervention: An Assessment of the US Experience. Washington: Board of Governors of the Federal Reserve System, February.

Fatum, Rasmus. 2000. *On the Effectiveness of Sterilized Foreign Exchange Market Intervention.* ECB Working Paper No. 10. Frankfurt: European Central Bank. Forthcoming in *Canadian Journal of Economics.*

Galati, Gabriele, Will Melick, and Marian Micu. 2002. *Central Bank Intervention and Market Expectations.* Bank for International Settlements, Basel. Photocopy.

Henderson, Dale W., and Stephanie Sampson. 1983. Intervention in Foreign Exchange Markets: A Summary of Ten Staff Studies. *Federal Reserve Bulletin* 69 (November): 830-36.

Hutchison, Michael M. 2002. The Role of Sterilized Intervention in Exchange Rate Stabilization Policy. University of California, Santa Cruz, June.

Ito, Takatoshi. 2002. *Is Foreign Exchange Intervention Effective? The Japanese Experiences in the 1990s.* NBER Working Paper No. 8914. Cambridge, MA: National Bureau of Economic Research.

Jurgensen, Philippe. 1983. *Report of the Working Group on Exchange Market Intervention.* Washington: US Department of the Treasury. Photocopy, March.

Kaminsky, Graciela L., and Karen K. Lewis. 1996. Does Foreign Exchange Market Intervention Signal Future Monetary Policy? *Journal of Monetary Economics* 37: 285-312.

Mussa, Michael. 1981. *The Role of Official Intervention.* New York: Group of Thirty.

Obstfeld, Maurice. 1995. International Currency Experience: New Lessons and Lessons Relearned. *Brookings Papers on Economic Activity*: 119-220. Washington: Brookings Institution.

Sarno, Lucio, and Mark P. Taylor. 2001. Official Intervention in the Foreign Exchange Market: Is It Effective and, If So, How Does It Work? *Journal of Economic Literature* 39 (September): 839-68.

Summit Finance Ministers, Central Bank Governors, and Representatives of the European Community. 1983. Statement on the Intervention Study, April 29.

Truman, Edwin M. 1994. Comment on "Concerted Interventions and the Dollar: An Analysis of Daily Data," by Pietro Catte, Giampoalo Galli, and Salvatore Rebecchini. In *The International Monetary System,* edited by Peter B. Kenen, Francesco Papdia, and Fabrizio Saccomanni. Cambridge, England: Cambridge University Press.

Truman, Edwin M. 2002. Economic Policy and Exchange Rate Regimes: What Have We Learned in the Ten Years Since Black Wednesday? Washington: Institute for International Economics, September.

Wadhwani, Sushil. 2000. The Exchange Rate and the MPC: What Can We Do? Speech to the Senior Business Forum at the Centre for Economic Performance, May 31.

13

Exchange Rate Manipulation to Gain an Unfair Competitive Advantage: The Case Against Japan and China

ERNEST H. PREEG

Article IV of the International Monetary Fund (IMF) Agreement states that members should "avoid manipulating exchange rates ... in order ... to gain an unfair competitive advantage over other members," and the related surveillance provision defines manipulation to include "protracted large-scale intervention in one direction in the exchange market." In other words, if a US trading partner makes protracted large-scale purchases of dollars and other currencies (that is, one-direction intervention) that leads to a lower-than-market-based exchange rate and a larger-than-market-determined trade surplus, there is prima facie evidence of IMF-proscribed exchange rate manipulation to gain an unfair competitive advantage.

In this context, this paper examines four questions: Have Japan and China, among others, been manipulating their exchange rates in recent years, as defined by the IMF? And if so, what has been the impact of such currency manipulation on the dollar exchange rate and the US trade deficit? What are the consequences for US economic and foreign policy interests? How should the US government respond?

Have Japan and China, Among Others, Been Manipulating Their Exchange Rates in Recent Years, as Defined by the IMF?

The answer begins with an assessment of the two adjectives applied to intervention in the IMF rules: "large-scale" and "protracted." In the cases

Ernest H. Preeg is a senior fellow in trade and productivity at Manufacturers Alliance/MAPI and a senior fellow at The Hudson Institute.

Table 13.1 Indicators of currency manipulation by Japan

	1998	1999	2000	2001	2002[a]
Foreign exchange reserves					
(billions of US dollars)					
Total, end of period	203	278	347	388	436
Increase from previous period		75	69	41	48
Cumulative increase from 1998		75	144	185	233
Trade, current, and FDI accounts					
(billions of US dollars)					
Trade balance, goods	122	123	117	70	
Current account balance	121	107	117	89	
FDI net flow	−21	−10	−23	−32	
Basic balance (current account balance plus FDI net flow)	100	97	94	57	
Foreign exchange reserve increase, as a percent of:					
Trade surplus		61	59	59	
Current account surplus		70	59	46	
Current account surplus plus FDI net flow		77	73	72	
Adequacy of reserves					
Foreign exchange (end of period) as a percent of imports (goods and services)	73	90	92	111	

a. January to July.

Source: International Monetary Fund, *International Financial Statistics.*

of Japan and China, as shown in tables 13.1 and 13.2, they unquestionably apply. Japanese one-direction intervention to buy dollars and other foreign exchange has totaled $233 billion since 1998, with large purchases each year, including $48 billion during the first seven months of 2002. Chinese cumulative purchases have been $98 billion since 1998, with a sharp upward trend to $46 billion in 2001 and $31 billion, or more than $5 billion per month, during the first six months of 2002.

Even with this clear evidence of protracted large-scale intervention, two other tests are appropriate before concluding that the motivation was to gain an unfair competitive advantage. The first test is of the "adequacy" of reserve holdings. If a country has run down its reserves through previous sales of foreign exchange, the motivation for purchases may simply be to restore an adequate level of reserves. There is no precise definition of "adequacy," although the World Bank benchmark over the years has been that a country should maintain reserves equal to at least 25 percent of annual imports. Japan and China, however, have levels of reserve holdings far above any comparable measure, as also shown in tables 13.1 and 13.2. Japanese foreign exchange holdings as a percentage of annual imports increased steadily from 73 percent in 1998 to 111 percent in 2001, while Chinese holdings have ranged between 81 percent and 104 percent of annual imports.

Table 13.2 Indicators of currency manipulation by China

	1998	1999	2000	2001	2002[a]
Foreign exchange reserves					
(billions of US dollars)					
Total, end of period	145	155	166	212	243
Increase from previous period		10	11	46	31
Cumulative increase from 1998		10	21	67	98
Trade, current, and FDI accounts					
(billions of US dollars)					
Trade balance, goods	47	36	34	23[b]	
Current account balance	31	21	21	21[b]	
FDI net flow	41	36	37	40[c]	
Basic balance (current account balance plus FDI net flow)	72	57	58	61	
Foreign exchange reserve increase, as a percent of:					
Trade surplus		28	32	200	
Current account surplus		48	52	219	
Current account surplus plus FDI net flow		18	19	75	
Adequacy of reserves					
Foreign exchange (end of period) as a percent of imports (goods and services)		104	93	81	91

a. January to June.

b. Data from *The Economist*.

c. Estimated.

Source: International Monetary Fund, *International Financial Statistics*, except as otherwise indicated.

The second test relates to balance-of-payments adjustment and whether a country is running a large deficit or surplus on current and long-term capital accounts. A country in a chronic large-deficit position, like the United States, could "manipulate" its currency to gain a competitive advantage, but such intervention might not be judged "unfair" if the objective is to bring external accounts back toward balance. Once again as shown in the tables, however, this rationale for justifying currency manipulation would not apply for Japan and China because they both run chronically large trade and current account surpluses, and China has a very large net inflow of foreign direct investment (FDI) as well. Japan had current account surpluses of $89 billion to $121 billion per year during the period 1998-2001, and even taking account of a net outflow of FDI, there was still a very large net overall inflow of foreign exchange of $57 billion to $100 billion on "basic balance." In the case of China, the current account surplus ranged from $21 billion to $31 billion, while a very large net inflow of FDI raised the basic balance net inflow of foreign exchange to $57 billion to $72 billion. Indeed, for the balance-of-payments test, the presumption would be for Japan and China, if anything, to be selling rather than buying foreign exchange in order to reduce chronically large surpluses on external accounts.

In conclusion, Japan and China, based on all criteria related to the IMF definition, have been persistently manipulating their currencies to gain an unfair competitive advantage.

There are also other likely official currency manipulators, but identifying the full list would require further research. The two most glaring suspects, however, are South Korea and Taiwan. South Korea increased its foreign exchange holdings from $52 billion in December 1998 to $103 billion in December 2001 and to $116 billion in July 2002. During the same period, Korea had a sustained current account surplus ($9 billion in 2001) and a large net inflow of FDI ($12 billion in 2001). Taiwan increased its foreign exchange holdings from $122 billion in December 2001 to $155 billion in July 2002, while running an annual current account surplus of $25 billion.

What Has Been the Impact of Such Currency Manipulation on the Dollar Exchange Rate and the US Trade Deficit?

IMF-defined currency manipulation, especially by Japan and China, is irrefutable, but how much impact this manipulation has had on exchange rates and the US trade deficit is a much more difficult question, and there is no precise answer. Although the unprecedentedly large market intervention by central banks from the late 1980s through 2002 might offer opportunity for econometric testing, the profession has not yet been able to meet the challenge. Thus the best that can be offered here are rough orders of magnitude based on the gross figures in play, and the conclusion drawn is that the protracted and very large-scale official intervention of the past several years, principally in East Asia, has had a substantial impact on exchange rates and the US trade deficit. The yen is probably at least 20 percent weaker than it would be based on market forces alone, while the Chinese renminbi is probably on the order of 40 percent weaker. As a consequence, the US trade deficit is probably about $100 billion larger than it would otherwise be, taking account of Japan, China, and other likely currency manipulators.

Before looking in detail at the derivation of these numbers, however, it is useful to make three analytic points that have often been ignored or misinterpreted by observers who conclude that currency manipulation has little actual impact on exchange rates and trade balances.

The great asymmetry. There is a world of difference between central bank sales of foreign exchange to keep a currency above market-determined levels and central bank purchases to keep a currency below market-determined levels. The former was the case for the series of financial crises since the mid-1990s (Mexico, Thailand, Indonesia, South Korea, Brazil, Russia, Turkey, and Argentina). They all failed because the central bank had a known quantity of foreign exchange to sell, and as reserves approached zero, speculation against the currency accelerated and a financial crisis was precipitated. In the case of central bank purchases of foreign exchange, which is the currency manipulation situation discussed here, there is, in sharp contrast, no limit to official purchases, as starkly shown in tables 13.1 and 13.2. Japan and China together have bought more than $330 billion of foreign exchange over the past three and a half years, and they could buy another $330 billion or more in the next several years, with no end in sight. This is the "great asymmetry" of official currency intervention, and those who claim that intervention cannot work for very long based on the experience of Mexico, Thailand, and so on, are at the wrong end of the feasibility curve. The fact is that intervention usually does not work for very long to maintain an overvalued currency, but it can work to prolonged and substantial effect to maintain an undervalued currency.

Net versus gross flows. Some observers conclude that currency manipulation has no significant impact on exchange rates because annual official foreign exchange purchases of $40 billion to $70 billion per year by countries such as Japan and China pale by comparison with a trillion dollars or more per day of international financial transactions. The error in this assessment is to compare net and gross financial flows. The very large majority of gross market financial transactions are offsetting inflows and outflows, just as most trade consists of offsetting exports and imports in its impact on exchange rates. What really counts for upward and downward pressures on exchange rates is the net dollar inflow or outflow on trade, current, and long-term capital accounts, as shown in the tables. These are more comparable in their impact on exchange rates with the net increases in official foreign exchange holdings, although, as explained below, official purchases of foreign exchange can have an even greater impact on exchange rates, dollar for dollar, than do trade or current account surpluses and net inflows of FDI.

Currency manipulation is only one part of the equation. Yet another misleading observation about currency manipulation is to compare official purchases of foreign exchange with apparently contradictory movements of the exchange rate. Japan intervened heavily in the spring of 2002 while the yen still appreciated from 130 to 120 to the dollar. At the time of the Asian financial crises in 1997-98, there was little intervention by any of the East Asian central banks, and yet the dollar rose substantially, as did the US trade deficit. The obvious explanation for such developments is that there are various forces in play that influence exchange rates and trade balances. The prospect of record-level, unsustainable US current account deficits and corporate scandals put overriding downward pressure on the dollar in the spring of 2002, while the dollar as "safe haven" for short-term capital inflow boosted the dollar rate in 1997-98 despite the temporary lull in currency manipulation. What is relevant for this discussion of the impact of "currency manipulation" is the *differential* impact of such intervention on exchange rates and the US trade balance. How much weaker would the dollar have been absent the protracted large-scale official intervention over the past several years, and how much smaller would the US trade deficit have been? It is to these questions that I now turn.

The Impact on Exchange Rates

As noted earlier, there are no precise estimates of the impact of official currency intervention on exchange rates. The gross figures on the relationship between such intervention and the balances of trade, current, and long-term capital accounts nevertheless provide indicators of the broad orders of magnitude involved. The way this interrelationship plays out, however, is very distinct between Japan and China, and each is thus addressed in turn.

In the case of Japan, official foreign exchange purchases equaled 59 to 61 percent of the trade surplus in the period 1999-2001 (table 13.1). For the broader basic balance measure of current account surplus plus FDI net flow, the figures rise to 72 to 77 percent. What this means is that the protracted intervention has directly offset, dollar for dollar, about 60 percent of the upward pressure on the yen from the very large trade surplus, and about 75 percent of the net inflow of dollars from the basic balance surplus. Moreover, in addition to this direct quantitative relationship, Japanese currency intervention policy has a strong reinforcing qualitative dimension, which can be called the "credible threat multiplier effect." The experience has been that when faced with upward pressure on the yen, not only does the Bank of Japan buy large quantities of foreign exchange, but also the Ministry of Finance states emphatically that Japan will intervene as much as necessary to keep the yen down, as an overriding economic policy objective to ensure continued export-led growth.[1] Such statements strongly dissuade currency dealers from intervening in anticipation of market-generated upward pressures on the yen. The overall result is currency manipulation through a combination of large-scale intervention plus credible threats of further intervention, with the latter constituting the "multiplier effect." A reasonable adjustment for this multiplier effect could raise the trade surplus offset from 60 percent to 75 percent and the basic balance offset from 75 percent to 100 percent.

---

1. Such statements, incidentally, constitute official admission that the intent of the intervention is to gain a competitive advantage in trade.

Based on these relationships, how much stronger would the yen be if currency manipulation were halted through a categoric statement by the government of Japan that it would indefinitely cease all purchases of foreign exchange? The rise in the yen would almost certainly be substantial, quite possibly by at least 20 percent, to 100 or fewer yen to the dollar. Such an assessment, moreover, is supported by another quantitative relationship related to the US trade deficit. The US trade deficit, as a share of total trade, is similar to that of the Japanese trade surplus, and considerable econometric work has produced the rule of thumb that a 1 percent decline in the dollar would reduce the US trade deficit by $10 billion, and thus a 20 percent decline would reduce the trade deficit by $200 billion, or by half of the total US trade deficit. This relationship can be compared with Japanese official intervention, to opposite effect, amounting to a 75 percent offset to upward pressures on the yen from the trade surplus, and thus to an implied strengthening of the yen from termination of the intervention of 30 percent. In other words, if a 20 percent decline in the dollar exchange rate can cause a 50 percent decline in the US trade deficit, currency manipulation to offset 75 percent of the Japanese trade surplus impact on the exchange rate would equate to a 30 percent weaker yen. To err on the conservative side, however, the conclusion drawn here is that Japanese currency manipulation probably results in a yen exchange rate at least 20 percent lower than it would be based on market forces alone.

In the case of China, the renminbi is fixed to the dollar but is nonconvertible on capital account. What this means in practice is that export earnings in foreign exchange, plus FDI not utilized for purchases on the current account, have to be sold to the central bank for renminbi at the fixed exchange rate. In effect, official intervention is carried out through mandatory foreign exchange sales to the central bank rather than central bank purchases in the market, as is the case in Japan and elsewhere. The net effect, nevertheless, is currency manipulation through protracted large-scale purchases of foreign exchange by the Chinese central bank.

As to how much stronger the renminbi would be if the central bank ceased to buy foreign exchange, the basic analytic approach would be the same as that applied to Japan, although with more indirect assumptions as to what would take place if the renminbi were freely convertible, and the appraisal is thus limited to an order of magnitude. The ratios of official foreign exchange purchases to the trade surplus and basic balance net dollar inflows have been rising sharply in 2001 and 2002. During the first six months of 2002, central bank purchases have been made at an annual rate of $62 billion, or roughly 200 percent of the trade surplus and about 100 percent of the basic balance inflow. These ratios, compared with Japan, indicate a rough order of magnitude for exchange rate impact almost double that caused by Japanese intervention. This should not be surprising, because in 2002 the dollar-linked renminbi has declined 10 percent vis-à-vis the yen and the euro, with a consequent strong positive impact on the Chinese trade surplus (up 55 percent in the first half of 2002) and FDI inflow (up 22 percent between January and July). Moreover, even with the $62 billion annual rate of mandatory sales to the central bank, market pressures from the huge foreign exchange net inflow stimulate underground cash flows out of the country of billions of dollars per year, linked to massive official corruption.[2] Taking all of these factors into account, the conclusion drawn here is that Chinese currency manipulation probably results in a renminbi exchange rate on the order of 40 percent lower than it would be with a convertible rate based on market forces alone.

The Impact on the US Trade Deficit

The bottom-line question is how much smaller the US trade deficit would be if others did not manipulate their currencies as described above. In this case, the analysis is more straightforward. Assuming the renminbi 40 percent stronger vis-à-vis the dollar, and the yen, the Korean won, and the Taiwanese dollar (the latter two with intervention/trade surplus ratios similar to that of Japan) 20 percent stronger, the dollar exchange rate, weighted by US imports, would be 7 percent lower. Based on the rule of thumb that a 1 percent decline in the dollar would lead to a $10 billion reduction in the trade deficit, the net result would be a $70 billion reduction in the US trade deficit if these four trading partners ceased currency manipulation.

This calculation, however, understates the trade impact for several reasons. Exports of these four trading partners are almost entirely in manufactures, which have relatively high price elasticities[3] compared with other sectors of trade, and therefore this trade would have an above-average quantitative response to a given exchange rate adjustment. Moreover, their exports have grown rapidly in recent years, and thus the $10 billion per 1 percent benchmark, based on earlier econometric work, should be adjusted upward. There has also probably been some additional currency manipulation beyond the four cited here, particularly in 2002, when the effects of the recession in the United States and a declining dollar have weakened export performance around the world and created

---

2. See the *Financial Times,* August 22, 2002, 5, "China Gears Up to Halt Capital Flight." The article cites estimates of capital flight as high as $20 billion per year, as well as a temper tantrum by Chinese Premier Zhu Rongji over the fact that nearly every corruption scandal in China in the past decade involves officials, or businessmen who have bribed them, fleeing overseas with large amounts of money.

3. The price elasticity relates percentage changes in relative prices and quantities of goods traded. For example, a -2 elasticity of demand for imports means that a 1 percent decline in the relative price of imports would lead to a 2 percent increase in the quantity of imports.

political pressures to intervene and keep currencies down relative to the falling dollar. For example, Russia, India, and Thailand made substantial official purchases of foreign exchange during the first half of 2002 even while running large current account surpluses. Bringing all of these factors together, the conclusion drawn here is that roughly $100 billion, or about one-quarter of the total US trade deficit, can be attributed to currency manipulation.

What Are the Consequences for US Economic and Foreign Policy Interests?

There are three distinct adverse consequences for US interests from the currency manipulation that has resulted in a US trade deficit roughly $100 billion larger than it would be based on market-determined exchange rates alone: the short-term impact on jobs and output; the longer-term economic impact on US productivity and growth; and the broader effects on US foreign policy interests. Only the first has received serious attention, while the second and third consequences are at least as important for overall US interests, and possibly more so.

The Short-Term Impact on Jobs and Output

The rising US trade deficit means less jobs and output for both US export and import-competing industries. The National Association of Manufacturers (NAM) estimates that since August 2000, 500,000 jobs have been lost from the decline in exports alone. Relating a $1 billion increase in the trade deficit to 15,000 jobs, a $100 billion larger trade deficit as a result of currency manipulation equates to 1.5 million fewer jobs, or more than 1 percent of the labor force, and a corresponding lower level of output.

Some observers contend that such lower levels of employment in export and import-competing industries are not a problem because they can be offset by more jobs created in other sectors. In effect, a larger trade deficit simply results in a shift of employment among sectors with no net loss of jobs. This analysis, however, is faulty on two counts. First, it assumes full employment, which has not been the case in 2001-02. Jobs lost to a rapidly growing trade deficit have not been offset by job creation elsewhere, as the unemployment rate has risen from 4 percent to 6 percent. Second, the composition of the labor force and output among sectors can have a substantial impact on longer-term productivity and growth in the US economy. The manufacturing sector is ten times more engaged in trade than the services sector, in terms of exports and imports as a ratio of domestic output, and has been bearing 80 to 90 percent of job losses from the rising trade deficit.[4] The net result from a $400 billion trade deficit—$100 billion of which is related to currency manipulation—is thus a relatively smaller manufacturing sector within the overall US economy. And this, in turn, has a significant adverse impact on longer-term productivity and growth in the US economy.

The Longer-Term Impact on US Productivity and Growth

The manufacturing sector has long been the engine for growth in the US economy, and this central role strengthened during the 1990s as accelerated new technology development and application spurred much higher levels of productivity and growth throughout the "new economy."[5] More than 60 percent of R&D and over 90 percent of new patents derive from the manufacturing sector. Productivity growth within the sector was two to three times higher than in the services sector throughout the 1990s, while productivity growth in other sectors is largely a result of new technology-intensive products developed and marketed by manufacturing industry. In addition, the manufacturing sector is restructuring rapidly to become even more high powered in generating productivity and growth. Since 1950, the share of value added by production workers has progressively declined by more than half to 18 percent, with value added becoming more and more concentrated in R&D, new investment in plant and equipment, and higher-skilled and professional employees. US manufacturing as the engine for growth is further reinforced by the economic globalization process. Rapid growth in international trade and investment increases competitive pressures to cut costs and develop new products faster and broadens global markets so as to spread out the large fixed costs of R&D and investment.

It is in this overall growth-oriented context that record US trade deficits of $400 billion per year, of which over $300 billion is in manufactures, can have substantial adverse impact on the US economic growth course ahead. A smaller manufacturing sector means a smaller engine for growth and fewer productivity gains. Likewise, the currency manipulators identified here—Japan, South Korea, Taiwan, and China most of all—are keenly aware of the fact that technology-intensive manufacturing industry is the primary engine for their growth as well. They each pursue the mercantilist approach of maintaining a large trade surplus as an overriding policy objective, with central emphasis on technology-intensive manufactured exports. And their favored policy instrument for pursuing such mercantilism is currency manipulation.

---

4. A full discussion of the contrasting roles of manufactures and services in trade is contained in Preeg (2001).

5. The transformation under way in US manufacturing summarized in this paragraph is analyzed in detail in Duesterberg and Preeg (2003).

The Broader Effects on US Foreign Policy Objectives

The motivation for protracted large-scale purchases of foreign exchange by currency manipulators is almost certainly to achieve the international competitive advantages described up to this point. In addition, however, there are a number of broader adverse consequences for US interests from the massive buildup of official holdings of dollars abroad, particularly in East Asia.[6] There is first the interest payments on official dollar holdings, which constitute a permanent flow of resources from the US to the other economies. At 5 percent interest, the $436 billion Japanese foreign exchange holdings, probably 80 to 90 percent in dollar-denominated assets,[7] would yield a United States-to-Japan annual payment of $17 billion to $19 billion. China is reported to hold some of its dollar holdings in Freddie Mac/Fannie Mae bonds in order to obtain a higher yield on its $243 billion of official foreign exchange holdings.

Other actual or potential adverse consequences for US interests are more in the foreign policy field. The huge official foreign exchange holdings of Japan and China provide a geopolitical opportunity to offer attractive trade and investment finance to regional trading partners, particularly in Southeast Asia, as a means of strengthening Japanese and Chinese economic engagement at the expense of the United States. A first step in this direction is the Chiang Mai Initiative, in which China, Japan, and South Korea have provided about $20 billion of bilateral financial swap agreements to Southeast Asian trading partners, or more than double the IMF quotas for these countries.[8] These initial agreements appear to be nondiscriminatory in financing imports from all sources, but such abundant financial support, with more in the offing, could provide leverage for preferential trading arrangements such as the recent Chinese initiative for a free trade agreement with the Association of Southeast Asian Nations. Press reports of these initiatives refer to the objective of weakening US economic hegemony in the region.

In the national security field, large Chinese purchases of weapons and other military equipment abroad, as regularly received from Russia in particular, can be made without financial constraint, having $243 billion of ready cash in the central bank.

More speculatively, China could use its official dollar holdings as foreign policy leverage against the United States by threatening to sell large

---

6. The effects on US-China policy, in particular, are elaborated in Preeg (2002).

7. The actual composition of official foreign exchange holdings is kept secret, as explained below.

8. See Henning (2002). As Henning explains, it is too early to assess how these swap arrangements will operate in practice, since there has been very little loan implementation thus far.

quantities of dollars on the market, or merely to shift its reserves away from dollars and into euros and yen. This will not happen anytime soon, because the result would be a decline in the dollar with an adverse impact on Chinese exports. At some future point, however, if China were to become less dependent on exports to the United States for economic growth, such a threat could become credible. For example, the threat of substantial Chinese sales of dollars, with the implications for a disruptive decline in the dollar and the US stock market, especially during a recession or an election year, could influence the course of US policy toward Taiwan. Chinese military officers, in fact, in their studies of nonconventional defense strategies, include reference to George Soros and his attack on the British pound in 1992 as a template for disrupting a rival's (i.e., the United States) economic system.

These are the wide-ranging economic and foreign policy adverse consequences for the United States from continued large-scale currency manipulation by others. They certainly add up to a strong case for action to curtail such manipulation. Fortunately, the specifics of such a policy response are readily at hand.

How Should the US Government Respond?

A US response designed to end exchange rate manipulation for unfair competitive advantage would consist of four steps pursued in parallel, with a fifth step held in reserve on a contingency basis.

Step 1: A clear statement of US policy. US exchange rate policy, in the broadest terms, is to let market forces determine exchange rates, and US official intervention is rare and of token size.[9] US policy has been in denial, however, about exchange rate manipulation by others, which is in fundamental conflict with a system of market-determined rates. This should be rectified through a clear statement of policy by the Secretary of the Treasury along the following lines:

"US exchange rate policy is to let market forces determine the rates. Official intervention in currency markets to counter short-term disruptive market conditions should be of limited duration and carried out in concert among major currency nations. In recent years, however, some others have engaged in protracted large-scale intervention to buy dollars and other foreign exchange, thus pushing their exchange rates substantially below market-determined levels. One important consequence has been a much larger US trade deficit than would prevail based on market-determined exchange rates alone. The IMF Agreement explicitly proscribes

---

9. US net currency intervention has averaged $3 billion per year since 1995, in some years net purchases, in other years net sales. In contrast, with six times as much trade as China, US net purchases on the current Chinese scale would amount to about $370 billion per year.

such exchange rate manipulation to gain an unfair competitive advantage, and the United States will actively seek to curb further manipulation through direct consultations with trading partners and IMF review procedures."

Such a statement would constitute a major change in US policy with respect to currency manipulation. The 1988 Omnibus Trade and Competitiveness Act requires the Secretary of the Treasury to report to Congress twice each year on currency manipulation by others, but the reports have been brief and essentially evasive. Japan, the most obvious manipulator, is routinely ignored. When Treasury officials are pressed, they dismiss the issue by claiming that the term currency manipulation is simply too vague and ill-defined. This, of course, is not the case, as explained in the first section above.

Step 2: G-7 consultations. The United States would pursue this newly stated line of policy among the Group of Seven (G-7) finance ministers, whose membership represents the principal international currencies. In fact, six of the seven—representing the US and Canadian dollars, the euro, and the pound sterling—do follow a market-determined floating rate policy, with very limited intervention, and they all suffer on the trade account from the mercantilist policies of currency manipulators. Japan, in contrast, would be the target within the group for curtailing manipulation, and the thrust of G-7 discussions would be about how Japan could restructure its growth strategy toward greater reliance on domestically generated growth and less reliance on a sustained trade surplus. Indeed, such a change would be as much in the Japanese interest as in that of the other six.

Step 3: Bilateral consultations. The United States would pursue bilateral consultations with targeted currency manipulators. Bilateral consultations with Japan would be an adjunct to the G-7 discussions. Consultations with such trading partners as South Korea and Taiwan would be along similar lines. Consultations with China would be more complex and would also be the most important, in view of the extreme degree of currency manipulation involved and the fact that the largest US bilateral trade deficit is with China. The short-term objective for China would be an upward adjustment of the fixed nonconvertible renminbi by at least 20 percent. The longer-term objective would be a transition by China to a fully convertible, freely floating renminbi, as a mutual economic interest and the best way to avoid trade conflict with the United States resulting from further unjustified currency manipulation.

Step 4: IMF transparency/consultations. The United States would approach the IMF to seek greater transparency in official market intervention and to curtail currency manipulation. As for transparency, members do not now publicly report currency intervention even though it is often the most important policy instrument utilized under a floating rate international financial system and has a significant impact on companies and banks engaged in international trade and finance. Current IMF disclosure is limited to a monthly statement of members' total foreign exchange holdings, with a two-to-three month time lag, in *International Financial Statistics*. The composition of the reserves—dollars, euros, yen, and so on—moreover, is never made public. In effect, China could shift $50 billion from dollars to euros, with a significant impact on the dollar/euro exchange rate, and the transaction would remain secret not only for private-sector traders but for other governments as well.[10] The United States, preferably together with like-minded free floaters, should therefore propose mandatory public reporting by central banks of significant purchases and sales of foreign exchange, including a breakdown by major currency.

Curtailment of currency manipulation would be pursued through the appropriate IMF review mechanism for Article IV commitments and related surveillance procedures. The specific objectives would be findings of currency manipulation against and commitments to cease such manipulation from targeted members, beginning with Japan and China. IMF Article IV stipulates "the right of members to have exchange arrangements of their choice consistent with the purposes of the Fund and the obligations under Section 1 of this Article." Section 1 includes the obligation to avoid manipulating exchange rates to gain an unfair competitive advantage. This means that China, in particular, is free to maintain its current fixed rate to the dollar only to the extent that it is consistent with avoiding prolonged large-scale purchases of foreign exchange. The implication, of course, is that the renminbi is currently undervalued and that China needs to revalue the currency upward in order to be able to cease such large-scale purchases and to be in full compliance with Article IV.

These four steps would be advanced in parallel and hopefully would lead to agreement to curtail currency manipulation to gain an unfair competitive advantage. The question remains, however, as to what the United States and other adversely affected trading partners should do if currency manipulators ignore the bilateral and IMF admonitions and continue their manipulative exchange rate policies. Under such circumstances, a contingent fifth step would be taken in the World Trade Organization (WTO).

Step 5: WTO dispute settlement. The General Agreement on Tariffs and Trade (GATT) Article XV, now incorporated within the WTO, addresses "Exchange Arrangements," and stipulates that members should not take exchange rate actions that "frustrate the intent of the provisions of this Agreement." The intent of the Agreement, in turn, as stated in broadest terms in the Preamble, is the objective of "entering into reciprocal and

---

10. The IMF publishes global official holdings by currency in September for the previous year, or nine months after the fact, but without a breakdown in such holdings by member country.

mutually advantageous arrangements directed to the substantial reduction of tariffs and other barriers to trade." Clearly, exchange rate manipulation that results in a $100 billion per year larger US trade deficit than would otherwise occur frustrates such reciprocal and mutually advantageous arrangements. The United States could thus file a complaint within the WTO dispute settlement mechanism against recalcitrant currency manipulators. GATT Article XV also provides for full consultation with the IMF, including that members "shall accept all findings of statistical and other facts presented by the Fund relating to foreign exchange," which would link any such US initiative in the WTO to prior IMF consultations as described in step 4.

This is the five-step policy response readily at hand. Step 5 should clearly be held in reserve, to be avoided if at all possible, but at the same time the United States should not be hesitant to state that it would be obliged to pursue this course if other actions proved fruitless. The rationale throughout all steps of the policy response would be derived from the adverse impact on US interests described earlier. Currency manipulation to gain an unfair competitive advantage has simply become too important an issue within the evolving international financial system to ignore any longer, and the practice therefore needs to be sharply curtailed or eliminated.

Epilogue: Systemic Implications

This chapter has been about currency manipulation and its direct impact on exchange rates and the US trade deficit. The issue of currency manipulation has broader implications for the international financial system as it evolves into a "two-corner" system of floating exchange rates and monetary unions.[11] In this context, a thorough appraisal of currency manipulation leading to its sharp curtailment or elimination would constitute a major step forward for realizing such a system within a cooperative multilateral framework.

The international financial system has been essentially undefined for three decades. The dollar fixed-rate system created at Bretton Woods ended in 1971 when the United States closed the window on dollar convertibility into gold. This precipitated a potpourri of exchange rate relationships from fixed to floating rates, with various forms of adjustable pegs and currency bands in between. The lack of systemic definition was highlighted in 1994 at the 50-year anniversary of Bretton Woods, when a Bretton Woods Commission group of 47 distinguished financial leaders and experts, chaired by Paul Volcker, called for the "establishment of a

---

11. The evolving two-corner system is analyzed in detail in Preeg (2000a), especially chapters 2 and 9.

new system . . . [because] the alternative to a new global system is to continue the present nonsystem." The commission report had little to offer, however, as to what form the new system should take except to note that "this system could possibly involve flexible exchange rate bands."

Five months later the Mexican peso crashed through the bottom of its dollar exchange rate band, and financial markets assumed the lead role in pushing governments toward a truly new postdollar floating rate system. Subsequent financial crises in Thailand, Indonesia, South Korea, Russia, Brazil, Turkey, and Argentina all resulted in shifts from some form of dollar-linked currencies to floating rates. Meanwhile, in the other monetary union corner, the European Monetary Union was launched and more modest steps were taken toward dollarization.[12]

The outstanding and indeed critical question for this new, predominantly floating rate system is to what extent the floating rates will be "managed" through official intervention in currency markets. Will rates be heavily managed, lightly managed, or allowed to float freely? Heavily managed rates, as described earlier, are subject to the "great asymmetry," wherein heavy intervention through foreign exchange sales to maintain a currency above the market-determined level has consistently failed, resulting in much higher foreign debt obligations and more painful ultimate adjustment. A lightly managed or free float is clearly preferable at this end of the asymmetric curve, although painful lessons are still being learned in Argentina, Brazil, and Turkey.

At the other end of the curve, there is the heavily managed float through official large-scale purchases to maintain an exchange rate lower than the market-determined level, which usually translates into currency manipulation. The case made in this paper is that such heavy management to gain an unfair competitive advantage should also be sharply curtailed if not eliminated.

The net result for the evolving international financial system should thus be definitive movement to lightly managed or freely floating rates. Heavily managed rates in one direction do not work, while in the other direction "currency manipulation" should be at least sharply curtailed. And this outcome, in turn, has important implications as to how the overall international financial system would work, including the IMF role within it. For example, there would be little need for foreign exchange reserves since their only purpose is for official intervention, which would be small to nil under lightly managed or free floating rates. The United States, in this regard, is ahead of the curve, with a rate close to free floating and only $30 billion of foreign exchange reserves, equal to a mere 2

---

12. Ecuador has dollarized and Central American leaders are considering it. Based on "optimum currency area" analysis, the small, highly open Caribbean Basin economies that are heavily dependent on trade with the United States would be optimal candidates for dollarization. See Preeg (2000b).

percent of annual imports.[13] A lightly managed or freely floating yen, in contrast, would make the $436 billion of Japanese foreign exchange reserves grossly redundant, raising the question as to what should be done with them.

There would also be little further need for large IMF loans, and the $30 billion loan package to Brazil in August 2002 could turn out to be the last hurrah for such lending. This would follow the longer-term process of IMF "graduation." None of the industrialized countries, which comprise two-thirds of world trade and investment, has taken out a large IMF loan in over 25 years. Emerging market economies that shifted to floating rates in the 1990s, such as Mexico, Thailand, and Russia, should not need further recourse to large IMF loans. Certainly the currency manipulators—Japan, China, South Korea, and Taiwan—who have accumulated such excessive reserve holdings, which would become even more excessive to the extent that they adopted lightly managed floating rates, will never need an IMF loan. Indeed, if the current financially troubled Argentina, Brazil, and Turkey, already with floating rates, could be nurtured away from largely counterproductive dependence on IMF lending, close to 90 percent of the global economy would be classified as IMF graduates.[14] And what would remain would mostly be the poorest countries, where highly concessionary loans and grant assistance from multilateral development banks and bilateral aid programs are more appropriate forms of official financial support than high-cost IMF borrowing.

There would still be a role for the IMF, but a much more modest role as a consultative forum, the repository for basic norms and financial market commitments of multilateral scope, and a provider of technical support for members adopting financial policy reforms. But the era of large-scale IMF loans, with all its political contention and painful economic aftermath, would be over. Members within the monetary union corner of the new financial architecture would by definition have no need for an IMF loan to defend internal national currency relationships that no longer exist, while members with lightly managed or free floating currencies would also have little or no need for IMF loans.

Graduation should be a joyous occasion, and graduation of the international financial system to a new cooperative order of floating rates and monetary unions would be worthy of celebration. We have not yet reached that point, however, and the biggest remaining obstacle is the persistent practice by some of currency manipulation to gain an unfair competitive advantage in international trade and investment.

---

13. The United States also holds $262 billion of gold reserves, but they are essentially useless. If even $10 billion to $20 billion of the gold were sold on the market to prop up the dollar, the market price of gold would crash and the value of reserves along with it.

14. This transition is elaborated in Ernest Preeg, "Argentina's painful graduation," *Financial Times,* August 3, 2001.

References

Duesterberg, Thomas J., and Ernest H. Preeg, eds. 2003. *US Manufacturing: The Engine for Growth in a Global Economy.* New York: Praeger, forthcoming.

Henning, C. Randall. 2002. *East Asian Financial Cooperation.* Washington: Institute for International Economics.

Preeg, Ernest H. 2000a. *The Trade Deficit, the Dollar, and the US National Interest.* Washington: Hudson Institute.

Preeg, Ernest H. 2000b. Dollar Rising Over the Caribbean. *American Outlook* (winter): 42-43.

Preeg, Ernest H. 2001. *Surging Yet Volatile Productivity Growth in US Manufacturing Industry: The International Trade Dimension.* Washington: MAPI (October).

Preeg, Ernest H. 2002. Chinese Currency Manipulation. Testimony Before the Senate Committee on Banking, Housing, and Urban Affairs, May 1. Washington: Senate Committee on Banking, Housing, and Urban Affairs.

About the Contributors

Martin Neil Baily, senior fellow at the Institute for International Economics, was chairman of the Council of Economic Advisers of President Clinton from 1999 to 2001 and a member of President Clinton's cabinet. Before joining the Council, he was a principal at McKinsey & Company's Global Institute in Washington, DC (1996 to 1999) and also a visiting fellow there (1993-94). He served as one of the three members of the President's Council from 1994 to 1996. He was senior fellow at the Brookings Institution (1979-89) and a professor of economics at the University of Maryland (1989-96). He has been an academic adviser to the Federal Reserve Board and the Congressional Budget Office. His research has focused on wage setting, macroeconomic policy, innovation, productivity, and economic growth.

C. Fred Bergsten has been director of the Institute for International Economics since its creation in 1981. He was also chairman of the Competitiveness Policy Council, which was created by Congress, throughout its existence from 1991 to 1995 and chairman of the APEC Eminent Persons Group throughout its existence from 1993 to 1995. He was assistant secretary for international affairs of the US Treasury (1977-81), assistant for international economic affairs to the National Security Council (1969-71), and a senior fellow at the Brookings Institution (1972-76), the Carnegie Endowment for International Peace (1981), and the Council on Foreign Relations (1967-68). He is the author, coauthor, or editor of numerous books on a wide range of international economic issues, including *No More Bashing: Building a New Japan-United States Economic Relationship* (2001), *Whither APEC? The Progress to Date and Agenda for the Future* (1997), *Global Economic*

Leadership and the Group of Seven (1996), *The Dilemmas of the Dollar* (2d ed., 1996), *Reconcilable Differences? United States-Japan Economic Conflict* (1993), *Pacific Dynamism and the International Economic System* (1993), and *America in the World Economy: A Strategy for the 1990s* (1988).

William R. Cline is senior fellow jointly at the Institute for International Economics and the Center for Global Development in Washington, DC. During 1996-2001 while on leave from the Institute, he was deputy managing director and chief economist of the Institute of International Finance (IIF) in Washington, DC. He has been a senior fellow at the Institute for International Economics since its inception in 1981. Previously he was senior fellow, the Brookings Institution (1973-81); deputy director of development and trade research, office of the assistant secretary for international affairs, US Treasury Department (1971-73); Ford Foundation visiting professor in Brazil (1970-71); and lecturer and assistant professor of economics at Princeton University (1967-70). He is the author of *The Economics of Global Warming* (1992), *International Economic Policy in the 1990s* (1994), *International Debt Reexamined* (1995), and *Trade and Income Distribution* (1997).

I. M. Destler, visiting fellow at the Institute for International Economics, is a professor at the School of Public Affairs, University of Maryland. He was formerly a senior fellow at the Institute, senior associate at the Carnegie Endowment for International Peace (1977-83) and at the Brookings Institution (1972-77), and visiting lecturer at Princeton University (1971-72) and the International University of Japan (1986). He is the author or coauthor of numerous books on American trade politics and foreign policymaking, and US-Japan economic relations, including *The New Politics of American Trade: Trade, Labor and the Environment* with Peter Balint (1999), *Renewing Fast-Track Legislation* (1997), *The National Economic Council: A Work in Progress* (1996), *American Trade Politics* (3d ed. 1995), and *Dollar Politics: Exchange Rate Policymaking in the United States* (1989).

Kathryn Dominguez is associate professor of public policy and economics at the University of Michigan and research associate at the National Bureau of Economic Research. She was associate professor of public policy at the Kennedy School of Government, Harvard University (1991-97), and visiting assistant professor and assistant director of the International Finance Section of the department of economics at Princeton University (1990-91). She was research consultant with AID and the World Bank and research scholar at the International Monetary Fund. She is coauthor of *Does Foreign Exchange Intervention Work?* with Jeffrey Frankel (1993).

Daniel Gros is director of the Centre for European Policy Studies in Brussels. He was an economist at the European and research departments of the International Monetary Fund (1983-86) and economic adviser at the Directorate General II of the European Commission (1988-90). He has taught at the European College (Natolin) as well as at various universities across Europe, including the Catholic University of Leuven, the University of Frankfurt, the University of Basel, Bocconi University, the Kiel Institute of World Studies, and the Central European University in Prague. His research concentrates on the impact of the euro on capital and labor markets and the international role of the euro, especially in Central and Eastern Europe. Since 2001 he has been a member of the advisory council of the French prime minister, the Conseil d'Analyse Economique. He is the author of *Winds of Change: Economic Transition in Central and Eastern Europe* (Addison, Wesley, Longman, 1995); *European Monetary Integration, from the EMS to EMU* (Addison, Wesley, Longman, 1992, 2d ed. 1998); *EMU and Capital Markets* (Wiley & Sons, 2000); and *Open Issues in European Central Banking* (Macmillan, 2000).

Catherine L. Mann, senior fellow at the Institute for International Economics since 1997, previously served in policymaking institutions in Washington, including at the Federal Reserve Board of Governors, Council of Economic Advisers, and the World Bank. She is coauthor of *The New Economy and APEC* (2001) and *Global Electronic Commerce: A Policy Primer* (2000) and author of *Is the US Trade Deficit Sustainable?* (1999). She is also an adjunct professor of management at the Owen School of Management at Vanderbilt University (on leave) and is teaching at the Johns Hopkins School for Advanced International Studies.

G. Mustafa Mohatarem has been chief economist at General Motors Corporation since 1995. He joined General Motors in 1982 as an economist in the Detroit office. He was promoted to director of trade and competitive analysis in 1987 and to general director of economic analysis in 1990. As the head of the corporation's trade team, he interacts regularly with officials from the United States and other countries on trade-related issues. He was the lead contact for General Motors with the United States and other governments during the Uruguay Round of General Agreement on Tariffs and Trade (GATT) negotiations, as well as the negotiations for the Canada-US Free Trade Agreement and the North American Free Trade Agreement. He has served as visiting assistant professor at the University of Notre Dame and as adjunct assistant professor at the University of Michigan and the University of Detroit.

Jim O'Neill has been head of global economic research at Goldman Sachs since September 2001. He joined Goldman Sachs in October 1995 as a partner and chief currency economist. After a brief spell with Bank of America in 1982-83, he joined International Treasury Management, a division of HSBC, and spent over six years with the group acting as a foreign exchange economist, initially in London and then in New York. In 1988, he joined SBC to start a fixed income research group in London, and in 1991, he became head of global research.

Thomas I. Palley is director of the Globalization Reform Project at the Open Society Institute (OSI) in Washington, DC. He has published extensively in numerous academic journals on financial policy, labor markets, the business cycle, Social Security, globalization, and economic development policy. Prior to joining OSI, he was assistant director of public policy at the AFL-CIO. He is the author of *Post Keynesian Economics: Debt, Distribution and the Macro Economy* (Macmillan, 1996) and *Plenty of Nothing: The Downsizing of the American Dream and the Case for Structural Keynesianism* (Princeton University Press, 2000).

Ernest Preeg is senior fellow in trade and productivity at Manufacturers Alliance/MAPI, and senior fellow at The Hudson Institute. He was deputy assistant secretary of state for international finance and development (1976-77); member of the US delegation to the Kennedy Round of GATT negotiations in Geneva (1965-67); US ambassador to Haiti (1981-83); and William M. Scholl Chair in International Business, The Center for Strategic and International Studies (1986-88). He is the author of numerous publications including *The Trade Deficit, the Dollar, and the US National Interest* (Hudson Institute, 2000) and *From Here to Free Trade: Essays in Post-Uruguay Round Trade Strategy* (University of Chicago Press/CSIS, 1998).

Stephen S. Roach is managing director and chief economist at Morgan Stanley, where he oversees the firm's team of economists in New York, London, Frankfurt, Paris, Tokyo, and Hong Kong. Prior to joining Morgan Stanley in 1982, he was vice president for economic analysis for the Morgan Guaranty Trust Company in New York. He also served on the research staff of the Federal Reserve Board in Washington, DC (1972-79), where he supervised the preparation of the official Federal Reserve projections of the US economy. He has also been a research fellow at the Brookings Institution. His published research covers a broad range of topics, with recent emphasis on globalization, corporate restructuring, productivity, and the macro paybacks of information technology.

Michael R. Rosenberg is managing director and head of global foreign exchange research at Deutsche Bank. Prior to joining Deutsche Bank in May 1999, he was managing director and head of international fixed income research at Merrill Lynch for 15 years. He also managed Prudential Insurance Company's global bond portfolio during 1982-84 and was a senior foreign exchange/money market analyst at Citibank (1977-82). He has written numerous articles on international bond diversification and the foreign exchange market for various academic journals and handbooks. He is the author of *Currency Forecasting: A Guide to Fundamental and Technical Models of Exchange Rate Determination* (Irwin/McGraw Hill, 1996).

Edwin M. Truman, senior fellow at the Institute for International Economics, served as assistant secretary of the US Treasury for international affairs from December 1998 to January 2001. Before joining the US Treasury, he was director and later staff director of the division of international finance of the Board of Governors of the Federal Reserve System beginning in June 1977. He was on the staff of the Federal Open Market Committee from March 1977 until he resigned from the Federal Reserve. He joined the staff of the Federal Reserve in July 1972. He has been a member of numerous international groups working on economic and financial issues, including the Financial Stability Forum's Working Group on Highly Leveraged Institutions (1999-2000), G-22 Working Party on Transparency and Accountability (1998), G-10-sponsored Working Party on Financial Stability in Emerging Market Economies (1996-97), G-10 Working Group on the Resolution of Sovereign Liquidity Crises (1995-96), and G-7 Working Group on Exchange Market Intervention (1982-83). He has published on international monetary economics, international debt problems, economic development, and European economic integration.

John Williamson, senior fellow at the Institute for International Economics since 1981, was project director for the UN High-Level Panel on Financing for Development (the Zedillo Report) in 2001; on leave as chief economist for South Asia at the World Bank during 1996-99; economics professor at Pontificia Universidade Católica do Rio de Janeiro (1978-81), University of Warwick (1970-77), Massachusetts Institute of Technology (1967, 1980), University of York (1963-68), and Princeton University (1962-63); adviser to the International Monetary Fund (1972-74); and economic consultant to the UK Treasury (1968-70). He is author, coauthor, or editor of numerous studies on international monetary and developing world debt issues, including *Delivering on Debt Relief: From IMF Gold to a New Aid Architecture* (2002), *Exchange Rate Regimes for Emerging Markets: Reviving the Intermediate Option* (2000), *The Crawling Band as an Exchange Rate Regime* (1996), *What Role for Currency Boards?* (1995), *Estimating Equilibrium Exchange Rates* (1994), and *The Political Economy of Policy Reform* (1993).

Index

structural adjustments of, 104-05,
111, 138
unions in, 107
zero-percent financing programs,
136-37

balance of payments
adjustments, and currency
manipulation, 269
broad basic (BBoP). *See* broad basic
balance of payments
crises, 61*n*
US, overall performance of, 17-18
balance of trade, US, 77-78
1959-2001, 112-16, 113*f*, 114*f*
GDP growth and, 83
and manufacturing sector, 83-85, 86*f*
long-term damage to, 151-56
short-term damage to, 146-51
merchandise, 78
real broad dollar index and, 147-50,
148*f*
strong dollar and, 157
Balassa-Samuelson model, 6-7, 17, 180
Bank of Japan, 53, 54
and banking sector, 178
exchange market interventions by, 5,
11, 13, 23-24, 159-60, 161, 162, 217,
221-22, 221*n*, 223, 223*f*, 225-31,
226*n*, 229*n*, 230*n*, 242
attitudes toward, 247*n*, 262
auto industry impacts of, 140-43
coordinated, 238*t*, 240*t*, 241, 242, 250,
254*n*
as currency manipulation, 11, 13,
142-43, 267-68, 272-73
efficacy of, 158, 161, 225-31, 249-50,
251*n*
with largest daily impact, 230, 230*t*
timing of, 224-25, 225*t*, 250*n*
volume of, 225-31, 226*f*
and yen-dollar rate, 226-31, 226*f*,
227*t*-228*t*, 230*t*, 236, 250
and Ministry of Finance, 221*n*, 262*n*
stock purchases by, 178, 178*n*, 195
banking sector, Japanese, 178, 178*n*, 195
BBoP. *See* broad basic balance of
payments
Boeing Corporation, 151
bonds
Europe-US net flows, 31, 33*f*
foreign, yield through 2017, 124*t*, 127,
128*t*
in US manufacturing sector, 97*n*

Brazil, 282, 283
exchange market intervention in, 158
steel industry in, 102, 104
Bretton Woods system, 162, 190*n*
British pound sterling
call for intervention in, 260*n*
dollar depreciation impacts on, 28, 28*t*
and euro, 25, 26
value of, oil sales and, 96
weight of, in trade-weighted dollar
index, 16*t*
broad basic balance of payments (BBoP),
22-23
vs. current account
of Europe, 29, 30*f*
of Japan, 23, 24*f*
of US, 18, 18*f*
in Europe, 29-33
vs. TWI, 30*f*
budget, US
1959-2001, 112-16, 113*f*, 114*f*
in national accounts identity, 112
surpluses, benefits of, 132
Bundesbank (Germany), 262*n*
exchange market interventions by, 217,
222-23, 222*n*, 224*f*, 231-33
coordinated, 238*t*, 240*t*, 242
and deutsche mark-dollar exchange
rate, 231-33, 231*f*, 232*t*, 234*t*
efficacy of, 249-50, 251, 252
with largest daily impact, 233, 234*t*
timing of, 224-25, 225*t*, 250*n*
volume of, 231-33
Bush administration (2001-04), 79

Canada
auto industry in, 111-12
dollar depreciation role of, 8, 17, 34
manufacturing employment in, 87, 88*f*,
111, 152, 153*f*
Canadian dollar, weight of, in trade-
weighted US dollar index, 16*t*, 17
capital consumption adjustment (CCA),
93, 94
capital flows. *See also* foreign capital
inflows
free, benefits of, 131
regulation of, 161, 162
transatlantic, and dollar-euro exchange
rate, 65*n*
capital income, US, 181, 181*n*
vs. Japan, 181
Caribbean Basin economies, 282*n*
Carter administration, 77, 259-60

case study methodology, 251-52, 251n
cash mergers and acquisitions pipeline,
    European *vs.* US, 31, 32f
central banks. *See also specific banks*
    attitudes toward intervention, 247-248,
        262
    conflicts with finance ministries, 262
    exchange market interventions by, 217,
        217n, 223-24, 242. *See also*
        exchange market interventions
    effectiveness of, 218-19, 241-43
    timing of, 224-25, 225t, 250, 250n
    stock purchases by, 178n
Chiang Mai Initiative, 277
Chile, 161
China
    currency manipulation by, 11, 13, 267-
        70, 269t, 271, 273-74, 276
        evidence of, 268-70, 269t
        recommended response to, 278-81
    dollar depreciation role of, 8, 17, 34
    economic policy of, 160, 161
    foreign direct investment in, 160
    foreign reserves of, 159, 159t
        in dollars, implications for US, 277-
            78
    service sector in, 130
    share of trade with Japan *vs.* US, 185-
        87, 187t
    trade surplus of, 159-60
    US interest payments on dollars to,
        277
    world exports share, 1989-2001, 21, 22f
Chinese renminbi
    manipulation of, 273-74
        and exchange value, 270, 273-74
    undervaluation of, 160, 161
    US objectives regarding, 279
Chinese yuan
    and Japanese yen, 21, 21t, 22
    weight of, in trade-weighted dollar
        index, 16t, 17
Clinton administration, strong-dollar
    rhetoric of, 2, 175
comparative advantage theory, 83
competition
    in auto industry, 104-06
    dollar exchange value and, 46, 83-99
    globalization and, 95
    against imports, 84
    in IT sector, 108-10
    in steel industry, 100-04
computer industry

in Asia, 108
    dollar swings and, 83
    employment in, 109, 110f
    investment, in 1990s, 90
    productivity in, 109, 109f
consumer price index (CPI)
    foreign, through 2017, in MA model,
        124t, 128t
    US
        in 1990s, in constant dollar
            simulation, 117, 117t
        through 2017, in MA model, 124t,
            126, 128t, 129
consumption, US
    in 1990s, under constant dollar, 117-18,
        117f
    through 2017, in MA model, 120, 121t,
        126-27, 128t, 129
    current slump and, 146
coordination channel, 13, 253-54, 253n,
    254-55
corporate profits, 1973-2002, 93-95, 94f
currencies. *See also specific currencies*
    involved in counterpart appreciation
        to dollar, 3-5, 8-10, 16-17, 34
    weights of, in trade-weighted dollar
        index, 16-17, 16t
currency appreciation
    as counterpart to dollar depreciation,
        3, 8-10, 16-17
    energy trade and, 96-97
currency depreciation, and inflation, 130
currency intervention. *See* exchange
    market interventions
currency manipulation, 11-12, 142, 267,
    270-72
    by China, 11, 13, 267-70, 269t, 271, 273-
        74, 276
        evidence of, 268-70, 269t
        recommended response to, 278-81
    curtailment of, recommendations for,
        11-12, 278-81, 282-83
    definition of, 267
    IMF role regarding, 11, 13, 142, 279-80,
        281
    impacts of, 270-78
        on exchange rates, 270, 271-72, 272-
            74
        on international financial system,
            281, 282-83
        on US auto industry, 143
        on US employment and output
            levels, 275-76

"new economy" forces and, 36, 40-
45, 44*f*, 179-80
vs. euro. *See* euro-dollar exchange rate
floating, US manufacturing and, 83-98
forces and factors in, 58
global wealth invested in US assets
and, 58-59, 60, 61-62, 63, 65-69, 70-
73
interventions affecting, in 1980s *vs.*
1990s, 219-23
issues surrounding, 5-12
needs of, conflicts with other
objectives, 256-61, 256*f*, 257*f*, 258*n*-
260*n*
"no-change scenario" for, 69-70, 171-72
vs. yen. *See* yen-dollar exchange rate
dollar holdings. *See* foreign exchange
reserves
dollar overvaluation, 36, 175-76, 179-80
extent of, 17-19
factors in, 96-98
global problems of, 156-57
impacts of, 145-46, 161
long-term, 151-56
short-term, 146-51
on US trade policy, 78-79
manufacturing sector impacts of
on employment, 87-89
long-term, 151-56
on profitability, 84
short-term, 146-51
"new economy" forces and, 36, 40-45
dollar risk, 171, 171*f*
dollar swings
amelioration of, 132
cost of, 131-32
impacts of, 81-132
through 2017, in MA model, 119-31,
121*t*-125*t*, 128*t*
in auto industry, 105
in IT sector, 109-10
in manufacturing sector, 81-98, 110-
12
in 1990s
counterfactual simulation, 116-19,
117*t*
macroeconomic adjustment, 112-16,
117-18
domestic demand
in Europe, with dollar appreciation,
211
in Japan, 21, 179

non-US, dollar depreciation impact on,
169-70
in postbubble economy, 166
US, 85
for goods, 1990-2002, 90-91, 91*f*
for goods, 2000-02, 111
policy on, 173
US-world disparities in, 169, 169*f*
"double-dip" recession, 5, 165

economic openness, international
comparison of, 208-09, 208*t*, 215*t*
economic policy. *See also* fiscal policy;
monetary policy
conflicts with exchange rate needs,
255-62
instruments for managing interest rate,
10-12
in Japan, dilemmas of, 177-78
monetary-fiscal mix, 54, 55*f*
in Japan, 177
in postbubble economy, 166
for price stabilization, in 1990s, 168-
69
objectives of, 255
recommendations for, 160-62
Ecuador, 282*n*
share of trade with Japan *vs.* US, 187,
187*t*
"elasticity pessimism," 190*n*, 191
employment
in agricultural sector, US, 152
in computer industry, 109, 110*f*
currency manipulation's impact on, in
US, 275-76
and dollar depreciation, 5, 6
euro-dollar exchange rate and, 214
exchange rate variability and, in
Europe, 214
in manufacturing sector, non-US
in Canada, 152, 153*f*
in developed nations, 87-89, 88*f*, 111
in developing nations, 87
dollar overvaluation and, 84-85
in manufacturing sector, US
1973-2000, 85-89, 88*f*
1990-2002, 89-92, 89*f*, 153*f*
auto industry, 103*f*, 105, 105*f*
balance of trade and, 146-47, 147*n*
importance of, 151-53
IT sector, 109, 110*f*
steel industry, 102, 103*f*
and productivity growth, 85, 152

energy trade, currency appreciation and, 96-97

equilibrium exchange rate
euro-dollar, 25, 25*n*, 26, 35, 36, 39, 40*t*
FEER models for. *See* fundamental equilibrium exchange rate (FEER) models
GSDEER. *See* Goldman Sachs dynamic equilibrium real exchange rate
long-term, definition of, 37-38
productivity growth differentials and, 6, 180
yen-dollar, 19, 19*f*

equilibrium exchange rate assessment(s), 35-56
FEER models for, 16, 19, 35, 38-39, 40*t*, 194-95
IMF macroeconomic balance approach to, 37-40, 38*f*
market participants and, 36-37
selected, 39, 40*t*
usefulness of, 37

equilibrium exchange value
of dollar, 35-56
depreciation beyond, 50-52
IMF macroeconomic balance approach to, 38-39, 38*f*
"new economy" forces and, 36, 40-45, 44*f*, 179-80
of euro, ECB models of, 36-37
relative productivity growth and, 6, 180
of yen, 36, 52-55

equity flows, net Europe-US, 31, 33*f*

euro
appreciation of, 6, 9-10
arguments for, 9-10, 161, 170
European productivity growth and, 29-31
BBoP and, 29-33, 30*f*
depreciation of, 211, 212*t*, 214-15
dollar depreciation impacts on, 28, 28*t*, 213
dollar depreciation role of, 8, 9-10, 24-27, 34
effective exchange value of, 9, 215
changes in, and euro-dollar exchange rate, 210-11, 212*t*, 213
and euro-dollar exchange rate, 210, 210*t*, 214-15
equilibrium value of, ECB models of, 36-37
exchange value of, 3, 4*t*, 205

September 2000 joint intervention for, 241
first four years, 205-15
inflation and, 156
target zones for, *81n*
weight of, in trade-weighted dollar index, 16*t*, 17
and yen, 21, 21*t*, 22

euro-dollar exchange rate
in 2002, 58, 59*f*
changes in
economic impacts of, 211-13, 213-14
macroeconomic models for, 211
and changes in effective exchange rate of euro, 210-11, 212*t*, 213
DAX-S&P 500 differential and, 69, 69*f*
with dollar at PPP value, 51
and effective exchange rate of euro, 210, 210*t*, 214-15
equilibrium
assessments of, 35, 36, 39-40, 40*t*
GSDEER, 25, 25*n*, 26
GSDEER, 25, 25*f*, 26
importance of, for euro zone, 205-06, 209-13, 210*t*, 215
interventions affecting, 233-35, 234*f*, 235*t*, 241
and transatlantic capital flows, 65*n*

Europe/euro zone. *See also* European Central Bank
BBoP, 29-33, 30*f*
cash mergers and acquisitions pipeline, 31, 32*f*
current account balance, 25, 29, 30*f*, 183*t*
deflation and, 167
dollar depreciation impacts on, 27-29, 28*t*, 34, 170
dollar depreciation role of, 6, 8, 9-10, 24-27, 34
economy of, 24-7, 205-15
openness of, 208-09, 215*t*
outlook for, 213
overvalued dollar and, 156
recovery, 161*n*
employment, exchange rate variability and, 214
exchange rate importance in, 208, 214-15
euro-dollar, 205-06, 209-13, 210*t*, 215
euro-dollar changes, 211-13, 213-14
exchange rate variability, 213-14
FDI-related flows, 29, 30*f*, 31, 32*f*

real broad dollar index *vs.* real major
currency index, 1995-2002, 59*f*
trade-weighted dollar index, 16-17, 16*t*
vs. import/export ratio, 147-50, 148*f*
vs. manufacturing profit share, 150,
150*f*
Working Group on Exchange Market
Intervention, 248
FEER models. *See* fundamental
equilibrium exchange rate (FEER)
models
finance ministries. *See also* Ministry of
Finance (Japan); US Treasury
and exchange market interventions,
247-48, 262, 262*n*
financial conditions, dollar depreciation
impacts on, 27-29, 28*t*
financial crises
in Asia, in 1997-98, 271, 282
based on balance of payments, 61*n*
since mid-1990s, 270-71, 282
financial markets. *See* stock market(s)
financial wealth, global. *See* global
financial wealth
first-mover advantage, in IT industry,
108
fiscal policy. *See also* exchange market
interventions
foreign, progrowth, 166, 170
in Japan, 177
mix with monetary policy, 54, 55*f*
in postbubble economy, 166
for price stabilization, in 1990s, 168-69
fixed exchange rates, 190*n*
flexible exchange rates, 190*n*
floating rate system
developing nations' fear of, 162
dollar in, US manufacturing and, 83-98
shift to, 281
Ford, 105, 106, 140, 143
forecasting models, for Japan's current
account, 190-92, 198-202, 200*f*, 202*t*
foreign assets
of Japan, 181, *181f*
of US, 154*t*, 155, 180-82, 181*f*, 182*f*
foreign borrowing, cost of, 118-19, *118f*
foreign capital inflows
and domestic savings-investment
imbalance, 39
in emerging markets, 47, 49*f*
and productivity growth, 7, 18
US, 65-67, 66*f*
through 2017, in MA model, 120

current recession and, 146
and dollar exchange rate, 89, 97-98,
99*b*-100*b*, 112, 115
net sustainable, 60
benchmarks for, 61-62
vs. net US debt, 118-19, 118*f*
and productivity growth, 7, 18
regulation of, 161, 162
relative to global savings, as
sustainability benchmark, 62
sustainability of, 61-62
and twin deficits, 114-15
US ability to attract, 47, 115
foreign direct investment (FDI)
in China, 160
and currency manipulation, 269
in Europe, 29, 30*f*, 31, 32*f*
in US, 47, 49*f*, 97-98, 98*f*, 119
foreign exchange market. *See under*
exchange market
foreign exchange reserves
"adequacy" of, 268
disclosure to IMF, 280, 280*n*
and floating rate system, 282-83
held by China and Japan, impact on
US, 277-78
of Japan, 141, 141f, 283
of US, 282-83, 283*n*
foreign income account, US, 118*f*, 119,
154-55, 155*f*
foreign liabilities, net, of US, 182
foreign policy, US, currency
manipulation's impact on, 277-78
foreign purchases of US assets, net, 65-
67, 66f. *See also* foreign capital
inflows, US
France, manufacturing sector
employment in, 88*f*
fundamental equilibrium exchange rate
(FEER) models, 16, 19, 35, 38-39, 40*t*,
158-59, 194-95

G-3 countries. *See also* Germany; Japan;
United States
economic changes in 1990s, 218
exchange market interventions by, 217,
219-43, 255
effectiveness of, 217, 241-43, 249-55,
263
vs. 1980s, and dollar exchange rate
movements, 219-23
G-7 countries
consultations on currency
manipulation, 279

and dollar's rise as disequilibrium
phenomenon, 45-46
in US in 1990s, *vs.* rest of world, 44
IT sector
in Asia, 108
hardware production, 108
US
competition in, 108-10
dollar swings and, 83, 109-10
employment, 109, 110*f*
investment, in 1990s, 90, 111, 113
productivity, 109, 109*f*, 111
profitability, 107*f*, 109-10
Italy, manufacturing sector employment
in, 88*f*

Japan. *See also* Bank of Japan; G-3
countries
auto exports to US, decline in, 139,
139*f*
auto industry
decline and recovery, 138-43
productivity, 104-05
Toyota production system, 104-05
banking sector, 178, 178*n*, 195
BBoP *vs.* current account of, 23, 24*f*
capital income, 181
currency manipulation by, 11, 12, 13,
142-43, 267-70, 271, 272-73, 276,
279
evidence of, 268-70, 268*t*
recommended response to, 11, 13,
278-81
and US auto industry, 143
current account balance, 181, 182, 183*t*,
184-85, 184*f*, 186*t*
vs. BBoP, 23, 24*f*
impact parameters for, 190-91, 191*t*
modeling, 190-92, 198-202, 200*f*, 202*t*
current account surplus reduction, 184-
98
alternative scenarios for, 192-94, 192*t*
appropriate extent of, 184-88, 188*t*,
197
and cyclical adjustment in exchange
rate policy, 194-95
economic impacts of, 176, 188-98
implications for yen, 176, 188-94
policy implications for, 197-98
real net import effects of, 196-97
recession and, 194-97
stock market effects of, 195-96, 196*f*
deflation, 53, 170

dollar depreciation impacts on, 28, 28*t*,
29, 170
dollar depreciation role of, 8-9, 9*n*, 19-
22, 34
domestic demand, 21, 179
economic policy dilemmas of, 177-78
economy
bubble in, 146
openness of, 208-09, 208*t*
performance of, 178-79
surplus reduction impacts on, 176,
188-98
weakness of, 21, 22, 177-79, 198
exchange market interventions by, 5,
11, 13, 23-24, 159-60, 161, 162, 217,
221-22, 221*n*, 223, 223*f*, 225-31,
226n, 229*n*, 230*n*, 242, 272
auto industry impacts of, 140-143
coordinated, 238*t*, 240*t*, 241, 242, 250,
254*n*
as currency manipulation, 11, 13,
142-43, 267-68, 272-73
efficacy of, 158, 161, 225-31, 249-50,
251*n*
with largest daily impact, 230, 230*t*
official attitudes toward, 247*n*, 262
timing of, 224-25, 225*t*, 250*n*
volume of, 225-31, 226*f*
and yen-dollar rate, 226-31, 226*f*,
227*t*-228*t*, 230*t*, 236, 250
foreign exchange purchases, 272
foreign exchange reserves, 141, 141*f*,
159, 159*t*, 283
implications for US, 277
import ratio
to exports, 199, 200*f*
to lagged real exchange rate, 189-90,
189*f*
inflation, 19
interest rates, 218
internal balance problems of, 52-55
IT industry, 108
manufacturing sector employment, 87,
88*f*
Ministry of Finance, 221, 221*n*, 242,
247*n*, 262*n*, 272
monetary base, 53
monetary policy, 53, 54, 54*f*, 159-60,
161
net foreign asset position, 181, 181*f*,
182, 182*f*
productivity growth in, 6, 9*n*, 20*f*, 22,
23*f*, 53, 178, 178*n*

instruments for, 10-12
of Japan, 53, 54, 54f, 159-60, 161, 177
mix with fiscal policy, 54, 55f
in postbubble economy, 166, 170
for price stabilization, in 1990s, 168-69
progrowth, need for in Europe and
    Japan, 166, 170
US, 79, 166
    conflicts with dollar exchange value
        needs, 256-61, 256f, 257f, 258n-
        260n
    and needs of real economy and real
        exchange rate index, 257-58,
        257f
MSCI-neutral portfolio, 67n, 72
Mundell-Fleming model, 54, 55f

NASDAQ index, 45, 119
national accounts identity, 112-16, 113f,
    114f, 157
National Association of Manufacturers,
    84, 84n, 147, 159, 275
national income and product accounts
    (NIPA), national accounts identity,
    112-16, 157
national income identity. See national
    accounts identity
national security, implications of large-
    scale dollar holdings by China for,
    277
NEER model. See nominal effective
    exchange rate (NEER) model
net international investment position
    (NIIP)
    negative, 60-61
    of US, 2, 15-16, 63-65, 64f
    relative to GDP. See NIIP-GDP ratio
"new economy" of 1990s. See also IT
    revolution
    corporate profits in, 93-95, 94f
    and deflation, 168
    dollar swings during
        counterfactual simulation of, 116-19,
            117t
        macroeconomic adjustment in, 112-
            16, 117-18
    and estimates of dollar's equilibrium
        value, 36, 40-45, 44f, 179-80
    expansion during, dollar overvaluation
        and, 145-46
    and US current account deficit
        sustainability, 44-45, 44f
NIIP-GDP ratio, 6, 7, 65

current account deficit impacts on, 60-
    61
stabilization of, 7, 176, 180
US, 6, 63-65, 64f, 180
    and dollar behavior, 62-63, 65
    and dollar value in 2003, 70
    in unchanged-dollar scenario, 70
Nikkei 225 stock index, 178, 195
    prices, and yen-dollar exchange rate,
        195-96, 196f
Nissan, 105, 140, 141, 142
Nixon administration, 77
nominal effective exchange rate (NEER)
    model, 198-99
nonaccelerating inflation rate of
    unemployment (NAIRU), 120
North American Free Trade Agreement
    (NAFTA), 87
    auto industry and, 111-12

oil
    UK sales of, 96
    US imports of, 96, 126
oil prices, and inflation, 131, 156
Omnibus Trade Act of 1988, 11, 142, 279
O'Neill, Paul H., 12, 84
open-mouth operations, 158
Organization for Economic Cooperation
    and Development (OECD), 17, 21, 65
    euro-dollar equilibrium exchange rate
        model, 39, 40t
    Net Financial Wealth data set, 73-75
Organization of Petroleum Exporting
    Countries (OPEC), 131
output, US, currency manipulation's
    impact on, 275-76
output gap, US, 256-57, 256f, 257n

Plaza Accord, 12, 78, 158, 219, 219n
    second, 161
Pohang Steel Company, 101
portfolio balance channel, 252-53
portfolio flows, in Europe, 29, 30-31, 31n,
    33f
pound sterling. See British pound
    sterling
price elasticity(ies), 274n
    in Japan
        in current account balance
            forecasting, 190, 191, 192, 200-
            01, 202t
        for exports, 200-01, 202t
price index. see consumer price index;
    GDP price index

exchange market interventions by, 23-
24, 217, 220, 220n, 222f, 223, 235-
41, 235n, 242
conflicts with other policy objectives,
256-61, 257f, 258n-260n, 263
coordinated, 231, 232t, 234, 236, 238t,
240t, 242, 250, 254n
and deutsche mark-dollar rate, 236f,
239t, 240-41, 240t
efficacy of, 235-41, 249, 250, 251, 252,
258-59
net size of, 278n
official attitudes toward, 248, 249
timing of, 224-25, 225t, 250n
and yen-dollar rate, 235-38, 236f,
237t, 238t
exports. *See* exports, US
financial crisis point, foreign debt and,
155-56
foreign asset position, net, 180-82, 181f,
182f
foreign capital inflows. *See* foreign
capital inflows, US
foreign demand, 85, 111
foreign exchange reserves, 282-83, 283n
foreign income account, 118f, 119, 154-
55, 155f
foreign liabilities, net, 182
foreign policy objectives, currency
manipulation and, 277-78
foreign yield spreads, and current
account deficit, 47, 48f, 50
GDP, real, growth in. *See* gross
domestic product (GDP), US real,
growth in
GDP price index, 117, 166-67, 167f
global financial wealth share, scenarios
for, 70-73, 71f
income distribution, manufacturing
jobs and, 152
interest payments on official dollar
holdings in Asia, 277
investment. *See* investment, US
monetary policy of, 79
output, currency manipulation's
impact on, 275-76
output gap, 256-57, 256f, 257n
productivity growth. *See* productivity
growth, US
trade
hysteresis in, 99b-100b
increase in, 148, 149f

recession stabilization and, 111
trade deficit
currency manipulation and, 270, 273
in goods, 84-85
in manufacturing, 2
trade in goods
deficit in, 84-85, 86f
and GDP growth, 92-93, 92t
trade policy, 5, 77-79
dollar's exchange value and, 77, 78-
79
trade relationships, 209, 215t
dollar holdings in Asia and, 277
by partner, *vs.* Japan, 185-88, 187t
shift in, since 1980s, 16-17, 16t
unions
in auto industry, 107
dollar overvaluation and, 84-85
in steel industry, 107-08
world exports share, 1989-2001, 21, 22f
world trade turnover share, *vs.* Japan,
185, 187f
US assets, in global investors' portfolios,
65, 66f, 67, 68f
allocation scenarios for, and dollar
behavior, 70-73, 71f, 71t
and dollar behavior, 2, 57-58, 60, 61-62,
63, 65-69, 70-73
factors determining, 62
sustainability analysis based on, 2, 57-
58, 60, 61-62, 63, 65-69, 70-73
in unchanged-dollar scenario, 70-71, 72
US economy. *See also specific sectors and
industries*
in 1990s. *See* "new economy" of 1990s
adjustment to trade, 83n-84n
Asian currency manipulation and, 270-
78
bubble in, 145-46
current slump in, and consumption,
146
dollar swings and, 81-132
euro-dollar exchange rate changes and,
211
and global economy, 156-57, 165, 171-
72
needs of, conflicts with exchange rate
needs, 256-61, 256f, 257f, 258n-
260n
openness of, 208-09, 208t, 215t
US Treasury
attitude toward intervention, 248

exchange market interventions by, 23-
24, 220*n*, 242, 262*n*
and conflicts with Federal Reserve,
260, 260*n*
response to currency manipulation, 11-
12
recommended statement for, 278-79
strong-dollar rhetoric of, 160
US Treasury note yield, through 2017,
124*t*, 127, 128*t*

wage insurance, 132
world exports shares, 1989-2001, 21, 22*f*
world net savings, US share of, 47
World Trade Organization, 13, 142, 280-
81
world trade turnover, Japanese *vs.* US
share of, 185, 187*f*

yen
appreciation of, 3-5, 8-9, 9*n*, 189-190
in 1995, 241-42, 242*n*
arguments for, 8-9, 170
with current account surplus
reduction, 197
real net import impacts of, 196-97
stock market impacts of, 195-96, 196*f*
currency manipulation's impact on,
270
depreciation of, arguments for, 8
dollar depreciation impacts on, 28, 28*t*
in auto industry, 1985-1995, 138-39
dollar depreciation role of, 8-9, 19-22,
34
equilibrium value of, 36, 52-55
and euro, 25
exchange value of, 1981-2002, 188*f*

Goldman Sachs trade-weighted index
of, 20*f*, 21, 21*t*
intervention policy regarding, 272-73
interventions affecting, 11, 13, 23-24,
140-43, 159-60, 161, 162, 252
monetary policy effects on, 53, 54*f*
real effective exchange rate (REER),
189-90, 189*f*, 199
ratio of non-oil imports to, 189*f*, 190
surplus reduction's impact on, 188-94
weight of, in trade-weighted dollar
index, 16*t*, 17
yen-dollar exchange rate, 3, 4*t*, 9, 19
after 2002, 52-55
in 2002, 58, 59*f*
in 1977-2002, 219, 220*f*
in 1981-2002, 188-89, 188*f*
in 1985-1995, 138-39, 139*f*
and US auto industry, 138-39
in 1985-2002, 139, 139*f*
in 1989-2001, 54*f*
adjustment of, views on, 8-9
changes in
in 1995, 241-42, 242*n*
with current account surplus
reduction, 197
impacts on auto industry, 138-43
GSDEER, 19, 19*f*
interventions affecting, 241-42, 250
by Japan, 226-31, 226*f*, 227*t*-228*t*,
230*t*, 236, 250
by US, 235-38, 236*f*, 237*t*, 238*t*, 250
long-dollar/short-yen positions, return
on, 54, 55*f*
and stock prices in US and Japan, 195-
96, 196*f*
and US imports of Japanese cars, 139,
139*f*

Other Publications from the Institute for International Economics

* = out of print

65 The Benefits of Price Convergence:
   Speculative Calculations
   Gary Clyde Hufbauer, Erika Wada,
   and Tony Warren
   December 2001   ISBN 0-88132-333-0
66 **Managed Floating Plus**
   Morris Goldstein
   March 2002   ISBN 0-88132-336-5
67 **Argentina and the Fund: From Triumph
   to Tragedy**
   Michael Mussa
   July 2002   ISBN 0-88132-339-X
68 **East Asian Financial Cooperation**
   C. Randall Henning
   September 2002   ISBN 0-88132-338-1

BOOKS

IMF Conditionality* John Williamson, editor
1983   ISBN 0-88132-006-4
Trade Policy in the 1980s* William R. Cline, editor
1983   ISBN 0-88132-031-5
Subsidies in International Trade*
Gary Clyde Hufbauer and Joanna Shelton Erb
1984   ISBN 0-88132-004-8
**International Debt: Systemic Risk and Policy
Response*** William R. Cline
1984   ISBN 0-88132-015-3
**Trade Protection in the United States: 31 Case
Studies*** Gary Clyde Hutbauer, Diane E. Berliner,
and Kimberly Ann Elliott
1986   ISBN 0-88132-040-4
**Toward Renewed Economic Growth in Latin
America*** Bela Balassa, Gerardo M. Bueno, Pedro-
Pablo Kuczynski, and Mario Henrique Simonsen
1986   ISBN 0-88132-045-5
Capital Flight and Third World Debt*
Donald R. Lessard and John Williamson, editors
1987   ISBN 0-88132-053-6
**The Canada-United States Free Trade Agreement:
The Global Impact***
Jeffrey J. Schott and Murray G. Smith, editors
1988   ISBN 0-88132-073-0
World Agricultural Trade: Building a Consensus*
William M. Miner and Dale E. Hathaway, editors
1988   ISBN 0-88132-071-3
Japan in the World Economy*
Bela Balassa and Marcus Noland
1988   ISBN 0-88132-041-2
**America in the World Economy: A Strategy for
the 1990s*** C. Fred Bergsten
1988   ISBN 0-88132-089-7
**Managing the Dollar: From the Plaza to the
Louvre*** Yoichi Funabashi
1988, 2nd ed. 1989   ISBN 0-88132-097-8

**United States External Adjustment and the World
Economy*** William R. Cline
May 1989   ISBN 0-88132-048-X
Free Trade Areas and U.S. Trade Policy*
Jeffrey J. Schott, editor
May 1989   ISBN 0-88132-094-3
**Dollar Politics: Exchange Rate Policymaking in
the United States***
I.M. Destler and C. Randall Henning
September 1989   ISBN 0-88132-079-X
**Latin American Adjustment: How Much Has
Happened?*** John Williamson, editor
April 1990   ISBN 0-88132-125-7
**The Future of World Trade in Textiles and
Apparel*** William R. Cline
1987, 2d ed. June 199   ISBN 0-88132-110-9
**Completing the Uruguay Round: A Results-
Oriented Approach to the GATT Trade
Negotiations*** Jeffrey J. Schott, editor
September 1990   ISBN 0-88132-130-3
**Economic Sanctions Reconsidered (2 volumes)
Economic Sanctions Reconsidered:
Supplemental Case Histories**
Gary Clyde Hufbauer, Jeffrey J. Schott, and
Kimberly Ann Elliott
1985, 2d ed. Dec. 1990   ISBN cloth 0-88132-115-X
                              ISBN paper 0-88132-105-2
**Economic Sanctions Reconsidered: History and
Current Policy**
Gary Clyde Hufbauer, Jeffrey J. Schott, and
Kimberly Ann Ellio
December 1990   ISBN cloth 0-88132-140-0
                    ISBN paper 0-88132-136-2
**Pacific Basin Developing Countries: Prospects for
the Future*** Marcus Noland
January 1991   ISBN cloth 0-88132-141-9
                   ISBN paper 0-88132-081-1
Currency Convertibility in Eastern Europe*
John Williamson, editor
October 1991   ISBN 0-88132-128-1
**International Adjustment and Financing: The
Lessons of 1985-1991*** C. Fred Bergsten, editor
January 1992   ISBN 0-88132-112-5
**North American Free Trade: Issues and
Recommendations***
Gary Clyde Hufbauer and Jeffrey J. Schott
April 1992   ISBN 0-88132-120-6
Narrowing the U.S. Current Account Deficit*
Allen J. Lenz
June 1992   ISBN 0-88132-103-6
The Economics of Global Warming
William R. Cline/*June 1992*   ISBN 0-88132-132-X
**U.S. Taxation of International Income: Blueprint
for Reform***   Gary Clyde Hutbauer, assisted
by Joanna M. van Rooij
October 1992   ISBN 0-88132-134-6

No More Bashing: Building a New Japan-United
States Economic Relationship
C. Fred Bergsten, Takatoshi Ito, and Marc Noland
October 2001   ISBN 0-88132-286-5
Why Global Commitment Really Matters!
Howard Lewis III and J. David Richardson
October 2001   ISBN 0-88132-298-9
Leadership Selection in the Major Multilaterals
Miles Kahler
November 2001   ISBN 0-88132-335-7
The International Financial Architecture:
What's New? What's Missing?   Peter Kenen
November 2001   ISBN 0-88132-297-0
Delivering on Debt Relief: From IMF Gold to
a New Aid Architecture
John Williamson and Nancy Birdsall,
with Brian Deese
April 2002   ISBN 0-88132-331-4
**Imagine There's No Country: Poverty, Inequality,
and Growth in the Era of Globalization**
Surjit S. Bhalla
September 2002   ISBN 0-88132-348-9
Reforming Korea's Industrial Conglomerates
Edward M. Graham
January 2003   ISBN 0-88132-337-3

SPECIAL REPORTS

1   **Promoting World Recovery: A Statement on
     Global Economic Strategy***
     by Twenty-six Economists from Fourteen
     Countries
     December 1982   ISBN 0-88132-013-7
2   **Prospects for Adjustment in Argentina,
     Brazil, and Mexico: Responding to the Debt
     Crisis***   John Williamson, editor
     June 1983   ISBN 0-88132-016-1
3   Inflation and Indexation: Argentina, Brazil,
     and Israel*   John Williamson, editor
     March 1985   ISBN 0-88132-037-4
4   Global Economic Imbalances*
     C. Fred Bergsten, editor
     March 1986   ISBN 0-88132-042-0
5   **African Debt and Financing***
     Carol Lancaster and John Williamson, editors
     May 1986   ISBN 0-88132-044-7
6   **Resolving the Global Economic Crisis: After
     Wall Street***
     by Thirty-three Economists from Thirteen
     Countries
     December 1987   ISBN 0-88132-070-6
7   **World Economic Problems***
     Kimberly Ann Elliott and John Williamson,
     editors
     April 1988   ISBN 0-88132-055-2

Reforming World Agricultural Trade*
by Twenty-nine Professionals from Seventeen
Countries
1988   ISBN 0-88132-088-9
8   **Economic Relations Between the United
     States and Korea: Conflict or Cooperation?***
     Thomas O. Bayard and Soogil Young, editors
     January 1989   ISBN 0-88132-068-4
9   **Whither APEC? The Progress to Date and
     Agenda for the Future***
     C. Fred Bergsten, editor
     October 1997   ISBN 0-88132-248-2
10   Economic Integration of the Korean
     Peninsula
     Marcus Noland, editor
     January 1998   ISBN 0-88132-255-5
11   **Restarting Fast Track***
     Jeffrey J. Schott, editor
     April 1998   ISBN 0-88132-259-8
12   **Launching New Global Trade Talks:
     An Action Agenda**   Jeffrey J. Schott, editor
     September 1998   ISBN 0-88132-266-0
13   **Japan's Financial Crisis and Its Parallels to
     U.S. Experience**
     Ryoichi Mikitani and Adam S. Posen, eds.
     September 2000   ISBN 0-88132-289-X
14   **The Ex-Im Bank in the 21st Century: A New
     Approach?**   Gary Clyde Hufbauer and
     Rita M. Rodriguez, eds.
     January 2001   ISBN 0-88132-300-4
15   **The Korean Diaspora in the World Economy**
     C. Fred Bergsten and Inbom Choi, eds.
     January 2003   ISBN 0-88132-358-6
16   **Dollar Overvaluation and the World Economy**
     C. Fred Bergsten and John Williamson, eds.
     February 2003   ISBN 0-88132-351-9

WORKS IN PROGRESS

**Deunionization in the United States:
The Role of International Trade**
Robert E. Baldwin
**Changing Direction: The New Economy
in the United States, Europe, and Japan**
Martin Baily
**New Regional Arrangements and the World
Economy**
C. Fred Bergsten
**The Globalization Backlash in Europe and
the United States**
C. Fred Bergsten, Pierre Jacquet, and Karl Kaiser
China's Entry to the World Economy
Richard N. Cooper
The ILO in the World Economy
Kimberly Ann Elliott

Australia, New Zealand,
and Papua New Guinea
D.A. Information Services
648 Whitehorse Road
Mitcham, Victoria 3132, Australia
tel: 61-3-9210-7777
fax: 61-3-9210-7788
email: service@adadirect.com.au
http://www.dadirect.com.au

United Kingdom and Europe
(including Russia and Turkey)
The Eurospan Group
3 Henrietta Street, Covent Garden
London WC2E 8LU England
tel: 44-20-7240-0856
fax: 44-20-7379-0609
http://www.eurospan.co.uk

Japan and the Republic of Korea
United Publishers Services, Ltd.
KenkyuSha Bldg.
9, Kanda Surugadai 2-Chome
Chiyoda-Ku, Tokyo 101 Japan
tel: 81-3-3291-4541
fax: 81-3-3292-8610
email: saito@ups.co.jp
For trade accounts only.
Individuals will find IIE books in
leading Tokyo bookstores.

Thailand
Asia Books
5 Sukhumvit Rd. Soi 61
Bangkok 10110 Thailand
tel: 662-714-07402 Ext: 221, 222, 223
fax: 662-391-2277
email: purchase@asiabooks.co.th
http://www.asiabooksonline.com

Canada
Renouf Bookstore
5369 Canotek Road, Unit 1
Ottawa, Ontario KIJ 9J3, Canada
tel: 613-745-2665
fax: 613-745-7660
http://www.renoufbooks.com

India, Bangladesh, Nepal, and Sri Lanka
Viva Books Pvt.
Mr. Vinod Vasishtha
4325/3, Ansari Rd.
Daryaganj, New Delhi-110002
India
tel: 91-11-327-9280
fax: 91-11-326-7224
email: vinod.viva@gndel.globalnet.
ems.vsnl.net.in

Southeast Asia (Brunei, Cambodia,
China, Malaysia, Hong Kong, Indonesia,
Laos, Myanmar, the Philippines, Singapore,
Taiwan, and Vietnam)
Hemisphere Publication Services
1 Kallang Pudding Rd. #0403
Golden Wheel Building
Singapore 349316
tel: 65-741-5166
fax: 65-742-9356

Visit our Web site at:
http://www.iie.com
E-mail orders to:
orders@iie.com